Economists in the Americas

Economists in the Americas

Edited by

Verónica Montecinos

The Pennsylvania State University, USA

John Markoff

University of Pittsburgh, USA

Edward Elgar

Cheltenham, UK • Northampton, MA, USA

Published by
Edward Elgar Publishing Limited
The Lypiatts
15 Lansdown Road
Cheltenham
Glos GL50 2JA
UK

Edward Elgar Publishing, Inc.
William Pratt House
9 Dewey Court
Northampton
Massachusetts 01060
USA

A catalogue record for this book
is available from the British Library

Library of Congress Control Number: 2009936736

ISBN 978 1 84542 043 7

Printed and bound by MPG Books Group, UK

Contents

Contributors

María José Álvarez-Rivadulla is *Profesora Principal* at the *Universidad del Rosario* in Bogotá, Colombia, where she teaches sociology. She did her undergraduate studies at the *Universidad de la República*, in Montevideo, Uruguay, and her PhD at the University of Pittsburgh. Her main research interest is urban inequality. She has also done work on global income inequality and the trans-American flow of economic ideas.

Sarah Babb is Associate Professor of Sociology at Boston College. She is author of *Managing Mexico: Economists from Nationalism to Neoliberalism* (Princeton University Press, 2001), *Behind the Development Banks: Washington Politics, World Poverty, and the Wealth of Nations* (University of Chicago Press, 2009), as well as a variety of scholarly articles. Her research interests include the origins and dynamics of economic policy ideas, international financial institutions and the role of multilateral organizations in globalization.

Glen Biglaiser is Associate Professor in the Department of Political Science at Texas Tech University. His research interests are on the effects of politics on economic development. He is the author of *Guardians of the Nation?: Economists, Generals, and Economic Reform in Latin America* (University of Notre Dame Press, 2002). His work has appeared in *Comparative Political Studies, International Organization, International Studies Quarterly, Latin American Research Review, Political Research Quarterly*, and other journals.

Luis Bernardo Flórez Enciso received his economics degree at the *Universidad Nacional de Colombia* where he served as dean of the *Facultad de Ciencias Económicas*. He is the author or co-author of various books and essays on macroeconomic policy, public finance, industrialization and urban development. He has been consultant for various international organizations and held many top government posts in Colombia: among others, economic adviser to the President of the Republic, Director of the National Planning Agency and Vice-Minister of Finance.

Marion Fourcade is Associate Professor of Sociology at the University of California Berkeley. She is a comparative sociologist, specifically interested in variations in economic and political knowledge and practice across nations. Her book, *Economists and Societies. Discipline and Profession in the United States, Britain, and France, 1890s to 1990s* (Princeton University Press, 2009), is an exploration of American, French and British society and culture through the lens of their respective economic institutions and the distinctive character of their economic experts. Recent work includes a comparative analysis of economic valuation techniques applied to the environment, the role of morality in markets (with Kieran Healy), the varying nature of political contention across nations (with Evan Schofer and Brian Lande) and the globalization of economics.

Adolfo Garcé is *Profesor Adjunto* of political theory at the *Facultad de Ciencias Sociales* and of political science at the *Facultad de Ciencias Económicas y Administración, Universidad de la República* (Montevideo, Uruguay). He is author of *Técnicos y política* (with Gustavo De Armas, Ediciones Trilce, 2000), *Ideas y competencia política en Uruguay: revisando el 'fracaso' de la CIDE* (Ediciones Trilce, 2002), *La era progresista* (with Jaime Yaffé, Editorial Fin de Siglo, 2004), *Think tanks y políticas públicas en Latinoamérica*, Editorial Prometeo, 2006), *Donde hubo fuego: el proceso de adaptación del Movimiento de Liberación Nacional-Tupamaros a la legalidad y a la competencia electoral* (Editorial Fin de Siglo, 2006) and many scholarly articles on the relationship between research and policy and the evolution of political and economic ideas in Latin America.

Maria Rita Loureiro is a Brazilian sociologist who teaches political science and economic sociology at the University of São Paulo and at the Fundação Getulio Vargas, where she conducts research on bureaucracy, democratic accountability and the political dimensions of policy-making. She is the author of *Os economistas no governo* (Editora Fundação Getulio Vargas, 1997) and several articles and book chapters on the role of economists in the Brazilian governments and on the political dimension of economic policies. She has also published in France (*Actes de la Recherche en Sciences Sociales*), the US (*History of Political Economy*), Argentina and Venezuela.

John Markoff is Distinguished University Professor at the University of Pittsburgh. He studies the history of democracy. His books include *Waves of Democracy: Social Movements and Political Change* (Pine Forge Press, 1996); *The Abolition of Feudalism: Peasants, Lords and Legislators in the*

French Revolution (Penn State University Press, 1996); and (with Gilbert Shapiro) *Revolutionary Demands: A Content Analysis of the Cahiers de Doléances of 1789* (Stanford University Press, 1998).

Verónica Montecinos is Professor of Sociology at The Pennsylvania State University, Greater Allegheny. She is the author of *Economists, Politics and the State. Chile 1958–1994* (CEDLA, 1998) as well as book chapters and articles that have appeared in such journals as the *International Journal of Politics, Culture and Society*, the *Journal of Economic Perspectives, Latin American Research Review* and *Studies in Comparative International Development*. She has recently served as consultant on gender and pension reform in Chile's Ministry of Finance and is part of an interdisciplinary group working on development and indigenous knowledge in Tanzania.

Preface

This book grew out of discussions between the editors that began more than twenty years ago when Verónica Montecinos was working on her doctoral dissertation on the management of the Chilean economy from the presidency of Alessandri to the government of Pinochet. We were fascinated by the trend toward an increasing presence of professional economists in high political office, including the occupancy of roles that were not limited to what one might have imagined as a delimited set of economic affairs. When Montecinos launched her dissertation research, this was not a subject many people were writing about. The dissertation was completed in 1988.

We then realized that the Chilean story was an instance of a much broader trend that showed up with interesting variations in country after country and not only in Latin America. We did not find that much was being written about the striking entry of members of this particular academic discipline into positions of political power, not in the literature on Latin America or elsewhere. We did not find that the sociological literature on the professions, which was entering a very creative period in the 1980s, was paying much attention to professional economists. Some economists thought a lot about economic ideas and the history of economics in some countries, but those of a historical bent were not writing much about Latin America and not much about the changing relationship of that profession to political power. While there was growing attention to the web of transnational connections that everybody seemed to be calling 'globalization', there were not many people who were writing about the important role of economists in forging these connections. Our conversations about all these matters turned into an essay on 'The Ubiquitous Rise of Economists' that appeared in the *Journal of Public Policy* in 1993. In the Spanish version that appeared the next year in *Desarollo Económico* we made it 'Irresistible' rather than ubiquitous. It was clear that, as the ultimate purveyors of policy initiatives for what was spoken of as the 'reform' of Latin American economies, economists had gained a political status they had not previously held.

By then others were increasingly addressing that professional history. There was an exciting efflorescence of what was being called 'economic sociology', some of whose many able practitioners were writing about not only economies but economists, for example, Richard Swedberg or Robin Stryker. Some economists were studying themselves as a profession and turning an empirical and, it turned out, critical eye on professional education. (The research of David Colander and Arjo Klamer and others was very valuable.) And the comparative and transnational dimensions began to be opened up. The work of Bob Coats in particular was a resource, a model and an inspiration. He sponsored important research and edited collections that energized the comparative study of professional economists in a variety of institutional contexts, moving the study of the profession beyond the national framework because that is where the profession was moving. Still more recently, Marion Fourcade, author of one of the chapters in this volume, summed it up in the title of her recent essay, 'The Construction of a Global Profession: The Transnationalization of Economics'.

We returned to these themes in several papers and examined the interplay of the changing character of public policy and the increasing role of Latin America's economists in the forging of that policy. It seemed to us that one useful way to address the Latin American policy changes was to see those changes in relation to the emergence of this global profession and we conceived this book accordingly. We focus on the Americas in the geographically broad sense of all the countries of the Americas as one component of the globalization of economics. To explore the transborder connections we brought together experts on particular countries. Their task would be twofold. They were to write about the history of the economics profession in one national case and about the role of that changing profession in national politics. We imposed no overarching framework for each chapter to follow and left it to our experts' judgment what to stress. Our own mission would be to tease out the similarities between and differences among the national instances, the traditional tasks of comparative analysis, but it would also be to examine the connections among those cases, the processes that connected national professions across national borders.

Throughout the Americas, North and South, broadly similar challenges to previous economic policies emerged, which we, like many, would sum up as 'more market, less state'. When the new prescriptions included dismantling previously established social safety nets, ending previously established protections for certain economic activities (sheltering industry from transborder competitions though tariff barriers, for example), eliminating previous barriers to transnational flows of investment, privatizing previously state-owned or state-managed enterprises, and loosening previously established mechanisms and agencies of state regulation of economic life, critics spoke of 'neoliberalism', a term used by practically no one to identify one's own position, and never used (as far as we have been able to discover) by professional economists as a self-description. A second commonality among all the cases in this book is that everywhere such shifts in policy occurred, the role of professional economists in political life was on the rise. And a third common feature of all the Latin American cases: the professional world of economics was changing, whether we look at training, or careers, or academic standards, or the forms of professional association. We could sum up these changes as a professional convergence on a common pattern, and if we are willing to call that model 'American', we can speak of the Americanization of Latin American economics. But in every Latin American country the process was uneven, and it advanced to different degrees and with a somewhat different timing in each.

But the chapters that follow also demonstrate that these are not simply parallel processes replicated, perhaps after some delay, in case after case, independently. For the cases are connected, not merely by some amorphous southward diffusion of ideas from the hegemonic north, but by connections forged as economists met at international conferences, as students from one country got educated in another, as Latin American economists learned to read journal articles in English, and to write them, too, as professors spent time in university appointments abroad and also in think tanks, consultancy firms, international banks and multilateral agencies. And, we think, and here our conclusions go against some common views of our global age, the picture of US-imposed patterns is too simple, partly because local actors had their own reasons for professionalization and for policy shifts (the main processes under study in this volume), and partly because not all important parts of the story invariably start in the US. Neoliberalism, if one accepts the term, may not have had a single birthplace at all. If one were to claim it did, it would make as much sense to call that place Chile as it would the US.

Early versions of some of these chapters were brought together in a panel at the 2001 meetings of the Latin American Studies Association a few days before the attack on the World Trade Center was a catastrophic reminder of the importance of transnational processes. Other papers were then invited to expand the range of cases. The rather long time between that date and the completion of the project altered the work. When we formed the project, our authors took it as their mission to explain where those neoliberal practices had come from and how they were connected across borders. We have a series of country studies, then, of the role of professional economists in forging new economic policies during a period in which their professions were changing and in which, in case after case, their political role in economic affairs, and beyond economic affairs, was expanding. We took as basic the shift from policies founded on the wisdom of the state's beneficent role in correcting the undesired potential consequences of the capitalist market to the view of the state as stupid or malign, a view commending much caution before interfering with the market's cunning.

How this change in dominant ideas played out differs significantly from case to case, as our country chapters show. For Mexico, Sarah Babb shows us, it is important to distinguish the economics taught in one important locale, UNAM, from the economics taught in another, ITAM. She stresses the profound transformative effect of the debt crisis of the early 1980s on Mexican economics. The relative standing of the most internationalized segments of the profession was enhanced, to the detriment of those whose policy influence and intellectual legitimacy had hitherto rested on the postwar developmentalist consensus and on academic degrees from public universities. Advancing hand in hand, the Americanization of economics in Mexico and the country's embrace of neoliberalism contributed to an over-crowded professional labor market for US-educated economists. In a nutshell, Mexico managed to generate more professional economists with the newly desired credentials than desirable positions for them. Babb predicts further declines in state patronage and an unprecedented exodus of economists seeking employment outside Mexico.

In Argentina, by contrast, brain drain has been the historical norm and its economists were known for their vast and visible networks abroad. By the 1960s, at any international agency full of Spanish-speaking economists you would surely have run into many Argentines. As Glen Biglaiser reports, that country's profession suffered the consequences of lengthy, repeated government attacks on academic freedom and other forms of official malice toward and neglect of higher education. Despite their success in Chile, early US efforts to transform the profession failed in Argentina. The number of foreign-trained economists rose only with the more recent proliferation of private universities and research centers.

The relative delay in the political ascent of cohesive pro-market economic teams during and after Argentina's military regime is traced by Biglaiser to political survival strategies and appointment patterns within fragmented governing institutions and to entrenched anti-US sentiments at the *Universidad de Buenos Aires* and elsewhere. By contrast, in Brazil economics was built against a strong tradition of state centralism. Maria Rita Loureiro explains how class and regional differences shaped enduring divisions in the profession's formative phases. Not until the 1970s did Brazil look toward the US, not France, for academic models. From the late 1960s on, the newly reformed university system began to replace the previously dominant influence of government and private institutions over the education of economists. Heterodox economics, despite its overall decline even under the presidency of Lula, longtime leader of the Workers' Party, has retained a remarkably vibrant presence within the Brazilian profession, as illustrated by the curriculum and faculty profile at the University of Campinas and other public institutions. It is sometimes said of this huge, varied country that one can find pretty much anything somewhere, and one might take Loureiro's detailed specification of the ways in which different Brazilian institutions harbor different kinds of economics and different kinds of economists' careers as a case in point.

Brazilian graduate-level economics programs, not surprisingly, vastly outnumber their counterparts in the rest of Latin America, but it was Chile where generations of economics students from all over Latin America flocked to study. Chile has played an outsized, even legendary, role in the diffusion of professional models in and beyond the region. Verónica Montecinos explores some of the reasons behind that country's unexpected centrality in the forging of successive waves of transnational convergence in economics education and policy-making as well as the unique paths leading so many Chilean economists to occupy positions of power. 'Unexpected', that is, if what you expect is that the US invents and those to the south mimic.

The evolution of the economics profession in Colombia and Uruguay has received less previous scrutiny than our other cases. Luis Bernardo Flórez, the only economist among our authors, depicts Colombia's pragmatic policy environment as the backdrop for the emergence of a largely depoliticized profession with a persistent propensity for gradualism. Only recently, as Colombia experienced great crises, have its economists' influence and internal divisions increased. For over a decade, as the country turned to pro-market policies, the public *Universidad Nacional* remained the only option for those seeking an economics doctorate. Exemplifying Colombian distinctiveness, the program was structured along European, not US lines. The more orthodox *Universidad de los Andes* did not initiate the country's second doctoral program in economics until 2008. Colombia has come to resemble the other cases in which multiple sites for the practice of economics sustain some multiplicity in the kinds of economics that are practiced.

As late as the 1980s, economists in Uruguay were trained in the country's single institution of higher education. The profession was slow to gain a clearly separate identity and credentials, Adolfo Garcé tells us. To the dearth of members, Uruguayan economics added an equivocal relationship with parties and politicians that constrained its influence. Education abroad was very circumscribed. Only in the past couple of decades has US-style economics made some inroads. After the military regime ended in 1985, a few private universities were created and Uruguay's preeminent university opened a second economics department with more international connections and more foreign-trained faculty.

In case after case, readers will find that central banks pushed decisively in favor of the Americanization of Latin American economics. If by cosmopolitan we mean openness to ideas from afar, in the adoption of certain economic ideas central banks often turn out to be beacons of cosmopolitanism, far ahead of many academic departments. Supplemental resources aimed at greater professional resemblance also came from local and international business interests, as well as foundations and public agencies.

Sometimes the terms and timing of this north–south hemispheric confluence occurred more or less in tandem with the US profession's own successive metamorphoses, the subject of Marion Fourcade's research. As portrayed by Fourcade, economic ideas, including economists' ideas, are pervasive in US culture and debates about policy, from criminal law to public health questions, despite a very limited occupancy of positions of formal political power, far more limited than in any of our Latin American cases. Her chapter on US economics shows an early and successful association of economics and science, undergirding the enormous, perhaps unparalleled influence of economists' ideas in that country. It is through the strict enforcement of the claims of science that US economics preserves its privileged standing. This chapter shows us a number of things about the US profession that not only distinguish that case from Latin American ones, but, as elaborated in Fourcade's other work, from Britain and France as well. Despite economists' relatively modest capture of positions of formal political power within US borders, our opening chapter suggests that their powerful abstract and universal formulations help account for the seemingly unobstructed international transmission of their ideas, which has done much to catapult to power economists abroad, as evidenced in this book.

But beyond these very important national particulars is a sense of the costs of three decades of reconfiguring the relationship of state and market that peeks out at us within those chapters. The critiques were present when our authors began their assignments, but in the 1990s the 'Washington Consensus' as it is commonly known was enjoying its still-recent triumph over the prevailing interventionism of not very long before. Just a few years after we conceived this book, that consensus is looking very frayed and people in many quarters are wondering what's next. As we were completing our preface, the financial crash of 2008 made a major pendulum shift in economic ideology look unavoidable. The sophistry of extreme deregulation seemed finally exhausted as the US conferred with other panicked governments on how to quell a fast developing global recession. Facing the specter of 1929, following the lead of the British government, US banks were partially nationalized. Market intervention was thus making a most spectacularly sudden comeback. This was all the more dramatic in that it was carried out by the most ostensibly pro-market administration of President George W. Bush. Coincidentally, the 2008 Nobel Prize in Economics was awarded to Paul Krugman, the academic economist turned public intellectual, a vocal advocate for a new direction in economic policy.

In Latin America, some sort of left party had been winning at the ballot box in quite a number of countries with promises to protect their societies from neoliberal globalization. Between the time we began this project and the writing of this preface, left parties of some sort won elections in four of the countries we take up, lost a bitterly contested election in a fifth, and are only without hope of electoral victory in the near future in the one remaining case. Our country cases have told the interesting tale of the rise of neoliberalism but in only one of our cases is that Washington Consensus not beginning to look like yesterday's news. Yesterday's news is well worth understanding and we hope our collection makes a contribution. But having found ourselves bringing this collection to a conclusion at this particular point, we thought we had to add a speculative epilogue that looks beyond that neoliberal moment because it is beginning to appear that it was but a moment.

In working so long on this project we have of course gone into debt for which 'thank you' is the conventional but inadequate form of academic repayment. We thank our country authors for their tolerance of how long we took as editors. We thank our universities for financial and our colleagues for intellectual support. We thank Florencia Tateossian for wonderful research assistance at an early stage until she took a job with the World Bank and María-José Álvarez for research assistance that mutated into welcome co-authorship of chapter one. In the final stages of manuscript preparation, we relied on Javier Vázquez-D'Elia's skills for word-processing. Despite the long-delayed completion of this book, and in fact because of it, it is quite clear that the work of understanding the political roles of economists in the hemisphere, not to mention the world, is hardly complete. The themes addressed here deserve and will no doubt receive further examination. As national and transnational political and economic circumstances change we expect a future flurry of historical and comparative research on the commanding stature of economists, their ideas and networks.

Verónica Montecinos and John Markoff

Abbreviations

BCU	Banco Central del Uruguay (Uruguayan Central Bank)
BID	Banco Interamericano de Desarrollo (Inter-American Development Bank)
BNDE	Banco Nacional do Desenvolvimento Econômico (National Bank of Economic Development, Brazil)
BROU	Banco de la República Oriental del Uruguay (Bank of the Republic, Uruguay)
CAEN	Centro de Aperfeiçoamento de Economistas do Nordeste (Center for the Professional Development of Economists in the North-East, Brazil)
CEA	Council of Economic Advisers (US)
CEIPOS	Centro de Estudios e Investigaciones de Posgrado (Center for Research and Postgraduate Education, Universidad de la República, Uruguay)
CEMA	Centro de Estudios Macroeconómicos de Argentina (Center for Economic Research, Argentina)
CEPAL	Comisión Económica para América Latina y el Caribe (United Nations Economic Commission for Latin America and the Caribbean)
CERES	Centro de Estudios de la Realidad Económica y Social (Center for the Study of Social and Economic Reality, Uruguay)
CESEC	Centro de Estudios Socio-Economicos (Center for Socio-economic Research, Chile)
CIAPEP	Curso Interamericano en Preparación y Evaluación de Proyectos (Inter-American Course on Project Formulation and Evaluation, IADB)
CID	Centro de Investigaciones para el Desarrollo (Center for Development Research, Universidad Nacional, Colombia)
CIDE	Centro de Investigación y Docencia Económica (Center for Research and Teaching in Economics, Mexico)
CIDE	Comisión de Inversiones y Desarrollo Económico

	(Investment and Economic Development Commission, Uruguay)
CIEDUR	Centro de Investigaciones y Estudios del Uruguay (Center for Research on Uruguay)
CIENES	Centro Interamericano (Inter-American Center for Statistical Training, Chile)
CIEPLAN	Corporación de Investigaciones Económicas para América Latina (Center for Economic Research on Latin America, Chile)
CINVE	Centro de Investigación Económica (Center for Economic Research, Uruguay)
CLAEH	Consejo Latinoamericano de Economía Humana (Latin American Council for Human Economics, Uruguay)
CNPIC	Conselho Nacional da Política Industrial e Comercial (National Council for Industrial and Trade Policy, Brazil)
COLMEX	El Colegio de México (Mexico)
CONACYT	Consejo Nacional de Ciencia y Tecnología (National Council for Science and Technology, Mexico)
CONADE	Consejo Nacional de Desarrollo (National Development Council, Argentina)
CONICET	Consejo Nacional de Investigaciones Científicas y Técnicas (National Council for Scientific and Technical Research, Argentina)
CORFO	Corporación de Fomento de la Producción (Economic Development Agency, Chile)
CPU	Corporación de Promoción Universitaria (Corporation for University Development, Chile)
DASP	Departamento Administrativo do Serviço Público (Agency for Public Administration, Brazil)
ECLAC	United Nations Economic Commission for Latin America and the Caribbean
EPGE	Escola de Pós-graduação em Economia (Graduate School of Economics, Brazil)
ESCOLATINA	Escuela de Estudios Económicos Latinoamericanos (Latin American Economics School, Chile)
FCEA	Facultad de Ciencias Económicas y Administración (School of Economics and Administration, Universidad de la República, Uruguay)
FGV	Fundação GetúlioVargas (Getulio Vargas Foundation, Brazil)

FIEL	Fundación de Investigaciones Económicas Latinoamericanas (Foundation for Latin American Economic Research, Argentina)
FNCE	Faculdade Nacional de Ciências Econômicas (National School of Economic Science, Brazil)
IAFFE	International Association for Feminist Economics
IBRE	Instituto Brasileiro de Economia (Brazilian Economics Institute, Brazil)
ICA	International Cooperation Administration (US)
IEERAL	Instituto de Estudios Económicos sobre la Realidad Argentina y Latinoamericana (Institute for Economic Research of Argentina and Latin America, Argentina)
ILDIS	Instituto Latinoamericano de Investigaciones Sociales (Latin American Institute for Economic Research, Chile)
IMF	International Monetary Fund
IPEA	Instituto de Pesquisa Econômica Aplicada (Institute for Applied Economic Research, Brazil)
IPES	Instituto de Pesquisa Econômica e Social (Institute for Economic and Social Research, Brazil)
ISEG	Instituto Superior de Economistas del Gobierno (Institute for Government Economists, Argentina)
ITAM	Instituto Tecnológico Autónomo de México (Autonomous Technological Institute of Mexico, Mexico)
IUPERJ	Instituto Universitário de Pesquisas do Rio de Janeiro (Research Institute of Rio de Janeiro, Brazil)
LACEA	Latin American and Caribbean Economics Association
MECESUP	Fondo Competitivo para el Mejoramiento de la Calidad y el Desempeño de la Educación Superior (Fund for the Improvement of the Quality and Performance of Higher Education, Chile)
MIDEPLAN	Ministerio de Planificación (Ministry of Planning, Chile)
NAFTA	North-American Free Trade Agreement
NBER	National Bureau of Economic Research (US)
ODEPLAN	Oficina de Planificación Nacional (National Planning Office, Chile)
OPP	Oficina de Planeamiento y Presupuesto (Office of Planning and Budget, Uruguay)

PAN	Partido de Acción Nacional (National Action Party, Mexico)
PJ	Partido Justicialista (Justicialista Party, Argentina)
PMDB	Partido do Movimento Democrático Brasileiro (Party of the Brazilian Democratic Movement, Brazil)
PPBS	Planning, Programming and Budgeting System
PREL	Programa en Economía para Estudiantes Latinoamericanos (Economics Program for Latin American Students, Catholic University, Chile)
PRI	Partido Revolucionario Institucional (Institutional Revolutionary Party, Mexico)
PT	Partido dos Trabalhadores (Workers' Party, Brazil)
PUC-RJ	Pontifícia Universidade Católica do Rio de Janeiro (Catholic University, Rio de Janeiro, Brazil)
PUC	Pontificia Universidad Católica de Chile (Catholic University, Chile)
PUC-SP	Pontifícia Universidade Católica de São Paulo (Catholic University of São Paulo, Brazil)
SEREX	Secretaría de Relaciones Económicas Exteriores (Agency for Foreign Economic Relations, Chile)
SNI	Sistema Nacional de Investigadores (Researchers National System, Mexico)
STN	Secretaría do Tesouro Nacional (National Treasury Secretary, Brazil)
SUDENE	Superintendência do Desenvolvimento Econômico do Nordeste (Northeast Economic Development Agency, Brazil)
SUMOC	Superintendência da Moeda e do Crédito (Money and Credit Agency, Brazil)
UBA	Universidad de Buenos Aires (University of Buenos Aires, Argentina)
UDELAR	Universidad de la República (University of the Republic, Uruguay)
UDLAP	Universidad de las Américas-Puebla (University of the Americas, Puebla, Mexico)
UEM	Universidade Estadual de Maringá (Maringá State University, Brazil)
UERJ	Universidade do Estado do Rio de Janeiro (Rio de Janeiro State University, Brazil)
UFBA	Universidade Federal da Bahía (Bahia Federal University, Brazil)

UFC	Universidade Federal do Ceará (Federal University of Ceará, Brazil)
UFF	Universidade Federal Fluminense (Fluminense Federal University, Brazil)
UFRGS	Universidade Federal do Rio Grande do Sul (Federal University of Rio Grande do Sul, Brazil)
UFRJ	Universidade Federal do Rio de Janeiro (Federal University of Rio de Janeiro, Brazil)
UFSC	Universidade Federal da Santa Catarina (Federal University of Santa Catarina, Brazil)
UNCU	Universidad Nacional de Cuyo (National University of Cuyo, Argentina)
UNAL	Universidad Nacional de Colombia (National University, Colombia)
UNAM	Universidad Autónoma de México (Autonomous University, Mexico)
UNB	Universidade Nacional de Brasília (National University of Brasilia, Brazil)
UNICAMP	Universidade Estadual de Campinas (Campinas State University, Brazil)
UNCTAD	United Nations Conference on Trade and Development
UNESP	Universidade Estadual Paulista Julio de Mesquita Filho/Araquara (State University Julio de Mesquita Filho/Araquara)
UNLP	Universidad Nacional de La Plata (National University of La Plata, Argentina)
UPAC	Unidad de Poder Adquisitivo Constante (Constant Purchasing Power Unit, Colombia)
USAID	US Agency for International Development
USP	Universidade do São Paulo (University of São Paulo, Brazil)
USU	Universidade Santa Ursula (Santa Ursula University, Brazil)

1. Economists in the Americas: convergence, divergence and connection

Verónica Montecinos, John Markoff and María José Álvarez-Rivadulla[1]

INTRODUCTION

This collection of essays, the first comparative study of economics and economists in the Americas, is published just as the crafting of a new hemispheric identity is widely debated. The United States and Latin America, with their centuries-old history of conflict and collaboration, offer a rich setting for comparative analyses. Both are important reference points in the field of economics. Since the Second World War, the US has provided the most richly endowed home for the expansion of modern economics. Within the global South, Latin America has been a major proving ground where theories are tested, rejected and created. With its unparalleled national wealth and power in combination with income inequalities well beyond those of other rich countries, the US is much discussed by both champions and foes of capitalism. Its universities attract economists who define, if anyone does, the world economics mainstream at the beginning of the third millennium. Latin America's economies are commonly taken as exemplars of various kinds of failure and its economists, known in the recent past for their challenges to that mainstream, more recently still have been oscillating among allegiance, rejection and compromise with it. Economic ideas and policies in the Americas, North and South, are often construed as models of what should and should not be thought and done in other parts of the world.

This project was inspired in no small measure by A.W. Bob Coats's comparative research on economics, which he has described as a 'virgin field' (Coats 2000, xiii; De Marchi 2001). Our own starting point for this book is the simple observation that economic ideas and the practice of economics are contingent upon the changing circumstances of political and economic regimes, including their transnational connections. Although the analytical framework of mainstream neoclassical economics often pays little attention to institutions, social relations and culture, contextual variations do matter (Mayhew 1999; McCloskey 1985; Ruccio and Amariglio 2003; Smelser and Swedberg 1994; Waller and Jennings 1991).

The country chapters that follow are authored by an interdisciplinary group of scholars working at the forefront of the comparative politics and sociology of economics. We expect that, presented side by side, these cases will illuminate the role of economists in the confluence of ideas, politics and policymaking. By tracing some of the contours of economics in the Americas, North and South, including the connections between economists in the North and the South, we hope to point to new avenues for future transnational studies.

A thorough comparison of economics in the Western Hemisphere requires building blocks that are often missing, scattered, or unusable in their present form. Before painting a complete picture of economics across the frontiers of time and space, more information is needed on such issues as professional membership, employment patterns and curricular reforms. To clarify parallels and contrasts between economics within the Americas and between the Americas and other world regions, more archival analyses, ethnographic studies, intellectual biographies and institutional histories will have to be done. We hope to make a start, and hope, too, that the results are interesting enough and at points unexpected enough that others will elaborate, improve upon, correct, or refute our contentions.

To our hope to make a modest start on comparison we add a larger ambition: to explore the interconnections among our national cases. Our aim is not simply to highlight striking differences and commonalities that a reader will find in the chapters ahead, but to point to the role of connections, not just many connections but many kinds of connection. Hemispheric flows of economic ideas have something to do with hemispheric flows of goods, loans, and investment, and something to do with relations among the hemisphere's states. But economics has also been shaped by connections among economists as policy-makers, students or professors, as colleagues at academic conferences and as policy wonks in think tanks. Many of these connections cross national borders, as funds flow to universities and research groups, professors go off to hobnob at conferences, students leave home on scholarships, and researchers publish in languages not their own. It is not just individual economists that establish cross-border connection but also the institutions that house them as universities in one country adopt, and adapt, standards for academic promotion or curricula from another; as careers move professionals among universities, government service, international organizations and think tanks, sometimes crossing borders in the process; as state institutions foster the study of ideas from abroad; as private think thanks emerge, with their own cross-border connections. We hope to make a beginning at describing the web of such connections in the Western Hemisphere.

Finally, we have a small contribution towards a third ambition. In the chapters that follow our authors will describe what we may call the neoliberal moment in their particular national cases. This moment arose from the confluence of many things – the position of the United States in the world, the policy changes in the wealthy countries associated with political leaders like Ronald Reagan and Margaret Thatcher, the dramatic redirection of Chinese economic strategy, and, closer to our core subject matter here, the displacement of models favored by economists by other models and the ongoing transformation of economists' professional worlds. And from other sources as well. But as we write in 2009, there are signs that this moment is passing. In using our introductory chapter to point to regional trends we hope not only to bring out some of the recent transformations in the economics professions of the Americas that were central components of the neoliberal moment, but some of the resources on which the next moment may build. Indeed there have been many important homogenizing forces in play, but there are countercurrents as well.

To propose an exploration of the interplay of economists' ideas, their professional lives, and their social and political contexts, and to look for differences as well as commonalities, change as well as inertia, and transnational connection as well as national circumstance, is to run counter to certain ways of thinking about economics. As Philip Mirowski (1989) formulates it, since its inception in the 1870s, neoclassical economic theory sought the authority of the natural sciences by borrowing their languages and metaphors.[2]

This borrowing had two important consequences. First a denationalized professional identity could be constructed around the search for the universally valid rules that govern economic phenomena, just as gravitation worked the same way in Boston and Buenos Aires and light has the same velocity in Louisville and Lima. But if economic science like physical science was the same in Boston, Buenos Aires, Louisville and Lima the resources to practice the search for the universal were greater in Buenos Aires than Lima and in Boston than Buenos Aires. The search for the universal had an intellectual geography that assigned an increasingly central position to US practice, a subject now attracting the attention of scholars (Coats 1997).

Mirowski (1989, p. 7) advances a second consequence of emulating physics. Mastery of the language of economics was restricted to advanced intellects shaped by years of study and 'impenetrable to the average literate layperson'. This has been an important mechanism creating deference to economists (Markoff and Montecinos 1993).

The future of economics sometimes appears as simply the culmination of a universal trend toward greater uniformity, often equated (positively or negatively) with the 'Americanization' of the discipline. The absorption of dominant professional rules and economic ideas has been eased by the multiplication of professional communication. At the center of transnational connections are a number of regional and global professional economic associations that sponsor periodic meetings and other events, distribute awards, journals, reports and other publications, maintain websites, sponsor research, and establish training standards. International professional organizations, such as the International Economic Association, contribute to the diffusion of a standard professional model. But the American Economic Association itself is far more internationalized than in the past. In 2002, 28.5 percent of its members resided outside the United States (Smith et al. 2004, p. 16). The Econometric Society, founded in 1930, described on its website as 'the most prestigious learned society in the field of economics' also has a worldwide membership. Indeed, 60 percent of its 3893 members reside outside the US.[3]

The Latin American branch differs from the parent body. According to the Econometric Society website, 'the Latin American meetings [LAMES] are more oriented to applied and policy-related topics than those in Europe or North America' (Gordon 2004). But despite such distinctiveness, much is standard. For example, the journal of the Latin American and Caribbean Economics Association (LACEA), *Economía,* only publishes in English (its first issue appeared in the Fall of 2000).[4] This journal, according to the LACEA website, 'demands the highest standards of theoretical and statistical rigor, but only publishes papers that are written in a style and language that make them accessible to policy makers'. The extent to which a foreign language is a significant obstacle for its Latin American readers is unknown, but the English-only practice serves the association's quest for international status and scope. One fifth of its members live neither in Latin America nor in the United States. Moreover, two of the first ten annual LACEA meetings were held in Europe: Madrid in 2002 and Paris in 2005.

Despite common trends, there is considerable geographic variation. Not all economists have equal access to travel and research funding. Professional networks and the resources they control are unequally spread around the globe. Not all regions are well represented in professional publications. Language barriers have not disappeared. Important dimensions of professional life, such as training and career paths, theoretical inclinations and scholarship patterns continue to follow national and regional traditions, either because Americanization has been out of reach, or because US imports are inevitably refracted through national and local practices, or because Americanization has been openly resisted. Even when dominant disciplinary norms are adopted in various national and institutional settings, emulation is partial and selective. Imported models are adjusted according to deeply entrenched customs and transient conjunctures. Policy challenges often inspire pragmatic responses and ideas are modified depending on institutional configurations and ideological compromises.

The implementation of structural adjustment programs in different parts of the world show, for example, that the drive toward market models that has been promoted as a standard package by powerful creditors and international advising agencies has not yielded the same results everywhere. Kurt Weyland (2004, pp. 15–17) has studied the international diffusion of policy models, using pension privatization as a pivotal case and Chile as the emblematic 'propagator' of the new paradigm. He concludes that experts, as members of 'epistemic communities', are 'most susceptible to the influence of foreign models'. Nevertheless, politicians retain the power to adapt the models to national conditions according to specific needs and political feasibility.

The data that we present in this chapter and the country chapters that follow this one will show this variation, including variation within countries (between public and private universities, between more leftist or 'structuralist'-oriented universities and those more open to free market ideas, between those who have many professors with US doctorates and those who do not). These nuances in the world history of economics, however, are often overlooked. Dissenting traditions and practices are decried as remnants of a less worthy past or pure manifestations of bad economics. Increasingly, Americanization is heralded as the only path to excellence.

Comparative studies are therefore important in the under-theorized and empirically under-studied geography of economics. A comprehensive mapping of world economics, especially when tackled by interdisciplinary teams of scholars, can reveal surprising and fascinating specificities within regional and national spaces and clarify the links between changes in the discipline and the worldwide evolution of capitalism in its many modalities.

Location shapes professional and disciplinary identities. Often inadvertently, cultural assumptions inform research premises and categories of analysis, to say nothing about policy preferences. Yet economic knowledge produced in many areas of the world, especially in non-English-speaking countries and in languages other than English, is hardly recognized. This gives a seriously distorted image of the state of the profession. The historian of economics Peter Groenewegen asks:

> Why is good applied economics based on peripheral countries not generally recognized elsewhere, let alone internationally appreciated and thereby implicitly considered as uninteresting for the world market? This is an issue worth contemplating, if only because it generates so many other problematic questions which ought to be dear to the minds of historians of ideas. (2003, p. 296)

Even in international associations with a decidedly unconventional approach to the discipline the representation from peripheral countries is limited. The International Association for Feminist Economics (IAFFE), founded in 1992, is open to people in all disciplines. IAFFE's website reads: 'We strive to be as inclusive, international, diverse and relevant as we can'. About half of the almost 700 IAFFE members are from countries other than the United States, but membership is drawn primarily from North America and Europe (53.3 and 25 percent respectively). Members in Asia represent only 8.8 percent of the total, Latin America and the Caribbean 5.8 percent and Australia/New Zealand 5.6 percent. Africa has less than 2 percent of IAFFE's members.[5]

Eminent economists from other regions are hardly mentioned in biographical dictionaries and other reference books. Table 1.1 from *Who's Who in Economics* (Blaug and Vane [1983] 2003) shows that of 743 economists for whom appropriate information is given, only 12 were born in Latin America.[6]

We can see the geography of eminence by constructing a simple pie chart displaying the birthplaces of those in *Who's Who in Economics* (Figure 1.1). Nearly three-quarters of those listed had been born in the wealthy English-speaking countries. In light of professional migration patterns, the proportion of the world's distinguished economists who are employed in those countries is surely even greater. Note that of the dozen eminent Latin Americans in Table 1.1, all had US doctorates and only one was still primarily affiliated with a Latin American institution.

While *Who's Who* claims to capture the mainstream, even a listing of economists rejecting the mainstream will have few from Latin America. The *Biographical Dictionary of Dissenting Economists* (Arestis and Sawyer 2000) pays Latin Americans scant attention as well. Only five economists are listed: Raúl Prebisch, Celso Furtado, Aníbal Pinto Santa Cruz, Luis Gonzaga de Mello Belluzzo and Carlos Díaz Alejandro.

Journals devoted to the history of economics showed a similar pattern. In our systematic search of two leading journals in the field, hardly any articles on Latin American economics were found in the years sampled

Table 1.1 Latin America's eminent economists, 1990–2000, according to Who's Who in Economics

Country	Name	Affiliation	1st Degree	PhD
Argentina	Calvo, G.A.	IADB	Yale, 1965	Yale, 1974
Argentina	Rotemberg, J.J.	Harvard	Berkeley, 1975	Princeton, 1981
Brazil	Scheinkman, J.A.	Princeton	Fed. Univ. Rio Janeiro, 1969	Rochester, 1974
Chile	Caballero, R.J.	MIT	U. Católica de Chile, 1982	MIT, 1988
Chile	de Gregorio, J.	U. Chile	Universidad de Chile, 1984	MIT, 1990
Chile	Edwards, S.	UCLA	U. Católica de Chile, 1975	Chicago, 1981
Cuba	Borjas, G.J.	Harvard	St Peter's College, 1971	Columbia, 1975
Cuba	Reinhart, C.M.	IMF	Columbia, 1980	Columbia 1988
Mexico	Mendoza, E.G.	Maryland	Anahuac, 1985	W. Ontario, 1989
Panama	Coe, D.T.	IMF	U. Maryland, 1970	Michigan, 1978
Uruguay	Spiller, P.	Berkeley	U. de la República, 1972	Chicago, 1980

Source: Our elaboration, based on Blaug and Vane (2003).[7]

between 1985 and 2005.[8] Only two out of 113 surveyed articles published in the *Journal of the History of Economic Thought* had some connection with Latin America. The co-author of one of the articles was Brazilian (Boianovsky and Tarascio 1998). The other article analyzed Juan Noyola's institutional approach to inflation (Danby 2005). In the journal *History of Political Economy*, none of the 246 surveyed articles dealt with Latin American economic thought and only one was authored by a Latin American, also from Brazil (Comim 2000).

Certainly, it is not only in the Americas that our knowledge of economics is woefully partial and incomplete. Although it was from its inception a highly transnational profession,[9] the gaze of scholars in the sub-discipline of the history of economic thought has been fixed on Great Britain and the United States, the countries that provide much of the dominant canon

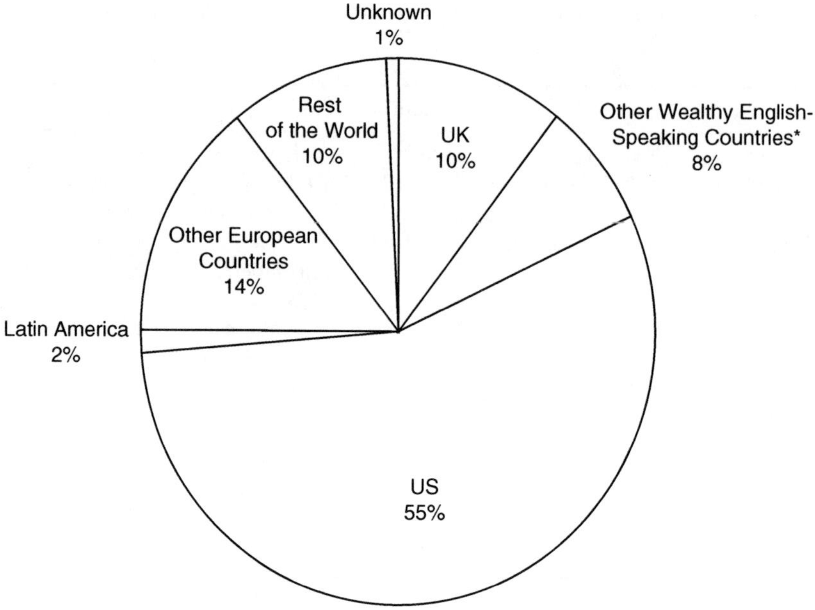

Notes: * Australia, New Zealand, Canada and Ireland.

Source: Our computation, based on data from Blaug and Vane (2003).

Figure 1.1 Country of birth of eminent economists, 1990–2000

in economics, coincidentally with their domination of the international system in the nineteenth and twentieth centuries. With the exceptions of Continental Europe and some of the English-speaking countries, the rest is terra incognita (Medema and Samuels 2001; Samuels et al. 2003; Weintraub 2002a). The central role of the US profession has the interesting consequence that much comparative information on world economics can be gathered from studies of economics in the US. As will be seen below, such is the case when studying foreign graduate students (Aslanbeigui and Montecinos 1998a), American Economic Association membership (Smith et al. 2004), or the extent to which the granting of economics doctorates is concentrated in a few universities (Barber 1997).

When students of economics have turned to inter-regional comparisons, they have mostly focused on the contrast between the economics profession in the United States and Europe. It is commonly accepted that professional practice in these two locations differ due to differences in market size, university reward systems and definitions of the proper role of economists in public life. In the less competitive atmosphere of European academia, economists tend to change employment less frequently and have a more active participation in policy and politics (Coats 2000, pp. 252–4; Frey and Eichenberger 1993; Frey and Frey 1995).[10]

For decades Latin American economists have produced interesting and innovative theoretical and policy work, but studies of the paths followed by economists and economic ideas in the region have focused on just a few institutions, primarily the UN Economic Commission for Latin America (CEPAL in its Spanish acronym) and a few countries (Brazil, Mexico and Chile have received the most attention). The history of the economics profession in Latin America has consisted mostly of partial accounts or anecdotal renderings, although the literature has grown since Hirschman (1961) wrote his seminal piece (Babb 2001; Biglaiser 2002; Camp 1975; Conaghan 1998; Drake 1993; Kay 1989; Loureiro 1997a, 1997b; Love 1980, 1996; Mallorquín 1998; Montecinos 1988, 1998a; Perez Caldentey and Vernengo forthcoming; Popescu 1997; Sikkink 1991; Silva 1991; Valdés [1989] 1995).[11] In addition, the history of economic thought became increasingly marginalized in Latin American universities themselves as the economics curriculum followed dominant trends abroad.

The relationship between Latin American economic thought and intellectual trends in other parts of the world has not been well studied. There is no survey of the Latin American economic literature, no specialized journals and no professional associations promoting the subject. The selective channeling of foreign funding to economics programs and research centers in Latin America is poorly documented. Biographies and autobiographies of eminent Latin American economists are few.

Sessions on Latin American economics or presentations by Latin Americans at the annual meetings of the History of Economics Society in the US are unusual. As we have shown, academic journals specialized in the history of economic thought include few articles on the region. Most references to economic knowledge produced in Latin American deal with one institution and one economist: CEPAL and Raúl Prebisch, the intellectual father of Latin American 'structuralism' and of the political economy of development from the perspective of the periphery. Structuralists criticized the theory of comparative advantage, calling for a strategy of import substitution industrialization to make the periphery less vulnerable to fluctuations in the world economy and reduce inequalities in international trade.

Prebisch, often celebrated as an inspiring teacher, an audacious thinker, an irreverent visionary, an accomplished diplomat, and even a prophet, was Executive Secretary of CEPAL from 1950 to 1963 and then the first Secretary General of the UN Conference on Trade and Development (UNCTAD) between 1964 and 1969. The image of Prebisch as the revered giant of Latin American economics continues to grow even today; a series of ceremonies and publications marked the centennial of his birth.[12] His contributions are being reprinted and reassessed, but within the professional mainstream Prebisch's ideas and those of his colleagues and collaborators remain unrecognized. Not many scholars other than the *cepalinos* themselves have analyzed CEPAL's intellectual production, despite its enormous and lasting influence (exceptions include Burger 1998; Love 1980). Such accounts have the invaluable knowledge of the insider, but their narratives are sometimes imbued with nostalgia for the institution's golden years and approach hagiography in discussing Prebisch (for thorough treatments, see Bielschowski 1998; Rosenthal 2004).

Mention economists and Latin America in the same sentence and someone will soon think of the University of Chicago. The Chicago tradition in Latin America has attracted considerable scholarly interest. Despite the important role they played in the transformation of economics and economic policy in Latin America – and they will figure in many of our country chapters – the 'Chicago Boys' and their ideas can hardly be counted as a home-grown Latin American current of economic thought. In any case, although a vast amount of what has been written on Latin American economics since the 1970s refers to the Chicago Boys, in our view much more research needs to be done to clarify the factors that made the Chicago network such an important component of the profession in the region.

HEMISPHERIC COMMONALITIES

Economic ideas have enormous influence on political life and Latin America is no exception. Economic notions have been invoked not only to regulate and deregulate markets but also to justify overthrowing democracy and establishing democracy, propose international alliances, foreign invasions, development priorities, loans, property transfers, and a long list of other actions and inactions of the private and public sectors.

Professional economists were assuming a role without precedent in politics and public policy in the last third of the twentieth century (Markoff and Montecinos 1993). In Latin America, as in Europe, the emulation of US-style professional norms, the wider use of mathematics both for theory and for the analysis of data as well as other international standards of professionalism have become more prevalent, although regionally distinctive professional profiles have not been totally abandoned, not even in institutions that closely follow the dominant canon. Economics journals and graduate programs advertise both their disciplinary rigor and their focus on Latin American issues (as illustrated by the *Programa Doctoral Latinoamericano* created in 2000 by the *Universidad de Chile* (Chile), *Universidad Torcuato Di Tella* (Argentina) and Mexico's ITAM).

In some ways, economics in Latin America is similar to continental European practice. As in Europe, the market for economics expertise is smaller and less competitive than in the US, the role of the state far more prominent in creating demand for economists' services and in consequence far more prominent as well in structuring the economics profession. In addition, as in Europe, academics in the social sciences, economics very much included, are far more likely to be public figures than in the United States,[13] as the growing literature on Latin American technocrats shows (for example, Centeno 1994; Centeno and Silva 1998; Domínguez 1997).

The distinctiveness of economics as developed and practiced in Latin America is rooted in the confluence of regional circumstances sketched below:

- subordinate position in the world-system;
- exclusionary class structures and elitist political systems;
- obtrusive but relatively ineffectual states;
- uneasy coexistence of nationalist and free market models of economic governance;
- persistent tensions among authoritarian, technocratic, clientelistic, and democratic orientations in decision making.

By the 1990s, Latin American economists had a strong voice in political and administrative affairs but the bases of their professional power were somewhat fragile. The precarious finances of universities and their level of politicization still precluded stable and well remunerated academic careers. Moreover, even those economists credited with the occasional economic 'miracle' were either prey to unexpected downfalls or permanently beholden to the favoritism of presidents and political patrons, especially during recurrent economic and political crises. Harvard-educated Domingo Cavallo was unceremoniously replaced after seven years as a cabinet member without even a phone call by Argentina's president, even though he was much celebrated in international circles for the implementation of major economic reforms.[14]

Despite such north–south differences, a number of threads are common to the practice of economics in the Americas, North and South alike. Consider the following:

1. In the first decades of the twentieth century, entrepreneurial technocrats worked on administrative and legal reforms and created new specialized agencies. The aim was to rationalize taxation, as well as budgetary and other aspects of economic policy, and was not altogether in accord with the economic orthodoxy of the time. In Latin America many of these technocrats were engineers and lawyers, whereas in the US the professional competence of economists was already getting recognition in government circles (see country chapters).[15]
2. The catastrophic impact of the Great Depression on unemployment and its disruption of international trade generally disheartened followers of economic liberalism and helped usher in an era of state activism, protectionist sentiment and a preference for planning techniques to face the crisis. 'Institutionalist' economists, particularly strong in the 1930s, challenged neoclassical orthodoxy and advocated a historical, pragmatic and reformist approach. But the boundaries between the main traditions were not clearly marked and most economists held eclectic views (Medema and Samuels 2003, p. 609). It was during the inter-war years that self-taught Latin American economists toured universities in the US and Europe, seeking ideas for modernizing the economics curriculum back home. They hoped to move the discipline beyond what they held to be its amateurish conditions. At this point Latin American economics was still largely housed in Schools of Law and Commerce, as illustrated in several of our country chapters.
3. Keynesianism, reigning supreme in the US from the late 1930s to the 1960s, shared common elements with Depression era policies in Latin America and later with the CEPAL school, founded in 1948 and dominant in the 1950s and 1960s.[16] The consensus at this time on the right combination of state and market favored public ownership of leading economic sectors, government controls, macroeconomic management to moderate economic cycles, and the promotion of class compromises, although the precise formula varied from country to country and over time. The transnational sway of developmentalism in the post-World War Two years contributed to the standardization of data collection methods, and the transferring of economic policy prescriptions from one country to another tilted toward state activism (on the UN role see Jolly et al. 2004). Throughout this period, state patronage in the form of commissioned research and non-academic employment was crucial for the reputation, legitimacy and growth of the economics profession.[17] Empirical, not theoretical, work was then prevalent in the US as well as everywhere else.

4. By the early 1960s, economics in the US had advanced rapidly in the direction of greater formalism and was rewarding the use of mathematics both in theory and in econometric modeling. Keynesianism was absorbed into these trends, especially after Paul Samuelson synthesized neoclassical and Keynesian theories and popularized his position through an enormously successful undergraduate text that became the world's best known introduction to economics. Samuelson's 1948 *Economics* is credited with facilitating the adoption of a common language for the profession. At the same time, the Cold War security concerns that affected the practice of economics in the US (Leonard 1991; Solberg and Tomilson 1997) also prompted a renewal of efforts to counter anti-capitalist and nationalist ideas in Latin America as a major emphasis of US foreign policy (Valdés [1989] 1995, p. 115). Healthy exports of market economic doctrines and scholarships for Latin Americans to pursue graduate studies in US departments were to contribute to this end. Thus, a new generation of US-trained Latin American economists in government positions began to apply modern economics, including the use of econometric techniques in planning.
5. This latter trend was powerfully amplified by the forms of economic aid supplied by the US under the auspices of the Alliance for Progress of the Kennedy years.[18] To qualify for aid, Latin American governments were required to produce appropriate plans to satisfy the American Keynesians. And produce these plans they did, and in doing so hired suitable economists to draw them up. They also began to educate an expanding cohort of economics students according to their canon. Intellectually and institutionally, these planning exercises tightened the connections of Latin America developmentalism and US Keynesianism.
6. At mid-century, the social sciences were flourishing in the US and Latin America, but the more 'scientific' economics discipline consistently took the lead in obtaining public and private funding for research and graduate programs and in providing policy advice to governments. Economists in the US took and were given credit for orchestrating economic recovery after the Depression and for the prosperity of the postwar years (Coats 1992, p. 409). In Latin America, the impressive results of import-substitution industrialization policies also gave economists much reason to take pride in and advertise their worth. Over the next generation there was an increasing presence of economists in policy domains that had not been their traditional strongholds (in ministries of health or foreign affairs, for example). Within the academy, what its devotees regarded as the

only true science among them expanded into intellectual turf previously occupied by other social sciences, a process some characterize as 'economic imperialism' (Hirshleifer 1985; Lazear 2000).

7. In the late 1960s, a gaping divide between conservative and radicalized intellectual and policy elites appeared in many quarters throughout the Americas. On the one hand, a more 'orthodox' delineation of the economics field was controlling the curriculum and enforcing theoretical and methodological conventions in the practice of economics. On the other, the 'heterodox', including CEPAL structuralists, Marxists and other radical schools of economic thought focused on the failures of capitalism, the plight of the poor and growing asymmetries in the international economic system.
8. Beginning in the mid-1960s a string of right-wing ideological movements, conservative politicians and generals came to power in the Americas, intent on freeing markets, curbing public expenditures, limiting welfare provisions and redistributive policies, and evicting labor from the political arena. We may take the Brazilian coup of 1964 as the starting date for this new trend. A new continental, even global, convergence pivoting around neoclassical economic orthodoxy emerged (Fourcade-Gourinchas 2006). A moribund developmentalism sought refuge in some of the UN agencies, smaller academic circles and private research institutes. Those who had pursued national and regional self-reliance or the creation of a more equitable international order were discredited and displaced by those seeking to mirror the American mainstream, a process that brought more economists into high places.
9. As in the US, a PhD became a marker of professional competence for economists in Latin America and mathematical skills became vital for securing that degree. One might alternatively describe this as an advanced stage in the emulation of physics or as the adoption of intellectually superior tools for theory construction and data analysis. One of the reasons that dissident economists converted to mathematized versions of the discipline, some have argued, was to avoid harassment and persecution (Fourcade in this book). This last option has a Latin American analogue in that leftist economists acquired impeccable academic credentials in the US to escape politically motivated marginalization, pursue stable professional careers, or even succeed in politics. This has produced an enormous selection of mathematically skilled economists in the US and Latin America, among other places. As David Colander (2003, p. 171) has it, US economics departments employ a 'mathematical filter' to recruit graduate students.[19] Colander and Klamer's (1987) survey of graduate

students in top US programs in the 1980s found that while 57 percent thought that 'excellence in mathematics' would 'put someone on the fast track in graduate school' a scant 3 percent thought that 'having a thorough knowledge of the economy' would have this happy consequence. Replicating the study in 2001–03, Colander (2005) found that among the newer crop of students, the great stress on mathematics had fallen to a still substantial 30 percent, but he concludes that recent 'students have been prescreened to be comfortable with the mathematics in the program' (2005, p. 193). Interestingly, as in the earlier study, among the US students only 2 percent thought a thorough knowledge of the economy important, but 13 percent of foreign students did so. In Latin America, students with a solid mathematical background are more likely to succeed in an academic environment designed to be equivalent to the best programs in the world and to prepare them to be admitted to the most highly competitive doctoral programs. But as mentioned earlier, even the most prestigious graduate programs in the region advertise not just a rigorous training in modern economic theory but emphasize their relevance to policy issues as well.[20]

10. No sketch of commonalities can neglect the transfer of social services from public to private providers, including the unpaid economy in which women are overrepresented as care givers and community organizers. This trend owes much to the influence of market-friendly economists in the policy apparatus and to the increasing prestige of applied microeconomics research in recent decades, a common trend in both the US and Latin America.

ECONOMICS IN LATIN AMERICA

Latin American economists, like others whose standing is not certain or fully accepted by the professional mainstream, have employed various strategies to enhance their status and establish their legitimacy. We will refer to two main professionalization modalities that we call the 'critical project' and 'economics mainstreaming'. Both stress knowledge and expertise as justifications for monopolizing policy decisions and both provide sets of symbols, beliefs and norms to be used as sources of self-identity, solidarity and differentiation from other professionals as well as from nonprofessionals. Although these strategies have coexisted, each of them has prevailed in successive periods. For example, in the 1950s, the ascendant structuralist school's critical project produced an influential interpretation of inflation that was passionately contested by an orthodox approach focusing on the money supply, the fiscal deficit and excessive demand. While structuralists were willing to tolerate moderate levels of inflation in order to promote growth, orthodox stabilization plans were willing to risk recession in order to limit public spending and eliminate difficulties in the balance of payments. Each of these strategies favored a different constellation of interests and social groups and each appealed to a different set of ideological principles. Then and now, divisions within the economics profession are inseparable from larger social and political cleavages. In the case of Latin America and other peripheral regions, conflicts within economics also reflect evolving international economic relations and transnational alliances.

Mainstreaming has been dominant since the early 1980s, when economists had a fairly consolidated jurisdiction over the economic policy domain. The profession successfully expanded that jurisdiction to social policy and other areas while excluding those whose languages and logics were different. During the military period, some observers held this as a trait of authoritarian regimes and saw 'technocrats' and generals as natural allies (for example, O'Donnell 1973, pp. 79–89). But the withdrawal of generals from presidential palaces revealed that the expanded role of economists continued, regardless of whether the political regime was democratic or not. On this point, see for example this volume's chapters on Brazil and Chile.

The two professionalization strategies compete, advancing alternative visions of how to deal with economic issues, of what economics is and of how economists ought to perform their professional and public roles. In the critical project, economic 'orthodoxy' is rejected. A new canon based on 'indigenous' interpretations challenges professional conventions and is judged more appropriate to Latin American themes than US doctrines. Separate channels of communication and professional associations are established to secure the critical project's enlargement. New sources of professional training and knowledge diffusion are created by dissident economists to set the historical record straight, new databases document heterodox contributions to the field, and funding is provided to study issues untouched or distorted by the professional mainstream.

CEPAL had a key role in the institutionalization of this project. A concerted campaign to 'Latinamericanize' economics was presented to redress power differences between the world's industrialized center and the Latin American periphery. Research on the historical and structural roots of the region's problems was used as a source of collective identity in international negotiations as well as in missions to rationalize antiquated government institutions and procedures. The practical applications of these ideas (for example, industrial 'programming' or planning, regional integration) allowed Latin American economists to gain self-confidence and policy influence, supported by a large international contingent of like-minded development specialists, then in high demand in academic and non-academic institutions.

Economics mainstreaming, by contrast, seeks greater professional recognition by embracing, not rejecting deviations from standard professional values, theories and methods of analysis. Economists pursue accepted professional credentials and join networks that include elite members of the profession. Historically, mainstreaming has been the preferred option among Latin American exporters and central bankers, international financial institutions, and more recently private universities and market-oriented think tanks. The recent turn toward emphasizing the self-correcting capacity of market mechanisms and international competitiveness led to the assumption that adopting 'good economics' would help cleanse the nefarious consequences brought about by protectionist populism and other wrongheaded and counterproductive heterodoxies. Those adhering to the neoclassical paradigm were promoted to the top of the profession, pushing other economists to less visible and influential positions. Also displaced to the margins were those working for government and international agencies whose policy preferences did not coincide with the orthodox directives issued by finance ministries, central banks, the World Bank and the IMF.

Mainstreaming is a more plausible strategy to the extent that there actually is a mainstream to follow. The prestige hierarchy of US economics departments is unusually clear by comparison with the other social sciences. A few journals are *the* places to publish and a few departments *the* places to be. Sociologists on deans' ad hoc promotion committees are reliably surprised to discover how much their economist colleagues value publication in a few specified journals over other journals or books. There are many reasons why Latin American sociologists, unlike their Latin American economist colleagues, do not follow US models as a route to power but among them is the absence of a US sociology mainstream (Han 2003; Whitley 1983). This does not mean that the economics mainstream is a fixed thing, a point to which we will return.

The most prestigious economics programs in Latin America have labored to follow more closely US models of professional training and academic careers, a theme apparent in every country chapter of this volume. In several departments, the economics curriculum was pruned of the remnants of statism, until many economists in the younger cohorts came to know little, if anything, about the innovative efforts of their forbearers, who were degraded as obsolete, parochial, ideologically biased and technically incompetent (Montecinos 1998b, p. 112).

Several universities have created their own state-of-the-art graduate programs to satisfy the growing demand for advanced economics credentials in their own and neighboring countries. Preparing students for entrance to the best graduate schools is considered an important mission of the region's best MA programs. These programs, which typically involve two years of full-time study, are an important option for mid-level government economists and private sector specialists, and are considered to be among the best in the world (Edwards 2003, p. 400).[21] Securing the return of foreign-trained economists to teach and practice in their country of origin is also driving reforms in economics education. Marketing strategies have been polished to recruit the brightest students, listing the credentials and publication records of their faculty, signing exchange agreements with foreign universities, and offering scholarships, contacts or letters of recommendation for graduate programs abroad. Students who cannot or will not spend years studying abroad enroll in the Latin American doctorates considered to be of high quality. These programs offer a similar set of core courses (micro and macro theory and econometrics) but also foster an applied, region-specific focus.

Table 1.2 lists doctoral programs from the countries treated in the chapters that follow. We see that countries with any doctoral programs at all invariably have more than one,[22] making it possible for departments in different universities to develop different identities, as data presented above and in the country chapters will clearly show.

Although in the past few decades there has been a dramatic increase in the number of economics faculty with doctoral degrees from US universities, there is a great deal of variation among and within countries. Our tabulations are presented in Table 1.3. Consider among other contrasting examples the 'un-Americanized' University of Campinas versus the graduate school at the Getúlio Vargas Foundation and PUC-Rio de Janeiro in Brazil. In Argentina, compare the public and much older Universidad de Buenos Aires with the newer, private and more US-influenced San Andrés and CEMA. In Mexico note the divergent paths followed by UNAM and ITAM. UNAM (with a minuscule 8 percent with US doctorates) was for decades a training ground for officials of the Institutional Revolutionary Party, whose fortunes have been declining with the opening up of the political arena, while ITAM (with its 69 percent) has become one of the central institutions nurturing the new technical elite. There is far less divergence among Chilean institutions. All three universities in our table have a majority with US degrees. Chile's narrower range of variation is (at least in part) testimony to the enduring legacy of Pinochet's many years of enforced mainstreaming, which included the systematic purging of dissident economists from university posts, among other punitive measures.

Table 1.2 Latin American doctoral programs in economics: six countries, 2003

Argentina	Universidad Nacional del Sur Universidad Nacional de La Plata Universidad del CEMA University Torcuato Di Tella (with ITAM and Universidad de Chile) Universidad Nacional de Córdoba
Brazil	Universidade Federal de Pernambuco Universidade Federal de Rio de Janeiro Universidade of São Paulo Universidade de Brasilia Fundação Getúlio Vargas, Escola de Pos-Graduação em Economia Universidade Federal do Rio Grande do Sul Universidade Federal do Ceará and Centro de Aperfeiçoamento de Economistas do Nordeste (CAEN) Universidade Federal Fluminense Universidade Estadual de Campinas, UNICAMP Pontifícia Universidade Católica do Rio de Janeiro
Colombia	Universidad Nacional de Colombia
Chile	Pontificia Universidad Católica de Chile Universidad de Chile (with ITAM and Di Tella)
Mexico	Universidad de las Americas-Puebla Instituto Tecnológico Autónomo de México (alone and in cooperation with U. de Chile and Di Tella) Universidad Nacional Autónoma de México
Uruguay	None

Source: University websites, 2003.

(See our Argentine, Brazilian, Mexican, and Chilean chapters for explanation of the processes producing these divergences, different in each national case.)

Table 1.4 presents data on publication patterns. It is becoming common to measure professional prestige and allocate salary raises according to the number of publications in well-known professional journals. We see that a great deal of economists' intellectual production is now in English, despite great variation among countries and among institutions within countries. The same institutions with many US PhDs are the ones with much publishing in English, with Mexico's UNAM having far fewer publications

Table 1.3 Full-time faculty with US doctorates in selected Latin American universities with graduate-level economics programs: six countries, 2003

	Fac.	Fac. w/ available info.*	% w/ US PhD
Argentina			
Universidad de San Andrés-UdeSA	10	10	70
Universidad Nacional de Cuyo-UNCU	15	14	14
Universidad Nacional de La Plata-UNLP	16	16	75
Universidad del CEMA	17	17	65
Universidad de Buenos Aires-UBA	31	25	20
Universidad Torcuato Di Tella-UTDT	20	19	63
Universidad Nacional de Córdoba-UNC	11	10	20
Brazil			
Universidade Federal Fluminense-UFF	18	18	11
Universidade do Estado do Rio de Janeiro-UERJ	21	21	33
Universidade Federal da Bahia-UFBA	16	16	19
Universidade Estadual de Campinas-UNICAMP	21	20	5
Pontifícia Universidade Católica do Rio de Janeiro-PUC-RJ	12	12	58
Universidade Federal de Santa Catarina-UFSC	16	16	6
Universidade Federal do Rio Grande do Sul-UFRGS	23	23	26
Universidade Federal do Ceará-UFC	14	14	57
Universidade de São Paulo-USP	21	21	29
Universidade de Brasilia-UNB	26	26	46
Fundação Getúlio Vargas-FGV/EPGE	18	18	67
Universidade Est. Paulista Julio de Mesquita Filho/Araquara-UNESP	15	15	7
Pontifícia Universidade Católica de São Paulo-PUC-SP	14	14	14
Pontifícia Universidade Católica do Rio Grande do Sul-PUCRS/FACE	8	8	25
Universidade Estadual de Maringa-UEM	17	17	12
Universidade Santa Ursula-USU Rio de Janeiro	12	12	50
Universidade Católica de Brasilia-UCB	12	12	8
Universidade Federal de Pernambuco-UFPE	19	19	32
Universidade Federal de Rio de Janeiro-UFRJ	5	5	0

Table 1.3 (continued)

	Fac.	Fac. w/ available info.*	% w/ US PhD
Chile			
Universidad de Chile	18	18	100
Universidad Alberto Hurtado-ILADES	10	10	60
Pontificia Universidad Católica de Chile-PUC	22	22	68
Colombia			
Universidad del Rosario-Urosario	6	6	67
Universidad Externado de Colombia-Externado	20	17	6
Pontíficia Universidad Javeriana-Javeriana	11	11	36
Universidad Nacional de Colombia-UNAL	19	17	6
Universidad de los Andes-Uniandes	7	7	57
Mexico			
Benemérita Universidad Autónoma de Puebla-BUAP	12	10	0
Universidad de las Américas-Puebla-UDLAP	12	12	75
Instituto Tecnológico Autónomo de México-ITAM	32	32	69
Universidad Nacional Autónoma de México-UNAM-Graduate Program**	72	24	8
Centro de Investigaciones y Docencia Económicas-CIDE	18	18	72
El Colegio de México, Centro de Estudios Económicos-COLMEX	20	20	45
Uruguay			
UdelaR-FCS – Departamento de Economía	36	36	17
Universidad de Montevideo-MA Program***	3	3	100

Notes:
*'Faculty with available information': this column gives us the Ns from which we calculated percentages. These numbers do not always coincide with the 'number of CVs available online' column from the next table (Table 1.4) because some websites indicate where doctorates were earned without presenting CVs or publication lists.
**These faculty are from the Division de Estudios de Posgrado only. We did not find other UNAM economists' CVs online.
*** Information available only for three faculty in charge of Master's program.

Table 1.4 Publications of economic departments in Latin America: selected universities, 1999–2003

	Average no. of publications* per faculty member 1999–2003	Percentage of those publications in English	Number of available CVs**	Number of full-time faculty listed online
Argentina				
University Torcuato Di Tella (UTDT)	8.3	76	6	20
Universidad del CEMA	3.2	75	5	17
Universidad de San Andrés	5.8	72	5	10
Brazil				
Fundação Getúlio Vargas (FGV/EPGE)	4.1	63	12	18
Universidade Estadual de Campinas (UNICAMP)	8.9	11	12	21
Universidade de São Paulo (USP)	7.3	39	19	21
Universidade Catolica de Brasilia (UCB)	3.0	53	10	12
Universidade de Brasilia (UNB)	3.5	46	11	26
Universidade Estadual Paulista Julio de Mesquita Filho/Araquara (UNESP)	2.2	10	14	15
Chile				
Universidad Alberto Hurtado-ILADES	2.8	11	3	10
Pontificia Universidad Católica de Chile (PUC-Chile)***	2.3	41	7	22
Universidad de Chile	5.9	61	16	18

Colombia				
Universidad Nacional	1.4	10	8	19
Mexico				
Instituto Tecnológico Autónomo de México (ITAM)	3.7	90	18	32
Universidad Nacional Autónoma de México (UNAM)****	7.1	17	24	72
El Colegio de México, Centro de Estudios Económicos (COLMEX)	3.6	58	17	20
Centro de Investigaciones y Docencia Económicas (CIDE)	3.2	52	17	18
Uruguay				
UdelaR-FCS – Departamento de Economía	6.2	35	6	36
Universidad de Montevideo-MA Program*****	2.5	60	3	3

Notes:
*Journal articles, book chapters and books.
** This column gives us the Ns from which we calculated the averages and percentages. These numbers may not coincide with the 'number of FT faculty with available information' from Table 1.3 because some faculty have just their degree on the website, including the university where they obtained it, but do not include the whole CV or any details about publications.
*** Only selected publications available online
****These faculty are from the División de Estudios de Post-grado only. We did not find other UNAM economists' CVs online.
***** Information available only for three faculty members in charge of Master's program.

Source: Faculty's CVs available at university websites, 2003 (with the exception of Uruguay, and UNAM-Mexico for which the information was retrieved in 2006).

in English than ITAM or Brazil's UNICAMP than its Fundação Getúlio Vargas. As we will discuss in a bit more detail, publishing in English does not necessarily mean publishing in US-based journals.

One important caution in studying Table 1.4 is that the publication computation is based on CVs located on websites. It is likely that the very existence of this data indicates some level of international orientation on the part of the faculty member, so it is likely that these figures inflate the proportion of all faculty who are publishing in English. Nonetheless, the differences among institutions are striking and are consistent with the other institutional differences we note here and that are developed in the country chapters.

Latin American economists now appear in prestigious journals, as Table 1.5 indicates, although not until recent years have their articles appeared in the top three (*Econometrica*, *American Economic Review* and *Journal of Political Economy*). But in journals with a development focus, such as *Journal of Development Economics* or *World Development*, there is a longer tradition of regional authorship.[23]

The presence of Latin American authors also reflects changes in the level of interest toward questions that require a detailed knowledge of the region as well as changes in editorial policies. The Latin American presence on the editorial boards of major journals has increased. Edwards (2003, p. 406) reports that to be the case in the following journals during the past twenty years: *Journal of Political Economy*, *Contemporary Policy Issues*, *Journal of Development Economics*, *Journal of International Economics*, *Journal of Law, Economics and Organization* and *Journal of Economics and Management Strategy*.

Latin Americans who publish in top economics journals tend to work at a US institution or co-author with someone who does. That was the case for almost 70 percent of a total of 75 articles in our sampled journals with at least one Latin American author. If we restrict ourselves to the top three journals, that proportion rises to almost 90 percent. However, in 56 percent of the articles at least one author was affiliated with an institution in Latin America. This proportion is much higher in the journals dealing with development (see Figure 1.2). These results must be taken with caution because many prominent Latin American economists hold positions in more than one institution, or even maintain institutional connections in more than one country, as discussed later.

Economics journals in Latin America are also mainstreaming the profession in several ways. More articles are being published in English. For example, the *Journal of Applied Economics*, published by CEMA University in Argentina, and *Economía*, the LACEA journal, publish only in English, thus attracting a substantial number of submissions by

Table 1.5 *Articles by Latin American authors in leading economics journals (percentage of total articles published in selected years), 1964–2004*

	American Economic Review	*Econometrica*	*Journal of Political Economy*	*Journal of International Economics*	*Journal of Development Economics*	*Journal of Comparative Economics*	*World Development*
1964	0.0	0.0	0.0	NA	NA	NA	NA
1974	0.0	0.0	0.0	3.3	6.3	NA	2.5
1984	0.6	0.0	0.0	0.0	12.9	0.0	10.7
1994	2.7	0.0	0.0	0.0	15.1	0.0	3.3
2004	4.5	4.8	3.3	11.9	17.6	0.0	3.4
Average	1.6	0.9	0.6	4.9	14.6	0.0	4.6
N	896	323	349	163	199	101	432

Note: All these journals are included in the ranking of economics journals by Kalaitzidakis et al. (2001), according to which the top three journals are *American Economic Review*, *Econometrica* and *Journal of Political Economy*. The other four are influential international or comparative journals. Articles with at least one Latin American author were counted. To detect Latin American authors we looked at the table of contents (and sometimes abstracts) of all issues published in 1964, 1974, 1984, 1994 and 2004. Authors' first and last names were used as a first approximation to their national origins. This was followed by an extensive search of CVs online for confirmation. We probably managed to exclude from the initial list most Spanish, Portuguese, Italian, and even some American economists with names like Victoria or Benjamin who were not born in Latin America. But we may have missed Latin Americans whose name did not suggest Iberian ancestry.

Source: Tables of contents of electronic version of journals.

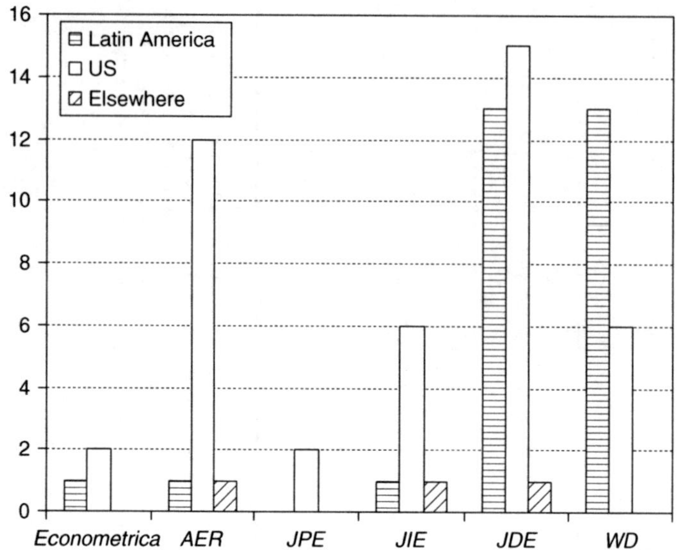

Source: Articles published in *Econometrica*, *American Economic Review*, *Journal of Political Economy*, *Journal of International Economics*, *Journal of Development Economics* and *World Development* in 1964, 1974, 1984, 1994 and 2004, which have at least one author born in Latin America (N=75 articles).

Figure 1.2 Place of employment of first author of articles in leading journals

people from outside the region.[24] Authors affiliated with prestigious Latin American institutions may submit their work in English, rather than in their native Spanish or Portuguese, in order to enhance their reputation and multiply their international contacts.[25] The decades-old *Cuadernos de Economía*, published by the Catholic University of Chile, now defines itself as a bilingual publication, having added *Latin American Journal of Economics* to its original name.[26] Regional journals appear in *EconLit*, the American Economic Association's electronic bibliography which makes articles accessible to an international readership.[27] Journals are being refurbished with international editorial boards and new procedures to referee submissions. In 2006, all members of the Editorial Board of LACEA's journal *Economía* were Latin Americans with US connections (World Bank, Harvard, MIT, Yale, Columbia, and Penn State); so were ten of the 18 board members of the *Journal of Applied Economics*. In *Trimestre Económico*, by contrast, the proportion is much lower (five out of 27). This journal accepts articles in English, but a search of the online version showed that during 1999–2004 it only published articles in Spanish (with abstracts in English).

The evidence thus far shows both a significant trend toward transnational standardization and significant variation from country to country, with individual universities differing markedly in the character of their economics departments. There are significant institutional bases for professional mainstreaming but this is hardly the only current. We will see more of these divisions in the next sections.

LATIN AMERICAN VARIATIONS[28]

Referring to Latin America as a whole is quite deceptive since a range of domestic and international processes generate important national differences in the economics profession. As the data in the previous pages hint at and as the case studies in this volume show convincingly, countries vary in the level of influence of economists, in the degree of adherence to dominant economic doctrines and ideologies, in the persistence and occasional resolution of professional conflicts, in the affinities and ties to external professional networks and institutions and in the changing academic and occupational profile of economists.

The origins of economics as a separate profession can generally be traced to the 1930s and 1940s in the larger countries, but the case of Argentina indicates that professionalization can be stalled due to political instability and the loss of university autonomy. Uruguayan economics, on the other hand, is a latecomer in which economics teaching began in the 1930s, but was clearly differentiated from accounting only in the 1960s. And in Peru, a case not covered in this volume, economics also emerged as a separate profession in the 1960s, although a department of economics and commercial sciences had existed since 1928 (Conaghan 1998, p. 144).

The founders of Latin America's economics professions were typically state modernizers less concerned with economic theory than with the quality of economic data, the design of new legislation and the skills of government personnel. The early generations of Latin American economists were often associated with nationalist and protectionist development projects, either as part of revolutionary experiences as in Mexico in the 1920s and 1930s or with technocratic efforts to expand state capitalism as in Brazil. Although advocacy of government interventionism and inward-looking development got a strong theoretical underpinning through CEPAL after the Second World War, there was significant skepticism, too, although more so in Argentina than in Brazil (Sikkink 1991), and more so in Mexico than in Chile. By the early 1970s, economics in Brazil, Chile and Mexico was polarized ideologically and institutionally, while in Colombia divisions did not grow strong until the 1980s and in Uruguay only in the 1990s. Centers of economic heterodoxy that currently remain academically and politically prominent and mostly untouched by Americanizing influences exist in Brazil and Uruguay, but are much weaker in Chile or Mexico. Chile and Mexico stand out as well for their large supply of economists with high academic credentials relative to available positions, but in other countries there is still a deficit of well-trained economists, to the extent that foreign experts are routinely hired as part of advising and consulting missions by private firms and international agencies.[29]

Foreign linkages differ from country to country, university to university, and over time. The University of Chicago's early training missions and professional mentoring, which began to alter the professional make-up in Chile in the 1950s and in Mexico in the 1960s, faltered in Argentina and Colombia, where its presence never reached beyond provincial universities, and even there its institutional influence was short-lived (Valdés 1995). Vanderbilt graduates are numerous in Brazil (thanks to an agreement signed with that university) but there is no Vanderbilt network in other countries. In fact, the number of US-trained economists in Argentina, Colombia and Uruguay stayed low much longer than in Brazil, Mexico or Chile. The differences are partly due to the uneven allocation of scholarships from national governments, private foundations and US agencies. In the 1970s, for example, the Ford Foundation awarded grants for economic research to four Latin American institutions. CIEPLAN, a major Chilean think tank got \$875000, the Latin American Institute for the Study of Transnationals (ILET) in Mexico \$250000, the Catholic University of Rio \$250000 and the Colombian Foundation for Higher Education and Development \$60000 (Ford Foundation 1982). Their relative amounts reflect the great attention paid abroad to Chilean affairs.

In several countries, US professors have played a major role teaching students, advising on curricular reforms, recommending students to US programs, influencing the distribution of scholarships, and setting up research programs. For a graphic example consider the view of a former Colombian president, who said that in his country there were two kinds of economics, B.C. and A.C., meaning before and after Currie, a Canadian Keynesian who advised President Roosevelt,[30] spent several decades in Colombia (de Vries 1997, p. 229), and whose presence looms large in our chapter on that country. Arnold Harberger recruited dozens and dozens of Latin Americans first to Chicago and later to UCLA in his more than forty year involvement with academic missions, consultancy networks, government advising and personal contacts throughout the region.

Our countries differ in their propensity to have their economists placed in international agencies. Until recently economists from Argentina, Uruguay, and Chile have been more likely to work for the UN and other international organizations in the region than have Brazilians, Mexicans or Colombians. During its first decade, headed by Prebisch, at the time in political exile from Perón's Argentina, CEPAL attracted many economists from nearby countries to its headquarters in Santiago.[31] This over-representation pattern continued in subsequent years due to the difficult conditions that economists faced in Argentina and Uruguay (on which see our chapters on those countries). Once nuclei of Argentine or Uruguayan economists found places abroad, others did as well through selective recruitment based on personal ties.

During the 1960s, leftist dissidents from nearby countries, economists included, left homelands occupied by their own militaries for the land of social experiment that was Chile between the election of President Frei in 1964 and the overthrow of President Allende in 1973 (Montecinos and Markoff 2001),[32] notably increasing the centrality of Santiago-based CEPAL. On the other hand, economists tended to stay in their own country when a sizeable and expanding professional market existed and when stable politics and prestigious technocratic niches offered adequate rewards, as was the case in Mexico (Babb 2001, pp. 203–7), or, to a lesser extent, in Colombia throughout the period under discussion. So we find few economists from those countries working for long stretches in international agencies.

The strength and nature of populist economic policies has varied much from country to country and over time, affecting government niches for economists of particular persuasions. Although theories of national and temporal variation in Latin American populism are abundant, we will avoid this interesting long detour here, except to note that factors affecting variations in populist economic policies – regime type, party structure (see, for example, Kaufman and Stallings 1991) – are also relevant to understand national and temporal variation in the role economists have played in the region.

The founding of influential journals is another indicator of the rate of professionalization of economics in different countries. Examples of specialized publications established during the first decades of the past century include the following: *Revista de Economía Política* in Argentina (1920s), *Trimestre Económico* in Mexico (1934),[33] *Panorama Económico* in Chile in 1947, *Revista de Ciências Econômicas* (1939), *Revista Brasileira de Economia* (1946), and *Revista Econômica Brasileira* (1955) in Brazil. Early on, these journals disseminated the works of internationally prestigious economists, promoted the careers of researchers and translated the most important professional debates for political and entrepreneurial constituencies. Some of these journals remain important outlets for the work of Latin American economists as well as vehicles for the hybridization of scholarly traditions and styles. Even those most eager to show technical rigor or to demonstrate similarities with US economics maintain an applied focus on the problems of Latin America or other less developed regions. As mentioned earlier, LACEA's journal *Economía* is devoted to policy-oriented matters.

If there has been a broad regional trend toward strengthening graduate programs, the strength of these programs has varied from country to country. In the 1960s there were several graduate programs. Some were designed to compete with universities abroad and attracted significant numbers of students from various countries. Examples are ESCOLATINA in Chile, which was created in 1954, and El Colegio de México, whose graduate courses date from 1961. Economics education at CEPAL was not a typical academic program, but it was the only graduate-level education that hundreds of Latin American economists received from the 1950s to the 1980s. Brazil, which has the largest number of graduate programs, created a National Association of Graduate Programs in Economics (ANPEC) in 1973. Economics education at the doctoral level is more recent, currently existing only in Argentina, Brazil, Mexico and Chile.

CONNECTIONS ACROSS THE AMERICAS

How are economic ideas and policy prescriptions prevalent in one country transferred to others? One might point to pressures from dominant states or international organizations, in control of needed resources or sometimes even force. One might point to the prestige of what seem models of success. One might point to common problems suggesting separate but similar solutions. Paul Drake (2005) has excellently catalogued a variety of such mechanisms operating in the Western Hemisphere We focus here on the linkages among economists and among institutions, the connections across borders formed as students from one country study economics in another, as professors teach abroad, as universities form agreements to foster such exchanges, as economics departments bring together people from different places, as professional economists' careers move them among university, government service, international institutions, and private think tanks, as proliferating think tanks forge connections with each other, as economists acquire facility in languages other than their own, as professional organizations bring economists together across national frontiers.

Mobile Students

Educating the elite of the profession in what is considered the most successful model requires well-financed efforts to support students, attract faculty and maintain international academic connections that both validate these efforts and provide channels for the transmission of ideas across borders. Early projects to Americanize economics training in Latin America received generous support from private foundations (especially Ford and Rockefeller; see Berman 1983) and from US government agencies. More recently, there has been a shift in geographic emphasis as large inflows of foreign funding have been devoted to revamping economics education in Russia and Eastern Europe (Bockman and Eyal 2002).

Latin American central banks and other government agencies have also financed large numbers of economics students every year, although accurate figures by country are not always available. From the US side, the recruitment of international students has helped counter the decline in graduate-level enrollment in the US.[34] The numbers are striking. US economics doctorates going to US citizens made up 67 percent of all economics doctorates in 1976–77, 56 percent in 1986–87, 43 percent in 1995–96, and had fallen to 38 percent in 2001 (Siegfried and Stock, n.d.). The percentage of foreign students in economics is much higher than in US graduate programs as a whole, which in 2000 was 26 percent (Fourcade-Gourinchas 2006, p. 172).

As students are drawn to the US, it is often assumed that they return intellectually remade in USA.[35] Transnationally mobile students would thus be a major vehicle for diffusion. But we wonder if that large student presence is only so much inert clay on which their professors imprint the doctrines of the finished science of economics or if they bring something to their studies, to their departments, and to economics as well. It has often been argued that the sequence of courses and the pedagogical style used in economics programs leave little room for the exploration of alternative theoretical paradigms, the creative and critical interpretation of course contents and the pursuit of students' broader interests (Aslanbeigui and Montecinos 1998a; Bartlett 1999; Colander and Brenner 1992; Fullbrook 2004; Hansen 1991). But although graduate student selection criteria place much emphasis on mathematical ability and strict curricular demands eventually change the students' initial preferences, available data suggest that women and foreign students tend to be more concerned with policy-related issues and macroeconomics and also generally favor a practical knowledge of the economy (Albelda 1997; Colander 2005).

Let us speculate a moment beyond the data we, or anyone, has gathered. As academic centers in North America (and to some extent in Europe) recruit increasingly cosmopolitan cohorts of graduate students, most of them with undergraduate economics degrees from their country of origin, perhaps the much criticized intellectual insularity of economics could be lessened and a more globalized discipline emerge instead. Foreign students enrich the pool of languages spoken within US economics departments. Their knowledge of national institutional and policy environments can moderate an excessive focus on US issues and practices. They may motivate their professors to become more interested and knowledgeable about other areas of the world, as evidenced in the proliferation of co-authored pieces on transition economies. This is by no means incompatible with those students buttressing the mathematization of economics. They enter with greater math skills, on average, than the US-educated (Colander 2005, p. 177), perhaps a reason why they expect to complete their degrees in less time than the median (Aslanbeigui and Montecinos 1998a, p. 173). In sum, the impact of foreign students on the ability of the economics profession to account for the complexities of economic phenomena may be far more salutary than usually acknowledged.

Not only might foreign students in US programs bring something as well as receive something, but the Latin American universities, newly sensing competitive possibilities, may continue to upgrade. New doctoral programs in Latin America are addressing the rising demand for graduate-level credentials in economics. These programs may be small (the one created in 2002 at the Catholic University in Chile admits a maximum of six students per year), but are especially important for talented people who do not want or cannot afford to go abroad, or who have family responsibilities that do not permit them to do so. In addition, there are recent signs that intra-regional academic exchanges are growing stronger among Latin American universities. At the *Programa Doctoral Latinoamericano*, which, as mentioned earlier, combines the resources of participating institutions in three countries, students can earn an MA at any of the three schools. During a second phase, students register for doctoral-level courses and spend four months in each program.

In general, the proliferation of graduate-level training programs has opened up attractive career opportunities in Latin America, enticing many holders of foreign doctorates to return to the region. The growing number of US-educated economists teaching in the Americas is a powerful predictor of the type of economics that will be practiced in the private and public sectors in the coming decades, but it does not predict simple mimicry.

Mobile Professors

As the number of US-trained economists living outside the US grows, so have the ranks of foreign-born economists in the US.[36] Many promising new PhDs (and even productive faculty members in universities outside the US) are attracted to professorships in the US, although not much is known about how the American economics profession is adapting to this phenomenon. In a tentative approximation, Aslanbeigui and Montecinos (1998b) confirmed this trend. Their June 1998 telephone survey of major economics departments showed, for example, that at MIT foreign faculty were 33 percent (out of 30) and that they were half of the six faculty hired in the previous three years; at Chicago, 32 percent (out of 28), including all six new hires; at Northwestern, 30 percent (out of 37) and two of four new hires; at Cornell, 48 percent (of 21) faculty were foreigners; at Brown 48 percent (of 25), including six of ten new hires.

Sebastián Edwards (2003) argues that the growing presence of foreign professors has contributed to reshaping US economics both in research and in teaching.[37] Our own data (Table 1.6) on the presence of Latin American economists in US departments indicate that their numbers are especially significant at the lower ranks, which promises a future of more senior professors than at present in the prestigious departments. The table also reveals some striking national differences. Argentine economists frequently stay in the US, a phenomenon that Glen Biglaiser's chapter suggests is due to the unattractiveness of Argentine academic careers (see also Biglaiser 2002). Conversely, very few Brazilian and Mexican economists hold positions in US institutions.

The largest bloc of the 51 US-based Latin American professors had been trained at Chicago (8), followed by Berkeley (5), Rochester (5), and then MIT, Minnesota, Pennsylvania, Wisconsin and Yale (4 each). The largest number employed in a single US department was at UCLA, followed by Maryland, Yale, Northeastern and Wisconsin. Whatever the past significance of the famous Chile–Chicago connection, the changing network of linkages is far more multiplex.

The different methodology of Siegfried and Stock (n.d.) gives parallel results. By their estimate, the number of new economics PhDs hired in the US has remained stable at about 700 annually over the past three decades, but the proportion of non-US citizens among them has risen.[38]

But now look at the last columns of Table 1.6, where we indicate whether the Latin American faculty in US departments maintained a position in their home countries. It turns out that although they were working in the best US programs, nearly half[39] remained involved in Latin

Table 1.6 Latin American faculty in top 50 US economics departments, 2006*

Country of origin**		Current position			Hold positions in home country***		
	No.	Prof.	Assoc. Prof.	Assist. Prof.	Yes	No	No data
Argentina	20	6	1	13	10	6	4
Bolivia	1			1	1		
Brazil	8	1		7	4	4	
Chile	5	4	1		1	3	1
Colombia	7			7	2	4	1
Costa Rica	1			1		1	
Cuba	1	1				1	
Mexico	4	3		1	2	2	
Peru	2	1		1		2	
Uruguay	2	1	1		1	1	
Total	51	17	3	31	21	24	6

Notes:
*We followed Dusansky and Vernon (1998) in identifying the top 50 economics departments.
**Country of origin: refers to country of birth when that information was available in the CV or some online source; failing that, we considered the country where the person obtained the undergraduate degree.
*** Includes academic and other positions held anytime since January 2000.

Source: Departmental and university websites and online faculty CVs. Data collected in 2003 and verified in 2006.

American academic and policy activities. Foreign economics professors in US universities seem to maintain a dual professional identity. They continue to publish in their mother tongue, cultivate connections and co-author studies with colleagues abroad. They also recruit students from their home countries and teach courses with a distinctive non-US flavor (courses such as 'Economic Problems in Latin America', or 'Economics in Emerging Markets'). Some of these economists seem prone to pursue a multi-dimensional research agenda: partly theoretical and partly applied and comparative, drawing on topics of interest in the countries they know. Multidimensional careers are also found among economists who regularly spend time teaching or consulting for international organizations or governments.[40] Their presence in US departments cannot be reduced to their 'Americanization' because they are bringing Latin American concerns with them. Or perhaps, if by 'Americanization' we may mean the establishment of linkages among the Americas rather than just the replication of the US, it is Americanization after all.

Professional Associations

Professional networks come alive when crowds of conference participants meet face to face in sessions, corridors and after hours, sharing thoughts, gossip and invitations. In the process, common beliefs are reinforced; the myths and legends of professional culture are displayed and reenacted; and the heart of the profession pulses with renewed vigor when members gather in these ceremonial occasions staged by the profession's leaders, in accordance with approved by-laws and traditions. No distant exchanges between authors and readers, no newsletters or websites adequately substitute for the excitement of seeing colleagues up close, for playing audience or performer in the ritual celebrations of the trade's doctrines and heroes. Professional associations' meetings help renew members' adherence, forge bonds of loyalty, help the young find mentors, the old disciples and the in-between collaborators. Those who do not participate in the right meetings may put their professional capital at risk.

No wonder that long trips do not dissuade economists from attending far away meetings. A sizeable group of Latin Americans (338) were members of the American Economic Association in 2006 according to the AEA database.[41] Many of them travel to the US every January to attend the AEA and the Allied Social Sciences Association meetings. In the late 1970s, Latin Americans, then a small fraction of the Econometric Society membership, established the Latin American Meetings of the Econometrics Society (LAMES). Since 1980, LAMES's reputation as the most esteemed of the regional gatherings continues to attract very high quality conference papers. Econometric Society Fellows, a highly select group of the profession's stars, frequently attend.[42] Perhaps one sign of the prestige of LAMES is that the connections with top US departments tend to be stronger than those of the other regional Econometric Society meetings, as shown in Table 1.7.[43] LAMES is seen by US professionals as something quite new. Arnold Harberger (1997, p. 309) comments that their debates are devoid of 'any ideological overtone', something he attributes to the society's 'brand name . . . which by itself probably serves as a repellent to most Latin American ideologues'.[44]

Founded in 1992, the Latin American and Caribbean Economics Association (LACEA) membership numbers a little over one thousand.[45] LACEA members reside more often in Latin America than anywhere else but as many as 37 percent live in the US, and a sizable 21 percent reside in other parts of the world, as shown in Figure 1.3.

Table 1.7 Regional meetings of the Econometric Society

	Total number of presentations	Percent with US affiliation*
South and Southeast Asia (2002 in Pakistan)	101	33
European Meeting (2002 in Italy)	681	13
Far Eastern Meeting (2004 in Korea)	522	28
Australasian Meeting (2002 in Australia)	156	7
American Winter Meeting (2003 in Washington DC)	479	86
Latin American Meeting (2002 in Argentina)	184	47

Notes:
*If more than one affiliation, we counted the first mentioned.
All presentations counted, except in the European Meeting, where individuals were counted once.

Source: Conference programs online.

LACEA membership within Latin America varies substantially, yet another indication of national variation in mainstreaming. Although Mexicans form the largest national contingent (Figure 1.4), Chileans are strongly represented in the association leadership. LACEA meetings tend to be organized by institutions that have close connections with US academia.[46]

The LACEA conference has become the largest academic conference on economics in Latin America (Fiszbein and Galiani 2005). In 2006, LACEA and LAMES were simultaneously hosted by ITAM, the *Instituto Tecnológico Autónomo de México*. If one takes both LACEA and LAMES as sites where a regional identity among professional economists is manifested, and forged, it is noteworthy that these two bodies are strongly invested in transnational mainstreaming, as is the Mexican host institution, ITAM (for more on ITAM, see our Mexico chapter). A term like 'hybridization' seems a better summary term than 'Americanization' pure and simple.

Table 1.8 compares the number of papers presented at LACEA and LAMES with the number of papers presented at the Econometric Society's European Meetings (ESEM). In 2006, ESEM was celebrating its sixty-first gathering. Considering the youth of LAMES, its membership and participation are significant.

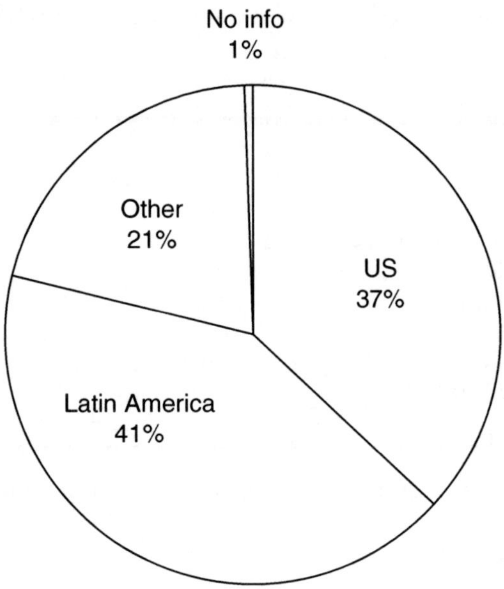

Source: LACEA online membership directory, available on its website, www.lacea.org. Retrieved on November 26, 2005.

Figure 1.3 LACEA members by place of residence, 2005

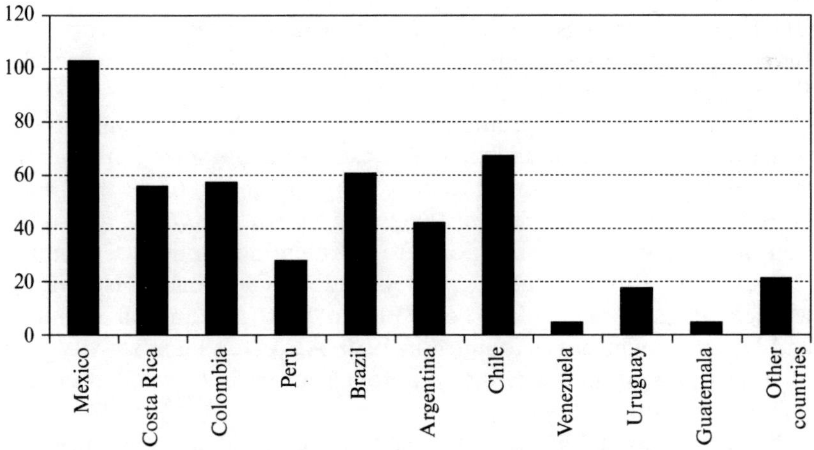

Source: LACEA online membership directory, 2005. Available on its website, www.lacea.org. Retrieved on November 26, 2005.

Figure 1.4 LACEA members in Latin America, by country of residence

Table 1.8 Number of papers presented at LACEA, LAMES and ESEM

	1997	1998	1999	2000	2001	2002	2003
Latin American and Caribbean Economics Assoc. (LACEA)	215	234	276	275	255	415	379
Latin American Meetings of the Econometric Society (LAMES)	186	194	367	*	167	305	185
Econometric Society European Meetings (ESEM)	526	633	599	373	625	629	536

Note: * World Congress. No regional meetings in 2000 (except for the North American winter meeting).

Source: Fiszbein and Galiani (2005).

The professional activity at LACEA and LAMES shows the economics profession in Latin America moving from the margins to the core of the mainstream at high speed. This is manifested in other ways as well. Edwards (2003, p. 412) lists 54 Latin American economists with more than 100 journal citations, based on the Social Sciences Citation Index (1975–2003). The list includes 21 Chileans, 16 Argentines, seven Mexicans, four Brazilians and the rest from Peru, Uruguay, Colombia and Venezuela. Eight had more than 1000 citations.

Beyond these very prominent professional bodies, some Latin American economists participate in transnational organizations that are less well known in the United States. The most important of them may be AEALC (*Asociación de Economistas de América Latina*), an association of professional organizations from Argentina, Bolivia, Colombia, Costa Rica, Cuba, Ecuador, El Salvador, Guatemala, Honduras, Mexico, Panama, Paraguay, Peru, Puerto Rico, Dominican Republic and Uruguay, which was founded in 1980. AEALC's main activity is to organize international meetings on globalization, but it also organizes regional meetings.[47]

These professional linkages suggest a certain 'regionalization' in Latin American economics. Connections are developing beyond the national level that link Latin American economists to each other. Transnationalization means more than connections to the US. This regionalization is likely to proceed along various channels, finding champions among the more conventional professional circles as well among those trying to rekindle more radical traditions in economic thought and practice.[48]

In addition to these transnational organizations, there is a proliferation of national professional associations, as the following list indicates:[49]

- Argentina: *Asociación Argentina de Economía Política*, founded in 1957.
- Bolivia: *Colegio Nacional de Economistas*, founded in 1964.
- Brazil: *Associacão Nacional de Centros de Posgraduacão em Economia* (ANPEC), founded in 1973.
- Chile: *Sociedad de Economía de Chile* (SECHI), founded in 2002.
- Colombia: *Sociedad Colombiana de Economistas*, founded in 1958.
- Costa Rica: *Colegio de Profesionales en Ciencias Económicas*, founded in 1970.
- Cuba: *Asociación Nacional de Economistas de Cuba*, founded in 1979
- Dominican Republic: *Colegio Dominicano de Economistas.*
- Ecuador: *Federación Nacional de Economistas del Ecuador.*
- El Salvador: *Colegio de Profesionales en Ciencias Económicas* (COLPROCE).
- Guatemala: *Colegio de Profesionales en Ciencias Económicas.*
- Haiti: *Association of Haitian Economists*, AEH.
- Mexico: *Colegio Nacional de Economistas*, founded in 1961.
- Panama: *Colegio de Economistas.*
- Paraguay: *Colegio de Economistas del Paraguay.*
- Peru: *Colegio de Economistas del Perú.*
- Puerto Rico: *Asociación de Economistas de Puerto Rico.*
- Uruguay: *Colegio de Contadores, Economistas y Administradores del Uruguay* (CCEA), founded in 1893.
- Venezuela: *Federación de Colegios de Economistas de Venezuela.*

The existence of these bodies testifies to a lot of geographically diverse activity on a variety of geographic scales and with varying degrees of connectedness to the US. Latin American economists are increasingly organized nationally, increasingly connected to the US, and increasingly connected to each other across national borders. The diversity of economics in Latin America is as much the product of national histories as it is of transnational bonds. As weighty as the US is, the recent Latin American trends cannot simply be reduced to US imposition.

THINK TANKS

Alongside universities, professional organizations and international agencies, think thanks have emerged as major sites for transnationalizing economics. The proliferation of think tanks adds new dimensions to the politics of expertise. Early US versions developed as non-governmental sources of expert policy advice prompted by the absence of the strong civil service common in Europe (Smith 1989, p. 181). Although they can be found from the early twentieth century, the term 'think tank' became widely known in connection with the Rand Corporation, established in 1948 and still one of the largest in the knowledge industry (Smith 1989, p. 179). RAND became a prototype for later think tanks, once the Truman administration began to provide generous funding to academic and independent research centers (Abelson 2004, p. 219). By the early twenty-first century, adaptations of the American model were observed around the world (Stone and Denham 2004), very much including Latin America.

Think tanks gained further momentum in the 1970s as platforms for debating the proper place of state and market, and especially for criticizing the still prestigious mix of Keynesianism and developmentalism, undercutting the appeals of state action to limit the harms of capitalism. Think tanks became an accepted part of the 'political architecture of policy making' (Rich 2004, p. 208; see also Stone 2004; Stone and Denham 2004; Stone and Maxwell 2005).

Although think tanks differ in the extent to which scholarly analysis and advocacy are combined (some stress technical expertise while others are unabashedly ideological), partisan and non-partisan activities are often hard to distinguish. The literature makes clear that in recent decades the boundaries between research and ideology, analysis and advocacy have blurred. And given the close relationship of some with governments or parties, they blur the private–public boundary as well. Because of definitional discrepancies and ambiguities, estimates of the number of think tanks in the US vary widely. In one estimate their numbers went from fewer than 70 in 1969 to more than 300 in the late 1990s (Rich 2004, p. 204). Abelson (2004, p. 216) puts the number at 1600.[50] In Latin America, too, their numbers have risen notably, as shown below.[51]

In the US and elsewhere an ever larger contingent of conservative think tanks has benefited from the growing political activism of businesses and corporations, merging anti-communism, libertarian anti-statism, neoconservative thinking and neoclassical economics. From this ideational platform a major offensive was launched against the Keynesian status quo, citizens' entitlements to social benefits and government financed developmentalist programs. Think tanks equipped the political right with new strategies to advertise their proposals and win the battle of ideas by changing public perceptions of governments, politics and the solution to social problems. According to Andrew Rich, in the mid-1990s, conservative think tanks in the US outnumbered liberal ones by 2 to 1 and outspent them by 3 to 1. A survey conducted by Rich in 1997 among congressional staff and journalists showed that the four most influential think tanks were the conservative Heritage Foundation, Cato Institute and American Enterprise Institute, and the liberal Brookings (Rich 2004, p. 231).

Think tanks connect experts and non-experts through internet web pages, media commentary, public lectures, books, scholarly reports, magazines and other publications, conferences and policy briefs. Their capacity to fund and commission research allows them to promote and publicize new ideas whose credibility is provided by their teams of experts. In the words of one observer, they claim to 'help government think' (Weiss 1992, p. viii). We may speculate that they are far freer to aim at and achieve coherence around ideologically defined identities than are either government agencies or university departments. Government agencies are enmeshed in bureaucratic structures, accountable to superiors involved in the give-and-take of actually carrying out policies, and, in many parts of the world in the early twenty-first century, at least nominally accountable to elected parliaments or presidents. University departments are places where traditions of devotion to the accretion of knowledge, the building of theory, and the examination of evidence through ever more refined methodologies are highly institutionalized agendas with complex relationships with any ideology. But think tanks provide a setting for thinking about society where the constraints of the academic or bureaucratic life are much relaxed, although they may have their own constraints.

While they are institutionally separate from the university and the government agency, they develop ties to political, academic, corporate and media elites. They thereby increase the influence of experts and their ideas among policy makers and the public at large. Think tanks can also catapult ambitious individuals into political careers, substituting for or complementing the institutional support of political parties or mass movements. In addition, they provide a resting place for those perhaps temporarily out of office to maintain their involvement with public issues. In other words, think tanks are full of past and future office-holders. Examples are found in many countries.

We can approximately track the growth of think tanks in Latin America and Figure 1.5 presents the results. We drew on two different sources: the National Institute for Research Advancement's World Directory of Think Tanks 2005 (NIRA 2005) and the Atlas Economic Research Foundation's Think Tank Directory (Atlas 2006). While NIRA's listing covers a broad

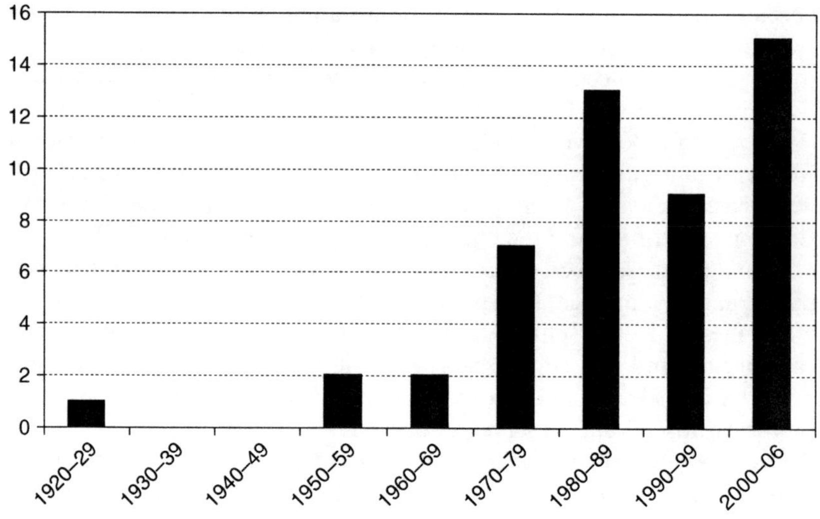

Note: * Argentina, Brazil, Chile, Colombia, Mexico and Uruguay.

Source: NIRA's World Directory of Think Tanks 2005 and Atlas Economic Research Foundation's Think Tank Directory.

Figure 1.5 Number of think tanks founded per decade: six Latin American countries, 1920–2006*

spectrum, Atlas focuses on pro-market advocacy. NIRA, a Japanese think tank itself, aimed at a comprehensive worldwide think tank directory. Atlas is a Virginia-based organization that 'serves the international market-oriented think tank movement by helping develop independent local think tanks and related programs that advance the ideas of freedom'.[52] Atlas itself turns out to be the central node in US–Latin American think tank connections (see below) and its president is Argentine.[53]

The timing suggests a process happening in parallel with US developments, not a delayed imitation: a small number founded before the Second World War, an increased rate of founding in the 1970s and 1980s, and a continuing proliferation of new ones since then.[54]

Experts are sometimes simultaneously affiliated with think tanks, universities, governments, businesses, parties and international organizations. The revolving door pattern is also common, as experts move in and out of institutions and across national borders, reinforcing professional communities and personal loyalties that cross the boundaries of institutions and national states. Consider, for example, the trajectory of the

Peruvian economist Pedro-Pablo Kuczynski, a naturalized US citizen, who served as Minister of Economy and Finance in 2001–02 and again in 2004–05, and who was later named Prime Minister in 2005. At other points in his impressive career he had major roles in government as Minister of Energy and Mines and deputy director of the Peruvian Central Bank; in the private financial sector as chairman of First Boston International and managing director of First Boston Corporation; in multilateral organizations with senior positions at the World Bank, as well as other top positions in transnational firms. He has published books on Latin American economic themes and has participated prominently at the Institute for International Economics in formulating and assessing the Washington Consensus (Kuczynski and Williamson 2003).

Economists, often in collaboration with political and foreign affairs specialists, appear prominently in think tanks as they advance market-centered agendas. For example, Milton Friedman and other prominent economics professors were on the academic advisory board or among the resident scholars of the Heritage Foundation and the American Economic Institute. The Mont Pelerin Society included Nobel laureates Hayek and Friedman, two emblematic figures at the University of Chicago. Ludwig von Mises of the Austrian School was even more hostile to government and his disciple Murray Rothbard was a founder of the Libertarian Party and the Cato Institute (Aune 2001, p. 102).

Many think tanks are becoming transnational, opening offices or sponsoring activities, individuals and organizations in other countries. But the international diffusion of think tank expertise and funding is not new. The Ford and Rockefeller foundations for example, have been actively involved in cross-border projects for decades. Since the end of the Cold War, developing and former socialist countries compete for think tank resources. American and European foundations are providing significant aid to emerging research centers in Central and Eastern Europe, as well as in Latin America (Wallace 2004, p. 284).

Think tanks circulate policy models from North to South without having to face directly the resentment and public resistance generated by financing conditionality (for example, the riotous mobilizations against the IMF and the World Bank; see Walton and Seddon 1994). But, and this has been much less appreciated, the think tank network provides vehicles for moving ideas and models of success and failure from South to North as well. From his tribune at Cato, José Piñera has for years extolled the benefits of pension privatization of the type adopted in Chile when he was Pinochet's Labor Minister in 1980. The Latin American Chicago Boys and other such groups have figured prominently in marketization campaigns carried out in former socialist and transition economies. In what

Stone has called the 'global agora' (2004, p. 41), scholars, advocates and consultants of varied national origins criss-cross local and transnational levels disseminating policy ideas and partisan doctrines. These webs do reflect differences between resource-rich and less affluent networks, but the global South has acquired a far from negligible presence in them, anchored in scholarly communities, promoted by transnational political parties, or courted by policy entrepreneurs in multilateral organizations. Some of these networks provide vehicles for the exploration of new research and policy models. An example of the latter is Joseph Stiglitz's Global Development Network initiative, the North-South network he promoted during his tenure as Chief Economist and Vice President of the World Bank. In his view, GDN would allow local institutions to play an important role, adapting 'development knowledge to local conditions and culture' (Stiglitz 2000, p. 32; see also King 2005).

We present some evidence that shows the extent of attention to Latin America on the part of US think tanks, as well as a snapshot of the state of transnational ties among these important institutions. We include the three most prominent think tanks associated with pro-market advocacy (Cato Institute, Heritage, American Enterprise), as well as the Institute for International Economics (IIE), which counts among its members the very coiner of the phrase 'Washington Consensus', John Williamson (2003). Figure 1.6 clearly shows a rise in generating ideas about Latin America on the part of major think tanks.[55]

But this is not because the gaze of think tankers turned away from somewhere else towards Latin America. As a proportion of all publications, the focus on Latin America has been more stable, as shown in Figure 1.7. Think tank intellectual production has simply been on the rise in general, with some devoting proportionately more and some proportionately less attention to Latin America. The Cato Institute and the Institute for International Economics have increased their proportional attention to Latin America while Heritage and American Enterprise have decreased theirs.[56]

As for the empirical delineation of the connections across borders, this is another very large subject of which we can present just a snapshot here. Let us define the universe whose connectedness we wish to illustrate. For the US, we will restrict ourselves here to the four important pro-market think tanks in Figures 1.6 and 1.7, plus Atlas. For Latin America we will restrict ourselves to the national cases that figure in our country chapters and we will use as a list of those countries' think tanks the organizations mentioned in the compilations of NIRA and Atlas as before.

We may get a good deal of information about these organizations from their websites. In our global age, we may take as one significant indicator

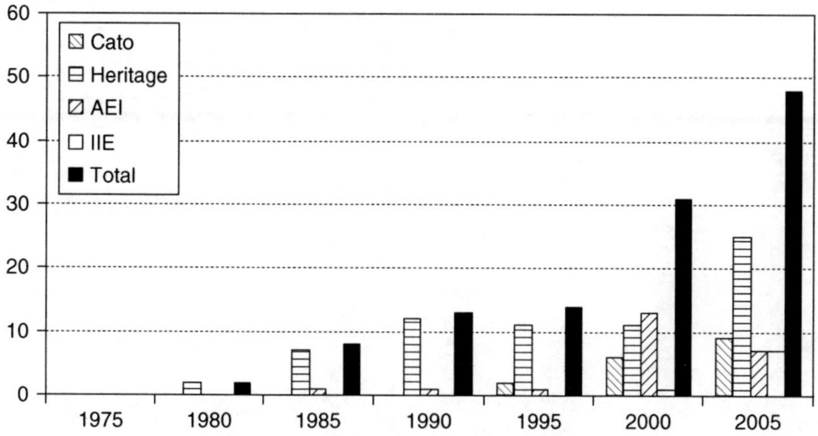

Source: Our counts, drawn from publication lists on think tank websites.

Figure 1.6 Annual number of US think tank publications related to Latin America, 1975–2005

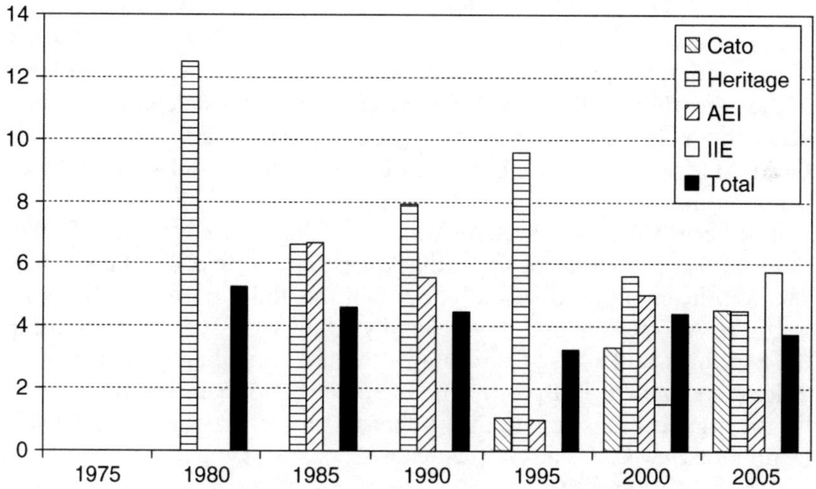

Source: Our counts, drawn from publication lists on think tank websites.

Figure 1.7 Annual percentage of US think tank publications related to Latin America, 1975–2005

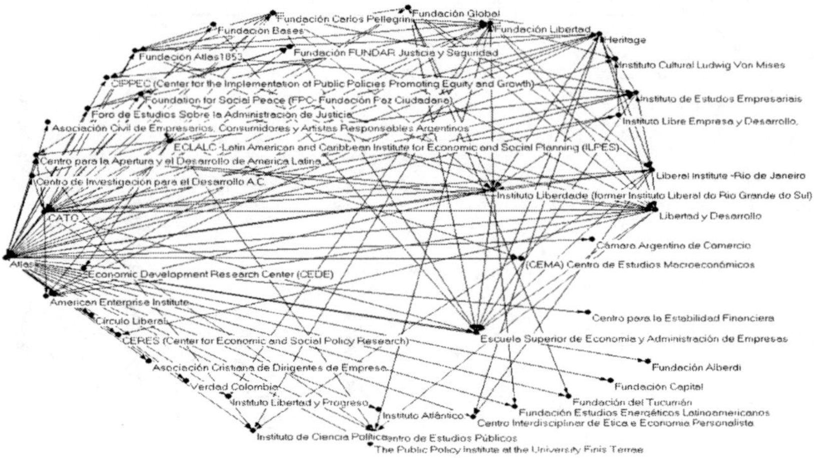

Note: *Argentina, Brazil, Chile, Colombia, Mexico, Uruguay, United States.

Source: Think tank websites.

*Figure 1.8 Think tanks' electronic connections in the Americas: 51 think tanks, seven countries**

of connection the presence of a link on that website to the website of any of the other think tanks in the little universe we have just defined. Our universe, thus defined, would have 53 organizations located in our half-dozen Latin American countries, but seven had no website and were excluded from the study.

In other words, we collected citations by think tank websites of other think tanks for a total of 46 Latin American and five US think tanks. The website citations are usually found in the 'links' pages of think tank websites. A hyperlink does not generally tell us what type of relationship the two think tanks have (for example funding, founding, and so on) but at least we know it is a positive tie of some sort. In general, think tanks list the organizations akin to their interests, those with which they actively identify or view as 'friends to their cause'.[57]

Figure 1.8 shows the web of connections linking our 51 think tanks. There are obviously a lot of connections. One can see many links for US think tanks like the Cato Institute, but a number of Latin American sites appear highly connected as well. Quite a few of these connections span national frontiers, but this is not so easy to discern through the web. As in many network studies, a simplified picture may help bring out essential elements.

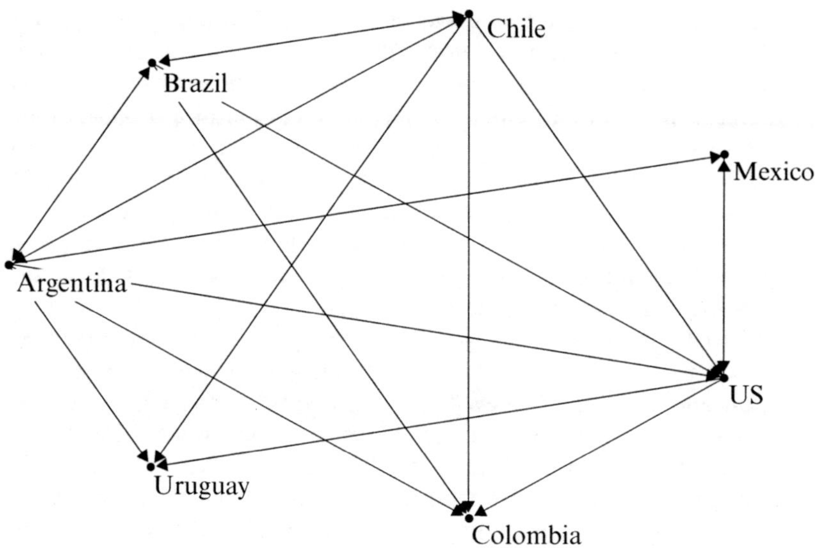

Source: Think tank websites.

Figure 1.9 Electronic connections among the think tanks of the Americas

For a broad snapshot we turn to the interconnections among countries, not individual institutions. If any of the five US cases had a link to any Mexican think tank, we called this an instance of the US naming Mexico and in our picture would have an arrow originating in the US and pointing to Mexico. If any Mexican instance names a US organization, we would then have an arrow running between the two countries pointing in both directions. We present the simplified picture in Figure 1.9.[58]

Puzzling our way through these network graphs is worth the effort because the proliferation of the think tank as an organizational form appears to be promoting interesting changes in the practice of economics. We highlight five:

1. First, a typical activity of think tanks is to bridge the gaps among specialists, political actors and the general public. This has now become an integral part of global strategies for economic policy change. Thinks tanks have contributed to the commercialization of economic advice through the worldwide expansion of the market for consultancy.
2. Second, think tanks bring together different kinds of expertise under one roof, often cemented by a political program. The mandates and

research agendas of policy agencies that used to focus mostly, even exclusively, on economics now officially proclaim the need to open interdisciplinary dialog on issues such as the quality of institutions, the level of political participation, and the inclusion of a broader range of variables in statistical models. (We hazard the guess that think tanks are more effective in promoting such cross-disciplinary research than universities, where professors' solidarities are often bounded by departmental affiliations.) Economists have therefore been called to go 'beyond economics' as they try to advance the success and sustainability of market reforms.

3. Third, think tanks sustain a different prestige structure than do university departments. Universities reward theoretical elegance or innovation and ingenuity in developing methodological esoterica, leading academics to a certain disdain for the demands of public service, though much more so in the US than in Latin America. The claim that even top US economics departments do not prepare students for real world policy advice is a common refrain (Colander 2003; Stock and Hansen 2004). But think tanks reward policy-relevant theory and presentations of data that can be communicated to policy makers or to the general public. Think tanks' access to corporate and other types of funding for applied economic research seems to temper pressures to conform to an academic professional system that rewards theoretical work above policy. It is no coincidence that the authoritative presence of economists in policy circles is now spilling over to legislatures, political parties and media outlets. This big generalization about trends needs to be softened with a lot of variation. The clout of economists with parties and the public, in our informal judgment, is less sweeping in the US than Latin America, and less in Brazil, say, than in Chile. Nonetheless, economists are not just devising conceptual frameworks for policy reforms but also translating them into guides for public deliberation.
4 Fourth, competition among think tanks for grants, contracts, public repute and political influence, and competition for recruiting the personnel who could attract grants and contracts, and earn the repute, may be a powerful element in reshaping the economics profession globally in some of the same ways that that competition among academic departments for resources and for the prestigious economists that would win these resources shaped the US profession (as discussed in our US chapter). This parallelism further encourages the transnational diffusion of styles of economic thought and policy advice associated with the US.
5. Fifth and finally, many organizations in which large numbers of economists are present, from academic institutions to development

agencies and professional associations, seem to be metamorphosing into think tanks (examples include LACEA, CEPAL and the World Bank), so one can reasonably expect that this form of fusing research and policy advice will be extending its reach into at least the near future.

But think tanks are not only important vehicles for the diffusion of dominant ideologies. They also play an important role in efforts to counter those ideologies, to challenge the sanctification of the market, contest global economic structures and oppose the narrow views of democracy advanced by orthodox policy elites. Non-governmental organizations, policy activists and dissident experts are joining forces in the dissemination of resources, information and alternative interpretations of the linkages among policy making, representative democratic and human rights. Think tanks are among the tools that centrists – and leftists – employ to regain some of their previous influence, challenge the currently accepted policy consensus, back a new generation of policy entrepreneurs, mobilize followers in their campaigns against the intellectual hegemony of market models, and weaken the grip of conservative media.[59]

BEYOND THE NEOLIBERAL MOMENT

In the chapters that follow, specialists describe the ways in which the development of the economics profession in national settings was a part of what we may call the neoliberal moment, when the strengthening of certain currents among professional economists and the strengthening of certain currents among the holders of political power worked in tandem. The broad trend was for a restructuring of the economics profession in Latin America to more closely resemble a US model, for that profession to be more visibly connected to political power in one country after another, and for the web of professional connections across national boundaries to be strengthened as well. We might summarize our country studies as showing the ways in which the economics professions of a group of countries helped shape this neoliberal moment and the ways they were shaped by it.

But before ceding the floor to our country specialists, we want to think a little beyond the neoliberal moment, for even before the global crisis that erupted in full force in 2008, there were many signs that this moment was coming to an end. References to a post-neoliberal phase in Latin America were becoming increasingly common (Cypher 2005; Gore 2002; Green 2003; Huber and Solt 2004). Even staunch defenders of market reforms were ready to concede the frequently disappointing character of policy outcomes, especially since the crises of the late 1990s (Kuczynski and Williamson 2003). It has been sometimes suggested that the champions of structuralism began to take less statist visions seriously when they confronted the empirical reality that the sorts of policies identified with CEPAL were failing to deliver the results that they were supposed to. By the early twenty-first century, much the same could be said of neoliberalism (Harvey 2005). In addition, the capacity of the United States to get its way was running into limits, as challenges mounted. In Latin America a new wave of leftist governments were elected, differing enormously from one another, but demonstrating that the US model was, perhaps, not the assured future of human society after all.

We cite the truism that the future grows out of the present, an uninteresting statement in itself, but one that invites the search for what there might be in the present that may be the seeds of a different future. As we look beyond the neoliberal moment described in its national variants in the chapters that follow, where do we see the resources for forging the next moment?

- We have seen the degree to which Latin American economics departments have opted for mainstreaming through hiring faculty with US degrees and promoting faculty who publish in English. Yet some universities have proven far more resistant to mainstreaming than others and maintain other strands of economic thought. Even countries where mainstreaming has gone far retain centers for what we have called the critical project, too.
- We have seen students head north to US classrooms, but we doubt that they are simply remolded *de novo*. We have seen some signs that they carry southern concerns northward and hybrid outlooks back home.
- We have seen the growth of transnational think tank networks as major carriers of neoliberal ideas and personnel, but we have suggested the possibility of other ideas carried by other think tanks, too.
- We see, too, that the US model itself undergoes change, in recent years, for example, imparting a far more empirical cast than earlier into graduate education (Colander 2005).

We do not believe that economic ideas are a fixed thing, or that the economics profession is a fixed thing, or that US hegemony will prove any more permanent than that of its predecessors. It is not only the hopeful foes of empire but the disappointed friends who are saying this.

The nostalgic souls who now tell us that the British used to do this sort of thing better are indicating as much. Economics is not an established body of ideas that having achieved perfection is now traveling various transnational highways and remaking the world on a set model. In transnational transmission, change happens. We see no reason to think the mainstream a generation hence will look more like the mainstream of today than neoliberalism resembles the doctrines, policies, theories, and understandings that it displaced. We therefore will follow our country chapters, rooted in empirical explorations of the recent past, with some speculative attempts to peek a little bit into the future.

NOTES

1. This chapter owes much to the splendid research assistance of Florencia Tateossian.
2. For more on late nineteenth century social analysts' claims to science see Heyck (1982) and Soffer (1978).
3. Computed from the society's membership directory. An important purpose of the Econometric Society is the promotion of the quantitative analysis of economic problems and 'rigorous thinking similar to that which has come to dominate the natural sciences' (http://www.econometricsociety.org; retrieved in May, 2006).
4. LACEA is an international association of economists with common research interests in Latin America. It is also a regional representative for the Global Development Network (GDN), a worldwide network of research and policy institutes designed to generate and disseminate knowledge on development issues. It was initially sponsored by the World Bank in 1999.
5. Data provided by IAFFE's Executive Director, December 2005.
6. The first edition of *Who's Who in Economics* (1983) included only three Latin Americans: Raúl Prebisch (Argentina), Carlos Díaz Alejandro (Cuba) and Keith Griffin (born in Panama of American parents).
7. The fourth edition of *Who's Who* lists 1168 living economists, whose selection was based on citation counts of articles published between 1990 and 2000, drawing on EconLit and the Social Science Citation Index to rank authors by citation frequency. Of these entries, 743 have data on nationality and careers.
8. For *History of Political Economy*, we studied online versions of tables of contents of all issues appearing in 1985, 1990, 1995, 2000, and 2005 and counted the total number of articles other than book reviews as well as the number of articles dealing with Latin America or with Latin American authors. For *Journal of the History of Economic Thought*, we could not find online versions prior to 1998. We therefore looked at tables of contents for 1990, 1995, 1998, 2000, and 2005.
9. Cosmopolitanism was a characteristic of the first economics societies in England and Continental Europe in the nineteenth century (Augello and Guidi 2001). As late as the 1880s, Americans received advanced economics training primarily in German universities, 'to which they migrated in considerable numbers' (Barber 2001, p. 218), and Germany was the preferred destination for American economists studying abroad until the later 1930s (Coats 2000, p. 7). Around the Second World War, trans-Atlantic economic debates and policy advice became even more institutionalized. German and other Central and East European exiles greatly contributed to transforming American economics. Development economics, of particular interest in Latin America, had very notable contributors with Central and East European origins (Love 1996, p. 6).
10. Only a handful of other international comparisons exist (Augello and Guidi 2001;

Coats 1981, 1997, 2000; Wagener 1998). Even rarer are comparisons of the economics profession in rich and less affluent countries: Camp (1977), Fourcade-Gourinchas and Babb (2002).

11. Important new material is in The Oral History Collection of the United Nations Intellectual History Project.
12. For example, UNCTAD instituted the Raúl Prebisch Lectures and CEPAL has the Raúl Prebisch Lecture Series and the Raúl Prebisch Ibero-American Prize in Economics. See *CEPAL Review* special issue (1998) and Dosman (2006). It is said that there have been repeated unsuccessful efforts to have Prebisch nominated for the Nobel Prize in Economics (Rosenthal 2004, p. 394).
13. Notwithstanding the enormous influence that conservative economists (Hayek, von Mises, Friedman, Buchanan) have exerted on the renewal of the conservative agenda in the US in the latter part of the twentieth century (Aune 2001; Waligorski 1990) or the role of Krugman for liberal critics of the Bush adminstration.
14. In an interview, Cavallo (2001, p. 210) claimed that in the five years since his dismissal from office he was invited to speak no less than 40 times in the US alone as well as in Portugal, Spain, France, England, Switzerland, Germany, Italy, Poland, Russia, Ukraine, Japan, Hong Kong, Taiwan, Singapore, Malaysia, India and most Latin American countries.
15. In the US the Federal Reserve was created in 1913. Various US specialists became involved in economic and institutional reforms in Latin America, often acting on behalf of American interests. The *Banco de la Reserva* in Peru, founded in 1922, had as its first manager William Cumberland, an American economist who previously supervised Peruvian customs. Princeton economist Edwin Kemmerer headed financial missions that resulted in the establishment of central banks in Colombia (1923), Chile (1925), Ecuador (1927) and Bolivia (1929). Argentina created its central bank in 1935.
16. According to Joseph Love (1980, p. 65), Prebisch's *Introducción a Keynes* (1947) enlarged his professional reputation, but his main thesis owed more to 'observation and experimentation' than to his reading of Keynes or other authors. On parallels of CEPAL's structuralism and 'US institutionalism', see Mallorquín (2001), Street (1962) and Sunkel (1989).
17. In Latin America state resources were mostly complemented by international organizations, although in some countries the domestic private sector and international foundations also played a part. In the US powerful private foundations, commercial consulting firms and universities generously financed what the government did not fund, especially prior to the creation of the National Science Foundation in 1958. The belief that more accurate factual knowledge would result in social improvements was a major justification for the funding of applied economic research (Fourcade 2009). Barber (1985) has famously disputed the characterization of inter-war institutionalists as atheoretical economists.
18. The economist W.W. Rostow, who worked then for the State Department, was sometimes known as the 'high priest of counterinsurgency' (Lodewijks 1991, p. 297).
19. Or as Colander (2003, p.171) puts it in a more dynamic formulation, 'the students have changed to fit graduate school, rather than graduate school changing to fit a broader student policy interest'.
20. The purpose of the Latin American Doctoral Program in Economics (offered jointly by ITAM in Mexico, Universidad Torcuato Di Tella in Argentina and Universidad de Chile) is described on its website as educating 'researchers with a solid theoretical background and a deep knowledge of the economy of Latin America'. For more on the mathematization of economics, see Laband and Piette (1994) and Weintraub (2002b).
21. Top-tier US programs typically do not offer master's degrees, which are treated primarily as an entry requirement for a doctoral program (Hansen 1991, p. 1062).
22. Colombia's *Universidad de los Andes* inaugurated its own doctoral program in 2008.

23. One cannot infer from these figures that such publication is typical, since a few active economists could be doing the lion's share of the publishing.
24. The *Journal of Applied Economics* receives 39 percent of submissions from Europe, 25 percent from the US and only 12 percent from Latin America (24 percent come from other places), according to the journal's website.
25. In 2005, a third of all articles (six out of 18) published in the *Revista Brasileira de Economia* were in English and the rest in Portuguese. All authors and co-authors were from Brazilian universities.
26. By contrast, the Brazilian journal *Economia* publishes only in Portuguese. Its mission statement stresses that the journal's goal is 'to build an independent, pluralist space . . . for theoretical and applied work in all fields of economics. It is not committed to any specific school of economic thought . . . academic excellence being its only guide' (our translation).
27. Mindful of the importance of professional visibility, the following Latin American journals are currently included in LogEc (which reflects usage statistics of articles and other work in economics): *Journal of Applied Economics* (Universidad del CEMA, Argentina); *Nova Economía* (U. Federal de Minas Gerais, Brazil); *Revista de Análisis Económico* (ILADES, U. A. Hurtado, Chile and Georgetown University); *Brazilian Electronic Journal of Economics* (U. Federal de Pernambuco, Brazil); *Colombian Economic Journal* (U. Javeriana, U. de Antioquia, U. de los Andes, U. del Valle, U. Externado de Colombia, U. Nacional de Colombia); *Economia* (ANPEC, Brazil); *Revista Brasileira de Economia* (Getúlio Vargas Foundation, Brazil).
28. Many of the specific claims made in this section about Argentina, Brazil, Chile, Colombia, Mexico and Uruguay are drawn from the chapters in this volume; for those claims we will not provide more specific references.
29. The diaspora of Argentine economists may be what prompted Economy Minister Cavallo during his tenure in office in the 1990s to create a two year training program for government economists that was offered by local universities.
30. According to William Barber, Currie was 'the first member of the profession to enjoy such exalted rank' (1981, p. 179).
31. To broaden CEPAL's geographic reach, a Mexico City office was added in 1951 to address Central America and one in Port of Spain in Trinidad in 1966 for the Caribbean. Tensions over representation, however, were not easily resolved. Víctor Urquidi, head of CEPAL-Mexico for most of the 1950s, complained that Prebisch paid insufficient attention to the area under his jurisdiction (Burger 1998, p. 102).
32. Osvaldo Sunkel, a first generation cepalino, commented: 'Dictatorships persecuted and expelled very good people. They thus contributed greatly to the intellectual activity that developed around CEPAL and other international organizations' (Interview with Jesús A. Treviño, Universidad de Monterrey, unpublished).
33. Modeled after the *Quarterly Journal of Economics* in the US (Burger 1998, p. 50).
34. Surveys of graduate economics programs in the United States by Aslanbeigui and Montecinos (1998a) and Colander (2005) show that the majority of students (52 percent and 62 percent, respectively) were foreigners. In some of the institutions studied that percentage was around 80 percent or higher.
35. Guillermo O'Donnell (1973, pp. 79–89) contended that '*técnicos* getting their degrees abroad' as well as others schooled following US models carried frustration-inducing expectations back home, as their new learning ran up against national realities. Jorge Domínguez (1997, p. 29), by contrast, argues that Latin American 'technopols . . . install a patriotic cosmopolitanism, grounding international experience in the empirical context of each country'.
36. An important precedent in the role played by foreign economists in the transformation of the American profession is the generation of 'illustrious immigrants', European economists who arrived in the US in the 1930s and the war period. Foreign-born American Economic Association presidents went from one before 1948 to 17 by 1978 (Coats 1992, pp. 417–31).

37. Edwards (2003) estimates that more than a dozen full professors from Latin America and many more at lower ranks are teaching in US programs, many in the best economics departments and business schools.
38. On the other hand, Finn (2003) has analyzed the number of foreign citizens who earned doctorates in the United States and stayed. Among disciplines, the highest stay rates were for computer/electrical and electronic engineering, computer science, and the physical sciences. The stay rates in economics and the other social sciences were the lowest.
39. This may be a low estimate since our sources may not have identified all Latin American connections.
40. Consider as an example the case of Andrés Velasco, Sumitomo Professor of International Finance and Development at Harvard's Kennedy School of Government. Soon after her election as president of Chile in January 2006, Michelle Bachelet surprised even her own circle by appointing Velasco as Finance Minister. His year-long involvement in the presidential campaign helped him prevail over several prominent economics PhDs whose policy experience and political credentials were far superior.
41. Data provided by Edda R. Leithner, Administrative Director, American Economic Association (February 2006).
42. Of the 37 invited speakers at the meeting of LACEA-LAMES in Mexico City in 2006, as many as 27 were on the list of 601 Fellows of the Econometric Society. Among them were Gary Becker, Robert Lucas, Jeffrey Sachs and Preston McAfee.
43. Regional meetings of the Econometric Society are held semi-annually in North America, annually in Europe, Australasia and Latin America, and bi-annually in the Far East and South and Southeast Asia regions. In addition, since 1965 the society has its world congress every five years.
44. Several Latin Americans have been elected Fellows of the Econometric Society (for example, Guillermo Calvo, José Scheinkman, Ricardo Caballero), although only two are affiliated primarily with institutions in Latin America: Marilda Sotomayor (U. São Paulo) and Aloisio Araujo (F.G.V.).
45. www.lacea.org. Retrieved November 26, 2005.
46. The list includes: FEDESARROLLO (Colombia), *Universidad de los Andes* (Colombia), *Universidad Torcuato Di Tella* (Argentina), *Instituto de Economía-Pontificia Universidad Católica* (Chile), *Centro de Economía Aplicada-Universidad de Chile*, *Pontificia Universidade Católica de Rio de Janeiro* (Brazil), CERES, Department of Economics of the *Universidad de la República* (Uruguay), *Universidad ORT* (Uruguay), *Universidad de las Américas*, Puebla (Mexico), *Universidad de Costa Rica* and INCAE (INCAE is a private, multinational institution of higher education in the fields of business and economics, founded in 1964 by Central American governments and business community, with the technical supervision of the Harvard Business School).
47. See the website of the Seventh Meeting on Globalization and Problems of Development, held in Havana in 2005: http://www.eleconomista.cubaweb.cu/globalizacion (Retrieved August 16, 2006). There is also ALEAR (Latin American and Caribbean Association of Environmental and Resource Economists). See http://www.alear.org (retrieved August 16, 2006).
48. For some interesting parallel suggestions on a growing 'Europeanization' among European economists, see Coats (2000, p. 12) and Fourcade-Gourinchas (2006, pp. 175–6).
49. Most of these organizations do not have websites. After an extensive internet search we were able to find some of the founding dates, but not all.
50. For a directory see Hellebust (2001).
51. There are several directories of Latin American think tanks such as those of NIRA, Atlas and GDN-CIPPEC (see the references for their websites).
52. http://www.atlasusa.org/aboutatlas/faq_do.php?refer=aboutatlas.
53. For both the NIRA and Atlas directories we used online versions. For Atlas we used

their 'focused' option in order to include roughly comparable organizations. Since Atlas is one of the two sources considered, we need to caution that its centrality may be to some extent an artifact.

54. One must be cautious about these conclusions. Since both sources give data only for presently existing think tanks, any think tank that went out of existence before 2005 would not appear in these graphs, raising the possibility that the earlier decades actually had more instances of founding than shown here. We note, however, that the data show more think tanks founded in the 1920s than in the next two decades and more in the 1980s than in the 1990s, which suggests that the data reflect more than just organizational demise.
55. To interpret Figures 1.6 and 1.7 we need to consider founding dates and availability of information, especially for the earlier years shown. Cato was founded in 1977, and we have information on publications available since 1980. For Heritage, the corresponding dates are 1973 and 1980, for American Enterprise 1943 and 1975, and for the Institute for International Economics 1981 and 1990.
56. A more refined analysis, which we defer to a subsequent publication, would take note of significant differences in the nature as well as the extent of attention to Latin America. All four think tanks have a pro-market agenda favoring such things as privatization and the reduction of trade barriers. But Heritage and American Enterprise are also extremely critical of Latin American governments and institutions.
57. Some pages lack a link list. The network analysis will therefore be an approximation, since the number of links depends not only on the real connections but also on the effort put into website development and in the choices organizations make in presenting themselves.
58. We drew this graph with the program Pajek (Slovenian for 'spider') and thank our colleague Patrick Doreian and his students, Spencer Foster and Jared Coopersmith, for their patient instruction in it.
59. Consider, for example, the World Social Forum, born as a grassroots mobilization in response to the success achieved by elite dialogues sponsored by the World Economic Forum. This is a vast subject that we can do no more than point to here (but see Jackie Smith 2008). For an enumeration of 'alternative globalization' networks see Díaz-Salazar (2002) whose account makes clear that such networks very importantly involve counter-hegemonic think tanks. Clifford Bob is currently researching the interplay of transnational networks of activists of the left and right (Bob 2006).

REFERENCES

Abelson (2004), 'The Business of Ideas: The Think Tank Industry in the USA', in Diane Stone (ed.), *Think Tank Traditions. Policy Research and the Politics of Ideas*, Manchester and New York: Manchester University Press, pp. 215–31.

Albelda, Randy (1997), *Economics & Feminism. Disturbances in the Field*, New York: Twayne Publishers.

Arestis, Philip and Malcolm C. Sawyer (2000), *A Biographical Dictionary of Dissenting Economists*, Cheltenham, UK and Northampton, MA, USA: Edward Elgar Publishing.

Aslanbeigui, Nahid and Verónica Montecinos (1998a), 'Foreign Students in US Doctoral Programs', *Journal of Economic Perspectives*, **12** (3), 171–82.

Aslanbeigui, Nahid and Verónica Montecinos (1998), 'The World and US Economics', paper presented at the History of Economics Society Annual Conference, Montreal, June 1998.

Atlas (2006), *Atlas Think Tank Directory*. Retrieved August 19, 2006 (http://www.atlasusa.org/V2/main/page.php?page_id=61).

Augello, Massimo M. and Marco E.L. Guidi (2001), 'Nineteenth-century Economic Societies in a Comparative Approach. The Emergence of Professional Economists', in Massimo M. Augello and Marco E.L. Guidi (eds), *The Spread of Political Economy and the Professionalization of Economists. Economic Societies in Europe, America and Japan in the Nineteenth Century*, London and New York: Routledge.

Aune, James Arnt (2001), *Selling the Free Market. The Rhetoric of Economic Correctness*, New York and London: The Guilford Press.

Babb, Sarah (2001), *Managing Mexico. Economists from Nationalism to Neoliberalism*, Princeton and Oxford: Princeton University Press.

Barber, William J. (1981), 'The United States: Economists in a Pluralistic Policy', in A.W. Coats (ed.), *Economists in Government. An International Comparative Study*, Durham, North Carolina: Duke University Press.

Barber, William J. (1985), *From New Era to New Deal: Herbert Hoover, the Economists and American Economic Policy, 1921–1933*, Cambridge: Cambridge University Press.

Barber, William J. (1997), 'Postwar Changes in American Graduate Education in Economics', in A.W. Coats (ed.), *The Post-1945 Internationalization of Economics*, Annual Supplement to Volume 28 *History of Political Economy*, Durham and London: Duke University Press, pp. 12–30.

Barber, William J. (2001), 'Economists and Professional Organizations in pre-World War I America', in Massimo M. Augello and Marco E.L. Guidi (eds), *The Spread of Political Economy and the Professionalization of Economists. Economic Societies in Europe, America and Japan in the Nineteenth Century*, London and New York: Routledge.

Bartlett, Robin L. (1999), 'Pedagogy', in Janice Peterson and Margaret Lewis (eds), *The Elgar Companion to Feminist Economics*, Cheltenham, UK and Northampton, MA, USA: Edward Elgar Publishing.

Berman, Edward H. (1983), *The Influence of the Carnegie, Ford, and Rockefeller Foundations on American Foreign Policy: The Ideology of Philanthropy*, Albany: State University of New York Press.

Bielschowski, Ricardo (1998), 'Evolución de las ideas de la CEPAL', *CEPAL Review*, Special Issue, October.

Biglaiser, Glen (2002), *Guardians of the Nation? Economists, Generals, and Economic Reform in Latin America*, Notre Dame, Indiana: University of Notre Dame Press.

Blaug, Mark and Howard R. Vane ([1983] 2003), *Who's Who in Economics*, Cheltenham, UK and Northampton, MA, USA: Edward Elgar Publishing.

Bob, Clifford (2006), 'Conservative Activism, Communications, and Global Civil Society', presented at University of Pennsylvania Annenberg School for Communication and London School of Economics Centre for the Study of Global Governance, Workshop on Global Framing of Democracy.

Bockman, Johana and Gil Eyal (2002), 'Eastern Knowledge as a Laboratory for Economic Knowledge: The Transnational Roots of Neoliberalism', *American Journal of Sociology*, **108** (2), 310–52.

Boianovsky, Mauro and Vincent J. Tarascio (1998), 'Mechanical Inertia and Economic Dynamics: Pareto on Business Cycles', *Journal of the History of Economic Thought*, **20** (1).

Burger, Hilary (1998), 'An Intellectual History of the ECLA Culture', PhD Dissertation, Department of History, Harvard University, Cambridge, MA.

Camp, Roderic A. (1975), 'The National School of Economics and Public Life in Mexico', *Latin American Research Review*, **10** (3), 137–51.

Camp, Roderic A. (1977), *The Role of Economists in Policy Making: A Comparative Study of Mexico and the United States*, Tucson: University of Arizona Press.
Cavallo, Domingo (2001) (in dialogue with Juan Carlos de Pablo), *Pasión por crear*, Buenos Aires: Grupo Editorial Planeta.
Centeno, Miguel Angel (1994), *Democracy within Reason: Technocratic Revolution in Mexico*, University Park PA: Pennsylvania State University.
Centeno, Miguel Angel and Patricio Silva (eds) (1998), *The Politics of Expertise in Latin America*, New York: St. Martin's Press.
Coats, A.W. (ed.) (1981), *Economists in Government. An International Comparative Study*, Durham, North Carolina: Duke University Press.
Coats, A.W. (1992), 'Economics in the US, 1920–70', in A.W. Coats (ed.) *On the History of Economic Thought. British and American Essays*, Volume I, London and New York: Routledge, pp. 407–55.
Coats, A.W. (ed.) (1997), *The Post-1945 Internationalization of Economics*, Annual Supplement to Vol. 28, *History of Political Economy*, Durham and London: Duke University Press.
Coats, A.W. (ed.) (2000), 'Preface', 'Introduction' and 'Concluding Reflections', *The Development of Economics in Western Europe since 1945*, London and New York: Routledge.
Colander, David (2003), 'The Aging of an Economist', *Journal of the History of Economic Thought*, **25**, 157–76.
Colander, David (2005), 'The Making of an Economist Redux', *Journal of Economic Perspectives*, **19**, 175–98.
Colander, David and Arjo Klamer (1987), 'The Making of an Economist', *Journal of Economic Perspectives*, **12**, 95–111.
Colander, David and Reuven Brenner (eds) (1992), *Educating Economists*, Ann Arbor: University of Michigan Press.
Comim, Flavio (2000), 'On the Concept of Applied Economics: Lessons from Cambridge Economics and the History of Growth Theories', *History of Political Economy*, **32** (4), 147–76.
Conaghan, Catherine (1998), 'Stars of the Crisis: The Ascent of Economists in Peruvian Public Life', in Miguel Angel Centeno and Patricio Silva (eds), *The Politics of Expertise in Latin America*, New York: St. Martin's Press, pp. 142–64.
Cypher, James (2005), 'Shifting Developmental Paradigms in Latin America: Is Neoliberalism History?', Paper presented at the Latin American and Caribbean Economic Thought Conference, New York, March 4–5.
Danby, Colin (2005), 'Noyola's Institutional Approach to Inflation', *Journal of the History of Economic Thought*, **27** (2).
De Marchi, Neil (2001), 'Bob Coats and the Historicizing of Economic Policy', in Steve G. Medema and Warren J. Samuels (eds), *Historians of Economics and Economic Thought. The Construction of Disciplinary Memory*, London and New York: Routledge, pp. 40–51.
de Vries, Barend A. (1997), 'The World Bank as an International Player in Economic Analysis', in A.W. Coats (ed.), *The Post-1945 Internationalization of Economics*, Annual Supplement to Vol. 28, *History of Political Economy*, Durham and London: Duke University Press, pp. 225–44.
Díaz-Salazar Rafael (ed.) (2002), *Justicia global: Las alternativas de los movimientos del Foro de Porto Alegre*, Barcelona: Encuentro Icaria-Intermón Oxfam.
Domínguez, Jorge I. (1997), 'Technopols. Ideas and Leaders in Freeing Politics and Markets in Latin America in the 1990s', in Jorge I. Domínguez (ed.),

Technopols: Freeing Politics and Markets in Latin America in the 1990s, University Park: Pennsylvania State University Press, pp. 1–48.
Dosman, Edgard J. (ed.) (2006), *Raúl Prebisch. Power, Principle and the Ethics of Development*, Buenos Aires: IDB-INTAL.
Drake, Paul W. (ed.) (1993), *Money Doctors, Foreign Debts, and Economic Reforms in Latin America from 1890s to the Present*, Wilmington, Delaware: A Scholarly Resources Inc. Imprint.
Drake, Paul W. (2005), 'The Hegemony of US Economic Doctrines in Latin America', in Valpy FitzGerald and Rosemary Thorp (eds), *Economic Doctrines in Latin America*, Palgrave Macmillan.
Dusansky, Richard and Clayton Vernon (1998), 'Ranking of US Economic Departments', *Journal of Economic Perspectives*, **12** (1), 157–70.
Econometric Society (2006), *Membership Directory*, Retrieved May 2006 (http://www.econometricsociety.org).
Edwards, Sebastián (2003) 'Latin American and US Universities: A Forty Year Analysis', *Cuadernos de Economía*, **21**, 399–412.
Finn, Michael G. (2003), 'Stay Rates of Foreign Doctorate Recipients from US Universities', Document prepared for the Division of Science Resources Studies of the National Science Foundation, November 2003, Retrieved August 2006 (http://orise.orau.gov/sep/files/stayrate03.pdf).
Fiszbein, Ariel and Sebastián Galiani (2005), 'On the Characterization of Research in Latin America', paper presented at the LACEA Annual Conference, Paris, October 2005. Retrieved June 2006 (http://wwwtest.aup.edu/lacea2005/system/step2_php/papers/fiszbein_afis.pdf).
Ford Foundation (1982), *The Search for a New Economic Order*, Retrieved August 2006 (http://www.fordfound.org/elibrary/documents/0174/toc.cfm).
Fourcade-Gourinchas, Marion (2006), 'The Construction of a Global Profession: The Transnationalization of Economics', *American Journal of Sociology*, **112** (1), 145–94.
Fourcade, Marion (2009), *Economists and Societies: Discipline and Profession in the United States, Britain, and France 1890s to 1990s*, Princeton: Princeton University Press.
Fourcade-Gourinchas, Marion and Sarah L. Babb (2002), 'The Rebirth of the Liberal Creed: Paths to Neoliberalism in Four Countries', *American Journal of Sociology*, **108** (3), 533–79.
Frey, Bruno S. and Reiner Eichenberger (1993), 'American and European Economics and Economists', *Journal of Economic Perspectives*, **7** (4), 185–93.
Frey, Bruno S. and R.L. Frey (eds) (1995), 'Is there a European Economics?', *Kyklos*, Special Issue, **48** (2).
Fullbrook, Edward (ed.) (2004), *A Guide to What's Wrong with Economics*, London: Anthem Press.
GDN-CIPPEC. *Directory of Policy Research Institutes in Developing Countries.* Retrieved 08/19/06 (http://www.researchandpolicy.org).
Gordon, Robert J. (2004), 'What is the Econometric Society? History, Organization and Basic Procedures'. Retrieved, May 12, 2006 (http://www.econometricsociety.org/society.asp).
Gore, Charles (2002), 'The Rise and Fall of the Washington Consensus as a Paradigm for Developing Countries', *World Development*, **28** (5), 789–804.
Green, Duncan (2003), *Silent Revolution. The Rise and Crisis of Market Economics in Latin America*, New York: Monthly Review Press.
Groenewegen, Peter (2003), 'Exemplary Economists of the Twentieth Century. A

Review Article of Thirty-six Economists' Autobiographies', in Peter Groenewegen, *Classics and Moderns in Economics. Essays on Nineteenth- and Twentieth-Century Economic Thought*, Volume II, London and New York: Routledge, pp. 278–96.

Han, Shin-Kap (2003), 'Tribal Regimes in Academia: A Comparative Analysis of Market Structure across Disciplines', *Social Networks*, **25**, 251–80.

Hansen, W. Lee (1991), 'The Education and Training of Economics Doctorates: Major Findings of the Executive Secretary of the American Economic Association's Commission on Graduate Education in Economics', *Journal of Economic Literature*, **XXIX**, 1054–87.

Harberger, Arnold (1997), 'Good Economics Comes to Latin America, 1955–95', in A.W. Coats (ed.), *The Post-1945 Internationalization of Economics*, Annual Supplement to Vol. 28, *History of Political Economy*, Durham and London: Duke University Press, pp. 301–11.

Harvey, David (2005), *A Brief History of Neoliberalism*, New York: Oxford University Press.

Heyck, Thomas William (1982), *The Transformation of Intellectual Life in Victorian England*, London: Croom Helm.

Hellebust, Lynn (ed.) (2001), *Think Tank Directory. A Guide to Nonprofit Policy Research Organizations*, US: Government Research Service.

Hirschman, Albert O. (1961), 'Ideologies of Economic Development in Latin America', in Albert O. Hirschman (ed.), *Latin American Issues: Essays and Comments*, New York: Twentieth Century Fund.

Hirshleifer, Jack (1985), 'The Expanding Domain of Economics', *American Economic Review*, **75** (6), 53–68.

Huber, Evelyn and Fred Solt (2004), 'Successes and Failures of Neoliberalism', *Latin American Research Review*, **39** (3), 258–74.

Jolly, Richard, Louis Emmerij, Dharam Ghai and Frédéric Lapeyre (2004), *U.N. Contributions to Development Thinking and Practice*, Bloomington and Indianapolis: Indiana University Press.

Kalaitzidakis, Pantelis, Theofanis P. Mamuneas and Thanasis Stengos (2001), *Rankings of Academic Journals and Institutions in Economics*, Report sent to the European Economic Association. Retrieved, May 9, 2006 (http://www.le.ac.uk/economics/research/rankings/eearank.pdf).

Kaufman, Robert R. and Barbara Stallings (1991), 'The Political Economy of Latin American Populism', in Rudiger Dornbusch and Sebastian Edwards (eds), *The Macroeconomics of Populism in Latin America*, Chicago and London: The University of Chicago Press, pp. 15–43.

Kay, Cristóbal (1989), *Latin American Theories of Development and Underdevelopment*, London and New York: Routledge.

King, Kenneth (2005), 'Knowledge-based Aid. A New Way of Networking or a New North–South Divide?', in Diane Stone and Simon Maxwell (eds), *Global Knowledge Networks and International Development across Boundaries*, New York: Routledge, pp. 72–88.

Kuczynski, Pedro-Pablo and John Williamson (eds) (2003), *After the Washington Consensus: Restarting Growth and Reform in Latin America*, Washington, DC: Institute for International Economics.

Laband, David N. and Michael J. Piette (1994), 'The Relative Impact of Economic Journals: 1970–1990', *Journal of Economic Literature*, **32** (2), 640–66.

Lazear, Edward (2000), 'Economic Imperialism', *The Quarterly Journal of Economics*, **115**, 99–146

Leonard, Robert J. (1991), 'War as a "Simple Economic Problem": The Rise of an Economics of Defense', in Craufurd D. Goodwin (ed.), *Economics and National Security. A History of Their Interaction*, HOPE Annual Supplement to Vol. 23, Durham: Duke University Press, pp. 261–83.
Lodewijks, John (1991), 'Rostow, Developing Economics, and National Security Policy', in Craufurd D. Goodwin (ed.), *Economics and National Security. A History of Their Interaction*, HOPE Annual Supplement to Vol. 23, Durham: Duke University Press, pp. 285–310.
Loureiro, Maria Rita (1997a), *Os economistas no governo. Gestão econõmica e democracia*, Rio de Janeiro: Editora Fundacão Getúlio Vargas.
Loureiro, Maria Rita (1997b), *50 Anos de Ciência Econômica no Brazil. Pensamento, Instituções, Depoimentos*, Petrópolis: Editora Vozes.
Love, Joseph L. (1980), 'Raúl Prebisch and the Origins of the Doctrine of Unequal Exchange', *Latin American Research Review*, **15** (3), 45–72.
Love, Joseph L. (1996), *Crafting the Third World: Theorizing Underdevelopment in Rumania and Brazil*, Stanford, CA: Stanford University Press.
Lowenthal, Abraham (1987), *Partners in Conflict. The United States and Latin America*, Baltimore and London: The Johns Hopkins University Press.
Mallorquín, Carlos (1998), *Ideas e historia en torno al pensamiento económico latinoamericano*, Mexico: Plaza y Valdés.
Mallorquín, Carlos (2001), 'El institucionalismo norteamericano y el estructuralismo latinoamericano: discursos compatibles?', *Revista Mexicana de Sociología*, **LXIII** (1), 71–108.
Markoff, John and Verónica Montecinos (1993), 'The Ubiquitous Rise of Economists', *Journal of Public Policy*, **1**, 37–68.
Mayhew, Anne (1999), 'Institutions Economics', in Janice Peterson and Margaret Lewis (eds), *The Elgar Companion to Feminist Economics,* Cheltenham, UK and Northampton, MA, USA: Edward Elgar Publishing, pp. 479–86.
McCloskey, Donald (1985), *The Rhetoric of Economics*, Madison: University of Wisconsin Press.
Medema, Steven G. and Warren J. Samuels (eds) (2001), *Historians of Economics and Economic Thought. The Construction of Disciplinary Memory*, London and New York: Routledge.
Mirowski, Philip (1989), *More Heat than Light. Economics as Social Physics, Physics as Nature's Economics*, Cambridge, Cambridge University Press.
Montecinos, Verónica (1988), 'Economics and Power: Chilean Economists in Government, 1958–1985', PhD dissertation, University of Pittsburgh.
Montecinos, Verónica (1998a), *Economists, Politics and the State. Chile 1958–1994*, Amsterdam: CEDLA.
Montecinos, Verónica (1998b), 'The Symbolic Value of Economists in the Democratization of Chilean Politics', in Kurt von Mettenheim and James Malloy (eds), *Deepening Democracy in Latin America*, Pittsburgh, PA: University of Pittsburgh Press.
Montecinos, Verónica and John Markoff (2001), 'From the Power of Economic Ideas to the Power of Economists', in Miguel Angel Centeno and Fernando López-Alves (eds), *The Other Mirror: Grand Theory through the Lens of Latin America*, Princeton: Princeton University Press, pp. 105–50.
NIRA (2005), *NIRA's World Directory of Think Tanks 2005*, Retrieved, August 19, 2006 (http://www.nira.go.jp/ice/nwdtt).
O'Donnell, Guillermo (1973), *Modernization and Bureaucratic-Authoritarianism.*

Studies in South American Politics, Berkeley: Institute of International Studies, University of California.
Perez Caldentey, Esteban and Matias Vernengo (eds) (forthcoming), *Ideas, Policies and Development in the Americas*, London and New York: Routledge.
Popescu, Oreste (1997), *Studies in the History of Latin American Economic Thought*, London and New York: Routledge.
Prebisch, Raúl (1947), *Introducción a Keynes*, Mexico City: Fondo de Cultura Económica.
Rich, Andrew (2004), *Think Tanks, Public Policy, and the Politics of Expertise*, Cambridge: Cambridge University Press.
Rosenthal, Gerth (2004), 'ECLAC: A Commitment to a Latin American Way Toward Development', in Yves Berthelot (ed.), *Unity and Diversity in Development Ideas. Perspectives from the U.N. Regional Commissions*, Bloomington and Indianapolis: Indiana University Press, pp. 168–232.
Ruccio, David F. and Jack Amariglio (2003), *Postmodern Moments in Modern Economics*, Princeton, NJ: Princeton University Press.
Samuels, Warren J., Jeff E. Biddle and John B. Davis (eds) (2003), *A Companion to the History of Economic Thought*, Malden, MA: Blackwell Publishing.
Samuelson, Paul A. (1948), *Economics: An Introductory Analysis*, New York: MacGraw-Hill.
Siegfried, John F. and Wendy A. Stock (n.d.), 'The Market for New Ph.D. Economists in 2002', Retrieved August 2006, (http://www.aeaweb.org/joe/articles/2004/2004_market.pdf).
Sigmund, Paul E. (1993), *The United States and Democracy in Chile*, The Twentieth Century Fund, Baltimore: The Johns Hopkins University Press.
Sikkink, Kathryn (1991), *Ideas and Institutions: Developmentalism in Brazil and Argentina*, Ithaca, NY: Cornell University Press.
Silva, Patricio (1991), 'Technocrats and Politics in Chile: From the Chicago Boys to the CIEPLAN Monks', *Journal of Latin American Studies*, **23** (2), 385–410.
Smelser, Neil J. and Richard Swedberg (1994), 'The Sociological Perspective on the Economy', in Neil J. Smelser and Richard Swedberg (eds), *The Handbook of Economic Sociology*, Princeton, NJ: Princeton University Press.
Smith, Jackie (2008), *Social Movements for Global Democracy*, Baltimore: Johns Hopkins University Press.
Smith, James A. (1989), 'Think Tanks and the Politics of Ideas', in David Colander and A.W. Coats (eds), *The Spread of Economic Ideas*, Cambridge: Cambridge University Press, pp. 175–94.
Smith, Vincent H., Philip G. Pardey and Connie Chan-Kang (2004), 'The Economics Research Industry', in Vincent G. Pardey and Vicent H. Smith (eds), *What's Economics Worth? Valuing Policy Research*, Baltimore and London: The Johns Hopkins University Press, pp. 12–66.
Soffer, Reba (1978), *Ethics and Society in England: The Revolution in the Social Sciences, 1870–1914*, Berkeley: University of California Press.
Solberg, Winton U. and Robert W. Tomilson (1997), 'Academic McCarthyism and Keynesian Economics: The Bowen Controversy at the University of Illinois', *History of Political Economy*, **29** (1), 55–82.
Stiglitz, Joseph (2000), 'Scan Globally, Reinvent Locally. Knowledge Infrastructure and the Localisation of Knowledge', in Diane Stone (ed.), *Banking on Knowledge: The Genesis of the Global Development Network*, London: Routledge, pp. 24–43.

Stock, Wendy and W. Lee Hansen (2004), 'Ph.D. Program Learning and Job Demands: How Close the Match', *American Economic Review*, **94** (2), 266–71.
Stone, Diane (2004), 'Think Tanks beyond Nation-states', in Diane Stone and Andrew Denham (eds), *Think Tank Traditions. Policy Research and the Politics of Ideas*, Manchester and New York: Manchester University Press, pp. 34–50.
Stone, Diane and Andrew Denham (eds) (2004), *Think Tank Traditions. Policy Research and the Politics of Ideas*, Manchester and New York: Manchester University Press.
Stone, Diane and Simon Maxwell (eds) (2005), *Global Knowledge Networks and International Development across Boundaries*, London and New York: Routledge.
Street, James (1962), 'The Latin American "Structuralists" and Institutionalists: Convergence in Development Theory', *Journal of Economic Issues*, **1**.
Sunkel, Osvaldo (1989), 'Institucionalistas y estructuralismo', *Revista de la CEPAL*, **38**.
Sunkel, Osvaldo unpublished interview with Jesús A. Treviño, Universidad de Monterrey.
The Oral History Collection of the United Nations Intellectual History Project, The Graduate Center, The City University of New York.
Valdés, Juan Gabriel ([1989] 1995), *La Escuela de Chicago: Operación Chile*, Buenos Aires: Grupo Editorial Zeta.
Wagener, Hans-Jurgen (1998), *Economic Thought in Communist and Post-Communist Europe*, London: Routledge.
Waligorski, Conrad P. (1990), *The Political Theory of Conservative Economists*, Lawrence: The University Press of Kansas.
Wallace, William (2004), 'Afterword: Soft Power, Global Agendas', in Diane Stone and Andrew Denham (eds), *Think Tank Traditions. Policy Research and the Politics of Ideas*, Manchester and New York: Manchester University Press, pp. 281–9.
Waller, William and Ann Jennnigs (1991), 'A Feminist Institutionalist Reconsideration of Karl Polanyi', *Journal of Economic Issues*, **25**, 485–98.
Walton, John and David Seddon (1994), *Free Markets & Food Riots: The Politics of Global Adjustment*, Cambridge, MA: Blackwell.
Weintraub, E. Roy (ed.) (2002a), *The Future of the History of Economics*, Durham, London: Duke University Press.
Weintraub, E. Roy (2002b), *How Economics Became a Mathematical Science*, Durham, London: Duke University Press.
Weiss, Carol H. (1992), *Organizations for Policy Analysis. Helping Government Think*, Newbury Park, CA: Sage Publications, Inc.
Weyland, Kurt (2004), 'Learning from Foreign Models in Latin American Policy Reform: An Introduction', in Kurt Weyland (ed.), *Learning from Foreign Models in Latin American Policy Reform*, Baltimore and London: The Johns Hopkins University Press.
Whitley, Richard (1983), 'The Structure and Context of Economics as a Scientific Field', *Research in the History of Economic Thought and Methodology*, **4**, 179–209.
Williamson, John (2003), 'Our Agenda and the Washington Consensus', in Pedro-Pablo Kuczynski and John Williamson (eds), *After the Washington Consensus. Restarting Growth and Reform in Latin America*, Washington, DC: Institute for International Economics, pp. 323–31.

2. The internationalization of ideas in Argentina's economics profession

Glen Biglaiser[1]

This chapter seeks to explain the philosophical change toward neoliberalism in Argentina's economics profession and the growing influence of economists in economic policy making. Building on work by Choi (1997), it stresses the supply of and demand for economists for promoting the diffusion of market-oriented ideas in Argentina's economics profession. From the supply side, I argue that decades of university intervention and ideological opposition under Juan Perón's rule and later military regimes stalled the profession's growth. However, in the mid-1950s to mid-1960s, when university autonomy returned, the profession developed largely because Argentine universities introduced more economics courses than ever before, most of them geared to structuralist, state-driven ideas. At the same time, US government agencies and private foundations funded Argentines to earn advanced economics degrees in the US, where neoliberal, market-based theory dominated, bringing a competition of ideas into the Argentine profession. US training of economists helped tilt the profession away from structuralism.

However, producing a supply of neoliberal economists[2] is only part of the socialization process that changed the profession and later affected economic policy making. Local demand for economists educated in the United States is also critical for understanding whether neoliberal ideas dominate the profession and influence policy making. Specifically, if economists educated in the United States cannot find full-time academic positions that pay reasonable salaries, they may choose to work outside academia or even abroad. Without these economists, students are likely to enroll in courses from professors opposed to neoliberal theory. Students also will receive less encouragement to study in the US, which impedes efforts to socialize future generations of neoliberal economists.

To explain when local demand for economists educated in the United States is likely to increase, public higher education and economic factors are important. If domestic higher education fails to supply competent economists to manage governmental and business affairs during ever increasing economic downturns, economic ministries and private sector interests have incentives to develop elite private institutes and universities. These institutes and universities offer high salaries and attractive employment opportunities, which motivate economists educated in the United States to return home. As more students attend these private institutes and universities because of better job prospects following graduation, academic positions for economists educated in the United States expand.

Job opportunities beyond academia are also an important consideration for neoliberal economists not only with regard to returning to Argentina but also for how they influence the country's economy. Recently, neoliberal economists have dominated top policy-making positions previously held by lawyers and even military officials during authoritarian regimes. This chapter explains why economists are now appointed to policy-making teams. Building on my previous work (2002b), I argue that presidents or military rulers use appointment strategies to serve their political survival interests. In the context of military rule, I contend that differences in long-standing characteristics of the military and in the kinds of governing institutions installed by military leaders shape the appointment of economic policy makers. A leader under one-man rule, whose military has little experience with factions, provides better opportunities for the appointment of neoliberal economists than collegial governments or factionalized militaries that require consensual agreement. Similarly, under democratic rule, centralized executive authority and executive party dominance in the legislature confer on the executive greater autonomy in economic policy-maker appointments.[3] Political survival strategies, based on different institutional settings, influence the executive's willingness to appoint economists.

The first section provides a brief historical overview of Argentina's limited economics profession before the 1950s. The second section explains Argentina's late introduction of an economics profession by stressing how liberal economic policy choice, 'money doctors' and university interventions constrained the supply of local economists. Growth of the profession and its initial support for structuralist ideas are presented in the third section. The effects of international funding and domestic demand for promoting market-oriented ideas in Argentina are detailed in section four. The fifth section considers policy-making appointment strategies used by presidents and military rules to stay in office. Section six concludes the chapter.

HISTORICAL OVERVIEW

Argentina presents an interesting nuance to the study of economics professions. Although Argentina was one of the first countries to broaden access to higher education, its economics profession developed relatively late (Balán 1998, p. 1). Ironically, Argentina had introduced an economics program early when the *Universidad Nacional de Buenos Aires* (UBA) created a doctorate in economic science in 1913, but for almost half a century the curriculum covered only two courses specific to economics (Dagnino Pastore 1989, p. 195; Lassalle 1943). Prior to the 1950s, a doctorate in economic science emphasized superior competency in accounting. Developing accounting skills necessary to manage the books for firms took precedence over original economic research. It was not until the late 1950s that 'public and newly founded private universities separated studies in economics from accountancy' (de Pablo 1999, p. 1). Besides accounting, economics students also enrolled in public law courses (Sikkink 1988, p. 110). In fact, economics training grew out of the accounting, commerce and legal professions.

From the 1900s to the 1940s, Argentine economics studies focused on 'the nature of "political economy" and came mostly within the province of historians, lawyers, public officials, politicians, or simply of cultured persons who were self-taught through reading the classical European texts' (Venezian 1982, p. 190). Economics students almost never engaged in debates over narrow analytical issues. Instead, students took a holistic approach to the study of economic problems that considered issues from a social, political, historical and religious bent. As Venezian (1982, p. 191) writes, 'The teaching of economics was very descriptive: learning current economic theories for general knowledge, rather than for their value as analytical tools for problem solving and policy purposes'.

Lack of a full-scale economics program does not imply that Argentina had no trained economists during the first half of the twentieth century.[4] Talented scholars including Luis Roque Gondra, Alejandro Bunge, Raúl Prebisch and José Barral Souto taught different aspects of the economics field. Gondra, for example, introduced the first course in mathematical economics in South America (Love 1996, p. 217). Julio Olivera of UBA and Oreste Popescu of the University of La Plata helped Argentines develop skills for conducting and publishing original research (Heymann 1994; Sjaastad 2002). Other economic scholars made their name through their governmental work. Juan J. Romero and Carlos Pellegrini, for example, addressed debt restructuring in the 1890s. Federico Pinedo and Raúl Prebisch managed the economic impact of the Great Depression in the 1930s (de Pablo 1999, p. 2).

Argentine scholars including Prebisch also wrote in *Revista de Ciencias Económicas*, *Revista de Economía Política*, and other professional journals to support the development of economic thought beginning in the 1920s (Popescu 1997, p. 273). In addition, a few Argentine economists earned advanced degrees abroad that stimulated new and innovative research. However, before the 1950s, Argentina had almost no 'well-organized economic research groups using sophisticated techniques and modern equipment' (Dagnino Pastore 1989, p. 196). The next section seeks to explain the constraints that slowed the profession's development.

SUPPLY CONSTRAINTS

Although Argentine economists developed innovative ideas and approaches, three factors limited the supply of economists and the subsequent progress of Argentina's economics profession in the 1900s to mid-1950s and beyond. Two factors are Argentina's historical preference for liberal economic policies and the availability of 'money doctors' from abroad prior to the 1930s. Once Argentines recognized the need to develop a homegrown economics profession, politicization and university interventions under Juan Perón and later, military regimes, proved to be a third factor that restricted the profession's growth.

Economic Policy Preferences

An important historical factor for the profession's late arrival relates to Argentina's economic policy preferences. During the 19th and early 20th century, Argentina's policy makers favored liberal economic theory with its bias toward open-market policies. Because of the Pampas' fertile land, Argentina developed profitable sectors tied to primary product exports in agriculture. Cattle, wheat, sheep and many of their by-products provided Argentina with abundant export opportunities, especially with Great Britain (Díaz Alejandro 1970, ch. 1). Given the relative vitality of Argentina's economy based on the classic liberal economic model, the impulse to create a homegrown economics profession laid dormant until the 1930s. In some exceptional years, Latin America abandoned liberal policies. During World War I, for example, when developed countries shipped few goods and closed off markets to most Latin American exports, countries in the Western Hemisphere engaged in an unconscious, import-substitution industrialization (ISI) strategy, producing goods for the local market that they previously imported.[5] However, by the early 1920s, bolstered by Britain's efforts to promote freer trade, Argentine policy makers returned to market-oriented policies. A focus on the invisible hand of the market and minimal role for the state lessened demand for local economists.

Imported Economists

The availability of economists from elsewhere is another reason for the profession's late arrival. Like many countries in the region, Argentina relied on 'money doctors', that is, foreign economists, or visiting professors, for advice on economic affairs (Hirschman 1963, p. 165). Governments also 'employed foreign advisers to improve their access to loans at reasonable rates' (Drake 1994, p. xiv).[6] Large debtors, such as Argentina in the early 20th century, welcomed the lower interest rates. The reputations of money doctors as free marketers certified the creditworthiness of borrowing governments, lowering the incentives to develop a local economics profession (Rosenberg and Rosenberg 1994, pp. 71–3).

Politicization and University Intervention

Politicization and university intervention in the 1940s to mid-1950s, and mid-1960s to early 1970s also impeded the profession's development. In the 1930s, prospects for a local economics profession appeared promising. Economic havoc caused by the Great Depression prompted initial interest by Prebisch and others to create an economics profession.[7] Fully exposed to the world market, Argentina experienced a decline in terms of trade on exports and a dramatic fall in export volume. As export markets closed, Argentina followed its liberal economic tradition and attempted to restart trade with its main trading partner, Great Britain. Backed by the agroexporter elite that helped the conservative regime of General Agustín Justo come to power via fraudulent elections, Argentina signed the Roca-Runciman Agreement in 1933. The agreement, with Prebisch actively involved in the negotiations, re-established bilateral trade with the British (Sikkink 1988, p. 93). However, because of the perceived unfair terms, the agreement fostered greater nationalist fervor against economic liberalism (Wynia 1992, p. 116).

Argentina responded by looking inward economically, in an attempt to insulate itself from the vagaries of world economic conditions (Thorp 1984).[8] As part of this insulation, state ownership of basic industries grew especially in the early 1940s. Even Prebisch, a fairly conservative man, remarked, 'During the Great Depression, although I had been a neoclassical economist, I realized that in light of the crisis, it was necessary to industrialize. I did this with misgivings, since all my ideas ran against it' (cf. Sikkink 1991, p. 76).

Policy makers also launched state development based on an economic strategy of ISI. Existing manufacturing firms expanded plants and established new firms to produce primarily for the domestic market

(Kaufman 1979, pp. 196–7). Shortages of manufactured goods during World War II reinforced interest in local production (Baer 1972, p. 97). Given Argentina's long trading relationship with Britain for intermediate goods, self-sufficiency in manufacturing took on heightened importance. Ranchers also supported the creation of state marketing boards in the 1930s, wherein the state served as an intermediary between farmers and the world market. Farmers sold goods to these boards at prices set by the state, guaranteeing them a profit, and protecting them from world market fluctuations (Wynia 1992, p. 23). Although ranchers initially supported an activist state, rural and urban communities would later take opposite sides over state intervention as the government used marketing boards to subsidize inefficient manufacturers at the expense of farmers. Indeed, from 1945 to 1975, manufacturing expanded 3.3 percent annually while agricultural product per capita fell 0.2 percent (Ramos 1986, p. 2).

The impulse toward state-led development stimulated demand for locally trained economists to manage these programs. Prebisch, founder and director of the Central Bank from 1935 to 1943, encouraged graduate students to seek education abroad at first-rate universities until Argentina developed a more formal economics curriculum.[9] The Central Bank sent graduates to Harvard University for two years in the 1930s and 1940s to supplement government staffing requirements and to develop better trained economists (Dagnino Pastore 1989, p. 210).

However, the profession's development regressed with university interventions and politicization especially during Juan Perón's first presidential administration (1946–55). Prior to Perón's coming into power, university autonomy generally carried the day. From 1884 to 1943, Decree Law 1420 granted universities complete autonomy 'in all matters of administration and academic policy' (Munger 1947, p. 275). Argentina's six universities remained outside the realm of politics, which provided professors with considerable academic freedom.

Beginning in October 1943 under military rule, General Pedro Ramírez 'intervened' Argentine universities – that is to say, he named 'interventores' to run them – and injected nationalism, militarism, and religiosity into the schools (Blanksten 1953, p. 187). In April 1945, the government moved to restore university autonomy, but such freedom proved short lived following Perón's win in 1946. Interestingly, the election of Perón reflected a temporary victory for democracy. Argentina's history of fraudulent elections, restrictions on popular participation and military coups produced, at best, restricted democracy. The expansion of the electorate and the scrupulously fair and open balloting contributed to a highly democratic election in 1946 (Crassweller 1987, p. 181). Sadly, once in office, Perón promoted authoritarian institutions. He also quashed the economics profession's development, as an independent and autonomous economics profession free of political interference strayed from Perón's goals of complete control over Argentina.

The loss of autonomy began in May 1946, when Perón appointed interventors to administer the universities (Blanksten 1953, p. 195). The interventors removed over 2000 university professors and administrators, who Perón replaced with his supporters (Ascher 1975, p. 40). Perón removed 70 percent of the professors (Crassweller 1987, p. 203) and attempted to eliminate courses in political economy and economics, among other subjects (Munger 1947, p. 282).

The most important step that abolished any semblance of university autonomy occurred on October 4, 1947, when Perón decreed the University Law. From then on, university rectors hand-picked by the president would be responsible for appointing administrative and academic personnel (Blanksten 1953, p. 196). The University Law also created a National University Council whose responsibilities 'would be to maintain a liaison between the government and the universities and to coordinate the curricula and administrations of the six campuses' (Blanksten 1953, p. 196). Perón swept out academic and technical economic staffs and appointed less proficient people for university chairs (Dagnino Pastore 1989, p. 196). Economic journals also 'either ceased to exist, or were published sporadically and their contents deteriorated' (ibid.). Perón also dismissed Prebisch from his official government posts, dismantled the economic team Prebisch had assembled at the Central Bank, and reversed some of the policies he had championed (Sikkink 1991, p. 76).

Perón's decision to sack Prebisch is important because Prebisch later played an immense role in international development debates. Not only did Prebisch serve as the first director for the United Nation's Economic Commission for Latin America (usually known by its Spanish acronym, CEPAL) in 1948 but he also acted as the first Secretary General for the United Nations Conference on Trade and Development (UNCTAD) in 1964. Prebisch also helped found the Group of 77 (G-77) and the New International Economic Order (NIEO), organizations that attempted to strengthen the hand of developing countries on commodity and trade issues. Prebisch earned a reputation as one of the best economists on development issues.[10] Given Prebisch's credentials, Perón's actions inspired many economists including Prebisch to leave Argentina. It was not until after the military exiled Perón in 1955 and Prebisch returned that economics bloomed into a full-fledged profession in Argentina.

Following Perón's ousting in 1955, the universities returned to their earlier condition. However, after the military coup in July 1966, General Juan Carlos Onganía intervened in the universities, replacing many administrators and causing more than 1000 university professors to resign (Ascher 1975, p. 55).[11] Seven years later, Perón returned to power and intervened in the universities, repeating the process he started nearly 30 years earlier. Perón removed qualified professors from the universities and inserted leftists and reputed sympathizers of the guerrilla group, the Montoneros, in the universities (Dagnino Pastore 1989, p. 199; Crassweller 1987, p. 356). Following Perón's death in 1974, the government attempted to 'weed out' sympathizers of the guerrillas from the universities (Rock 1987, p. 367). From 1974 to 1976 and during the subsequent military period, the government maintained strict controls over the universities in an effort to defend against guerrilla unrest. It was only in 1986 that the universities regained full autonomy. Not surprisingly, lack of academic freedom during the Peronist years and much of the military period stunted the economics profession's development. Many Argentine economists resisted academic circles and often stayed abroad.

SUPPORT FOR STRUCTURALISM

Although political actions taken by Perón and the military regimes harmed the profession, the brief period of university autonomy in the mid-1950s to mid-1960s supported the growth of economics and the spread of structuralist ideas. Following the fall of Perón in 1955, autonomous Argentine universities began to offer new courses and curricula to support economic research. From these courses and research came the development of a profession.

Based on philosophical debates raging in the profession worldwide, Argentine economists chose between two schools of thought: structuralism or classical liberalism, which later came to be called neoliberalism[12] (Harberger 1997, p. 306).[13] Whereas structuralism advocated state intervention and controls over the economy, neoliberalism espoused free trade and comparative advantage to promote economic growth.[14]

Most economists in Argentina, much like the rest of Latin America in the 1950s–1970s, subscribed to the structuralist position tied to CEPAL. Structuralism attracted many Argentine economists because of its break with national economic dependence. Free of interference from developed countries, Argentines expected economic prosperity to arrive shortly. The fact that structuralism grew out of ideas produced regionally also appealed to them. Indeed, Argentine and Latin American economists favored their own theory to promote professional prestige and to enhance their autonomy from foreign economists (Montecinos and Markoff 2001, p. 118).

Under Prebisch's leadership, CEPAL developed a doctrine that explained the economic disparities between developed and developing countries. According to this doctrine, the world's economic system was divided into an industrial center in the developed world and a primary-product export periphery in the developing world.[15] Developing countries produced goods that experienced declining terms of trade and erratic prices relative to the industrial goods they imported (Prebisch 1947). CEPAL theorists proposed to solve the developing world's plight by having the state promote the domestic manufacture of industrialized goods through import substitution. CEPAL supporters claimed that by adopting ISI measures developing countries could obtain the benefits of industrialization. CEPAL offered courses to policy makers and economics students in Latin America 'to put the doctrine into practice' (Bruce 1980, p. 3). CEPAL's 'practical' theories appealed to local policy makers (Pinto and Sunkel 1966, p. 82).

Not coincidentally, the rise of Argentina's economics profession occurred almost simultaneously with CEPAL offering courses in Argentina. In the late 1950s, Argentina adopted policies proposed a decade earlier by Prebisch to separate the accounting and economics specializations. In addition, the School of Economics at UBA introduced new curricula and texts that systematically incorporated CEPAL materials into the classroom (Sikkink 1988, p. 110). CEPAL-trained economists also received some policy-making positions in Argentina's national planning agency (CONADE), founded in 1961, and received other government and university positions, acquiring many local employment opportunities (Wynia 1978, pp. 115, 163). Although CEPAL's ideas appeared to conflict with policies initially adopted by President Arturo Frondizi in the late 1950s, producing a potential schism between 'desarrollistas' and 'Cepalinos' (persons favoring CEPAL's philosophy), these groups shared many of the same goals (Sikkink 1988, p. 109). Argentines supported CEPAL's ideas against conservative elements (Heymann 1994). Thus, as in other Latin American countries, structuralist ideas almost immediately dominated Argentina's nascent economics profession.

Since the late 1970s, structuralist ideas have been less popular among Argentine economists, with market ideas gaining many adherents. In contrast to state-led development, Argentine economists now emphasize a minimal state. Only under limited conditions including the protection of property rights, the provision of resources for police, defense and infrastructure, and the regulating of natural monopolies do neoliberals favor an activist state. Neoliberalism endorses the application of market mechanisms to promote economic development (Johnson 1975). The shift to a market philosophy does not suggest that Argentine economists believe in the exact same economic policies. However, guiding principles of freer trade, more open markets, and a limited state role in the economy receive solid backing from neoliberals in the economics profession. What explains the switch from structuralism to neoliberalism in Argentina's economics profession?

THE SHIFT TO NEOLIBERALISM

Explanations for the Rise of Neoliberalism in Argentina

The literature on changes in the beliefs of economics professions offers several promising explanations that either focus on the supply of or demand for economists. Among supply-side arguments, some argue that incentives from international sources including US government agencies and private foundations explain the growing influence of neoliberal ideas. Whether it is through coercive or voluntary means, US assistance affects higher education abroad (Levy 1999). During the Cold War era, well-coordinated socialization efforts by US government agencies and private foundations attempted to challenge CEPAL's supremacy in Latin America (Valdés 1995). As part of an agreement between the University of Chicago and Argentina's Universidad Nacional de Cuyo, Argentine economics students received graduate training and immersion in free market philosophies at the University of Chicago. Following the completion of their studies, Argentines were expected to return as professors at local universities to train another generation of economists in their way of thought. US-based foundations also supported graduate study at many US universities in the 1950s–1970s, where most economics faculty members backed neoliberalism. In addition, 'free-market' professors from Chile and the US taught courses at Argentine universities to support the socialization process. Although the influence of international actors differentiates the training of economists, international training leaves unexplained when change would occur in Argentina's economics profession. Despite strong US efforts to convert Argentine economists to neoliberalism in the 1960s, more than a decade passed before market ideas took hold in its economics profession.

Alternatively, others build explanations based on the demand for economists. Some contend that the economics profession's shift toward neoliberal ideas occurs because of the failure of Keynesianism (Harberger 1997; Iglesias 1992; Williamson 1994). Economic problems caused by protectionism and ISI led a 'consensus' of economists to reconsider their beliefs about economic development. The more serious the economic problems faced by the country under structuralist policies, the greater the likelihood that the profession would shift toward neoliberal ideas. In the early–mid 1970s, Argentina experienced severe economic dislocation. High inflation and budgetary deficits contributed not only to the fall of democratic rule but also produced growing dissatisfaction with state-led growth. Although economic failure led to different policy choices, economic misfortune by itself does not explain the timing of the change in Argentina's profession. The ideas held by Argentine economists shifted in the late 1970s and 1980s, not when the economic difficulties first appeared.

Others argue that domestic interest groups engineered the shift toward neoliberalism in the economics profession.[16] Business groups, aware that economists trained abroad might play a growing role in their firms, provided funds for students to earn graduate degrees in economics. Businesses also sponsored private educational institutes that favor market-oriented ideas. In Argentina, some firms hired economists trained abroad, and a few sponsored private institutes in the 1970s. Although businesses stimulate incentives for students to receive advanced degrees abroad and provide job opportunities for economists, it is also important to understand how international and domestic financing combine to support shifts in the professions' views.

Business financing is part of a larger economics socialization process. Drawing on work by Choi (1997), I develop an argument that links the supply and demand side to understand Argentina's shift toward neoliberalism. Although the argument presented here emphasizes Argentina, it has application to other countries, including Chile, Mexico and Uruguay. Differences in the amount of US assistance and job opportunities for returning economists educated in the United States help explain Chile's early switch to neoliberalism and its later arrival in Uruguay (Biglaiser 2002a). Declining public education and demand for technically trained economists during an economic downturn suggest many parallels between Mexico's and Argentina's economics professions (Biglaiser 2002b).

Specifically, economics training in US universities nurtures support for neoliberalism. Economists educated at any American university after the 1950s share a commitment to open market policies.[17] Although there are differences among economics departments, with University of Chicago faculty historically known as the most orthodox followers of laissez-faire economics, the training of economists over the past 40 years in American universities and/or by local academics that were themselves trained in US universities promotes a free-market ideology. Similar training is important because 'the perception of belonging to the same community of shared ideology, basic values, or religion generates a trust that facilitates transfer of products of social sciences from producers to users' (Boeninger 1982, p. 273). The economics training of Argentines in the US, or in universities in Argentina by economists educated in the United States, helps inculcate market-oriented ideas in the profession.

The degree of influence such economists will have in the profession, however, also depends on domestic demand for their services. When economists educated in the United States are not able to secure full-time academic positions in Argentina, they may accept fairly lucrative jobs from international organizations headquartered abroad, which affects their ability to socialize future generations of economists. Without these economists educated in the United States, economics students are likely to take courses from professors who are less sympathetic to neoliberal theory and who assign course readings that bolster their own views. Students also receive less inspiration to study in the US. In the end, if economists educated in the United States decide not to return to Argentina, this inhibits the creation of a cohesive 'critical mass' of economics faculty members who favor neoliberal ideas.

Government and business demands influence whether job opportunities are available to these economists. When public educational systems fail to provide enough qualified economists to manage governmental and business affairs and conduct research, Argentine economic ministries and private sector interests have strong incentives to support the founding and growth of elite private institutes and universities. Economic crisis, and the inability to provide adequate solutions, brings the ineffectiveness of the economics education into full view. In addition, prospective students attend these expensive private institutes and universities because of better job opportunities after graduation. High tuition charges and governmental and private sector support enables elite private institutes and universities to pay salaries that attract economists educated in the United States. Once these economics programs are in place, economists educated in the United States encourage more students to earn advanced degrees abroad, leading to a constant flow of students to the US, and eventually to economists educated in the United States dominating the profession.

US Training and Neoliberalism

As previously stated, Argentina's economics profession developed in the mid–late 1950s largely because of the availability of new economics courses. Business needs for increasing sophistication helped expand economics course offerings (Weil et al. 1974, p. 116). CEPAL also encouraged more economics programs and classes. In 1956–57 CEPAL carried out a mission to examine Argentina's economy. The mission, headed by CEPAL's Executive Secretary, Raúl Prebisch, led to a short-term economic program based on his diagnosis of Argentina's problems, the so-called Prebisch Plan (Sikkink 1991, p. 77). Complementing Prebisch's efforts, the mission sponsored economics and training courses attended by university and government scholars (Sikkink 1988, p. 113). Although UBA introduced a three-year course program in economics in 1953, the course material did not differ much from courses offered in public accountancy (Weil et al. 1974, pp. 116–18). The program prompted UBA to offer many economics courses and to create an economics department separate from accounting (Canitrot 1994). Congress's passage of legislation that recognized private university degrees in the late 1950s and early 1960s further opened academic opportunities in economics (Leonard 1989).

This expansion of economics courses encouraged student interest to earn advanced economic degrees, which stimulated more modern professional training. Between 1957 and 1959, US universities including Harvard, Chicago, Yale, Columbia, MIT and Texas received their first Argentine doctoral students in economics (Dagnino Pastore 1988, p. 3; de Pablo 1999, p. 1). The creation of the National Resource Council (CONICET) in 1958 complemented efforts to upgrade academic achievement in all fields. CONICET financed many full-time academic positions, and supported research through a network of newly created research institutes (Gertel 1997, p. 58).

Important changes occurred in the early 1960s that produced a supply of US-trained Argentine economists. To combat CEPAL's dominance over Latin American economics departments, US officials facilitated agreements between the University of Chicago and Latin American universities. During the Cold War era, US officials feared the spread of communism at universities. From the US perspective, CEPAL's sympathy with more leftist policies matched its anti-US views. In fact, certain US government circles viewed Executive Secretary Prebisch, 'with suspicion as a leftist critic of standard economic wisdom' (Sikkink 1988, p. 91). Ironically, some of his countrymen identified him with both conservative groups and liberal ideas (ibid.). Aware of Argentina's shift away from liberalism since the mid-1940s and its aversion to US policies during the Peronist years, US officials wanted Argentina to return to its liberal economic traditions, support US policies, and reject CEPAL ideas.

The US also had opposed CEPAL's formation since it believed that CEPAL 'duplicated and competed with work that was being carried out under the Organization for American States, an entity more open to US influence' (Sikkink 1991, p. 58). Because CEPAL discouraged newer generations from attending economics training programs abroad, US policy makers saw this as further proof of CEPAL's anti-US position.

To stem communist support and CEPAL's dominance in the region, US officials created programs for Latin American students to study in the US

(Packenham 1973, p. 109). Through the auspices of the US's International Cooperation Administration (ICA) and its Point Four Program,[18] precursor to the Agency for International Development (AID), the US established agreements with Latin American universities to send their best economics students to earn advanced degrees at the University of Chicago, in an intellectual atmosphere highly averse to Marxist economic teachings. Following the completion of their studies, these students were supposed to return to their home country as professors whose mission was to train a new generation of students in free market economics.

The first exchange program developed between the University of Chicago and Chile's *Universidad Católica* in 1956.[19] In an effort to reproduce the Chilean program elsewhere, AID created Project Cuyo in Argentina (Valdés 1989, p. 263). With some of the same actors responsible for the agreement with Chile, Professor Arnold Harberger of the University of Chicago negotiated with Dr Corti Videla, dean of the economics faculty at the Universidad Nacional de Cuyo in Mendoza, to establish a scholarly exchange program (Valdés 1989, p. 262). The agreement, signed in 1961, included not only the *Universidad de Cuyo* and University of Chicago, but also the *Universidad Católica* in Chile. As a major US participant in these events recalls, although an agreement with UBA, the largest and most important university in Argentina, offered better opportunities to influence the profession, such an agreement was impossible given opposition from UBA faculty and students alike (Harberger 1999).

Under the direction of Larry Sjaastad with the support of H. Gregg Lewis, both from the University of Chicago, as well as Ernesto Fontaine and Raúl Yver, Project Cuyo attempted to counteract CEPAL's influence (Sjaastad 2002). As part of the agreement that began in 1962 and ended in 1967, AID allocated funds to Argentina that ranged between $1.3 and $2.9 million annually (see Table 2.1). Although AID allocated more funds to Chile than to Argentina or Uruguay, AID funded 27 Argentines to study in Chicago (Valdés 1989, p. 263). The money also supported professors from Chile's Universidad Católica, who had earned graduate degrees in Chicago, to teach courses at the *Universidad de Cuyo*. Their commitment to Chicago ideas made them well suited to create a curriculum modeled after the University of Chicago.

A 'Chicago' curriculum also developed at the *Universidad de Tucumán*. Backed by Adolfo Diz, a former Chicago student and chair of Tucumán's economics department, Diz encouraged students to pursue graduate studies at Cuyo and Chicago (Harberger 2001). Once they arrived in Chicago, the Argentines learned the importance of the free market for economic development. These students also developed cohort and social ties through the exchange program, which intensified the coherence of their

Table 2.1 Assistance and grants from AID to Latin America, 1961–1970 (value as of June 30, 1970: US$1 000 000)

Year	Argentina	Chile	Uruguay
1961	0.8	22.9	0.1
1962	2.0	2.4	0.3
1963	2.9	5.4	1.9
1964	1.3	2.9	0.8
1965	1.5	2.5	0.9
1966	1.5	2.8	0.8
1967	1.3	2.8	2.6
1968	1.8	2.9	1.2
1969	1.8	2.7	1.3
1970	0.9	2.9	1.5

Source: Unión Panamericana, 1972.

economic ideas.[20] Having spent at least two years in courses that stressed the benefits of free market economics, and having many occasions to interact with professors in formal and informal settings about the importance of economic liberalization, most students came to espouse monetarism.

In addition to AID's support for Project Cuyo, private foundations funded Argentine studies in the US. The Ford Foundation, Fulbright Commission, Organization of American States and Rotary Club provided scholarships for Argentine students to enroll in US graduate programs in the 1960s and 1970s (Sturzenegger 1994).[21] Not all US funds went to US universities. Some Argentines were able to use the support to attend programs that favored a large state, such as ESCOLATINA, a graduate economics program at the University of Chile in which many Cepalinos taught. But in general US donors encouraged US training.

Demand Considerations and Neoliberalism

Although US government agencies and private foundations, motivated by political goals, succeeded in fostering a critical mass of free-market Argentine economists, most in the profession preferred structuralism.[22] Several demand factors limited the effectiveness of the US's socialization program.[23] As Argentine Julio Berlinsky, who earned both his master's degree in 1967 and doctorate in 1970 at Harvard, points out, only a few of the 50 economics students who left the country for US training in the 1960s ever returned to teach in Argentina (Berlinsky 1994). Lack of job opportunities in desirable locations reflected a key obstacle. For instance,

Table 2.2 Average Salaries for Full-Time Professors in Argentina, 1974–1985 (in Australes of June 1985)

Year	Monthly Salary	Index
1974	630	100.0
1975	575	91.3
1976	326	51.8
1977	532	84.5
1978	722	114.7
1979	746	118.5
1980	1013	160.9
1981	906	143.9
1982	511	81.2
1983	442	70.2
1984	592	94.0
1985	334	53.1

Source: World Bank (1988, p. 96).

Buenos Aires did not have many academic jobs, especially full-time ones.[24] Full-time academic positions could be found in such places as Mendoza and Tucumán, cities not as popular for professors who wanted the excitement of Buenos Aires. In addition, economists educated in the United States who served on the faculty in the provinces had relatively little impact on the profession. The absence of intellectual contact between the provincial universities and Buenos Aires curtailed the spread of neoliberal ideas (Harrison 1967, p. 21; Valdés 1989, p. 263).

Low salaries also discouraged many economists educated in the United States from accepting teaching positions in Argentina. Prior to 1989, a full-time professor at UBA might earn as little as $250 per month (Pessino 1994). As Table 2.2 shows, average teaching salaries for full-time faculty fell for most years between 1974 and 1985. Full-time professors' salaries at public universities decreased at an average annual rate of 5.1 percent between 1971 and 1990 (Gertel 1997, p. 64). As economist Juan Carlos de Pablo (1992) notes, it was nearly impossible to live solely on a public sector wage over the past twenty years.[25] Unlike in Chile, where universities paid their faculty high enough salaries so that they earned a living without seeking additional employment, in Argentina more than 70 percent of the faculty worked part-time and close to 10 percent worked full-time in the 1960s–1980s (Gertel 1997, p. 66).[26] Faculty needed to supplement their income, which left little time to inculcate students with neoliberal ideas (García de Fanelli 1995, p. 6).

Government intervention under democratic and military rule in Argentina also made university life difficult (Rein 1998; Reisberg 1993, p. 40). As mentioned before, generals and presidents intervened in the universities for much of the 1940s–1970s (Ascher 1975, p. 55; Crassweller 1987, p. 356). In sharp contrast to Chile, where universities provided a professional atmosphere largely free from governmental interference and where professors could do research and teach regardless of which party was in power, in Argentina, many faculty members lost their positions based on their political ideas (Ascher 1975, p. 67; Leonard 1989, p. 273).

Undesirable job locations, low salaries and lack of university autonomy prompted many of the best economists to abandon the Argentine university system and accept better paying positions abroad with international agencies such as the World Bank and International Monetary Fund (IMF). The preponderance of Argentines in international organizations is well known.[27] Based on its population, the Argentine diaspora holds many more positions relative to other Latin American countries. The significant difference in salaries measured in dollars between Argentina and abroad greatly influenced the decision to seek employment in international organizations (Sturzenegger 2002). Some economists educated in the United States also found employment at universities and private think tanks in the US, contributing to the so-called 'brain drain' of Argentina's economists. Others returned to Argentina to work in the private sector, in private consulting firms, or in the Consejo Nacional de Desarrollo (National Development Council) (de Pablo 1994). However, few economists educated in the United States taught in Argentine universities, which hampered opportunities to promote a new generation of neoliberal economists.

Other obstacles also worked against a consensus forming around neoliberal ideas. In the early 1960s, Chicago-trained economists from Chile, sent to Mendoza as faculty members, received cold receptions from their colleagues at the Universidad de Cuyo. Ideological disputes raged between Chilean and Argentine faculty members, which interfered with the development of a coherent curriculum for economics students at Cuyo (Valdés 1989, p. 263). For years, courses taken as part of Project Cuyo did not earn academic credit or count toward a degree. Members of Cuyo's academic council and senate blocked validation for course credit (Harberger 2001). Students thus earned few incentives to enroll in courses through Project Cuyo.

Students in economics and other disciplines at UBA also appeared unreceptive to neoliberal ideas from US universities. As Albion Patterson (1995), director of the ICA, who spearheaded the technical assistance program that sent Chilean economists to study at the University of

Chicago, remarked, when AID and the Ford Foundation provided funds to send visiting scholars from Columbia University to UBA in the early 1960s, UBA students insisted on leftist scholars. US intellectual imperialism spurred student protests against faculty visits (Harrison 1967, p. 22). In addition, most professors at UBA and *Universidad Católica Argentina* in Buenos Aires advocated structuralist views identified with Prebisch, in part because of his personal influence (Canitrot 1994). Although political skirmishes reduced Prebisch's impact on Argentina's economics profession in the 1950s and early 1960s (Sikkink 1988, p. 109), evidence suggests he left a substantial legacy. According to Mallon (1988, p. 123), 'An intellectual leader's most durable influence is that affecting individuals, and I know from personal experience that economic policy-making after the mid-1950s would have been far different without the influence of the ideas of CEPAL and Prebisch on Argentina's political leaders and economists'. Former Economy Minister Adalbert Krieger Vasena (1988, p. 116), an internationally-respected economist, concurred, stating that a goal of Prebisch was 'to stimulate younger economists to follow in his footsteps'. Until the late 1970s, the University of Chicago and other US universities had little influence in Buenos Aires and the other provinces (Heymann 1992).

In the late 1970s–1980s, changes occurred that brought about the founding of new institutes and universities supportive of neoliberal policies that enhanced demand for economists educated in the United States. According to Chicago-trained economist and former finance minister Ricardo López Murphy (1994), rising inflation in the mid 1970s spurred the private sector and government to develop a growing interest in the role of economists. Economic pressures prompted the opening of elite private institutes and universities in business and economics in the late 1970s to meet the rising demand for economists and MBA students in the Central Bank and private sector (Rodríguez 1994). Ironically, these institutes grew at the same time as thousands in the science and intellectual community left the country following the military's intervention of the universities (Pozzi 1987, p. 16). However, the junta government's (1976–83) support for some market-oriented reforms complemented the economic positions of new institutes and universities, thus availing them of significant autonomy (see Table 2.3 for a brief history of Argentina's attempts to initiate economic reforms between 1966 and 2004).

In the mid 1970s, severe economic problems plagued government and business groups alike. Inflation rates nearing 500 percent, a record high for Argentina at the time, made it clear that the Central Bank needed a technically trained staff (World Bank 2003). Business groups, too, reeled from the crisis. Many in the private sector perceived their nations' major

Table 2.3 Economic reforms in Argentina, 1966–2004

Key Economy Minister	1966–70 Krieger	1971–75 Ferrer	1976–80 Martínez de Hoz	1981–84 Grinspun	1985–88 Sourrouille	1989–90 González	1991–2001 Cavallo	2002–04 Lavagna
Stabilization	Yes (2)	No (1)	Yes (2)	No (1)	Yes (2)	Yes (2)	Yes (2)	Some (1)
Capital reform	Yes (2)	Little (1)	Yes (2)	Some (1)	Some (1)	Some (1)	Yes (2)	Some (1)
Tariffs	Fell (1)	High (0)	Fell (1)	Same (1)	Same (1)	Low (2)	Low (2)	Low (2)
Privatization	None (0)	None (0)	Little (0)[a]	None (0)	None (0)	Some (1)	Yes (2)	Same (2)
Price controls	Yes (0)	Yes (0)	Few (2)	Yes (0)	Few (2)	None (2)	None (2)	None (2)
Industrial promotion	Some (1)	High (0)	High (0)	High (0)	Reduced (1)	None (2)	None (2)	None (2)
Total	6	2	7	3	6	10	12	10

Notes:
2 = Strong Neoliberal Policies; 1 = Gradual Neoliberal Policies; 0 = Non-liberal Policies.
a. While the government privatized some small firms, it nationalized others.

public universities largely as failures (Levy 1986, p. 226). For both Central Bank officials and private sector members, the declining quality of university education and the need for technically qualified personnel made the development of elite private institutes/research centers and universities, modeled on the US example, imperative.[28]

Argentina experienced the ascent of private universities and research centers because of negative perceptions about public education (Levy 1996, p. 84). Specifically, instruction students received at public universities did not relate to the country's economic and technical requirements. Argentina had an oversupply of lawyers and a shortage of economists (Leonard 1989, p. 264). Many of its economists also lacked the technical skills necessary to conduct research and administer solutions in a complex world economy. The growing complications of high inflation and budget deficits and the inability to propose remedies indicated the inadequacy of the country's public educational system (Levy 1986, p. 46).

Public financing and enrollment figures help confirm the worsening state of Argentina's higher public education. From 1960 to 1990, student enrollment in public education rose 5.9 percent, but funds for public education declined 1.5 percent (Gertel 1997, p. 58). Budgetary woes are painful for public education since 99.75 percent of the national universities' income comes from the state (Levy 1986, p. 221).[29] As Table 2.4 indicates, funds budgeted for the national universities declined for most years between 1972 and 1994 as student enrollment continued to expand. The budget per student dropped from a high of 3978 pesos in 1980 to a low of 1397 pesos in 1990 (in 1994 constant pesos).[30] The combination of increasing enrollment and scarce resources led to poorer quality public education (Balán 1998, p. 2; Bonasegna 1988, p. 40).[31] Declining educational funds also fostered a fall in public university salaries (Levy 1997, p. 14).

Changes in admission and tuition policy in the early 1980s provide stunning examples of public education's difficulties. Following the democratic transition in late 1983, President Raúl Alfonsín approved an open admission and tuition-free policy for all national universities. Open enrollment and free tuition led to an explosion in the number of students attending public universities (see Table 2.4). State enrollments climbed as severe economic decline beset Argentina for much of the 1980s, leading to deteriorating conditions at public universities.[32]

Economic misery at the public universities produced windfalls for the creation of elite private institutes and universities, funded primarily by business associations and the international philanthropic community, some of the most important of which are discussed later. These institutes and universities significantly increased the number of better paying jobs for scholars in the field, luring economists educated in the United States to

Table 2.4 Budget and enrollment for the national universities, 1972–94

Year	Budget			Number of students	Budget per student
	1994 Pesos	Period	Change (%)		
1972	927 647 451	1972–73	31.89	245 789	3774
1973	1 223 450 696	1973–74	19.74	312 110	3920
1974	1 464 999 456	1974–75	−8.87	417 876	3506
1975	1 335 092 237	1975–76	−46.68	447 380	2984
1976	711 884 091	1976–77	−0.23	461 187	1544
1977	710 264 888	1977–78	33.43	407 125	1745
1978	947 672 232	1978–79	3.53	402 422	2355
1979	981 096 018	1979–80	22.50	397 643	2467
1980	1 201 807 310	1980–81	−11.31	302 110	3978
1981	1 065 835 426	1981–82	−27.09	301 085	3540
1982	777 085 390	1982–83	38.79	318 299	2441
1983	1 078 544 071	1983–84	3.22	337 998	3191
1984	1 113 258 611	1984–85	−5.44	443 441	2510
1985	1 052 650 668	1985–86	0.52	524 590	2007
1986	1 058 077 001	1986–87	30.70	581 813	1819
1987	1 382 926 820	1987–88	−4.58	618 651	2235
1988	1 319 556 968	1988–89	−25.81	652 997	2021
1989	979 035 016	1989–90	−3.04	661 315	1480
1990	949 267 351	1990–91	2.80	679 403	1397
1991	975 839 615	1991–92	19.69	681 990	1431
1992	1 168 023 346	1992–93	8.12	699 293	1670
1993	1 262 817 219	1993–94	10.54	657 545	1921
1994	1 395 958 000	1994–95	7.57	615 796	2267

Source: Balán (1998, p. 20).

work in academia (García de Fanelli 1995, p. 17; Reisberg 1993, p. 93). The preference for economists educated in the United States over most scholars educated elsewhere occurred, in part, because of reputational effects. Based on the technical emphasis in US graduate schools, economists educated in the US developed rigor and mathematical skills, which enhanced their employment prospects in the public and private sector. Advanced US degrees also acted as a sign of credibility, enhancing the institute's image with prospective students and employers. These skills and prestige factors boosted job opportunities for economists educated in the United States.

Demand for quality education allowed institutes and universities to charge higher tuition than at public universities. Whereas UBA and other public institutions are virtually free for students and depend on scarce state revenues, the cost of tuition in these self-financed private schools can run into the thousands per year. For wealthier patrons and their children as well as highly qualified students on scholarship, these institutes and universities provided excellent educational opportunities, often comparable to the best universities abroad. Based on their education, students from these private universities secured top jobs in the public and private sector (Levy 1999, p. 34).[33] High tuition charges also supported better faculty salaries.

Business demand for trained economists also enabled these institutes and universities to obtain corporate sponsorships and endowments that backed higher salaries and more faculty positions. Firms recognized the value of higher education and research for their corporate bottom line (Levy 1997, p. 14). Because of the declining system of public education, these elite institutes and universities attracted major corporate donations (Levy 1986, p. 226).

The state also played an important role in funding economics training and in the return of economists educated in the United States. Aware of the declining standards at the public universities, the Central Bank took an active role in training economists, sending many abroad for professionalization in the 1970s (Dagnino Pastore 1989, p. 199). Sponsorships and higher tuition enabled these institutes and universities to offer high enough salaries to attract faculty members trained in the US who might otherwise not work in academia or possibly live in Argentina.[34]

Among elite private institutes and universities that formed in the 1970s, one of the most important is the *Centro de Estudios Macroeconómicos de Argentina* (CEMA) that evolved into the *Universidad del CEMA* in 1995. Founded in 1978 by four former University of Chicago PhD students, and located in Buenos Aires, CEMA developed a postgraduate program in economics and an MBA program in the 1980s that helps to generate more neoliberal adherents to the profession.[35] CEMA today offers four undergraduate degrees, ten graduate level programs, and three executive programs. Among its 21 full-time faculty members in the economics program, 15 hold advanced degrees from US universities, and the current rector, Carlos Rodríguez, and vicerector, Edgardo Zablotsky, earned PhDs from the University of Chicago (http://www.cema.edu.ar/academica/ full_time.html). Curricula in the graduate economics program are comparable to US universities, with courses in mathematical economics, econometrics, microeconomic and macroeconomic analyses, financial analysis and capital markets, and price theory. CEMA also funnels prospective doctoral students to the US. After completing their studies, many return to Argentina to train another generation of economists.

Other private universities and institutes created near the same time as CEMA also are proliferating neoliberal economics. *The Instituto de Estudios Económicos sobre la Realidad Argentina y Latinoamerciana* (IEERAL) in Córdoba, a non-profit organization founded under the auspices of the *Fundación Mediterránea*, is an important institute that provides job opportunities to economists who might not otherwise have stayed in the profession or even lived in Argentina. Created in 1977 by two Córdoba businessmen for research on national and Latin American economics, the guiding principles of the Foundation are to support a strong market economy and social progress. Staff members of the IEERAL conduct research in several areas including: short-run economic analysis, growth, institutions and development, governance, and social policy. Research staffers have also held high-level government positions (Levy 1996, p. 156). Domingo Cavallo served as first president of the think tank, where he recruited highly trained and internationally oriented economists based on their loyalty to antistatist ideas (Corrales 1997, p. 56). Later, as Economy Minister in the Menem administration, Cavallo enlisted members of IEERAL for government positions. Policy positions bolstered IEERAL's prestige, allowing them to expand their research branches to six that operate in different regions of the country. The IEERAL's growing number of research centers has created additional faculty slots for internationally trained economists, primarily from the US. Among the top four authorities of the IEERAL, two hold advanced economics degrees from the US, as do eight of its top staff researchers (http://www.fundmediterranea.org.ar/).

Private universities and institutes created years earlier also supported the profession's shift to neoliberalism. The *Fundación de Investigaciones Económicas Latinoamericanas* (FIEL), founded in the early 1960s, has UCLA and Chicago-trained economists holding the position of director. In the *Instituto Torcuato Di Tella*, founded in 1958, 7 of its 15 faculty members hold PhDs from US universities including its director, Adolfo Canitrot (http://www.aaep.org.ar/itdt/). The *Universidad Torcuato Di Tella* founded in 1991 by the Di Tella Foundation and the *Instituto Torcuato Di Tella*, with support from the international philanthropic community, and its economic center are composed of faculty with doctorates from US universities (Levy 1996, p. 176). In fact, the former rector (Gerardo della Paolera 1991–2001), and the current rector (Juan Pablo Nicolini) of the university are products of the University of Chicago.[36] Of the 49 faulty members in the entire university, 28 have advanced degrees from US universities, with most holding economics PhDs (http://www.utdt.edu/profesores/index. php3).

The *Universidad de San Andrés*, founded in 1988, and *Universidad de Belgrano* are increasing the number of neoliberal proponents in the profession (Bonasegna 1988, p. 40). Of the 23 full-time, visiting and invited faculty members, 16 hold PhDs from US universities (one holds a masters), and the director, Mariano Tommasi, is a former PhD from the University of Chicago (http://www.udesa.edu.ar/). Through their teaching, these faculty members are producing another generation of neoliberal economists. Work opportunities in government, private institutes and universities are motivating more students to earn advanced degrees abroad, furthering the cause of neoliberalism.

Government programs complement the spread of neoliberal influence in Argentina's economics profession. In his capacity as Minister of the Economy, Cavallo established the *Instituto Superior de Economistas del Gobierno* (ISEG) in 1994 to upgrade the training of upper level government officials and to prepare officials entering government service. Cavallo, who earlier worked as Minister of Foreign Affairs, admired the training and preparation diplomats received from the foreign-service institute. Cavallo developed the ISEG to mirror the foreign-service training. With Arnold Harberger, who helped negotiate Project Cuyo, serving as external advisor for the program, the ISEG offered master's level courses in micro and macroeconomics at CEMA, UBA, the Universidad de San Andrés, and the *Universidad Torcuato Di Tella.* Although a few Cepalinos attacked some market-oriented positions, most professors taught courses that proliferated neoliberal ideas. In fact, some Chicago-trained professors from Chile's *Universidad Católica* (for example, Ernesto Fontaine and Alvaro Donoso) taught courses for ISEG. Harberger, who helped develop the curriculum and served as general auditor of the training program, devoted 90 hours to classroom teaching (Harberger 2001). These courses facilitated the spread of neoliberalism to students and government officials.

APPOINTMENT OF NEOLIBERAL ECONOMISTS TO POLICY-MAKING POSITIONS

Economists educated in the United States at elite institutes and universities also earned job opportunities at the Central Bank and economic ministries, providing another funding source and incentive to return to Argentina. As Argentine economist Juan Carlos de Pablo (1999, p. 1) proclaimed, 'Economic policy is too important not to be left to professional economists'. However, historically, most Argentine presidents or military rulers appointed relatively few economists to serve as top economic policy makers. Indeed, prior to 1976, executives selected less than 50 percent of economists to serve in top economic policy-making positions, with some supportive of structuralism (see Figure 2.1). The percentage of neoliberal economists increased to just over 50 percent between 1976 and 1980, only

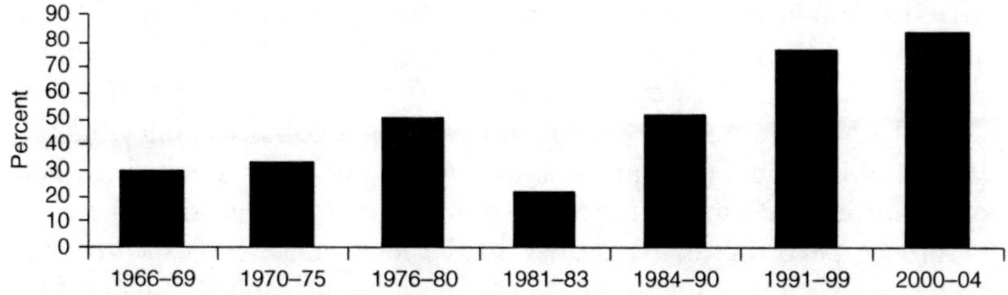

Note: Economic policy-making positions in Argentina for 1966–99 are: secretary and subsecretary of finance, minister and subsecretary of the economy, secretary and subsecretary of SEPCE (the planning office), secretary and subsecretary of commerce, and president, first vice president and second vice president of the central bank. Because of data limitations, only the secretary of the economy and president of the central bank are used for 2000–04. I counted as economists anyone who earned a graduate economics degree regardless of where they received their training. Although a few of the economists in policy-making positions in the 1960s–mid 1970s favored structuralist philosophies, educational backgrounds of policy makers would change. Since the early 1980s, nearly all economists in policy-making positions either hold graduate degrees from US universities or received their training from others educated in the US.

Source: Biglaiser (2002b, pp. 103, 167), with updates from Argentina's economics ministry and central bank.

Figure 2.1 Percentage of economists in economic policy making in Argentina

to decline again in 1981–84. The massive influx of neoliberal economists occurred in the early 1990s.

To explain the appointment decisions of political leaders, it is important to examine the effects of political institutions. Building on an assumption that military and democratic leaders have political survival as their main goal, I argue that different institutional configurations constrain the appointment strategies of survival-minded leaders. Specifically, under military rule, differences in longstanding characteristics of the military and in the kinds of governing institutions installed by military leaders shape the appointment of policy makers. Leaders under one-man rule, whose military has little experience with factions, have more autonomy in their appointments than collegial governments or factionalized militaries that require consensual agreement. This autonomy enables leaders to follow medium-term appointment strategies based on technical merit rather than serving immediate political concerns. Technical merit criteria are likely to contribute to the appointment of neoliberal economists.

Using a similar theoretical structure for democratic rule, governing institutions and characteristics of the legislature helps in understanding policy-making appointments. Differences in governing institutions and party strength in legislatures influence the appointment decisions of political leaders. Complementing work by Haggard and Kaufman (1995), I contend that centralized executive authority is important for overcoming political stalemates, and selecting and backing a cohesive policy-making team. Building on Mainwaring and Shugart (1997), in countries where governing institutions confer much power on executives and where the executive's party holds a majority in the legislature, the executive has greater autonomy in the appointment of economic policy makers. Like one-man rule and a less factionalized military, a strong executive and a legislature dominated by the executive's party provide executives with more means to do whatever they want. Political survival strategies, based on different institutional settings, influence the executive's willingness to appoint economists.

Argentina's military regimes appear consistent with the appointment strategies predicted by our model. Following many years of unstable democratic and authoritarian governments, Argentina imposed a more permanent military regime in 1966, with General Juan Carlos Onganía serving as a one-man ruler. However, Argentina's long history of factional disputes between the army and navy affected Onganía's discretion in cabinet appointments. Based on the many counter-coups and military interventions of democratic governments, Onganía hoped to use policy-making appointments to reduce the countercoup threat from competitor officers. Attempts to appease military challengers worked against the selection of neoliberal economists opposed by most military officers. Military officers rejected neoliberal economists on at least two fronts. First, officers worried about the survival of *Fabricaciones Militares* (FM), the military-run enterprises, if neoliberal economists held top policy-making positions (Lewis 1992, p. 283). Created in 1941, FM included both heavy industrial and light manufacturing sectors. To survive, these enterprises depended on subsidies and protection from external and internal competition, policies anathema to neoliberal economists. Second, the neoliberal goal of reducing the state contrasted with the military's security concerns and strong state needs. As a result, Onganía selected diverse policy makers to satisfy various military interests (see Figure 2.1).

In 1970, the military replaced Onganía with General Roberto Levingston, who worked in a collegial setting as one of four participants in making important decisions. Much like Onganía, Levingston appointed relatively few economists in order to appease different military factions. Levingston's successor, General Alejandro Lanusse, followed a similar appointment strategy, using concessions in an attempt to attract support for his future presidential goals.

After a three-year democratic interregnum with the septuagenarian

Juan Perón returning to office in 1973 followed by his death and succession of his wife and vice president, Isabel Perón, to office in 1974, a military junta took power in 1976. The head of the junta, General Jorge Videla, supported the appointment of neoliberal economists (Videla 1992). However, collegial power among service chiefs and within each service branch implied arduous inter-branch negotiations on cabinet appointment (Fontana 1987, pp. 44, 49). Admiral Emilio Massera, chief of the navy, and General Díaz Bessone, head of a sector of the army, especially opposed market-oriented economists.[37] As a power struggle ensued among the service chiefs, none of these men would compromise on the direction of the economy. This lack of cohesion in Argentina's state apparatus further weakened the chance of choosing a coherent team of experts (Stepan 1985, p. 330). Although Videla selected economists who received slightly more than half the policy-making appointments, tensions persisted that undermined the consistency of policy choices. Videla's successors would have even greater difficulties appointing economists without risking countercoups. Broad-based opposition to market-oriented policies by most military and business groups as well as traditional political parties led the military leaders to sack many neoliberal economists (Fontana 1987, p. 120).

The appointment strategies under the democratically-elected Raúl Alfonsín in late 1983 followed a similar pattern based on institutional constraints. Although Alfonsín's Radical Party held a majority of seats in the Chamber of Deputies, and a strong 'contingent [in the Senate] that could construct agreements from a position of relative strength', the president still needed to satisfy interests within his party and the opposition (Jones 1997, p. 267). Fear of democratic rule not being consolidated, or worse, of a return to military rule, was Alfonsín's prime concern. This fear, complemented by weak executive powers, prompted Alfonsín to appoint a diverse group of policy makers in 1984. Over the next year, Alfonsín's economy minister, Bernardo Grinspun, proclaimed his program to reflate the economy and promote equitable income distribution. Grinspun's program led to economic disaster, with inflation rising over 600 percent and external debts climbing near $50 billion (World Bank 2003). Economic crisis forced Alfonsín to replace old-time party stalwarts with extraparty technocrats (neoliberal economists) including Adolfo Canitrot, José Luis Machinea and Juan Sourrouille in 1985 (McGuire 1995, p. 230). However, pressures from interests in Alfonsín's party and from opposition Peronists restricted the number of economists. In addition, the Radical Party's loss of many seats in 1987 midterm elections eliminated any appointment leverage Alfonsín might have with the legislature.

The appointment strategies of Alfonsín's successor, Carlos Menem, suggest that political institutions can support greater executive autonomy. Based on Menem's sizable margin of victory,[38] the swelling in the number of legislative seats held by his party that increased at midterm elections, and the fall in seats held by the main opposition party, Menem earned much freedom in his economic appointments. Menem also held executive decree and veto powers that supplemented his formal and partisan powers, enhancing his executive powers. During his presidential campaign in the spring of 1989, Menem stressed ideals commonly endorsed by previous Peronist leaders. He proposed state intervention in the economy and support for workers as keys to economic revitalization. His electoral victory, however, led the already faltering economy into a hyperinflation. Investor concerns over the decisions Menem might make once he took office contributed to capital flight and economic chaos.

In an attempt to calm investors, Menem appointed an economic team that consisted of business leaders from Bunge and Born along with some economists, who initiated a gradualist neoliberal strategy (Smith 1991). Menem's initial appointments also served to marginalize the institutionalization of the Justicialista Party (PJ). Menem, a former governor of La Rioja and political outsider, wanted to limit the institutionalization and organization of the PJ and redesign it in his own image. Menem reduced party influence by appointing 'minor Peronist figures connected personally to him or extraparty technocrats committed to liberalizing the economy' (McGuire 1995, p. 232). In December 1989, Argentina experienced a second bout of hyperinflation. Menem selected another team headed by Antonio Erman González to address these economic difficulties, but economists still did not dominate the economic ministries. Menem waited until January 1991, with his survival at stake,[39] to select Harvard-trained economist Domingo Cavallo as his new economic minister. Bringing with him 'Cavallo Boys', economists from the IEERAL, an economic think tank he helped to launch, Cavallo assembled an economic policy-making team of neoliberal economists (Corrales 1997, p. 56). From 51 percent of economists holding policy-making positions from 1984 through 1990, the percentage of economists rose to 74 percent from 1991 through 1993 and 83 percent from 1994 through 1999. Menem's appointment of Cavallo and his team suggests the role of a strong executive and control of the legislature by the executive's party for autonomy in policy-making appointments.

Menem's successor, President Fernando de la Rua, also selected many neoliberal economists, with Cavallo later returning as Minister of the Economy. Since December 2001, when economic crisis contributed to de la Rua's stepping down from power, anti-neoliberal forces have grown in Argentina. President Eduardo Duhalde (2002–03) and President Néstor Kirchner faced intense domestic pressure from the jobless as well as countless Argentines who lost money because of the peso devaluation. Many wanted Kirchner to battle the IMF and other creditors who were owed billions. Despite Kirchner's strong rhetoric against the international lending community, the president continued to appoint economists educated in the United States with Harvard-educated Roberto Lavagna serving as economic minister, and Harvard-trained Martín Redrado, who replaced University of Pennsylvania-trained Alfonso Prat-Gay as Central Bank President. Even under the worst economic circumstances, the influence of economists educated in the United States persists.

CONCLUSION

This chapter detailed the history of Argentina's economics profession to explain the shift from structuralism to neoliberalism. Building on Choi's (1997) work, it identifies the effect of supply and demand considerations. From the supply side, the influence of international organizations is significant in supplying economics students with financial resources to enroll in US graduate programs. As a counterweight to CEPAL's support for more leftist policies and influence in Latin America, US government agencies and private foundations funded Argentines to study in the US. Based on similar economics curricula in most US universities, the more students a country sent to the US for economics training, the more likely that neoliberal ideas affected the economics profession in the foreign country.

However, the chapter also demonstrated that US training alone does not guarantee that the economics profession in the home country accepts neoliberal ideas. From the demand side, the chapter indicates the importance of employment prospects in the home countries. If economists educated in the United States cannot find positions in academia, they are likely to accept employment abroad, which limits their ability to train a second generation of economists.

Despite assistance from USAID and private US foundations that sent many Argentines to study economics in the US, the Argentine profession remained committed to structuralism in the 1960s and through most of the 1970s. A lack of desirable full-time academic positions resulted in fewer economists educated in the United States holding academic jobs. Many decided to work for international organizations overseas. Since the late 1970s, however, increased demand for well-trained economists by the private sector and the central bank led to the founding of private institutes and universities by economists educated in the United States. Greater demand for economists allowed institutes and universities to charge high tuition fees and to secure corporate sponsorships and endowments that enabled them to offer competitive salaries to attract US-trained faculty members. Through their teaching, faculties at these institutes and universities have produced another generation of economists who advocate neoliberal ideas.

In addition to academic positions, economists have also been rewarded with top economic policy-making positions in the past decade. Unlike the 1960s–1980s, when military and democratic leaders tended to appoint few neoliberal economists because of institutional constraints and political survival goals, the past decade has provided opportunities to select economists for policy making. Rather than work abroad, academic and government posts provide neoliberal economists with incentives to return to Argentina.

Whether neoliberalism will remain popular with the Argentine economics profession merits close scrutiny. Growing economic inequalities and unstable growth in Argentina have fostered growing anger toward the neoliberal model. No one knows if the inability of free-market reforms to promote greater welfare for all is short term or if it will lead to an anti-neoliberal backlash within the economics profession. Despite the uncertain benefits, US influence in Argentina's economics profession has important implications. First, as Argentine executives appoint economists educated in the United States for economic policy-making positions, it is critical to examine how these policy makers affect economic development. More studies are needed to assess the impact of different policy-making teams on economic growth and prosperity. Second, as economists educated in the United States come to dominate Argentina's universities and professions, this has the potential to extend US influence for generations. On the basis of advice and encouragement they are receiving from faculty in their home countries, more economics students from Argentina and Latin America, in general, are earning advanced degrees from US universities, which affects the creation of communities within the economics professions of Latin America. Third, the employment of economists educated in the United States in the private sector widens the potential reach of US influence abroad. Socialization programs designed to defeat rival ideologies can have a long-lasting impact on societies.

NOTES

1. I am grateful to the following for their comments and suggestions: Juan Carlos de Pablo, Jeff Frieden, Barbara Geddes, Daniel Heymann, Ricardo López Murphy, John Markoff, Verónica Montecinos, Carola Pessino and Adolfo Sturzenegger. Special thanks to Al Harberger and Larry Sjaastad who clarified the connection between the University of Chicago and the spread of market-oriented ideas in Argentina.
2. The term neoliberal economist is not without controversy. However, based on the

comments of Argentine academics, I define neoliberal economists as those who were socialized to favor market-oriented ideas during their graduate studies, whether they were American-trained or studied under others trained in the US.

3. While constitutions confer on executives the ability to select their own cabinet, political considerations and pressures affect their choices. Strong executive powers and legislatures dominated by the executive's party, however, may shield executives from these pressures.
4. For a thorough treatment about the early history of economic thought in Latin America, and in Argentina, in particular, see Popescu (1997).
5. See Montecinos and Markoff (2001) for a good discussion of economic liberalism in Latin America.
6. See also Mallon (2000, p. 21), who argues that foreign policy advisers are sometimes used today 'as window dressing to justify requests for more foreign aid'.
7. On the anti-liberal economic trends that antedated the world economic crisis, see Montecinos and Markoff (2001). Latin Americans followed debates in the Soviet Union, France, Germany and Spain, where strong opposition to liberal policies intensified.
8. In addition to the Great Depression, the specific trade crises during World Wars I and II also inspired the shift toward inward-oriented, economic development (Schneider 1999, p. 284).
9. Unlike Mexico's Central Bank, which helped to create elite private economic programs through the *Instituto Tecnológico Autónomo de México* (ITAM) in the 1940s, Argentina's Central Bank waited until the early 1970s, under economic crisis, to foster elite private institutes.
10. For more details on Prebisch's development ideas, see Prebisch (1984).
11. Onganía also closed the *Instituto Torcuato Di Tella*, a multidisciplinary institution founded in the 1950s that conducted research in the social sciences.
12. In the 1950s, few used the term neoliberal to identify economists who favored more open markets. During that time and even today, these economists are sometimes referred to as monetarists. Analysts popularized the term neoliberal to describe free-market economics in the 1970s and 1980s.
13. A few Argentines also subscribed to a third economic school, namely Marxism. However, unlike in Mexico and Chile, Marxist influence came fairly late to Argentina and appeared more as a political rather than economic movement (Sjaastad 2002).
14. For a discussion about the conflicts between structuralists and monetarists, see Silva (1991). For the different perspectives on economic development policies, see Hirschman (1968).
15. See Mitchell (1967) and Iglesias (1992) for details about CEPAL's influence in Latin America. For a thorough treatment of CEPAL and Prebisch's impact, see Love (1996).
16. See Silva (1993) for the influence of business coalitions on economic policy.
17. According to Piñera (1991, p. 7), economists trained at any American university after the 1950s shared similar philosophies because of the use of Samuelson's textbook in introductory economics courses. See also Amsden (1992, p. 353) who states that between 1953 and 1991 free market theory triumphed both intellectually and politically within the economics profession in the United States.
18. For information about the Point 4 Program, see Packenham (1973, pp. 43–9).
19. For useful insights on the agreement, see Correa (1985) and O'Brien (1983).
20. See Pion-Berlin (1986, p. 320) and Hecht Oppenheim (1993, p. 148) who discuss the coherence of Chicago economic ideas. Although they focus specifically on the Chilean students, Argentines trained in Chicago developed a similar fondness for market reforms.
21. For instance, the Ford Foundation created a program called *Pro Economía Agraria*, which trained many economists in agricultural economics at US universities (Sjaastad 2002).
22. See Mallon (2000, p. 80) on the importance of creating a critical mass of reform advocates.

23. Regardless of the limitations with Project Cuyo, it did train Pedro Pou, a past president of the Central Bank, and Claudio Loser, head of the Western Hemisphere Department of the IMF.
24. See Suárez (1969) for more details on the part-time status of economics faculty members. The *Instituto Torcuato Di Tella* is an important exception for economists educated in the United States seeking full-time academic work in Buenos Aires.
25. According to University of Chicago Professor Larry Sjaastad, an Argentine math professor trained in the US informed him that during the early days of the Alfonsín regime the number of students in his UBA classes was greater than his monthly salary (when converted to dollars).
26. Approximately 15 percent worked half-time. See Bonasegna (1987, p. 41) for additional information on the percentage of faculty employed full-time at the national universities. See Harberger (1997, p. 307) for Latin America's reliance on part-time faculty.
27. A staff member from the Inter-American Development Bank also confirmed the significant influx of Argentine personnel at the Bank.
28. See García de Fanelli (1996, p. 23) for a discussion of Argentina's graduate education modeled on the US.
29. See also Balán (1997, p. 197) who contends that Argentina's national universities are almost entirely funded by the state.
30. According to Gertel (1997, p. 58), per student expenditure fell from $1800 in 1963 to $225 in 1989, with an annual 7.5 percent rate of decline.
31. See also Levy (1986, p. 47) who claims that booming enrollments have produced lowered average quality of student preparation, higher student/instructor ratios, and worse job prospects.
32. Although laws introduced in the 1990s eliminated open enrollment and a free tuition policy, because of political concerns, the state rarely collects more than a nominal tuition fee.
33. Graduates from elite universities also have good job prospects in multinational enterprises (Levy 1997, p. 87).
34. For instance, full-time faculty members at the private *Universidad de Belgrano* earn three times as much as their public university counterparts.
35. Money earned in CEMA's MBA program helps subsidize its economics master's program.
36. Gerardo della Paolera is currently the Rector of the American University of Paris.
37. Rock (1987, p. 370) discusses a third faction, headed by General Carlos Suárez Masón and General Luciano Menéndez, who opposed economic policies preferred by Videla.
38. Menem garnered over 47 percent of the vote in 1989, while his nearest competitor won barely 32 percent.
39. Mounting corruption scandals against high officials and signs of another hyperinflation made Menem's survival appear in jeopardy. Indeed, speculation surfaced from high-placed members of his government that Menem might be eased out of the presidency before his term expired (*Latin American Regional Reports: Southern Cone*, March 14, 1991, p. 1).

REFERENCES

Amsden, A. (1992), 'The Globalization of the Crisis in American Economic Education', *The Journal of Economic Education*, **23** (4), 353–6.

Ascher, William (1975), 'Planners, Politics, and Technocracy in Argentina and Chile', PhD dissertation, Yale University.

Baer, W. (1972), 'Import Substitution and Liberalization in Latin America', *Latin American Research Review*, **7** (1), 95–122.

Balán, Jorge (1997), 'Governance and Finance for National Universities in Argentina: Current Proposals for Change', in Lewis A. Tyler et al. (eds), *Contemporary Higher Education: International Issues for the Twenty-First Century*, New York: Garland Publishing, pp. 195–210.

Balán, Jorge (1998), 'Higher Education Policies in Argentina in the 1990s: Regulation, Coordination, and Autonomy', in Jorge Balán et al. (eds), *Higher Education Reform in Latin America*, Washington, DC: Latin American Program Working Papers #235, The Woodrow Wilson Center.

Berlinsky, Julio (1994), Interview of March 28 with the Argentine economist.

Biglaiser, G. (2002a), 'The Internationalization of Chicago's Economics in Latin America', *Economic Development and Cultural Change*, **50** (2), 269–86.

Biglaiser, Glen (2002b), *Guardians of the Nation? Economists, Generals, and Economic Reform in Latin America*, Notre Dame: University of Notre Dame Press.

Blanksten, George I. (1953), *Perón's Argentina*, Chicago: University of Chicago Press.

Boeninger, Edgardo (1982), 'Application of the Social Sciences to Public Policies: Producers, Consumers, and Mechanisms of Mediation', in Laurence D. Stifel et al. (eds), *Social Sciences and Public Policy in the Developing World*, Lexington, MA: Lexington Books, pp. 251–76.

Bonasegna, C. (1987), 'Professions in Argentina Reject Government's Salary Offer and Extend Exam Boycott', *The Chronicle of Higher Education*, **7**, January, p. 41.

Bonasegna, C. (1988), 'Argentina: Debt, Scarcity, and Overcrowding Saddle a Public University System in Crisis', *The Chronicle of Higher Education*, **13**, January, p. A40.

Bruce, D. (1980), 'The Impact of the United Nations Economic Commission for Latin America: Technocrats as Channels of Influence', *Inter-American Economic Affairs*, **33** (4), 3–28.

Canitrot, Adolfo (1994), Interview of March 28 with the Director of the Institute Di Tella.

Choi, Young Back (1997), 'The Americanization of Economics in Korea', in A.W. Coats (ed.), *The Post-1945 Internationalization of Economics, Annual Supplement to Volume 28, History of Political Economy*, Durham: Duke University Press, pp. 97–122.

Corrales, Javier (1997), 'Why Argentines Followed Cavallo: A Technopol Between Democracy and Economic Reform', in Jorge. I. Domínguez (ed.), *Technopols: Ideas and Leaders in Freeing Politics and Markets in Latin America in the 1990s*, University Park: Pennsylvania State University, pp. 49–93.

Correa, S. (1985), 'Algunos Antecedentes Históricos del Proyecto Neoliberal en Chile (1955–1958)', *Opciones*, **6**, 106–46.

Crassweller, Robert D. (1987), *Perón and the Enigmas of Argentina*, New York: W.W. Norton & Co.

Dagnino Pastore, José María (1988), *Crónicas Económicas: Argentina 1969–1988*, Buenos Aires: Editorial Crespillo.

Dagnino Pastore, José María (1989), 'Argentina', in Joseph A. Pechman (ed.), *The Role of the Economist in Government: An International Perspective*, New York: Harvester Wheatsheaf, pp. 195–212.

de Pablo, Juan Carlos (1992), Interview of November 17 with the Argentine economist.

de Pablo, Juan Carlos (1994), Interview of March 29 with the Argentine economist.

de Pablo, Juan Carlos (1999), *Economists and Economic Policy: Argentina since 1958*, http://www.cema.edu.ar/publicaciones/download/documentos/149.pdf.

Díaz-Alejandro, Carlos (1970), *Essays in the Economic History of the Argentine Republic*, New Haven: Yale University Press.

Drake, Paul W. (1994), *Money Doctors, Foreign Debts, and Economic Reforms in Latin America from the 1890s to the Present*, Wilmington: Scholarly Resources.

Fontana, Andrés (1987), 'Political Decision Making by a Military Corporation', PhD dissertation, University of Texas, Austin.

García de Fanelli, A. (1995), 'Institutional and Program Differentiation in the Argentine Higher Educational System: The Outcome of the Public Policies in the 1980s', presented at the Annual Meeting of the Latin American Studies Association, The Washington DC Sheraton.

García de Fanelli, A. (1996), 'Estudios de Posgrado en la Argentina: Alcances y Limitaciones de su Expansión en las Universidades Públicas', *Documento CEDES*, 114.

Gertel, Hector R. (1997), 'Issues and Perspectives for Higher Education in Argentina in the 1990s', in Lewis A. Tyler et al. (eds), *Contemporary Higher Education: International Issues for the Twenty-First Century*, New York: Garland Publishing, pp. 57–75.

Haggard, Stephan and Robert R. Kaufman (1995), *The Political Economy of Democratic Transitions*, Princeton: Princeton University Press.

Harberger, Arnold C. (1997), 'Good Economics Comes to Latin America, 1955–95', in A.W. Coats (ed.), *The Post-1945 Internationalization of Economics, Annual Supplement to Volume 28, History of Political Economy*, Durham: Duke University Press, pp. 301–11.

Harberger, Arnold C. (1999), Interview on December 28 with the Professor of Economics at UCLA.

Harberger, Arnold C. (2001), Interview on August 28 with the Professor of Economics at UCLA.

Harrison, John P. (1967), *A Report to the American Academic Community on the Present Argentine University Situation*, Austin: Special Publication of the Latin American Studies Association, pp. 17–28.

Hecht Oppenheim, Lois (1993), *Politics in Chile: Democracy, Authoritarianism, and the Search for Development*, Boulder: Westview Press.

Heymann, Daniel (1992), Interview on October 26 with the Argentine economist.

Heymann, Daniel (1994), Interview on March 29 with the Argentine economist.

Hirschman, Albert O. (1963), *Journeys Toward Progress: Studies of Economic Policy Making in Latin America*, New York: The Twentieth Century Fund, Inc.

Hirschman, A. (1968), 'The Political Economy of Import-Substitution Industrialization in Latin America', *Quarterly Journal of Economics*, **82**, 1–32.

Iglesias, Enrique (1992), *Reflections on Economic Development: Toward a New Latin American Consensus*, Washington, DC: IDB.

Johnson, Harry G. (1975), *On Economics and Society*, Chicago: The University of Chicago Press.

Jones, Mark P. (1997), 'Evaluating Argentina's Presidential Democracy: 1983–1995', in Scott Mainwaring and Matthew Soberg Shugart (eds), *Presidentialism*

and Democracy in Latin America, New York: Cambridge University Press, pp. 259–99.
Kaufman, Robert R. (1979), 'Industrial Change and Authoritarian Rule in Latin America: A Concrete Review of the Bureaucratic-Authoritarian Model', in David Collier (ed.), *The New Authoritarianism in Latin America*, Princeton: Princeton University Press, pp. 165–253.
Krieger Vasena, Adalbert (1988), *El Programa Económico Argentino 1967/69*, Buenos Aires: Academía Nacional de Ciencias Económicas.
Lassalle, Edmundo (1943), *Argentina*, Washington, DC: Higher Education in Latin America, Vol. 1, Division of Intellectual Cooperation, Pan American Union.
Leonard, Virginia W. (1989), *Politicians, Pupils, and Priests: Argentine Education Since 1943*, New York: Peter Lang.
Levy, Daniel C. (1986), *Higher Education and the State in Latin America: Private Challenges to Public Dominance*, Chicago: The University of Chicago Press.
Levy, Daniel C. (1996), *Building the Third Sector: Private Research Centers and Nonprofit Development in Latin America*, Pittsburgh: University of Pittsburgh Press.
Levy, Daniel C. (1997), 'Issues and Concepts', in Lewis A. Tyler et al. (eds), *Contemporary Higher Education: International Issues for the Twenty-First Century*, New York: Garland Publishing, pp. 3–16.
Levy, Daniel C. (1999), 'When Private Higher Education Does not Bring Organizational Diversity', in Philip G. Altbach (ed.), *Private Prometheus: Private Higher Education and Development in the 21st Century*, Westport, CT: Greenwood Press, pp. 15–43.
Lewis, Paul (1992), *The Crisis of Argentine Capitalism*, Chapel Hill: University of North Carolina Press.
López Murphy, Ricardo (1994), Interview of March 30 with the Argentine economist and former Minister of the Economy.
Love, Joseph L. (1996), 'Economic Ideas and Ideologies in Latin America Since 1930', in Leslie Bethel (ed.), *Ideas and Ideologies in Twentieth Century Latin America*, New York: Cambridge University Press, pp. 207–75.
Mainwaring, Scott and Matthew Soberg Shugart (eds) (1997), *Presidentialism and Democracy in Latin America*, New York: Cambridge University Press.
Mallon, R. (1988), 'The Influence of Raúl Prebisch on Argentine Economic Policy-Making, 1950–1962: A Comment', *Latin American Research Review*, **23** (2), 120–23.
Mallon, R. (2000), *The New Missionaries: Memoirs of a Foreign Adviser in Less-Developed Countries*, Cambridge, MA: Harvard Institute for International Development, Harvard University Press.
McGuire, James W. (1995), 'Political Parties and Democracy in Argentina', in Scott Mainwaring and Timothy R. Scully (eds), *Building Democratic Institutions: Party Systems in Latin America*, Stanford: Stanford University Press, pp. 200–248.
Mitchell, C. (1967), 'The Role of Technocrats in Latin American Integration', *Inter-American Economic Affairs*, **21** (1), 3–29.
Montecinos, Verónica and John Markoff (2001), 'From the Power of Economic Ideas to the Power of Economists', in Miguel A. Centeno and Fernando López-Alves (eds), *The Other Mirror: Grand Theory through the Lens of Latin America*, Princeton: Princeton University Press, pp. 105–50.

Munger, W. (1947), 'Academic Freedom Under Perón', *Antioch Review*, **7** (2), 275–90.
O'Brien, Philip J. (1983), *Chile: The Pinochet Decade: The Rise and Fall of the Chicago Boys*, London: Latin American Bureau.
Packenham, Robert A. (1973), *Liberal America and the Third World: Political Development Ideas in Foreign Aid and Social Science*, Princeton: Princeton University Press.
Patterson, Albion (1995), Interviews with the former director of AID's Point Four Program on February 27 and May 17 in Ojai, California.
Pessino, Carola (1994), Interview of March 30 with the Argentine economist.
Piñera, J. (1991), 'Political Economy of Chilean Reform', *International Economic Insights*, **2** (4), 6–9.
Pinto, A. and O. Sunkel (1966), 'Latin American Economists in the US', *Economic Development and Cultural Change*, **15** (1), 79–86.
Pion-Berlin, David (1986), 'The Defiant State: Chile in the Post-Coup Era', in Abraham F. Lowenthal and J. Samuel Fitch (eds), *Armies and Politics in Latin America Revised Edition*, New York: Holmes and Meier, pp. 317–34.
Popescu, Oreste (1997), *Studies in the History of Latin American Economic Thought*, New York: Routledge.
Pozzi, P.A. (1987), 'The University of Buenos Aires: Social Crisis and Democratization', Amherst, MA: Program in Latin American Studies Occasional Papers Series No. 20.
Prebisch, Raúl (1947), *Introducción a Keynes,* México: Fondo de Cultura Económica.
Prebisch, Raúl (1984), 'Five Stages in my Thinking on Development', in Gerald M. Meier and Dudley Seers (eds), *Pioneers in Development*, New York: Published for the World Bank, Oxford University Press, pp. 175–204.
Ramos, Joseph (1986), *Neoconservative Economics in the Southern Cone of Latin America, 1973–1983*, Baltimore: The Johns Hopkins University Press.
Rein, Mónica Esti (1998), *Politics and Education in Argentina, 1946–1962* (Translated by M. Grenzeback), New York: M.E. Sharp.
Reisberg, Liz A. (1993), *Argentina: A Study of the Educational System of Argentina and a Guide to the Academic Placement of Students in Educational Institutions in the US*, Washington, DC: World Education Series Publication.
Rock, David (1987), *Argentina, 1516–1987: From Spanish Colonization to Alfonsín*, Berkeley: University of California Press.
Rodríguez, Carlos (1994), Interview of March 28 with the Director of CEMA.
Rosenberg, Emily and Norman Rosenberg (1994), 'From Colonialism to Professionalism: The Public–Private Dynamic in US Foreign Policy Advising', in Paul W. Drake (ed.), *Money Doctors, Foreign Debts, and Economic Reforms in Latin America from the 1890s to the Present*, Wilmington: Scholarly Resources, Inc., Jaguar Books on Latin America, 3, pp. 59–84.
Schneider, Ben Ross (1999), 'The Desarrollista State in Brazil and Mexico', in Meredith Woo-Cummings (ed.), *The Developmental State*, Ithaca: Cornell University Press, pp. 276–305.
Sikkink, K. (1988), 'The Influence of Raúl Prebisch on Economic Policy-making in Argentina, 1950–1962', *Latin American Research Review*, **23** (2), 91–114.
Sikkink, Kathryn (1991), *Ideas and Institutions: Developmentalism in Brazil and Argentina*, Ithaca: Cornell University Press.
Silva, E. (1993), 'Capitalist Coalitions, the State, and Neoliberal Economic Restructuring: Chile, 1973–88', *World Politics*, **45** (July), 526–59.

Silva, P. (1991), 'Technocrats and Politics in Chile: From the Chicago Boys to the CIEPLAN Monks', *Journal of Latin American Studies*, **23** (2), 385–410.
Sjaastad, Larry (2002), Personal correspondence on August 22 with the Professor of Economics from the University of Chicago.
Smith, W. (1991), 'State, Market, and Neoliberalism in Post-Transition Argentina: The Menem Experience', *Journal of Interamerican Studies and World Affairs*, **33** (4), 45–82.
Stepan, A. (1985), 'State Power and the Strength of Civil Society in the Southern Cone of Latin America', in Peter B. Evans, Dietrich Rueschemeyer and Theda Skocpol (eds), *Bringing the State Back In*, Cambridge: Cambridge University Press, pp. 317–46.
Sturzenegger, Adolfo (1994), Interview of March 29 with the Argentine economist.
Sturzenegger, Adolfo (2002), Personal correspondence on August 28 with the Argentine economist.
Suárez, Francisco M. (1969), 'Institutionalization of New Professions in Developing Countries: The Case of Argentine Economists', PhD dissertation, Indiana University.
Thorp, Rosemary (ed.) (1984), *Latin America in the 1930s: The Role of the Periphery in the World Crisis*, New York: St. Martin's Press.
Unión Panamericana (1972), *América en Cifras; Situación Económica*, Washington, DC: Unión Panamericana.
Valdés, Juan Gabriel (1989), *La Escuela de Chicago: Operación Chile*, Buenos Aires: Grupo Editorial Zeta, S.A.
Valdés, Juan Gabriel (1995), *Pinochet's Economists: The Chicago School in Chile*, Cambridge: Cambridge University Press.
Venezian, Eduardo (1982), 'The Economic Sciences in Latin America', in Laurence D. Stifel et al. (eds), *Social Sciences and Public Policy in the Developing World*, Lexington, MA: Lexington Books, pp. 189–210.
Videla, Jorge (1992), Interview of November 25 with the former Argentine junta leader from 1976 to 1981.
Weil, Thomas E. et al. (eds) (1974), *Area Handbook for Argentina*, Washington, DC: Foreign Area Studies of the American University.
Williamson, John (ed.) (1994), *The Political Economy of Policy Reform*, Washington, DC: Institute for International Economics.
World Bank (1988), *Argentina: Social Sectors in Crisis, A World Bank Country Study*, Washington, DC: The World Bank.
World Bank (2003), *World Development Indicators*, Washington, DC
Wynia, Gary (1978), *Argentina in the Postwar Era: Politics and Economic Policymaking in a Divided Society*, Albuquerque: University of New Mexico Press.
Wynia, Gary (1992), *Argentina: Illusions and Realities, 2nd ed.*, New York: Holmes & Meier.

3. Economists in the Brazilian government: from developmentalist state to neoliberal policies

Maria Rita Loureiro

INTRODUCTION

From the beginning of the military regime (1964–84) economists have occupied leading positions in the Brazilian government. They have been ministers of Finance and Planning, presidents and directors of the Central Bank, as well as heads of development banks and other important agencies. This chapter will analyze the emergence of the economists as a political elite in Brazil. This elite is identified and legitimized not through political party and electoral representation but through technical and scientific competence. Although this process was historically connected with the consolidation of the developmentalist state in the 1950s and 1960s, it has paradoxically been reinforced by recent neoliberal economic reforms in a democratic context.

The participation of economists in government is not a process that automatically follows from the interventionist and regulatory role of the state. It has varied patterns. After World War II, as a result of the spread of Keynesian ideas, economists were participating in government in several Western countries. But in contrast to Brazil and other Latin American countries, economists in Europe, Japan and United States have occupied mainly middle level positions (Coats 1981). In France, economics was traditionally taught in law schools and only achieved autonomy at a very late date, in the 1950s. The recruitment for macroeconomic agencies took place not among economists but among professionals from the *Grandes Écoles* (the *École Nationale d'Administration*, the *Polytechnique*, the *École Libre de Sciences Politiques* and others) (Suleiman 1970; Birnbaum 1977; Fourquet 1980; Pollak 1976). In the United States, the economists remained scholars, despite the development of state regulatory activities. Though they may work as consultants, they do not stay for long in government positions to avoid the loss of academic prestige (Swedberg 1990; Klamer and Colander 1990).

In Brazil the emergence of the economists as a ruling elite is the result of the actions of a variety of institutions and groups. It was carried out over several decades in government agencies, international commissions and university circles. Thus, this analysis distinguishes domestic factors as well as international trends in order to explain the rise of the economists and the shift of their orientation from state to market. It takes into account two interconnected historical processes: (a) the expansion of government agencies in charge of economic regulation and development from the 1930s until the 1970s, along with the changing patterns of macroeconomic policymaking; and (b) the modernization of university programs and the internationalization of economics. We will be looking therefore at transformations in the social environment where economists are formed and where different groups compete to impose their theoretical and ideological viewpoints.

This study also examines the ways in which the Brazilian presidential system presented opportunities and risks for technocratic policymaking. Characterized by a strong presidency and weak parties, the political system has permitted the emergence of insulated macroeconomic agencies where economists have made decisions with great autonomy from the rest of the political system, particularly the legislature. This analysis highlights authoritarian aspects of macroeconomic decision-making even in democratic times.

This chapter is organized in three parts. The first treats the period from the 1930s to 1964 and discusses several processes that contributed to the rise of economists as a new group of policymakers: (a) the creation and expansion of new agencies in charge of development and macroeconomic policies in the context of building the national devolopmentalist state in Brazil; (b) the activities of research institutes and international economic agencies in fostering economic expertise; and (c) disputes among economists, including disagreements over academic curricula as well as theoretical and ideological controversies. The second part considers the consolidation of these processes during the military regime (1964–84) and lays particular emphasis on the modernization of university courses and the internationalization of economics in the context of technocratic legitimation of authoritarian rule. The third part examines patterns of macroeconomic policymaking in the post-military democratic period, comparing the Cardoso (1995–2002) and Lula (2003–) administrations.

THE RISE OF ECONOMISTS AS A NEW RULING ELITE (1930–64)

The social field of the economists and their identity as a segment of the ruling elite developed not only inside the university system, but also – and above all – in government agencies and institutes of applied research.[1] It developed through the ideological struggles that characterized the political environment in Brazil from the 1930s to the 1960s. The consolidation of the university curriculum was a long and difficult process, and it was only completed in the 1970s with the establishment of graduate programs.

Building a Space for Economists within Government Agencies

The emergence of economists as an important segment of the ruling elite in Brazil is connected to the political centralization and increasing state control over the economy that occurred under the first administration of Getúlio Vargas (1930–45). These changes were in part generated by internal economic and political crises that followed the 1929 crash and the decline of international coffee prices. But they were also influenced by the pre-World War II ideological climate that discredited liberal and democratic institutions. There is a large body of literature on this subject. Two ramifications are particularly important to us: first, the transformation of technical competence into a political tool and second, the displacement of decision-making from the political arena to new agencies for economic regulation and planning. These had become the loci of disputes among entrepreneurial groups and also vehicles for the formation of nationalist and developmentalist ideologies (Lafer 1970; Leff 1968; Mantega 1985; Martins 1976; Sola 1982; Souza 1976; Wirth 1970). Economic knowledge in both its theoretical and instrumental dimensions was not a matter of consensus, but rather an object of dispute among different groups of 'technicians', as the economists were known at that moment.[2]

The major turning points of twentieth century Brazilian politics may be briefly sketched: the Revolution of 1930 weakened the agrarian oligarchies that had dominated the country during the First Republic (1889–1930) and significantly advanced political and adminstrative centralization under Getúlio Vargas's first government (1930–45). In 1937 Vargas established a dictatorial state – the 'Estado Novo' – that lasted until he was forced out at the end of World War II as a democratic period began. Under Brazil's 'populist democracy' Vargas returned to power in 1951 when he was elected to office and carried out nationalist economic measures. Under enormous opposition pressure, he committed suicide in August 1954. This democratic period ended with a military coup d'état in 1964. After 20 years of military rule, a civilian government was reestablished in 1985. In 1988 a democratic constitution was approved and since 1989 all presidents of the republic have been elected by direct popular vote.

The rise of the economists is related to the reinforcement of the state economic role and the expansion of the government apparatus in Brazil that began during Vargas's first, authoritarian administration (1930–45). From the 1930s, many important agencies were created or expanded, including technical councils or committees to organize federal finances and regulate external trade,[3] such as: DASP (Administrative Department of the Public Service), the so-called 'superministry' that controlled the government budget during the 'Estado Novo' (1937–45); SUMOC (Superintendency of Money and Credit), established in 1945 with the functions of a central bank, which Brazil still did not have. These processes continued during the next two decades. Some highlights were the creation of BNDE (National Economic Development Bank) in 1952 during the second Vargas administration and the creation of executive groups to regulate new industries during the Kubitschek administration (1955–60) (Sikkink 1991, pp. 174–6).

The rise of the economists is also connected to new trends in international relationships after World War II, especially the growing United States hegemony in Latin America. In the wartime and post-war periods, there were several commissions that brought together Brazilian and US technicians and politicians for discussion of national economic issues (Miceli 1990; Moura 1984). These international commissions had decisive repercussions for Brazilian economic debates. They stimulated the systematic collection of data on the Brazilian economy and studied the effects of the global situation on Brazil's domestic problems. Among these international commissions, the most important was CEPAL (the Economic Commission for Latin America), which played a prominent role in the formation of economic ideas in Brazil as it did in Latin America generally.

All these government agencies (controlled by bureaucrats with some knowledge of economic matters) and international commissions were centers of economic decision-making, and they also functioned as practical schools of economics for engineers, lawyers and other high-level employees involved in economic regulation, planning and development.

The following discussion of the National Development Bank shows how it promoted the development of a specific skill – conceiving of economic activities in aggregate terms – on the part of those later known as economists. Furthermore, it reveals the legitimization of the technicians as a new segment of the ruling elite based on their technical competence.

> Since its establishment, and most clearly during the Kubitschek administration, almost all requests for the financing of industrial investment in both the public and the private sectors were evaluated by the BNDE . . . The extent [of its financial resources] and its autonomy from Congress . . . thus made the control of the BNDE an important part of the elite power game. As a category, the technicians had the best location in this dispute. Briefly, this was because they had access to the technical information brought by 'international cooperation'.

> This was needed for the effective exercise of one of the functions of the bank: the analysis of investment projects, particularly those to be presented to international financing agencies. In a country like Brazil, this apparently banal fact takes on a considerable degree of importance, since the number of people able to satisfy such demands is extremely small. Thus, those who are able to do so acquire immediate authority. (Martins 1976, p. 398)[4]

For its part, SUMOC made decisions about exchange rates, which had a great influence on Brazilian industrialization in the 1950s. But it also had an important role in training future economists. In the words of its founder, Otávio Bulhões, this agency was a preparatory step for the establishment of the future *Banco Central.*

> SUMOC was preparing the basic conditions for its transformation into a central bank, but above all it needed to train personnel. Basically it served this purpose. It had this great virtue: it brought employees who had specialized in credit problems from the *Banco do Brazil.* (Bulhões 1990, p. 93)[5]

In addition to the agencies already discussed, there were still other organizations established from the 1930s to the 1950s that were important both as places where economists acted and where they were trained. These agencies were: the mixed BNDE-CEPAL group,[6] the Economic Advisory Board of Vargas,[7] the *Plano de Metas* (Target Plan) and the executive groups in the Kubitschek administration.[8]

Some of the professionals in these agencies gradually came to be known as 'economists'. They were not a homogeneous group. There were profound divergences among them on the direction of economic policies and even on the economic role of the state. In an analysis of Brazilian economic thought in the period 1945–64, Bielschowsky (1988) characterizes 'developmentalism' as 'the project for overcoming underdevelopment by way of industrialization through planning and strong state support'. The most important authors of the period were engaged in debates about this developmentalism and may be grouped into no less than five currents of thought. The liberals under the leadership of Gudin and Bulhões were strongly opposed to the developmentalists. For their part, the developmentalists came in three variants: that of the entrepreneurial sector, represented by Roberto Simonsen; that of the non-nationalist public sector, represented by Roberto Campos; and that of the nationalist public sector, headed by Celso Furtado. Finally there was the socialist current. We may even consider the economic ideas of Ignácio Rangel, often classified as socialist, as constituting a sixth current.

Development, nationalism, protectionism, state intervention and planning were all recurrent themes of the political and ideological debates of that period. Theoretical questions mixed with political disputes. Stuggles between the 'entreguistas' of the right and the nationalism of the left were intertwined with theoretical divergences between monetarists and structuralists.[9]

INTELLECTUAL CONTEXT: GROUP STRUGGLES

The Controversy over Economic Planning

The social environment of the economist-technicians was characterized from its very earliest days by disputes. There were the disputes of technicians with members of congress and representatives of industrial associations (Martins 1976; Sola 1982); disputes between different segments of the economic bureaucracy, such as those among groups in the *Banco do Brasil* and in the Finance Ministry (Bulhões 1990; Maxfield 1997); and there were the internal struggles within different currents of thought.[10]

At the beginning of the 1940s, this social field began to take shape with the polemic between Eugênio Gudin and Roberto Simonsen, later revived as 'the controversy over economic planning'. The debate had great repercussions in the media and in entrepreneurial circles. Simonsen was an entrepreneurial leader and member-chief of the CNPIC (National Council for Industrial and Commercial Policy); Gudin was an engineer and self-taught economist, who took part in the Committee for Economic Planning, even though he was a defender of economic liberalism. While Simonsen proposed increased state intervention, planning and protectionist measures for Brazilian industry, Gudin rejected Simonsens's ideas and proposed monetary and fiscal reforms that would limit state intervention to correcting market tendencies.[11]

It is important to stress here the symbolic effect of the debate. The 1940s saw the recognition of the economist as a legitimate participant in politics.[12] This helped Gudin, who held a distinguished position in academic circles as a full professor in the country's most important school of economics, and who was also president of the center for economic studies (IBRE) of the *Fundação Getúlio Vargas* (FGV). During the next decade Gudin and his colleagues were to face attacks from members of CEPAL. In Celso Furtado's (1985) view, this permitted Gudin to aim at 'monopolizing the scientific aspect' of economic analysis in Brazil in the 1950s.

To understand the disputes between CEPAL and FGV, and their effects on the establishment of this social field, it is first necessary to take a look at the academic circles within which the schools and research centers in economics were born.

Dilemmas and Difficulties in Setting up University Courses

The first programs in economics were set up in Brazil in the 1940s. Previously, the teaching of economics had been incorporated into law and engineering, and also formed part of a professionalized business education.

The political transformations which occurred with the Revolution of October 1930 and the arrival of Getúlio Vargas in power had important repercussions in intellectual circles. These had been simmering since the previous decade, and there was active debate about the design of university programs for training a new ruling elite to be entrusted with modernizing the country.

The first project for establishing an advanced school in economics grew out of the reforms of Francisco Campos, the first Minister of Education in the Vargas administration in 1931. His intention was to create a School of Political and Economic Sciences. The school was never established under the intended name and it was the object of considerable dispute among various interest groups. On the one hand there were those who had completed a secondary education in commerce and accounting. For them, the purpose of the new school would be to obtain university status for their studies and to gain social recognition for their profession. For others, the school was to be a nucleus for training the ruling classes in order to modernize the Brazilian government. Eugênio Gudin and Otávio Bulhões were the principal representatives of this latter orientation, which triumphed in establishing the National School of Economic Sciences at the University of Brazil in Rio de Janeiro in 1945.

The conditions which brought about the victory of this project are worth noting. The accountants and administrators, organized into the unions of professional economists in Rio de Janeiro and São Paulo, had brought great pressure to bear on the Minister of Education, Gustavo Capanema. They mobilized their members in large numbers and drew up documents in support of their claims. Even so, the social trump cards of Gudin and Bulhões carried great weight.[13] They occupied high-level positions in the Vargas administration and they had connections with the intellectuals involved in the new university projects. Gudin, for example, was in 1937 a member of the Brazilian Society for Economic Policy, entrusted with planning an advanced school of economics in Rio de Janeiro that in 1938 became the first private faculty of economics in Brazil, under the name of *Faculdade de Ciências Econômicas e Administrativas*. He passed the competitive examinations for a post in this faculty and became the first occupant of its Chair of Money and Credit.[14]

Gudin and Bulhões submitted their plan for a program in economics to Harvard University in August 1944, soon after the Bretton Woods Conference, in which they had represented Brazil. Although I have been unable to discover whether Harvard faculty were actually involved in the program, the mere submission of the plan to Harvard added legitimacy, a valuable resource in dealing with Brazilian adversaries.[15]

What was at stake in the question of separating (even physically) a school of economics from a school of accounting was the broader matter of affirming the distinction between two specific social segments and their different interests. First, there were the lower classes, coming up through the business schools, who wanted to raise themselves socially by way of the university degree that might be obtained through the new program. And second, there was an upper-class segment whose long professional practice in high-level posts in government or in large private companies showed it the need to train a new elite qualified in economic matters.

It was the latter group which came to define the direction of the new school. For them, it was a matter of creating a new steering body with modernizing tendencies inspired by rational principles and scientific rigor. Hence there was a rejection of 'mixed' curricula, made up of a variety of legal and administrative disciplines and more accessible to those social groups with less economic and intellectual capital. The curriculum was to lay great emphasis on mathematics, statistical methods and economic theory. These subjects demanded superior academic preparation and were, therefore, less accessible to those from lower social strata who had been educated at what Brazilians call 'escolas técnicas', which at that time did not carry the prestige of a university degree.

Once the *Faculdade Nacional de Ciências Econômicas* (FNCE) had been founded at the University of Brazil in 1946, its teaching staff was recruited from among the ranks of the self-taught, some of whom were already teaching in the somewhat older *Faculdade de Ciências Econômicas e Administrativas*. They were also already involved in the practical problems of managing the economy in various government agencies set up under Vargas.[16]

It was not an easy task to train new elite professionals in economics. Surveys carried out in the archives of the Faculty of Economics and Adminstration show that in its first few years students were recruited mostly among accountants (60 percent and 89 percent of the classes of 1939 and 1940 respectively). The social basis of recruitment had not changed significantly in 1946, even after Gudin's reform brought in the new four-year curriculum but retained the evening schedule. The lack of a tradition for a university program in economics and its low prestige compared to engineering, law and medicine, meant that it held little attraction for young people from higher social backgrounds. Such desired students amounted to only 11 per cent of all those who entered the Faculty of Economics in 1946. In addition, the dropout rate was very high. In the early years it reached about two-thirds of registrations, and from 1946 to 1950 about half (data from the archives of the *Faculdade de Ciências Econômicas e Administrativas of the Federal University of Rio de Janeiro*).

In São Paulo, the creation of a higher school of economics was also no great success at first. The School of Economics (part of the University of São Paulo) was founded in 1946 in parallel with the one in Rio. There was no intention of just going on with the traditional teaching of economics and finance. As shown by Canabrava (1981), the São Paulo plan sought a 'new cultural experience', an intellectual break with the past. But in its early years, this school suffered from many problems. Rather than following the example of the Department of Philosophy, which recruited its first high-quality staff mainly in France, the School of Economics opted for recruitment from within the university, particularly from the School of Law. Pinho (1981, p. 39) shows that in 1946, 19 of the 37 of those teaching in the newly-opened school came from law. Furthermore, much of their experience had been in 'escolas técnicas' or other secondary schools in São Paulo, where the skills of the staff were not very high.

In its early years, the School of Economics at USP was characterized by its orientation to law. Until the 1960s, it suffered from a persistent shortage of students. Its drop-out rate was high, attendance was low, and even when night courses began in the 1950s enrollments were declining. This was because the very limited professional value of the program did not allow it to compete with more established fields. In fact, the School of Economics was largely sought after by young people from lower social backgrounds who lacked the financial resources for an education in law or engineering[17] and who had instead gone through the 'escolas técnicas' in accounting that did not grant university degrees.

In Rio de Janeiro, the initial problems surrounding the training of economists were alleviated by proximity to the seat of power. A quantitative assessment of research in economics at the time shows that most of the authors and most of the publications came from there. This occurred because a large proportion of the graduating students found positions with the new agencies of economic management, such as the Center for Economic Studies of the *Fundação Getúlio Vargas* (FGV), set up in 1946 and later transformed into the Brazilian Institute of Economics (IBRE).[18]

For several decades, IBRE/FGV was the single most important institution for producing economic knowledge. It was where the discipline of economics took on its practical dimension and where training in that discipline came to be a basic requisite for running the economic affairs of the country. It was noteworthy for developing national accounts, in which it was an innovator (even compared to developed countries) and which was a result of the implantation of Keynesian macroeconomic theories. It was also important in creating price indexes, which years later permitted monetary correction. This had significant political implications. It made it possible to carry on daily life under high inflation, and it was also a decisive element in establishing public and private income in the form of salaries and return on investments. According to statements made at the time, the members of IBRE were perfectly aware that they were creating 'a quantitative mark in the Brazilian economy', as someone put it in an interview. And at the same time they knew their activities to be highly politicized, above all the calculation of price indexes.

Among the professionals recruited by FGV were many recent graduates as well as trainee-grantholders from FNCE. They worked on National Income in the Center for Economic Analysis and later in the Centers for National Accounts, Fiscal Studies, and other agencies. They also worked on two journals sponsored by FGV, the *Revista Brasileira de Economia*, devoted to theoretical articles by Brazilian and foreign authors, and *Conjuntura Econômica*, which published FGV's statistical indicators, following the model set up in Germany by Ernest Wageman, who founded the Institute for the Economic Situation in Berlin in the 1920s (Furtado 1985, p. 47).

To strengthen the training of its personnel, IBRE/FGV (sometimes in partnership with FNCE) from its very beginning kept in close contact with foreign universities. It hosted visiting professors, such as Haberler, Jacob Viner, and many others. It also was systematically sending its own staff for training in international economic agencies and in universities in the US and Europe. Thus the institution was distinctly cosmopolitan by nature and was a center for the diffusion of information from abroad.[19]

Over several years, the IBRE/FGV group developed an extensive network of relationships within government agencies, academic institutions and business.[20] The data show that this collection of social actors was able to carry out broad and well-organized institution building.[21] Their success may owe something to their social characteristics. Its members mainly came from upper class Rio families. The IBRE members had backgrounds in business, as high-level government personnel, as military officers and as professionals among whom engineering predominated. Most completed their studies of economics at American universities or in agencies such as the International Monetary Fund or the World Bank, where monetary problems were emphasized and mathematical modelling was established as a professional skill par excellence.[22]

The disputes between this group and their opponents were characterized at various times as monetarists vs structuralists or as right-wing 'appeasers' vs nationalists. These disputes were fundamental in the constitution and consolidation of the economists' social field.

The Dispute between Monetarists and Structuralists: FGV versus CEPAL

The debate between Gudin and Simonsen, which occurred when the field was still at an embryonic stage, reveals that their intellectual and political disputes can be traced to their different business connections. Simonsen, an engineer from the industrial upper class and business leader in São Paulo, represented the interests of industrial companies that were still consoliding and thus dependent on state protection. Gudin represented the interests of foreign capital. But to propose the same type of analysis for understanding the debate during the 1950s between Brazil's CEPAL group and IBRE/FGV would be simplistic reductionism. In this case it was not just a question of external connections. There were also internal conditions at stake in the constitution of the economists' field in Brazil, and in the positions occupied by the disputing groups.

CEPAL is well known for its great influence on developmentalist thinking in Latin America. In Brazil, CEPAL was more important in legitimizing and providing strong analytical arguments for policies already in place than as a source of new policy ideas (Sikkink 1991, p. 59). Nonetheless, its impact has been well recognized in economic history and in economic thought. Writing produced at CEPAL or written by authors connected with it became foundational works. Prebisch's manifesto 'inaugurated Latin American structuralism' (Bacha 1985, p. 13) and Celso Furtado's book *A Formação Econômica do Brazil* 'was a landmark in Brazilian economic thought' (Mantega 1985, p. 11).

In Brazil, when CEPAL began to publish its studies it came up against the existing FGV group that was identified with neoclassicism. This group had consolidated its position in the schools of economics and in IBRE over several years. It had considerable visibility not only through its own journals, but also in the non-specialized press. For example, Gudin had for many years been writing for such important Rio newspapers as *Correio da Manhã* and *Globo*. Together with Bulhões, he also published in other journals such as the *Digesto Econômico* of the São Paulo Commercial Association and in the monthly newsletter of the National Commercial Confederation. The number of lecture invitations the two received from schools of economics throughout the country is a further indication of their prestige in the nascent field of economics.

The members of CEPAL represented a new institution, whose intention was to affirm its Latin American identity and to assume a position of autonomy with respect to the US government. Most were recent graduates from schools of law, economics or social sciences in a variety of Latin American countries. Some had studied in American universities. They had gathered in Santiago, Chile, under the leadership of the Argentine Raúl Prebisch, the 'Grand Heresiarch', founder of his country's Central Bank and expelled from Perón's Argentina. Thus the possibilities of theoretical innovation and of the assumption of heterodox positions were very high. Prebisch himself was politically persecuted. Many of the others, such as Celso Furtado, were just beginning their careers.[23]

CEPAL orientations were introduced into Brazil by Celso Furtado, by way of his own articles and those of Prebisch, published in the *Revista Brasileira de Economia* (FGV) at the beginning of the 1950s. This reopened the debate of the previous decade. The questions of economic planning and protectionism, together with new interpretations of problems such as backwardness, poverty and inflation were taken up once more, this time with greater theoretical consistency.

Even though they had agreed to the publication of the articles by Prebisch and Furtado in their journal, the members of the FGV – above all Gudin and Bulhões – reacted to the challenge. They arranged lectures by foreign economists (including Viner and Haberler) in reaffirmation of neoclassical precepts. They also published their own critiques in the *Revista Brasileira de Economia*. Their criticisms also appeared in the newspapers and were of particular interest to government officials and businessmen. Furtado and Prebisch, who had no access to university circles or even to other areas of the media, sought support for their ideas from businessmen, from the National Confederation of Industry and from some nationalist technicians, such as Rômulo Almeida, Cleanto Paiva Leite and Ignacio Rangel, members of Vargas's Advisory Board. It was in the course of this debate that the CEPAL group gave the name of 'monetarists' to the members of the FGV, because of the role of monetary factors in their analysis of inflation. They called themselves 'structuralists', claiming that by contrast their own approach was to seek out structural determinants. When Gudin criticized the CEPAL group (whom he called 'leftists'), the primary target was the concept of structuralism, claimed as the Latin American economic science. Confirmation of the structuralist thesis would end the dominance of Gudin and his group over Brazilian economists, since they were known as the introducers and disseminators of neoclassical theory.

The theoretical differences among economists were intensified by the political disputes of Vargas's second administration (1951–54). 'Aware that the orthodox counter-offensive was gaining ground', as Celso Furtado recalled, he decided to go on the offensive. In his 1953 book, *A Economia Brasileira* (The Brazilian Economy), he systematically set out the ideas of CEPAL. Soon after his return to Brazil, he decided to join with others who shared his nationalist thinking and opposed the 'entreguista' right. Furtado also had close intellectual and political connections with the former Economic Advisory Board of Vargas[24] and with ISEB.[25] Together with several members of these bodies he founded the *Club de Economistas* (Economists' Club) in 1955. The Club included Américo Barbosa de Oliveira, Furtado's former colleague in editing *Conjuntura Econômica.* Barbosa de Oliveira had been editor-in-chief of *Conjuntura Econômica* before falling out with the FGV personnel. There were also numerous employees of government agencies such as Eduardo Sobral, Sidney Latini, Domar Campos, Ewaldo Correa Lima and Almeida Magalhães. The primary aim of this group was to put out *Econômica Brasileira,* soon considered the journal 'of heterodox, progressive, or leftist thought'. Furtado saw this journal as fundamental for diffusing the ideas of CEPAL: 'since we had practically no contact with the university world, the debates around this new line of thought were limited to places with little power to spread them'. The publications of the Fundação Getúlio Vargas, by contrast, were dominated by orthodox positions (Furtado 1985, pp. 172–3).

The Economists' Club differed socially and professionally from the monetarists in that its members' connections to each other were less strongly institutionalized. Celso Furtado, one of the few associated with CEPAL, tried to assert influence through the mixed BNDE-CEPAL Group, through SUDENE (Superintendency of Northeastern Economic Development) at the end of the 1950s, and through the Planning Secretariat of the Goulart administration, where he worked briefly before the military coup. But it was not possible to sustain the connections between the members of the Economic Advisory Board within other agencies. The Economists' Club, moreover, was in a precarious situation right from the beginning, due to difficulties in obtaining money to support *Econômica Brasileira.* Those involved held no stable positions in teaching or research institutions. Their economic writings therefore were essentially essays emphasizing such broad economic issues as development, poverty and industrialization, all seen as problems from a nationalist viewpoint.

It is striking that the principal members of this group came from elite families in Brazil's North-East. They migrated to Rio de Janeiro in the 1930s and 1940s in search of opportunities in government. Some, like Ignácio Rangel and Rômulo Almeida, were driven by political persecution (Almeida 1988). Most had degrees in law or other subjects but they had no specific training in economics, apart from Furtado.

Rangel's preface to his most important work, *A Inflação Brasileira (Brazilian Inflation)*, written in 1963, reveals these features:

Table 3.1 Social field of economists in the 1950s and 1960s: main characteristics of institutions and members

Left	Right
CEPAL, ISEB	SUMOC, BNDE
Vargas's Economic Advisory Board	IBRE/FGV, FNCE
Structuralism	Monetarism
Nationalists and developmentalists	Free market ideologues
Works done mainly on economic history and essay format	Mathematical modeling
Celso Furtado, Ignácio Rangel, R. Almeida	E. Gudin, O. Bulhões, R. Campos
Social background: families from Northeast	Social background: elite Rio families
Educational background in law	Educational background in engineering

> I am not a monetary specialist . . . . My work in economics has from the beginning been motivated by legal and political concerns. I have worked in industry and in the BNDE on project analysis, I have accustomed myself to raising, indiscreetly, the so-called 'monetarist veil' which hides more than it reveals. My infancy and childhood were peopled, through my father, a provincial magistrate, the son and grandson of other provincial magistrates, with legends of our national history. . . . According to family tradition, I was destined to take up the law. . . . It was the cult of the law that inspired me . . . . My professor of Introduction to the Science of Law showed me the connection between law and economics. This discovery of the economic foundation of our laws came to be my central aim. (pp. xi–xiii)

In sum, the disputes between monetarists and structuralists must be seen in the broader context of intellectual and political debate in Brazil in the 1950s and early 1960s. They concerned such themes as nationalism, industrial development and agrarian reform. They also defined political and ideological positions, with the right entrenched in organs such as BNDE, SUMOC and FGV, and the left in Vargas's Economic Advisory Board, in CEPAL and in ISEB. Table 3.1 summarizes the main institutions and members on each side of the ideological spectrum at that time.

The intensification of these disputes was to imply vigorous political mobilization by those involved. The FGV group would support initiatives such as the IPES (Institute for Economic and Social Research, created in early 1960s). IPES became an important center of political, ideological and financial coordination for the movement which led to the 1964 coup (Dreifus 1981). Among outstanding leaders and important supporters of IPES were members of FGV, such as Bulhões, Dênio Nogueira, Mário

Henrique Simonsen, Garrido Torres, Alexandre Kafka, Julian Chancel, as well as Roberto Campos, Lucas Lopes and Glycon de Paiva. Under the military, members of this group rose to leading positions in the Finance and Planning Ministries (such as Bulhões and Campos, under General Castelo Branco's administration and Simonsen under General Geisel's), as well as to the presidency of the *Banco Central* (Nogueira, under Castelo Branco). The intensifying struggle after the coup would also lead to the loss of political rights for Celso Furtado, who was in exile for several years, and for many other leftist or nationalist economists, such as Rômulo Almeida, Jesus Soares Pereira and Ignácio Rangel.

UNIVERSITY MODERNIZATION AND THE INTERNATIONALIZATION OF ECONOMICS

The participation of economists in government increased enormously with the installation of the military regime in 1964. Increased political centralization, the enlargement of the Executive in general and of its control over the economy in particular, and the need to provide legitimacy for an authoritarian government on the grounds of economic efficiency led to an increase in government positions dominated by economists. Between 1964 and 2004, 10 of 17 finance ministers were economists. In the Planning Ministry, starting from 1963 when it was created and headed by Celso Furtado, 10 of 14 ministers were economists. Economists had a near-monopoly on the positions of president and director of the Central Bank and of the National Economic and Social Development Bank (BNDES), as well as of the directorships of organs such as IBGE (Brazilian Institute for Statistics) and IPEA (Institute for Applied Economic Research, associated with the Ministry of Planning). In this part of the chapter, I will link this participation of economists in government to the development of their academic training as well as to the internationalization of Brazilian economics.

Until the 1950s and 1960s the preparation of professionals for economic management occurred mostly outside of the university system: in international agencies such as CEPAL, in applied economic research centers such as the IBRE, and within government agencies, the so-called 'practical schools' of economic knowledge. But since the 1970s, university courses, especially graduate programs, have become the principal mechanisms for training economists. As economists have risen to high positions these university programs have become privileged paths into government policymaking. As a result of these changes, upper-class students have been entering schools of economics.

Along with the industrialization and modernization of Brazilian society and the expansion of the university system, several new academic disciplines have emerged since the 1960s including business, psychology and urban planning. It was economics, however, that was most privileged by the military government in expanding job opportunities and in funding academic research. According to data collected by the Federal Economic Council in the mid-1980s, 42 percent of Brazilian economists worked in government. In the North, North-East and Federal District, respectively, 67 percent, 68 percent and 86 percent of economists were in government agencies. Only in the southern states were the majority of economists working in private industrial and financial enterprises. In São Paulo, 21 percent were in government, 36 percent in business.

With the university reform of 1968, the system of higher education in Brazil experienced substantial modification. The French model of public universities organized around chairs held for life was replaced by North-American style teaching departments. There was also an enormous expansion in the overall number of schools of higher education (especially private establishments) and a corresponding increase in enrollments.[26] Another significant element of the Reform of 1968 was the establishment of graduate programs in all areas. These programs received significant support from federal agencies in the form of funding and institutional support for improving the academic qualifications of faculty. The creation of graduate programs was a considerable step forward in advancing scientific skills as a whole in Brazil. Between 1969 and 1982, the number of graduate programs in Brazil in all fields increased from 125 to 1324, and by the 1990s, there were about 290 graduate programs in the humanities alone and 13 in economics, according to official statistics from MEC (*Ministério da Educação*).

Among the new graduate programs, economics was especially privileged in government funding. Besides the regular funds allocated to all graduate programs in the country, economics was provided with additional financial resources from agencies such as BNDES and IPEA.[27] Economics also received privileged benefits in the international exchange programs sponsored by such US agencies as USAID (US Agency for International Development) and the Ford Foundation in the 1960 and 1970s.

Since 1966 several graduate programs in economics have been created around the country.[28] Among them, five stand out as the most selective. Three were in Rio de Janeiro: the graduate school in economics (EPGE) of the Getúlio Vargas Foundation, founded in 1964; the Department of Economics of the Catholic University (PUC); and the graduate program in economics of the Federal University of Rio de Janeiro (UFRJ). This last replaced the first National School of Economics discussed earlier. In São

Paulo there were the Institute of Economic Reserach (FEA/USP), founded in 1964 by the Faculty of Economics and Business of the University of São Paulo, widely considered the most important university in the country, and the Institute of Economics of the State University of Campinas (IE/UNICAMP).

The establishment of graduate courses, together with the other changes that occurred in the university teaching of economics (the increase in both students and courses at all levels, the growth of academic production, the development of a system to support research, the launching of new journals), should be seen within the broader context of the modernization of this discipline in Brazil. These transformations are part of the internationalization or North Americanization of economics that occurred from the 1960s on through two basic mechanisms.

The first and most important step toward the integration of Brazilian economics into the mainstream of international economics involved young Brazilian students systematically pursuing doctoral studies abroad, particularly in the United States. Table 3.2b indicates that, until the early 1990s, 60 percent of teachers of graduate courses in economics were credentialled outside Brazil. Of these, 46 percent (158 professors) went to US universities, 7.6 percent studied in France, and 5.5 percent in England. Seven US universities were particularly important in the training of economists. Eighteen Brazilian professors completed their PhDs at Vanderbilt. Sixteen got doctorates from Chicago (13 from EPGE and 3 from USP); 12 got doctorates from Berkeley, 11 from Harvard, 8 from Yale and 7 each from Michigan and Illinois. Interuniversity agreements played a major role in establishing these connections, as discussed below.

A second mechanism was the arrival of American professors to teach in Brazil's new graduate programs. These arrangements were subsidized by USAID (US Agency for International Development) and by the Ford Foundation, which signed cooperative agreements with several schools in Brazil. The faculty of economics of the University of São Paulo (FEA/USP) was one of the beneficiaries. Its graduate program was established in 1964 through agreements with USAID and with the Council for Technical Cooperation of the Alliance for Progress. By contractual agreement, USAID assumed responsibility for the expenses of North American professors and Vanderbilt University undertook 'the duty to advise in the creation of the program, the development of its curriculum, the planning for research and student grading' (FEA/USP 1981, pp. 229–30). The Ford Foundation provided grants for several faculty members to pursue graduate studies in Brazil and abroad, funds for the purchase of equipment and books, and financial suport for visiting professors to teach graduate courses in the new programs. Indeed, the Ford

Table 3.2a *Faculty members affiliated with graduate programs in economics in Brazil: national origins of Master's and/or PhD Degree, 1991; principal programs*

Graduate Program[a]	Total	US		France		UK		Brazil		Others	
	N	N	%	N	%	N	%	N	%	N	%
Principal programs											
EPGE/FGV	30	24	80.0	–	–	–	–	4	13.3	2	6.7
PUC/RJ	17	14	82.3	–	–	2	11.9	1	5.8	–	–
IPE/USP	55	21	38.2	3	5.4	–	–	31	56.0	–	–
IEI/UFRJ	20	5	25.0	1	5.0	4	20.0	10	50.0	–	–
IE/UNICAMP	28	2	7.2	–	–	–	–	26	92.8	–	–
Subtotal: all principal programs	150	66	44.0	4	2.7	6	4.0	72	48.0	2	1.3

Notes:

[a] EPGE/FGV – Getúlio Vargas Foundation at Rio de Janeiro; PUC/RJ – Catholic University at Rio de Janeiro; IPE/USP – University of São Paulo; IEI/UFRJ – Federal University of Rio de Janeiro; IE/UNICAMP – State University of Campinas; PIMES – Federal University Pernambuco; IEPE – Federal University of Rio Grande do Sul; UNB – Federal University of Brasília; FGV/SP – Getúlio Vargas Fondation at São Paulo; CEDEPLAR – Federal University of Minas Gerais; NAEA – Federal University of Pará; UFBA Federal University of Bahia; CAEN – Federal University of Ceará.

Source: Catalogues from graduate programs associated with ANPEC. Does not include the newly created programs at Fluminense Federal University and PUC-São Paulo.

Table 3.2b *Faculty members affiliated with graduate programs in economics in Brazil: National origins of master's and/or PhD degree, 1991; other programs*

Graduate Program[a]	Total	US		France		UK		Brazil		Others	
	N	N	%	N	%	N	%	N	%	N	%
Other programs	194	92		22		13		65			
PIMES	27	13	48.0	1	4.0	5	18.0	8	30.0	–	–
IEPE	27	17	63.0	2	7.4	1	3.6	7	2.6	–	–
UNB	32	14	43.8	8	25.0	2	6.2	6	18.8	2	6.2
FGV/SP	14	8	57.1	–	–	1	7.1	5	21.4	–	–
CEDEPLAR	35	15	43.0	3	8.5	3	8.5	14	40.0	–	–
NAEA	24	5	21.0	5	21.0	1	4.0	13	54.0	–	–
UFBA	17	7	41.1	3	17.8	–	–	7	41.1	–	–
CAEN	18	13	72.2	–	–	–	–	5	27.8	–	–
Total: all other programs	194	92	47.4	22	11.3	13	6.7	65	33.5	2	1.0
Totals	344	158	45.9	26	7.6	19	5.5	137	39.8	4	1.2

Notes:
[a] EPGE/FGV – Getúlio Vargas Foundation at Rio de Janeiro; PUC/RJ – Catholic University at Rio de Janeiro; IPE/USP – University of São Paulo; IEI/UFRJ – Federal University of Rio de Janeiro; IE/UNICAMP – State University of Campinas; PIMES – Federal University Pernambuco; IEPE – Federal University of Rio Grande do Sul; UNB – Federal University of Brasília; FGV/SP – Getúlio Vargas Fondation at São Paulo; CEDEPLAR – Federal University of Minas Gerais; NAEA – Federal University of Pará; UFBA Federal University of Bahia; CAEN – Federal University of Ceará.

Source: Catalogues from graduate programs associated with ANPEC. Does not include the newly created programs at Fluminense Federal University and PUC-São Paulo.

Foundation played a quite decisive role in the internationalization of Brazilian economics.

As far as government agencies are concerned, the University of California at Berkeley sent some faculty to advise economists at IPEA, a think tank associated with the Ministry of Planning. Outstanding in the Berkeley group was Albert Fishlow, noted especially for his extensive work on Brazilian income distribution, a topic of great controversy in the 1970s.

According to a Brazilian professor involved in these arrangements, the US economists were more concerned with transplanting their model of organizing teaching and research than with the content of advanced economic theory. In his view, Brazilian academia was already well endowed with professional economists who had extensive theoretical backgrounds, so that 'what was really missing at the time was the adequate diffusion of attitudes and positions that might characterize a solid scientific community. And it was here that the North American economists really contributed' (Ekerman 1989, p. 127).

Professional Impact of Internationalization: The Polarization of Economics in Brazil

For its adherents the internationalization of economics was a salutary importation of superior theoretical and methodological tools from developed countries, particularly the United States (see Coats 1996). But in some Brazilian institutions it was seen as just another form of cultural colonialism carried out by North American imperialists. There was strong resistance, in particular from groups on the political left, so that not all graduate programs in economics adhered with the same intensity to the international academic patterns. As shown in Table 3.2a UNICAMP has the lowest percentage of faculty with doctorates from abroad. Only two have US PhDs, as compared with 26 doctorates from UNICAMP itself or from the University of São Paulo. The largest numbers of faculty with US doctorates are to be found at PUC-RJ, with more than 82 percent and EPGE/FGV, with 80 percent.

These figures indicate a quite complex process of polarization on the part of the local schools of economics around theoretically divergent positions. This polarization, as discussed above, dates back to the antagonisms of the 1950s and 1960s, when economics as a separate discipline was taking shape and economic development was the key issue in the conflicts in intellectual and political circles. Despite the stronger academic credentials of more recent times, the growth of academic production (in the form of theses, articles and books), and the creation of several research institutions, the current polarization continues that old opposition between structuralists and monetarists.

One way to classify the most representative local graduate programs in economics is as follows. At one pole there is the EPGE/FGV in Rio de Janeiro, which even today is considered the home of the most orthodox strand of neoclassical thought in Brazil and whose faculty attribute a great deal of importance to mathematical modeling and the tools of econometrics. It is not just by chance that 72 percent of its members majored in engineering and mathematics. In the same camp is PUC-RJ, made up of ex-students from EPGE and dissident professors from FGV and other universities. Most of their professors have degrees in engineering and mathematics and their programs also emphasize mathematical modeling. These two schools constitute the most internationalized pole and the one most fully integrated with the professional mainstream. Four-fifths of their faculty hold PhDs from US universities.

At the opposite pole stand the graduate programs in economics offered by UNICAMP and UFRJ, most of whose faculty members are former disciples of CEPAL and are concerned with issues that can be broadly defined as structural. This group includes a considerable number of professors trained in law and the social sciences. Their work, especially at UNICAMP, is carried on with little mathematical formalization and emphasizes a historical and sociopolitical approach to economic processes.

Between these two poles lies the graduate program at the University of São Paulo, the largest in terms of faculty numbers. Although most professors (31) hold doctorates from USP itself, a significant number studied in the United States (21). Only EPGE has more US doctorates (24).

Tables 3.3 and 3.4 reveal other aspects of the varying character of the internationalization of graduate programs and resistance to it. While 90 percent and 78 percent respectively of the readings in EPGE/FGV and PUC-RJ graduate courses are in English, English accounts for less than 10 percent at UNICAMP. Almost 70 percent of the readings at UNICAMP are written in Portuguese or are in Portuguese translation. Some 22 percent are in Spanish (generally by CEPAL authors) or French.

As for fields within economics, EPGE and PUC have high percentages of readings in either theory or quantitative methods: 98 percent and 95 percent respectively. By contrast, UNICAMP has only 55 percent of such references and 45 percent in the areas of economic history, history of economic thought, and political economy. Since each program was asked to send to ANPEC (National Association of Graduate Programs in Economics) only information on those courses most representative of the program's profile, these data are very indicative of the polarization.

Table 3.3 Language of readings from selected Brazilian graduate programs in economics, 1990–91

Selected graduate programs	Readings in Portuguese			Readings in English		Readings in Spanish and French	
	Written in Portug.	Transl. into Portug.	% Written/ transl.	N	%	N	%
EPGE/FGV	18	0	8	208	90	4	2
PUC/RJ	39	9	16	233	78	19	6
UNICAMP	280	53	69	45	9	108	22

Source: Franco (1992), using data from ANPEC catalogue.

Table 3.4 Theoretical and methodological approach of readings from selected Brazilian graduate programs in economics, 1990–91

Selected graduate programs	Theory and quantitative methods[a]		Economic history/ history of economic thought and political economy[b]	
	N	%	N	%
EPGE/FGV	226	98	5	2
PUC-RJ	286	95	14	5
UNICAMP	266	55	220	45

Notes:

[a] Includes macroeconomic and microeconomic theory (including game theory), monetary theory, international trade theory, industrial organization theory, agricultural economic theory, labor market economic theory (the two latter as applied microeconomic theory), economic development theory, mathematics, statistics, econometrics.

[b] Includes general economic history, history of economic thought, Brazilian economy, philosophy of science, methodology, sociology, political science, Marxist theory.

Source: Franco (1992), using information from ANPEC catalogue.

Table 3.5 shows the weight each graduate program gives to the various sections of the national examination for prospective students. 'Microeconomics' and 'macroeconomics' get about the same weight in all programs, although the small variations are interesting. But 'mathematics', 'statistics' and 'Brazilian economy' – essentially historically oriented – show a great deal more variation. Looking at the information as a whole, we see that at one extreme, EPGE attributes greater weight to economic

Table 3.5 National selection examination (organized by ANPEC) for admission of candidates to programs: weighting of exams, 1992 (percentages)

Programs	Micro-economics	Macro-economics	Math	Stats	Brazilian economy
Right					
EPGE	22.5	22.5	22.5	22.5	10.0
PUC-RJ	20.0	20.0	20.0	20.0	20.0
In-between					
IPE/USP	20.0	20.0	15.0	20.0	25.0
Left					
UFRJ	20.0	20.0	15.0	15.0	30.0
UNICAMP	17.5	17.5	12.5	12.5	40.0
Other centers (*)					
CAEN	25.0	25.0	15.0	15.0	20.0
CEDEPLAR	20.0	20.0	15.0	15.0	30.0
FGV-SP	20.0	20.0	15.0	15.0	30.0
IEPE	20.0	20.0	20.0	20.0	20.0
NAEA	20.0	20.0	10.0	10.0	40.0
PIMES	20.0	20.0	20.0	20.0	20.0
UFBA	20.0	20.0	15.0	15.0	30.0
UFF	20.0	20.0	20.0	20.0	20.0
UNB	20.0	20.0	20.0	20.0	20.0

Note: (*) These centers have no clear ideological identification.

Source: ANPEC (1992).

theory (both macro- and microeconomics) and quantitative methods, and less to the Brazilian economy; at the other extreme, UNICAMP gives the greatest weight to the Brazilian economy and assigns the least weight to mathematics and statistics among all graduate programs.[29]

Another important aspect of internationalization is the differentiation of the career strategies of economists at each pole. Economists at EPGE/FGV and PUC-RJ have more intense participation in international scientific networks. To a greater extent than other economists, they are members of scientific societies, attend international conferences, publish articles and books abroad, especially in the United States,[30] and spend time in international agencies such as the International Monetary Fund.

Tables 3.6 and 3.7 show that faculty from these two schools published the most in English-language journals. In contrast to an impressive 60 percent of publications from PUC-RJ that are in English, only 6 percent

Table 3.6 Publication by Brazilian professors from selected graduate programs

Graduate programs (N faculty)	Articles in Eng.		Books in Eng.		Articles in Portuguese		Books in Portuguese		Total	
	N	%	N	%	N	%	N	%	N	%
EPGE (20)	11	22	3	6	21	41	16	31	51	100
PUC-RJ (7)	9	45	3	15	4	20	20	20	20	100
USP (33)	9	10	4	4	43	48	34	38	90	100
Federal U. Rio (24)	3	6	2	4	34	73	8	17	47	100
UNICAMP (18)	1	3	1	3	15	38	22	56	39	100

Source: Catalogue from graduate programs in economics in Brazil published by ANPEC (1992). Percentages are approximate.

of the publications from UNICAMP professors are. When UNICAMP professors do publish abroad they generally are focused on specifically Latin American issues. But they published mostly in Brazilian journals and books: 38 per cent of their articles and 56 per cent of their books appeared in Brazil.[31]

In terms of the differentiation of professional strategies, the pole constituted by EPGE/FGV and PUC-RJ might be called 'privatizing', not only because of the theoretical value placed on the role of the market in the economic system (many of the professors affiliated with EPGE/FGV got their doctorates at the University of Chicago) but mainly because its faculty members have close relationships with the private sector, in particular with financial institutions, for which several work as consultants.

The less internationalized pole constituted by UNICAMP and UFRJ might be called the 'public' pole. Their studies stress the political aspect of the economy, the work of their members is carried out in public universities, and in general they offer consulting to government agencies and public sector enterprises. Finally, the intermediate position between these two poles represented by the faculty of economics of USP is displayed in a wide variety of professional careers and consulting practices in both private and public organizations.

Political Impact: Careers and Legitimation of Economists in Government

Besides the professional impact, we must note that the internationalization of economics, when regarded as a dimension of economic globalization,

Table 3.7 Publications in international journals by Brazilian professors from selected graduate programs in economics

	Graduate programs		
	EPGE/FGV	PUC-RJ	UNICAMP
English-language journals			
Journal of Development Economics	–	15	–
World Development	–	8	–
Economic History Review	–	1	–
Journal of Mathematical Economics	3	–	–
Journal of Econometrics	1	–	–
Econometrica	4	–	–
Journal of Economic Theory	6	–	–
Quartely Journal of Economics	4	2	–
The Bell Journal of Economics	–	1	–
The Economics Journal	–	1	–
All English-language journals	18	13	–
Spanish-language journals			
El Trimestre Económico	4	13(*)	6
Revista de la CEPAL	1	3	5
All Spanish-language journals	5	16	5
Total Publications	23	29	11
Number of professors	30	17	28
English articles per professor	0.6	0.7	0.0

Note: (*) A single professor from PUC-RJ, Edmar Bacha, published seven articles in *Trimestre Económico* during 1984–92. He also wrote two articles in *Trimestre Económico* when he was at FGV (1970–71) and another three when he was at UNB (Brasilia National University) (1974–77).

Source: Data collected in the most important international economics journal, from the 1970s on. The journals in the list are the ones where there are articles from Brazilian professors.

also has significant political effects. It opens up new channels of access to government positions in the economic area. In the past, most finance ministers came from political parties or from the business world, or if they did have degrees, were engineers or lawyers. At present they are mostly economists, many of whom have obtained their degrees abroad. The Central Bank's top positions are also mostly held by economists. Of a total 78 officials at the bank (presidents and directors), on whom information was available, 44 are economists, almost 60 per cent.[32]

Table 3.8 Careers and educational background of Central Bank officials, 1965–2004

Positions and careers	Total		Officials with graduate education				
	N	%	Brazil	US	Other countries	% with graduate courses	% graduated in the US
Presidents	21	100.0	2	15	2	90.4	78.9
Scholars	10	47.6	1	9	–	100.0	90.0
Bureaucrats	6	28.5	–	2	1	50.0	66.6
Banks and Corporations	5	23.9	–	4	1	100.0	80.0
Directors	57*	100.0	16	17	3	63.0	47.2
Scholars	17	29.8	2	13	2	100.0	76.4
Bureaucrats	27	47.3	10	2	–	44.4	16.6
Banks and Corporations	13	22.8	4	2	1	53.8	28.5

Note: (*) The available data refer only to 57 out to 74 directors.

Source: Brazilian Central Bank; Dicionário Historico e Biográfico, CPDOC, 1983.

Table 3.8 presents data on the educational background of Central Bank officials. It shows that they are not only graduates from domestic universities but have also obtained postgraduate degrees in economics abroad. Of 21 presidents, 11 can be called scholars, that is, their pre-Central Bank careers were mostly in academia; 5 had worked in private banks and 6 came out of the public bureaucracy. Seventeen presidents (more than 80 per cent) had postgraduate degrees, two from Brazil, 13 others from the United States. Although data on the directors are incomplete, of the 57 officials on whom information is available, 36 (or 63 per cent) had postgraduate degrees, 17 in the US and 16 in Brazil (among them 10 of the Bank's career bureaucrats). In addition, even those managers of the Central Bank who graduated in Brazil have foreign professional activities in their backgrounds.[33]

One may distinguish two different types of government careers for economists. The first is a career as economist-employee; that is, a government employee qualified in economics. Young economists get a position with a government agency involved in management of the economy either by competitive examination or on direct contract. Most of those who follow this career path do not rise to the top levels in their agencies but remain in midlevel positions, as has been shown for other countries (Coats 1981).

The second career type, and more important in this chapter, is that of economist-scholar as policymaker. It is filled by scholars who are appointed to positions in the government as ministers or presidents and directors of federal banks. They are in general 'brilliant' professors (some of them still young) who, on finishing their theses, are eager to put into practice the theories and models they have just learned. Their theses tend to have been devoted to the more immediate needs of the economy. To be invited to participate in government demonstrates recognition of an economist's academic competence. These scholars are recruited from the university or from the international agencies by politicians or by colleagues already in government posts.

Each career has a distinct relationship between the economist and the public post. While the economist-employees remain in government for most of their professional careers, scholars only pass through government. Regardless of the length in government service, their relationship with their posts is transitory, a stage in a broader career, usually organized from university to government to private sector. Each new stage is considered more important than the previous one. After a greater or lesser time in government, most scholars do not return to their universities. Instead, they move on to banks or consulting firms, where they profit from the accumulated capital of knowledge acquired in the course of their experience. To sum up, the increasing participation of economists in government and the consolidation of a modern and international academic system for their training and qualification created a new ruling elite in Brazil: the economist-scholars. This elite has inaugurated a new path to power in which academic prestige carries great weight. This prestige is sustained by: (a) strong links with the international economist network and with international economic agencies, such as the IMF and World Bank, (b) visibility in the local press and (c) strategic relationships with political and entrepreneurial leaders. In other words, the consolidation of an international system of education became a crucial mechanism of legitimization of this new ruling elite. The more integrated into international networks, the more likely a minister of finance will have his decisions approved by IMF or World Bank officials and consequently the more legitimate he will be in the national political arena.

I quote at length a journalist's account that illustrates these mechanisms well. This passage describes the efforts of two Brazilian economists to win international approval (and therefore domestic recognition) for their inertial inflation theory, which was later transformed into a plan for inflation control.

> September 1984, at the IMF meeting. Persio Arida was here with his proposal of monetary reform. Lara Resende arrived with his Brazilian article. The

> papers were distributed among the authorities. One copy was sent to Alexandre Kafka, the IMF Brazilian representative, who did not make any comments, as it was fine. Another copy was sent to Peter Knight from the World Bank, who said to the authors that their idea was splendid. Lara Resende explained the proposal to the Federal Reserve officials, who were reasonably receptive to his ideas. Persio Arida was invited to speak at a seminar at the Woodrow Wilson Institute, where he is working at the moment.[34] The audience was composed of World Bank, State Department, and IMF officials, people interested in Brazil for academic or professional reasons. Ana Maria Jul of IMF listened to Persio Arida's proposal in silence and did not take part in the discussion. . . . The proposals resonated and the papers eventually fell into John Williamson's hands.[35] . . . He met Lara Resende and Persio Arida and they decided to organize an international seminar about the experience of inflation control in Europe and countries such as Brazil, Argentina, and Israel. . . . The seminar took place in December 1984 and brought together several economists who would later lead reforms in Israel, Argentina, and Brazil. The international connection was being shaped. . . . After the IMF meeting, Resende came back to Rio de Janeiro. He arrived to find a tumultuous and even hostile climate [on the part of some orthodox economists]. . . . His articles were published and gained the explicit approval of Professor Simonsen [from EPGE]. This changed the nature of the controversy, at least for the general public. Resende and Arida were respected academic professors but not great public personalities as Simonsen was. The latter had been minister twice and his name was respected not only in the international academic community, but also in entrepreneurial and financial circles. He was a frontline public man. [Following Simonsen's acceptance of inertial inflation theory] the press became excited. The news was in the headlines, with TV networks and the weekly magazines involved as well. (Sardenberg 1987, pp. 42–3)

Both Persio Arida and Lara Resende were at that time economists from PUC-RJ and both had studied in the United States, where they established contacts with the international economist network as well as with agencies such as the IMF and World Bank. When they were appointed to high positions in the Ministry of Finance and the Central Bank during the Cruzado Plan (February 1986), they put into practice their inertial inflation theory through heterodox shock by freezing wages and prices.

The Cruzado Plan's failure not only had economic and political consequences, but also a professional one as well since it generated criticism about the competence of government economists. But that criticism was stronger against the professors from UNICAMP than against those from PUC-RJ.[36] This can be explained by two factors. First, when economists from UNICAMP were active in economic policymaking through their relationships with the leaders of the center-left Party of the Brazilian Democratic Movement they were called PMDB's economists. Economists from PUC participated only in their professional capacity. Second, the PUC economists resigned their government positions before the press and public opinion fully realized the plan's failure, and they could circulate political explanations for that failure that were accepted by academia. According to common explanations at the time, 'the Cruzado Plan was a good plan in terms of its theoretical coherence or technical correctness; its failure was due to the political constraints and to the populism of President Sarney and his party' (Pereira 1992; Sardenberg 1987).

Thus it is not by chance that the Real Plan, the successful program of monetary stabilization organized by Fernando Henrique Cardoso as Minister of Finance under the Franco administration in 1994, and the neoliberal reforms under Cardoso's own administration (1995–2002) were carried out by the very economists from PUC who had prepared the Cruzado Plan. By contrast, UNICAMP economists were no longer invited to join the economic team of the Ministry of Finance. Persio Arida, Gustavo Franco and Armirio Fraga, presidents of the Central Bank under Cardoso, came from PUC, as did Edmar Bacha, who held the post of president of BNDES and Pedro Malan, Cardoso's Finance Minister.

The example of Pedro Malan also shows clearly a political career in which the internationalization of Brazilian economics played a strong role. He is a member of an elite Rio family, an engineer, who received his PhD in economics from Berkeley in 1973. During the 1970s he worked at PUC-RJ and in IPEA, the Planning Ministry think tank. In this period he obtained notoriety through articles published in Brazilian journals with Albert Fishlow, his professor at Berkeley, about the inequality of Brazil's income distribution that were critical of Brazil's macroeconomic policies. These articles generated a debate with Langoni, a professor of EPGE linked to the military government's economic team. In the context of an authoritarian regime academic debates had political repercussions.

At the beginning of the 1980s, Malan went to the US, where he pursued various professional activities at the United Nations, at the World Bank and at the Inter-American Development Bank (BID). In 1991, he participated in negotiations over Brazil's foreign debt. In 1993, when Cardoso became president Franco's minister of Finance, Malan became the president of the Central Bank and one of the leaders of the Cardoso economic team that elaborated and implemented the Real Plan.

Malan stayed in office the entire eight years of Cardoso's two terms as president. He was considered the economic czar, that is, a powerful man who carried out economic policies formulated and implemented by his staff with hardly any account taken of pressures from the rest of the political system. This is much the role Delfim Netto had played during the military regime. In his period as Minister of Finance, the Brazilian Central Bank, even though formally dependent, gained *de facto* autonomy (Sola et al. 2002).

TECHNOCRATIC PATTERNS IN DEMOCRATIC BRAZIL

In the authoritarian periods of Brazil's twentieth-century history (1930–45 and 1964–84) economic management was characterized by strong centralization in which insulated government agencies made decisions with few checks from other powers. It did not change much with democracy. During the populist democracy (1945–64), leftist nationalist economists acted through Vargas's Economic Advisory Board, which was in charge of building new economic agencies and forming developmentalist policies. Here they used to work silently backstage. They stressed the technical aspects of their decisions in order to empty Congress of initiative in these matters (D'Araujo 1982, p. 427). During the democratic administration of Kubitschek (1955–60), technicians had great freedom and autonomy to elaborate his Target Plan and to manage the executive groups (Martins 1976). After the postmilitary democratization of the 1980s, even economists who had been strongly critical of the military regime's economic policies practiced technocratic policymaking once it was their turn to hold the government posts. This was especially the case when the 'economic miracle' ended and rates of growth declined.

Indeed, macroeconomic policies in democratic times continue to be managed in restricted decision-making arenas, particularly through the so-called economic teams. Made up primarily of economists recruited straight from academia or from the financial markets, they wielded broad power in formulating and implementing economic measures or plans. They worked behind a sort of insulation, protected from outside pressures by the president's personal interventions, shielded from public oversight and without having to coordinate with political parties.

This technocratic decision-making pattern has been historically justified in several ways, whether by the need to develop the country (1950s and 1960s), to control the inflation 'monster' (1980s and 1990s), or more recently, to deal with external vulnerability. Arguing that development, monetary stability and other issues are technically complex (that is, demand the exclusive competence of specialists and, therefore, cannot be open to competition among political forces), economists, regardless of their theoretical or ideological orientation, have thereby reinforced nondemocratic patterns of political action.

In addition to the historical legacy of authoritarianism, these characteristics of economic management are encouraged by the institutional framework of the Brazilian presidential system. As in other Latin American countries, the executive branch in Brazil is stronger than the Congress, even in democratic times. This strength arises from the president's legislative power to issue provisional measures, a power maintained by the democratic Constitution of 1988. At the same time, political parties are fragmented and Congress is weak, particularly in budgetary matters.[37] In addition, as pointed out above, the president has great discretion in spending because congressional funding authorizations leave actual spending up to the president's discretion. Thus Brazilian presidents have institutional resources to protect their economic team, even though they have to continuously negotiate to secure Congressional support for their agendas (Loureiro and Abrucio 1999). With appointments not subject to congressional vote, and endowed only with academic prestige or financial credibility, it is largely because of the presidential umbrella (directly or through the Minister of Finance) that the economic team can operate with such great autonomy in such crucial matters as monetary, fiscal and foreign exchange.

A new element has further enhanced the autonomy of the economic team, the backing of international economic organizations (especially IMF and the World Bank). Sharing the liberal creed with these institutions and following their recommendations, government economists have often been complimented by leaders of such agencies for their accurate guidance of the country's macroeconomic policies, something widely reported in the local press. Such statements certainly add to the economic team's capacity to resist pressures for reducing interest rates or loosening the fiscal adjustment.

And last but not least, the external vulnerability of the economy has been used as another important argument to reinforce autonomy for economic policymakers. This has been especially the case after 1998, when a severe financial crisis hit the country. With unregulated international flows of financial capital, the Brazilian economy has been vulnerable to external crises, as have many other 'emerging markets', such as Mexico, Argentina, Russia and Turkey (Whitehead 2003).

This external vulnerability became a crucial dimension of economic policymaking. The need for financial credibility in order to access global markets helps explain the continuation by the Lula da Silva administration of Cardoso's most important macroeconomic policies. In order to achieve inflation targets both Cardoso and Lula kept interest rates high and even intensified fiscal adjustments. Cardoso's second term began deeply constrained by financial crisis and agreements with the IMF. In response, the government has been running a surplus under both Cardoso and Lula through an increase of the tax burden with, in consequence, a reduction of economic growth and employment.[38]

The 1998 crisis had a major impact on macroeconomic management, which embraced a stronger fiscal adjustment, a floating exchange rate, and the regime of inflation targets. This last was an important step towards a more transparent monetary policy. The central bankers have to monitor interest rates in order to achieve inflation targets established by the National Monetary Committee, made up of the Minister of Finance, the Minister of Planning and the President of the Central Bank. In order to produce financial credibility, other rules for transparency were also instituted. These include a formal explanatory report from the president of the Central Bank if inflation targets are not achieved and the publication of the proceedings of the Monetary Policy Committee, the agency in charge of establishing monthly interest rates whose members are the president and directors of the Central Bank. Such new monetary institutions were designed to constrain decisionmakers to be accountable to the financial markets.

Monetary policymakers are of course very sensitive to financial markets, but in Brazil the relationships of policymakers to those markets threaten democratic order and republican values. These relations are too intimate, since many members of the Central Bank, as discussed above, are tied by previous and future careers to banks and consulting firms. But decisions about interest rates have an impact on a much broader public and so issues of transparency in monetary decision-making have a broad significance.

Despite the similarities, there are some important differences between the Cardoso and Lula administrations, in respect to their economic challenges and to the logic that guides the recruitement of their economic teams. Cardoso was faced with the challenge of curtailing a long and persistent hyperinflation. Since this required technical knowledge, new ideas (the inertial theory of inflation), and new political solutions (the Real Plan), the choice of his economic team was strongly driven by its academic competence. As already mentioned, Malan, Arida, Lara Resende, Bacha, Franco and others had great prestige in Brazilian university circles and even abroad.

The Lula administration was faced with a different challenge, that of overcoming a lack of financial credibility due to positions previously taken by his party against IMF views and against the repayment of the public debt (Sola 2004). This challenge determined in great part the criteria by which the economic team was chosen. The government formed by the leftist Workers' Party (PT) had to choose as its central banker a former president of Bank Boston. Many other officials of this bank and of the Ministry of Finance had careers in finance or in more conservative academic circles. Even though the Minister of Finance, Antonio Pallocci, is a PT member (a medical doctor, who started his political career as mayor of a rural village in the State of São Paulo), his staff is made up of economists known for their involvement with monetary issues as well as others with backgrounds in banking or consulting.[39]

Consider some other examples. The *Secretaria do Tesouro Nacional* (STN) is an extremely important agency. To understand the role of STN we need to realize that the budget approved by the Brazilian Congress is not mandatory. In other words, the executive branch can impound funds if the estimated revenues are not realized or when fiscal adjustments are necessary. STN is the executive agency in charge of these measures. The head of STN is Joaquim Levy, a former staff member of the Cardoso administration, who got his PhD from Chicago, taught at EPGE/FGV and worked at the IMF. Another important member of the Minister of Finance's staff, Marcos Lisboa, head of the Secretariat of Economic Policy, is a young professor at EPGE, who got his PhD in economics from the University of Pennsylvania and was an assistant professor at Stanford. Lula's choice as Central Bank president had previously been World President of Bank Boston (1996–99) and President of Global Banking at FleetBoston Financial from 1999 to 2002. Among the eight directors of the Central Bank, two from PUC-RJ got their PhD in American universities. Two other directors, also with graduate courses in the US, are from the financial markets. In short, the careers of Lula's economic staff give his administration financial credibility.

Lula's economic team includes almost none of the heterodox and leftist economists from UNICAMP or UFRJ that one might have expected. There was a single exception: the president of the BNDES, Carlos Lessa, a former professor of UFRJ and disciple of CEPAL. He was recommended to President Lula by his colleague Maria Conceição Tavares, a renowned economist from CEPAL, professor of UFRJ and UNICAMP, member of the Workers Party and one of its former congressional deputies. But he stayed in this position for less than two years. In December 2004 he was dismissed after an interview in which he strongly attacked Central Bank policies and was replaced by another developmentalist economist, Guido Mantega, the Lula administration's first Minister of Planning, who was politically more moderate. Indeed, in the Lula administration, Carlos Lessa remained as a solitary national developmentalist Don Quixote in the midst of a team oriented mainly to monetary issues. This was dramatically highlighted in September 2004, two months before Lessa's dismissal, when Tavares gave up her column in an important São Paulo newpaper, and declared with bitterness that she was disappointed with the government's economic positions and tired of fighting against the dominant financial market viewpoint.

When we observe Lula's administration continuing and even extending Cardoso's policies, we are inclined, on the one hand, to agree with the thesis of convergence of national macroeconomic policies in the present global economic context (Boix 1998). The inherent instability of 'emerging markets', due to the post-Bretton Woods international arrangements, imposes on governments of different ideological positions enormous external constraints that carry more weight than domestic partisan forces and social demands.

But, on the other hand, we can not forget that most of these 'emerging markets' are also new democracies which 'are bound to govern with one eye looking towards the changing moods and expectations of markets, and the other checking up on perceptions and demands of the electorate' (Sola 2004, p. 2). The great challenge for emerging market democracies is to find a way to build institutions sufficiently flexible to absorb external shocks without crumbling that at the same time are committed to principles of accountability and democratic control.

FINAL CONSIDERATIONS

The economics profession has developed in Brazil in close connection with government. The ties between academic circles and government have remained strong. The emergence of a modern and internationalized field of economics did not change this and actually reinforced earlier polarizations. In other words, along with the emergence of a scholar-policymaker identity, the social field of the economists has been historically characterized by profound disputes and internal struggles between different theoretical approaches and political ideologies, and remains so.

Despite the strong participation of mainstream economists in government positions, and their support by international agencies, this mainstream has never held complete hegemony in Brazil. On the contrary, their opponents have been continually present in the academic and political arenas. Developmentalist and heterodox schools like UNICAMP and UFRJ continue to recruit many undergraduate and graduate students and several of their leading members have weekly bylines in major newspapers. Their opinion still has repercussions in the media and they are in demand as consultants. When the *Biographical Dictionary of Dissenting Economists*, published in London, included three Brazilian economists in the early 2000s (Celso Furtado, Maria Conceição Tavares and Gonzaga Belluzzo), it was well publicized in Brazil. Even considering the fact that heterodox economists have not participated in Lula's economic team, it is impossible not to recognize their presence in the theoretical debate over present economic policies as well as their media visibility.

During Lula's second administration (from 2006 on) poor economic performance led to changes in the economic team and in policy. The new Minister of Finance, Guido Mantega, replaced his high-level staff and

BNDES[40] increased support for industrial policy. At IPEA, too, there was a renewed emphasis on social inclusion.

The neoliberal concept of extreme adjustment as a precondition for growth was abandoned. The Growth Acceleration Program (PAC) was announced in January 2007. Focused mainly on public investment in infrastructure and other priority areas and on stimulating public credit, the program also set forth tax cuts, changes to the tax system and a long-term reorientation of the role of fiscal policy to support growth as well as solvency in the public sector. Growth would increase public revenues and financial credibility. It would also generate funds for public investments with no need to reduce social programs such as *Bolsa Família* and Social Security. Politically, higher growth would meet the demands of Lula's constituencies.

However, the Lula administration's response to the international financial crisis of 2008 maintained the ambivalent profile of its earlier macroeconomic policy. On the one hand, the main measures seemed intended to deal with the issue of domestic and international credit contraction. On the other hand, the Central Bank continued to uphold the same interest rate policy, keeping the prime rate at 13.75 percent until January 2009, despite the striking drop in inflationary pressure.

Regarding macroeconomic decision-making, we can say it has been characterized since the very beginning of the Brazilian experience by centralized and authoritarian patterns. Even in democratic times, the policymaking arenas are restricted to very small groups insulated against demands from the rest of the political system. Policymakers are not constrained by effective mechanisms of control and democratic accountability. As they do not have an electoral mandate nor a bureaucratic career there are no mechanisms of sanction in cases of errors or bad decisions.

At a moment when macroeconomic policies are oriented towards investors in order to guarantee access to external capital, new practices of transparency and accountability have developed, but they are addressed mainly to financial markets and not to the public in general. Macroeconomic policymaking in countries like Brazil brings about a serious democratic deficit. Working with a large margin of autonomy, policymakers have great influence over crucial policies that affect the lives of millions of citizens without adequate institutional mechanisms to make them politically accountable.

NOTES

1. Bourdieu (1976) conceived of a social field as a social space structured by relationships of competition and power among individuals, groups and institutions. In such

struggles, each group of individuals or set of institutions mobilizes different kinds of social 'capital' or attributes.

2. As will be discussed later, 'economist' was not a professional identity in Brazil until the 1960s. Engineers and lawyers who performed some kind of economic role or had public finance knowledge were labeled 'technicians' in government and political circles. On the other hand, people who got a degree from schools of economics worked mostly as accountants.
3. These councils or committes were charged with balancing the consumption and production of agricultural goods, creating incentives for industrial firms, and improving infrastructure for industrialization (Souza 1976). Among them were the National Coffee Council, the National Sugar Cane Council, the Brazilian Commercial and Industrial Council, and the National Road Committee.
4. It is interesting to mention that the BNDE as well as the Plano de Metas (Target Plan) of the Kubitschek government were spin-offs from one of the international commissions, the Joint Brazil–USA Economic Development Commission of 1951.
5. It is important to note that Banco do Brasil is not a government authority but a public commercial bank created in the nineteenth century. It is the Banco Central do Brasil that is the monetary authority and it was not created until 1965.
6. The mixed BNDE-CEPAL group was set up in 1953 under the direction of the Chilean economist Aníbal Pinto. It was of fundamental importance in spreading the ideas of CEPAL and in training Brazilian economists. It offered courses in economics and planning in several cities (Ekerman 1989, p. 116).
7. Vargas's Advisory Board had important responsibilities for industrial development programs and state oil and energy enterprises starting in the 1950s (D'Araújo 1982).
8. The executive groups set up during the period included: GEIA (Executive Group for the Automobile Industry); GEICOM (Executive Group for the Shipbuilding Industry); and GEIMAPA (Executive Group for the Heavy Machinery Industry and for Capital Goods). Several studies have stressed the innovative role of these executive groups in coordinating decision-making under Kubitschek so as to combine economic development and political stability (Benevides 1976; Lafer 1970). For a more detailed analysis of the 'dual bureaucracy' (a part of which operated under a merit system and a part under political patronage) see Sikkink (1991, pp. 175–7).
9. 'Entreguista' was an expression used by the nationalists to identify their opponents. It means the people who hand over the country's wealth to foreign capital, that is, to foreign companies.
10. The conflicts within the economic bureaucracy led to the creation of a Superintendency of Money and Credit (SUMOC) inside the Banco do Brasil as a 'halfway' step toward a central bank. This was a political solution that circumvented the opposition to a central bank on the part of the Banco's directing board because that would threaten its power to control foreign exchange and monetary policy. This resistence explains why the Brazilian Central Bank was created so late in comparison to other Latin American countries, in 1965 after the arrival of the military regime (Maxfield 1997).
11. The disputes between Gudin and Simonsen had important repercussions in Congress, in business associations in Rio and São Paulo, and in the press. Gudin's criticisms were published in March 1945 in a book titled *Rumos da Política Econômica* (Directions in Economic Policy). In August of the following year, Gudin struck again with the publication of the 'Letter to the Planning Commission' which closed the debate (Bielschowsky 1988; Magalhães 1961; Sola 1982).
12. The importance of the Gudin–Simonsen debate can be seen by noting that it was to be updated three decades later in the 1970s with the publication of a new edition by the Planning Ministry's think tank, the Institute for Applied Economic Research (IPEA).
13. Gudin came from an important family of the French commercial *bourgeoisie* that provided luxury goods for the Brazilian aristocracy during the Empire (1822–89). As an engineer, he was director and partner in a number of large foreign companies involved in civil construction and urban services (dams, railways, telegraph services). Bulhões

was a high-level employee of the Finance Ministry. He came from a family of politicians during the First Republic (1989–30). His father was a diplomat and his uncle had been Finance Minister during the presidencies of Rodrigues Alves and Nilo Peçanha.

14. This school would be transformed in 1945 into the National Faculty of Economic Science at the public University of Brazil in Rio de Janeiro. Gudin relates his involvement with initiatives for the study of economics: 'I went into the planning of the economy with no project, no particular plan. (President) Getúlio had a lot to do with this. He never set up a committee – and he set up quite a few – without putting me on it. And then, at a certain point, some friends looked me up in the office to ask me to join the teaching staff of the school they wanted to found, a school of economics. I didn't much want to at first, but in the end I gave in . . .' (CPDOC/FGV, 1984, p. 91)
15. In 1979, Gudin remembered the visit and the disputes surrounding the creation of the school: 'I went to the Bretton Woods Conference and on my return, instead of coming back the usual way, I stopped off at Harvard. There you have the School of Economics and, on the other side of the Charles River, the School of Business Administration. I told my Harvard colleagues: 'I'm battling away in Brazil to separate economics from accounting, but they don't want it like that; they want it all together. What do you think?' They said, 'I don't know if you have a Charles River in Brazil. If you haven't, then make one and separate'. I got them to tell this to Capanema (Minister of Education), and it was the decisive argument for him to carry out what I had proposed' (CPDOC/FGV, 1984, pp. 89–90).
16. During the 1940s Gudin became professor of Money and Credit. Bulhões took on Value and Price Formation. Dias Leite, an engineer who had been with Gudin on the Economic Planning Commission, taught Structure of Economic Organizations. Jorge Kafuri, Dias Leite's brother-in-law, also an engineer and member of the Economic Planning Commission, taught Evolution of the Economic Situation. Jorge Kingston, a member of the Brazil–US Mixed Commission, taught Economic Statistics. Gudin, Bulhões and Dias Leite were also publishing: Gudin's *Princípios de Economia Monetária* in 1943, Bulhões *Orientação e Controle em Economia* in 1941, and Dias Leite's *Renda Nacional* in 1948. Gudin's text became a basic work in a number of schools of economics in Brazil and went through a number of editions; its author became a Brazilian pioneer in writing economics textbooks.
17. Delfim Netto, Minister of Finance for more than ten years during the military regime, was one of the most successful examples of this career path. A former student, he was professor at USP in the 1960s when he led the reform of its curriculum. He recognized new demands for economic development activities in the government and fought 'against the overdevelopment of the less important chairs at the expense of those which were fundamental'. He therefore proposed new guidelines for the program with an emphasis on mathematics and economic theory (Pinho 1981, p. 48).
18. FGV was founded in 1944 at the initiative of top-level officials of the first Vargas government (1930–45) connected with DASP and especially with its first Director-General, Simões Lopes, who became president of FGV for several decades. As Sikkink (1991, p. 175) puts it, 'DASP became "a sort of superministry" in charge of installing a new bureaucratic apparatus and creating an elite civil service'. FGV was also to provide qualified personnel for modernizing public administration. From its founding, then, FGV was closely linked with government and could count on substantial financial support.
19. Both Gudin and Bulhões had lived abroad. Gudin studied in Paris, while Bulhões lived in France and Austria as a child. From the 1940s on, both frequently travelled abroad as Brazilian representatives to the IMF. They maintained their contacts with Harvard and other American universities. Aware of the importance of such contacts in academic circles, they promoted the systematic practice of sending IBRE personnel abroad for training. This had already been taking place at DASP under Simões Lopes.
20. Examples of this network: in the 1950s, Bulhões worked with Roberto Campos (a diplomat and later his colleague in the cabinet of Castelo Branco, the first military

president, 1964–67) in the consulting firm, CONSULTEC, where there were also colleagues of Campos from BNDE, such as the engineers Lucas Lopes and Glycon de Paiva. Mário Henrique Simonsen, an engineer and later Finance Minister, was a relative of Gudin and worked with Dias Leite, professor at FNCE and also minister in the Castelo Branco government, in his consulting firm, ECOTEC (CPDOC/FGV 1984, pp. 503 and 3.199).

21. The 'orchestrated' work of this group is well demonstrated in the articulation of economic policies, even before 1964. Gudin, as Finance Minister under the Café Filho government, and Bulhões, as Director of SUMOC, set up Instruction 113 in 1955, which enormously facilitated industrialization under the Kubitschek government by means of the Plano de Metas (Target Plan), of which Roberto Campos was one of the principal coordinators.
22. Consider the career trajectory of Roberto Campos. Born in the state of Mato Grosso, he worked as a small-town teacher before going to Rio de Janeiro in 1939. There he entered the diplomatic service through public examination. After a time he was sent to the US, where studied economics in Washington DC and at Columbia University. He was a brilliant participant in a number of international economic committees, including Bretton Woods, where he had his first contact with Gudin and Bulhões. From that time, he maintained close connections with the group. At the beginning of the 1950s he was a participant in CEXIM (a commission in charge of export activities), under the direction of FGV's president, Simões Lopes. He replaced Gudin when the latter retired from FNCE. Before joining Bulhões in 1964 in the Castello Branco government, he was a member of the Joint Brazil–US Economic Development Commission (1951) and was one of the founders and president of the BNDE (see Sikkink 1991, p. 128).
23. Celso Furtado, Brazil's main representative at CEPAL, came from a family of lawyers on his father's side and on his mother's from a family of large landowners and farmers in the Sate of Paraíba. He graduated in law in Rio de Janeiro, and after experience in journalism and at DASP, he did his doctorate in Political Economy in Paris in the mid-1940s. He then spent some time in England, where he encountered Keynesian ideas. Returning to Rio in 1948, he participated for a while in the FGV group, working on *Conjuntura Econômica*. Dissatisfied, in his own words, with the trifling nature of his task, he saw CEPAL as a chance for career improvement. On the recommendation of Bulhões, then the 'big chief' in the Economic and Financial Division of the Finance Ministry and president of the Brazilian group with the Abbink Mission, he obtained a post at CEPAL (Furtado 1985, p. 49). On the contribution of CEPAL to Brazilian economics see Bielschowsky (1988), Mantega (1985) and Oliveira (1975).
24. During the second Vargas government there were efforts at conciliation between the interests of foreign capital and nationalist groups carried on by the Joint Brazil–US Economic Development Commission and the Economic Advisory Board, made up of nationalist technicians, such as Rômulo Almeida, Ignácio Rangel and Cleantho de Paiva Leite (D'Araujo 1982).
25. ISEB (Instituto Superior de Estudos Brasileiros) was created in the Ministry of Education in 1955 to train high-level employees, political party members and union members. It acted as a catalyst for the nationalist positions of the time. Its deep internal disputes led to the resignation of some of its members, including Roberto Campos. In 1958 it allied with the Communist Party and other groups on the left, which led to its disbandment by the military in April 1964 (Sikkink 1991, pp. 127–8).
26. According to Ministry of Education statistics, in 1968 Brazil had 84 programs in economics with 17000 enrolled undergraduates; in 2000, 249 programs with more than 65000 students.
27. BNDES is the new name of the former BNDE, where the added final 'S' indicates a social dimension added to the bank's activities. This bank also gives annual awards for the best theses in economics (master's and doctoral levels), while IPEA provides funds for the annual conference of ANPEC (National Association for Graduates in Economics) and its publications.

28. According to Ministry of Education statistics, in the 1990s there were 13 graduate programs in economics in Brazil. In 2002 this increased to 27 with more than 2500 enrolled, including both master's and PhD students.
29. See Loureiro and Lima (1996) for other aspects of the internationalization of Brazilian economics, such as the curricula and syllabi of the local graduate programs as well as the kinds of articles in the main Brazilian journals.
30. Six professors from PUC-RJ and three from FGV are mentioned as members of the *American Economic Review* and as fellows of the Econometric Society (see the survey of the members of *American Economic Review* and of *Econometrica*, respectively, in 1989 and 1993). Three other professors from USP are also on this list. Not a single professor from UNICAMP is mentioned.
31. According to Whitley (1991), scientific fields vary in the importance given to books or journal articles for communication of research to peers. Distinguishing three types of scientific field – 'fragmented adhocracies', 'polycentric oligarchies' and 'partitioned bureaucracies' – this author states: 'In fragmented adhocracies, for instance, the relatively low degree of skill and concept standardization, limited autonomy from lay elites and ordinary discursive language and variety of legitimate audiences for intellectual contributions, limit the ability of particular groups to dominate the reputational system and establish their goals and standards. . . . The lack of technical standardization means that research outputs are not easily communicated through brief journal articles . . . [In fields such as management studies, sociology, etc.] journals do not dominate the formal communication system . . . but monographs, general books and semi-popular articles are still legitimate means of communicating research' (1991, pp. 24–5)
32. Although the Brazilian Central Bank is not formally autonomous, it has been operating as if it were since the Cardoso government. Although the president and directors are named by the Minister of Finance and the Brazilian President and do not have the protection of a fixed mandate, they have conducted monetary policy in the last several years with considerable autonomy, especially in the face of pressures coming from the political arena (Sola et al. 2002).
33. Former Central Bank president Affonso Pastore had been an aide to the Brazilian government delegation to CIAP *Comitê Interamericano da Aliança para o Progresso*, held in Washington and to its delegation to the IMF, in 1967 and 1968. In the 1970s he also took part in of international bodies such as IFRI International Financial Research Institute as a member of the Board of Trustees, as well as USAID missions to Uruguay. All this was before he became Central Bank president.
34. The paper discussed in the meeting was Arida's article, written in English, 'Economic Stabilization in Brazil'.
35. John Williamson, of the International Economic Institute in Washington, had been a professor at PUC-RJ.
36. Besides the economists from PUC, the economic team that managed the Cruzado Plan was made up of economists from UNICAMP with close links with the entrepreneur and Minister of Finance, Dilson Funaro and with the president of PMDB, Ulisses Guimarães.
37. Figueiredo and Limongi (1999, p. 146) point out that 53 percent of provisional measures issued in Brazil between 1989 and 1995 concerned economic matters, especially monetary stabilization plans.
38. According to official statistics, the tax burden was around 25 percent of GDP at the beginning of the Cardoso administration in 1995. In 2003, at the end of the first year of Lula's administration, it reached over 35 percent and in 2004 it is estimated to have surpassed 37 percent.
39. An informant with financial market contacts told me that the PT's election campaign document 'Letter to the Brazilian People' was written in collaboration with people from the private banks. Published in June 2002, it committed the party to economic stability and fiscal and monetary responsibility.

40. In 1982, BNDE changed its name to BNDES (*Banco Nacional de Desenvolvimento Econômico e Social*) to emphasize the social dimension of development policies.

REFERENCES

Almeida, R. (1988), *Depoimento*, Rio de Janeiro: CPDOC/FGV.

ANPEC (1992), *Programas de Pós-graduação em Economia no Brasil*, ANPEC/IPEA.

Bacha, E. (1985), *Resenha do livro de Celso Furtado, A fantasia organizada*, Sao Paulo: Leia.

Benevides, M.V. (1976), *O governo Kubitschek: desenvolvimento econômico e estabilidade política*, Rio de Janeiro: Editora Paz e Terra.

Bielschowsky, R. (1988), *O pensamento econômico brasileiro. O ciclo ideológico do desenvolvimentismo*, Rio de Janeiro: IPEA/INPS.

Birnbaum, P. (1977), *Les Sommets de L'Etat*, Paris: Ed. du Seuil.

Boix, C. (1998), *Political Parties, Growth and Equality.Conservative and Social Democratic Economic Strategies in the World Economy*, Cambridge: Cambridge University Press.

Bourdieu, P. (1976), 'Le champ scientifique', *Actes de la recherche en sciences sociales*, 2–3.

Bulhões, G. (1990), *Depoimento*, Rio de Janeiro: CPDOC/FGV.

Canabrava A.P. (1981), 'As condições sociais, econômicas e políticas da fundação', *História da Faculdade de Economia e Administração da USP (1946–1981)*, São Paulo: USP.

CPDOC/FGV (1984), *Dicionário histórico–biográfico brasileiro*, Rio de Janeiro: FGV/Forense Universitária, FINEP.

Coats, A.W. (1981), *Economists in Government. An International Comparative Study*, Durham, NC: Duke University Press.

Coats, A.W. (1996), 'The Post-1945 Internationalization of Economics', in *Annual Supplement to Volume 28 of History of Political Economy*, Durham, NC: Duke University Press.

D'Araujo, M.C. (1982), *O segundo governo Vargas. Democracia, partidos e crise política*, Rio de Janeiro: Zahar Editores.

Dreifus, R. (1981), *A conquista do Estado. Ação política, poder e golpe de classe*, Petrópolis: Ed. Vozes.

Ekerman, R. (1989), 'A comunidade de economistas do Brazil: dos anos 50 aos dias de hoje', *Revista Brasileira de Economia*, **43** (2).

FEA/USP (1981), *História da Faculdade de Economia e Administração (FEA/USP) da Universidade de São Paulo (1956–1981)*, São Paulo: FEA/USP.

Figueiredo A. and F. Limongi (1999), *Executivo e Legislativo na Nova Ordem Constitucional*, Rio de Janeiro: Editora Fundação Getúlio Vargas.

Fourquet, F. (1980), *Les comptes de la puissance. Histoire de la comptabilité et du plan*, Paris: Ed. Encre.

Franco, G. (1992), *Cursos de Economia*, Rio de Janeiro: ANPEC.

Furtado, C. (1954), *A Economia Brasileira*, Rio de Janeiro: A Noite.

Furtado, C. (1985), *A fantasia organizada*, Rio de Janeiro: Paz e Terra (4a. Edição).

Gudin, E. (1979), *Depoimento*, Rio de Janeiro: CPDOC/FGV.

Klamer, A. and D. Colander (1990), *The Making of an Economist*, Boulder, San Francisco and Londres: Westview Press.
Lafer, C. (1970), *The Planning Process and the Political System in Brazil: A Study of Kubitschek's Target Plan*, Ithaca: Cornell University Press.
Leff, N. (1968), *Economic Policy-making and Development in Brazil 1947–1964*, New York: John Wiley & Sons.
Loureiro, M.R. and F. Abrucio (1999), 'Política e burocracia no presidencialismo brasileiro: O papel do Ministério da Fazenda no primeiro governo Cardoso', *Revista Brasileira de Ciências Sociais*, **41**, pp. 69–89.
Loureiro. M.R. and G.T. Lima (1996), 'Searching for the Modern Times: The Internationalization of Economics in Brazil', *Research in the History of Economic Thought and Methodology*, **14**, pp. 277–305.
Magalhães, J.P. (1961), *Controvérsia brasileira sobre desenvolvimento econômico*, Rio de Janeiro: CNI.
Mantega, G. (1985), *A economia política brasileira*, São Paulo e Petrópolis: Polis/ Vozes.
Martins, L. (1976), *Pouvoir politique et dévellopement économique*, Paris: Anthropos.
Maxfield, S. (1997), *Gatekeepers of Growth. The International Political Economy of Central Banking in Developing Countries*, Princeton: Princeton University Press.
Miceli, S. (1990), *A desilusão americana*, São Paulo: Editora Sumaré.
Moura. G. (1984), *Sucessos e ilusões: relações internacionais do Brasil durante e após a segunda guerra mundial*, Rio de Janeiro: Fundação Getúlio Vargas.
Oliveira, F. (1975), 'A economia brasileira, crítica à razão dualista', *Seleção Cebrap*, 1. São Paulo.
Pereira, L.C.B. (1992), 'Problematizando uma experiência de governo: contra a corrente no ministério da Fazenda', *Revista Brasileira de Ciências Sociais*, **7** (19).
Pinho, D. (1981), 'O departamento de ciências econômicas', in *História da Faculdade de Economia e Administração da USP (1946–1981)*, São Paulo: USP.
Pollak, M. (1976), 'La planification des sciences sociales', *Actes de la Recherche en Sciences Sociales*, 2–3.
Rangel, Ignácio (1963), *A Inflação Brasileira*, Rio de Janeiro: Tempo Brasileiro.
Sardenberg, C.A. (1987), *Aventura e agonia: nos bastidores do Plano Cruzado*, São Paulo: Companhia das Letras.
Sikkink, K. (1991), *Ideas and Institutions. Developmentalism in Brazil and Argentina*, Cornell University Press.
Sola, L. (1982), *The Political and Ideological Constraints to Economic Management in Brazil, 1945–1963*, Oxford: University of Oxford Press.
Sola, L. (2004), 'Financial Credibility, Legitimacy and Political Discretion: Lula da Silva Government, First Year', Paper presented in 4th Annual meeting of Brazilian Political Science Association, Rio de Janeiro.
Sola, L., Kugelmas, E. and L. Whitehead (eds) (2002), *Banco Central. Autoridade Políticaa e democratizaçã. Um equilíbiro delicado*, Rio de Janeiro: FGV Editora.
Souza, M.C.C. (1976), *Estado e partidos políticos no Brasil*, São Paulo: Editora Alfa-Omega.
Suleiman, P. (1970), *Les élites en France*, Paris: Ed. du Seuil.

Swedberg, R. (1990), *Economics and Sociology. Redefining their Boundaries: Conversations with Economists and Sociologists*, Princeton: Princeton University Press.

Whitehead, L. (2003), 'The Political Dynamics of Financial Crises in 'Emerging Market Democracies', Paper presented at the 19th IPSA Word conference, Durban, South Africa, June 29th–July 4th.

Whitley, R. (1991), 'The Organisation and Role of Journals in Economics and Other Scientific Fields', *Economic Notes by Monte dei Peschi di Siena*, **20** (1), 6–23.

Wirth, J.D. (1970), *The Politics of Brazilian Development (1930–1954)*, Stanford: Stanford University Press.

4. Economics: the Chilean story

Verónica Montecinos[1]

Chilean economists have made history well beyond the country's frontiers. In the second half of the twentieth century, the economics profession in Chile, inventive and influential by many standards, grew surprisingly original and cosmopolitan. Economists gradually displaced other professional groups and rose to celebrity status by mastering their role as mediators between domestic and external forces, becoming a seductive instance of professional hegemony.

As Chile gained an unexpected significance in the international connections among economics, politics and diplomacy, the chapters of the Chilean story became a staple in policy debates.[2] Tales of Chile's anti-capitalist and pro-capitalist reforms often read like propaganda pamphlets and profuse journalistic coverage brought echoes of the Chilean story to ordinary citizens the world over. Moreover, the largesse of foreign foundations and governments reinforced Chile's worth as an exemplary case of policies to be avoided and of policies to be rewarded. This suggests that the character of a nation's economics profession not only reflects internal disciplinary dynamics but is affected by the country's politics and by wider geopolitical calculations.

Arguably, nowhere else in Latin America has economics reached the same degree of historical significance and nowhere else has such a small national profession mirrored so closely and consequentially the overall battles and phases of the discipline. Versions of the intra-professional debates of the day were staged in Chile and relayed to other countries during the developmentalist wave associated with the Keynesian consensus as well as during the counterattack of neoliberalism. General accounts of the history of economics, however, have failed to recognize the active involvement of countries like Chile in the twists and turns of the profession. Rectifying that narrowly constructed narrative can sharpen portraits of economics as seed and fruit of much broader transnational processes.

Since the late 1940s, the profession and some of its constituencies far from Chile found in that country a convenient theater for their own dramas. At various junctures, this small but expertise-laden country with an active foreign policy proved to be a valued testing-ground for those seeking to export models of economic governance. Chile's technocratic reformism seemed to show something of value to other developing regions and even to richer countries. The Chilean case became a point of reference in wide-ranging East/West debates as well as in North/South confrontations. When the Cold War clouded development diplomacy and Inter-American relations, anticommunist crusaders focused on Chile, along with propagandists of social Catholic, social democratic and socialist variants of reform, as did champions of social revolution in several versions. 'Chile was a laboratory in which contenders for legitimate state expertise in the North invested heavily. . . . What happened in Chile, therefore, played directly into northern debates fought in the media and in the universities and think tanks' (Dezalay and Garth 2002, p. 141).

Chile has operated as a stepping stone in the international transmission of professional resources and a regional hub for economics training programs, international development agencies, think tanks, foundations and other disciplinary constituencies. Its prestigious, highly subsidized but independent universities which underwent a process of modernizing reforms in the 1960s made of Chile an attractive destination for foreign experts, academics and students. A tradition of democratic politics, available research funding and scholarships as well as exchange agreements with foreign universities added to the country's appeal. With such an exceptionally favorable growing ground, by the 1960s if not earlier, the social sciences in Chile and economics in particular were considered the strongest in the region (Puryear 1994, p. 164). Recent assessments confirm the high productivity of Chilean economists compared with the rest of Latin America and even the world average (Koljatic and Silva 2001; Contreras et al. 2006). The impact of their work has been significant (Edwards 2003; see also the papers presented at the annual conference of the *Sociedad de Economía de Chile*, posted on line).

Chile's status in the world hierarchy of economics was elevated by the convergence of material and symbolic resources, often of foreign provenance. It has been estimated that Chile in the 1960s, with less than 4 percent of the region's population, received as much as 14 percent of all US economic aid. The Ford and Rockefeller foundations were especially generous (Puryear 1994, pp. 11–15). European governments and foundations also focused on Chile. The Friederich-Ebert-Stiftung, a German social-democratic foundation, established its first Latin American office there, in 1967; its activities included scholarships and the creation of the *Instituto Latinoamericano de Investigaciones Sociales* (ILDIS), a research center. The Chile office of the Konrad-Adenauer-Stiftung, linked to the Christian Democratic Party, also offered scholarships and financed research, for example, through the

Corporación de Promoción Universitaria (CPU). And in the past couple of decades, the transnationalization of think tanks again selected Chile ahead of others in the region (Alvarez-Rivadulla et al. forthcoming).

The first part of this chapter reviews the expansion of the economics profession within various institutional spheres and the second part examines aspects of economics education. The ties with international actors and trends are emphasized throughout.

THE ASCENT OF ECONOMICS IN CHILE: A SYNOPSIS

Remarkable for its pro-economist bias, Chile is a paradigmatic case on several counts. The profession's extraordinary sway in public life, already well consolidated by 1970, has since risen further, enduring changes in political regime and various economic cycles of depression and prosperity. The influence of economists is partly a matter of professional demography. In Chile the number of highly qualified economists is much higher than one could expect given the country's size. Forty years ago only a handful of Chilean economists possessed a doctoral degree. Deficit turned into surplus, as currently shown by the credentials of government, academic and business economists, not counting those employed in international agencies in Chile and abroad. As the economist-lawyer ratio changed, Americanized economicism gradually replaced the Euro-centric, legalistic traditions of Chile's public discourse. The composition of national elites, policy processes and debates, and even the conduct of foreign affairs became thoroughly permeated by the language and conventions of economics. Eventually, the country's image as a site of bold policy experimentation became indistinguishable from that of its well-regarded economists.

Not only is the profession unrivaled in its authority over policy matters but its social prestige and political influence are enormous. There are families with two or three generations of well-placed economists. Some families count spouses, siblings and cousins, parents and children with graduate economics degrees. It is not uncommon to observe members of these families serving simultaneously in the executive and legislative branches, in ministries and other public agencies, private banks, political parties and universities.[3] Of course, the large contingent of certified economic experts is a reflection of the extraordinary level of resources allocated to the education of Chilean economists and the hospitable environment they find in their home country after graduation.

The history of economic thought in Latin America features Chile prominently. Liberal economic ideas were initially rooted in the country's export-based economy of the nineteenth century. Threads of economic thought were rewoven with full force in the interventionist era of protected industrialization. During the golden years of state-led developmentalism, many heterodox economic ideas were crafted in Chile. Those ideas cycled radically back to laissez-faire orthodoxy after the 1973 coup d'état that deposed Salvador Allende. In the 1980s and 1990s, panegyrics of the Chilean market 'miracle' proliferated. Although typically associated with the Chicago Boys and Pinochet's authoritarian regime, the visibility of Chile's market reforms only increased after the dictatorship ended in 1990.

By the late 1980s, the country's economics profession had been deeply transformed by years of censorship, massive repression, and exile, as well as by a less confrontational international environment.[4] With the rising number of foreign-trained economists, the economic discourse of the center-left had lost its previous adversarial tone and its economic ideas closely resembled the US-centered professional mainstream. A 1980s survey sent to 228 Chilean economists showed that although economists remained clustered in otherwise ideologically homogeneous institutions, they largely agreed on previously controversial topics (price fixing, exchange rate) and showed no substantial divisions in terms of positive and normative questions (Morandé 1986).

A broad national consensus on trade openness, fiscal discipline and market-centered policies continued through the 1990s. A series of microeconomic measures – the so-called second generation reforms – were adopted to further competition and efficiency. Contrary to warnings of populist excesses, democratic politics heightened macroeconomic performance and Chile's lustrous image among economic analysts and investors shone even brighter. For the past two decades, inflation has been kept at historically low levels. Fiscal surplus and economic growth rates have been among the highest in the region. Policy disagreements persist, primarily on how best to quell poverty and income inequality and how to make the economy less vulnerable to external economic turbulences and long-term environmental stress, but it is not a matter of dispute that the prosperity cycle initiated in the 1980s has lasted longer than any other in Chile's modern history (Ffrench-Davis 1999; Gallego and Loayza 2002; Meller 2005). The approbation of international economists can be illustrated with the following quote:

> Chile of all Latin American countries best documents how much of a shift in thinking has taken place. In the 1970s orthodoxy was tantamount to Pinochet, Chicago, conservatism, and antisocial policy. Today, in the aftermath of some

> tempering of the policies, but mostly in view of the sheer success of these policies and of the pressure of world opinion, Chile has espoused these policies and rejected populism and interventionism. (Dornbush and Edwards 1994, p. 104)

Many such reports of what went on in the Chilean laboratory have continued to inspire corresponding lessons for policy makers around the world.

From Development Diplomacy to Trade Diplomacy

Chronic inflation had been a central issue in Chile since the nineteenth century but economic controversies on this and other topics radicalized positions in tandem with the 'reform vs. revolution' debate of the 1960s and 1970s. As the United States invested in alternatives to Castro's revolutionary model, Chile's political economy shifted with ever greater passion along the right–left axis, very much shaped by external dynamics.[5] To a large degree, policy dogmatism in Chile reflected and was promoted by rising dogmatism in hemispheric affairs.

Intense cleavages within economics were both cause and effect of that intransigency as issues of security and development assistance became tightly linked.[6] Economists' authority in strategic reasoning had been boosted during the Second World War and so had their collective confidence (Leonard 1991). Economists were no strangers to the defense of market capitalism; conversely, few others could so well paint the pitfalls of markets (Johnson 1977; Lodewijks 2001). Not coincidentally, by the 1940s, following the US lead, world economics was revamping its scientific status with a new emphasis on mathematics and econometric modeling. Neoclassical economics was rising at the expense of previous theoretical pluralism when ever-larger numbers of economists from around the world arrived in the United States, some as students, others as observers of the ongoing revolution in professional economics.

The postwar expansion of graduate-level training generated much doctrinal and curricular controversy among academic economists (Barber 1997). Outside academia, economists gained from opportunities in the emerging multilateral system, including the United Nations. Their preferred analytical tools (cost–benefit analysis, game theory) were reshaping international alliances, redefining institutional frameworks and visions of the future. A telling example is the spread of PPBS (Planning, Programming and Budgeting System), the budgeting technique developed at Rand and widely adopted by the Johnson administration, which was exported to the rest of the world as a system that linked budgeting and economic planning.

The comparatively brawny Chilean economics is best understood in this broader ideational and geopolitical context.[7] Chilean economists, who were outspoken critics of the emerging mathematization of the discipline and its irrelevance to address the challenges of Latin American development (Pinto and Sunkel 1996), benefited more than most from the post-1945 internationalizing trends in economics. Consider, for example, that starting in the 1950s, Chile's rapidly expanded universities and research institutes received a large contingent of local and foreign economists seeking training and employment.

The very concept of periphery was crafted in CEPAL, the United Nations Economic Commission for Latin America, when few were challenging orthodox neoclassical prescriptions with autochthonous economic doctrines. CEPAL was established in 1948 as one of the first United Nations Economic Commissions. One of several multilateral agencies with regional headquarters in Santiago, CEPAL became a fulcrum of economic creativity and internationalism, mounting an ambitious platform where '"thinkers" and "doers" could meet' (Rosenthal 2004, p. 170). From its center of operations in Santiago, CEPAL disseminated development theories through multiple publications and advisory missions aimed at transforming the region and more broadly the world economic order. CEPAL organized multiple training programs. Between the 1960s and the 1990s, over 12 000 participants had attended CEPAL courses and seminars (Montecinos 1997a, p. 289).[8]

While fashioning its own distinctive identity, CEPAL altered the course of economics in Chile through multiple forms of direct influence rather than simply ideational affinity, as in the case of Mexico, where CEPAL had a sub-regional office but where national authorities kept external influences at bay (Babb 2001, p. 77). From the start, CEPAL benefited from Chile's liberal hospitality and, in turn, it afforded Chileans unequalled opportunities to work side by side with fellow Latin American economists (Hira 1999).[9] The first director of CEPAL's year-long training program in economic development was the Chilean Jorge Ahumada. The renowned Celso Furtado, Juan Noyola, José Serra, Aldo Ferrer, Pedro Paz, Víctor Urquidi, Felipe Pazos, among others, were affiliated with CEPAL, and so were economic experts from Europe and the US who came to Santiago as consultants and visiting luminaries. The list includes Jan Tinbergen, Nicholas Kaldor, Dudley Seers, Paul Rosenstein-Rodan and Hollis Chenery.[10] These pioneers in development theorizing were hosted in Chile when the professionalization of economics in the region was still incipient (Love 1996, p. 113).

Chile was obtaining for itself not just a privileged position in the world of economics but it was simultaneously assuming a role in development diplomacy.[11] Chileans played a protagonist role in the promotion of Latin American integration during the period of protected industrialization and were active participants in various international economic organizations. It had been one of the 23 founding countries of the General Agreement on Tariffs and Trade, in 1948. Prebisch and other economists with ties to Chile labored to redefine inter-American relations, for example, by helping to legitimize the Alliance for Progress, often mistakenly understood as a unilateral US initiative adopted by the Kennedy administration (Burger 1998; Porzecanski 2005).[12] In fact, Chile was identified as the country that would showcase the type of progressive, anticommunist reforms proposed. After all, Chile had the strongest Socialist and Communist parties in the region and in coalition these parties had almost won the presidency in 1958, just ahead of Castro's triumph in Cuba. Although loyalty toward Washington was maintained for most of the Cold War, Presidents Frei and Allende pursued an increasingly independent foreign policy that valued multilateralism and supported Third World movements like the Group of 77 and the Non-aligned Movement.

In the 1960s, Santiago had already become 'the crucible of dependency analysis' (Love 1996, p. 191). Rebellious, anti-imperialist postures had been strengthened by exiled leftist intellectuals from Brazil, Argentina and other neighboring countries (Celso Furtado, Fernando H. Cardoso, Theotonio Dos Santos, Ruy Mauro Marini, Vania Bambirra). Their arrival in Chile gave a stronger voice to Marxism and radicalized versions of developmentalism. Allende's so-called 'second path to socialism' further increased Chile's international visibility, diversifying external and trade relations to include socialist countries. More intense demands were made for fair rules in international trade, along with higher and more stable prices for export commodities and more development assistance and reduced protectionism in developed countries. Much of the early enthusiasm for indigenous economic theorizing was recaptured and the community of leftist economists grew increasingly contemptuous of the mainstream professional canon. Economists became more interested in class analysis, history and sociology. In fact, many of Allende's own advisers have attributed analytical and policy errors to the official neglect of monetary and financial variables, seen as 'policy instruments subordinated to the attainment of structural transformations' (Bitar 1986, p. 57; Griffith-Jones 1981).

Allende's economists placed politics over economics because of ideological convictions, but also because few alternative options were left. Chile's confrontation with multinational corporations incensed the Nixon administration into starting a sort of 'economic warfare' by convincing banks, including the World Bank and the Inter-American Development

Bank, to deny credits to Chile (Sigmund 1993, p. 83).[13] Meanwhile Chile's actions were greeted enthusiastically in the developing world. In 1972 for example, Chile was invited to host the Third United Nations Conference on Trade and Development (UNCTAD), an important forum for discussions of North–South problems. And some European governments provided substantial funds (Bitar 1986, p. 83; Sigmund 1993, p. 64). François Miterrand reportedly said: 'The Chilean regime represents the experience closest to what could happen in France' (Palacios 1979, p. 79).

When Pinochet seized power in 1973, not only did the pivot of economics shift radically in favor of CEPAL's critics but CEPAL itself was threatened with expulsion (Rosenthal 2004, p. 177). With Pinochet's fundamentalist embrace of market reforms Chile abandoned third-worldism to court international financiers and foreign investors who celebrated the undoing of heterodox economics. Unilateral, rapid trade liberalization was seen as a catalyst for a form of internationalism based on an outward-oriented market economy.

The military regime relied on the extreme orthodoxy of its economists to counterbalance political ostracism. Its disdain for constitutional norms led to an arms embargo and trade and financial sanctions, all of which were used to chastise Pinochet for his dismal human rights record. The country's reputation was shattered to new extremes with the 1976 murder of Chilean economist Orlando Letelier in the heart of Washington. Letelier was a former senior official at the Inter-American Development Bank, a Chilean Ambassador to the US and Allende's Foreign Minister. His assassination intensified international condemnations of military rule and made it more difficult to secure external loans.

In response, the professional prestige of economists was more widely used in international negotiations, consolidating a tendency to place economists in posts traditionally reserved for professional diplomats or politically skilled individuals. In 1976 Finance Minister Jorge Cauas was appointed ambassador to Washington and in 1978 Harvard-trained José Piñera (the son of Frei's former ambassador to the United Nations) was named Labor Minister. The latter hastily devised a plan to avert an imminent international boycott of Chilean exports proposed by the AFL-CIO in solidarity with Chilean union leaders and to protest deteriorating labor conditions.

By the late 1970s, the international press heralded Pinochet's economists as a trend-setting example for their swift implementation of trade opening, financial deregulation and decentralization, and privatization of state assets. Visits by personalities like Milton Friedman, Gordon Tullock, Frederick von Hayek and others from the libertarian Mont Pelerin Society seemed to confirm the merits of 'the Chilean miracle'.[14]

Variations of the Chilean narrative were diffused to so-called emergent and transition economies. The worldwide Americanization of economics and the proliferation of conservative think tanks, along with the expansion of the specialized economic press in the 1970s and 1980s, contributed to inflate the renown of market success – Chilean style. The patronage of the International Monetary Fund and the World Bank was also important. As Patricio Meller, then an opposition economist, has commented, Chile's dutiful compliance with the recommendations of the IMF during the Pinochet period was unparalleled. Chile became '*más fondista que el Fondo*', he said, paraphrasing the popular maxim of 'more papist than the Pope' (Meller 1990, p. 23). As a result, Chile began to receive abundant external resources from banks and multilateral institutions.

The demand for economists in the private sector grew as banks, corporations and entrepreneurial associations professionalized their operations and became more connected with global businesses and conservative transnational networks. While economic diplomacy marched in to conquer the heart of Chilean foreign policy, economists' jurisdiction expanded in that area too.

Economists' first formal (and contentious) entry into the Foreign Ministry occurred under Allende with the creation of SEREX (*Secretaría de Relaciones Económicas Exteriores*), an agency that was partly dependent on the Central Bank. Later, the Chicago Boys formed a more powerful technocratic niche with the creation of the General Directorate for International Economic Relations, which, according to a former diplomat, amounted to a 'parallel ministry' (Montecinos 1997b).[15]

Under President Aylwin (1990–94) the rivalry between diplomats and the economic team became intense. Chile was then the first to adhere to a US-proposed hemispheric free trade area in the Americas. Many expected that negotiations to join NAFTA as the agreement's fourth partner would succeed. Tellingly, those negotiations were managed from the Finance Ministry. NAFTA did not expand but Chile persisted in its active and diversified commercial policy, signing free trade agreements with an impressive list of countries. Critics have complained that the country's foreign policy suffers from an excessive dose of economicism. The process culminated with the appointment of Alejandro Foxley, the former economics professor, opposition leader and Finance Minister, as Foreign Minister in 2006.

Chicago Economics in Chile

CEPAL was a crucial but not the sole contributor to the internationalization of economics in Chile. An altogether different tipping point was marked by the arrival of a University of Chicago mission in 1955. At the time, both the University of Chicago and the Catholic University economics departments were outsiders seeking to enhance their market and doctrinal competitiveness. The University of Chile had a much stronger economics department than the Catholic University and Chicago's position was marginal compared to economics departments in the Ivy League institutions. The latter needed students but also funding for the Cowles Commission for Research in Economics, which had underwritten the founding of *Econometrica* and supported mathematical economics and had just moved from Chicago to Yale, taking its generous support for quantitative economic research (Barber 1997, p. 19).

The Chicago mission to Chile was sponsored by the US government and private entities interested in building a platform in Latin America from which to change the training of Latin American economists and promote free trade and free markets in the region. The Chile project achieved enormous success (Valdés 1989). Defined by a particular brand of market fundamentalism, the Chicago Boys were soon deployed to other countries. They went to Cuyo, Argentina and also to Cali, Colombia, where Sergio de Castro, a group leader and Pinochet's future Finance Minister, was hired by the Rockefeller Foundation to teach in the early 1960s. By 1958 they had conquered the presidency of the student association at the Catholic University (long-controlled by the Christian Democrats) and by 1965, the group was explaining economic theory to entrepreneurs gathered at one of Chile's major business associations (Fontaine Aldunate 1988, pp. 27–8). Eventually, the export of Chicago economics put Chilean economics onto a new path to fame and forced a reappraisal of the development literature, at least as understood by the promoters of market reforms (Williamson 1994, pp. 21–3).

In the post-coup years, these economists moved from the relative obscurity of writing opinion columns in conservative periodicals and teaching at the Catholic University to Pinochet's cabinet and other top government positions. Many of them had begun working for the research divisions of private conglomerates toward the end of Allende's presidency. Eight of the ten authors of 'The Brick', an economic plan to be implemented after Allende's fall, had studied in Chicago. The group met secretly at the offices of one of the country's peak entrepreneurial associations (Silva 1996, p. 74). Although initially closer to the Navy, the Chicago Boys gained Pinochet's decisive backing, which allowed them to orchestrate an ideological, even a cultural project. Around the ideal of economic freedom the essence of citizenship was redefined as consumer choice. In a sense, by spinning marketization into an overarching anti-statist dogma, the neoliberal formula came of age in Pinochet's Chile, ahead of the Reagan and

Thatcher crusades (Fourcade-Gourinchas and Babb 2002; Harvey 2005, p. 9).

Over the years, having received dozens of scholarships and research grants, the Chicago group widened the impact of its proselytism through academic training programs, publications, think tanks and advisory missions in and out of the region. As of this writing, the vast Chicago network in Latin America can still boast of Professor Arnold Harberger, one of the original members of the Chile Project, as its mentor. The network is recognized for its categorical distinction between 'good' and 'bad' economics, its ideological cohesiveness, its links to business and financial interests, and its efforts to include the general public in its market campaign.

The Catholic University became a sort of subsidiary of Chicago, reproducing its curriculum and science-centered notions of professionalism. Their leftist colleagues were condemned for intellectual parochialism. Only the rigor of neoclassical orthodoxy, it was argued, would lead to Chile's development. The prevailing economic doctrines of the 1950s were countered with an emphasis on price and monetary theory that devalued historical, cultural and social factors. Economic imperialism was defended against multidisciplinary ventures. Consider the statement of a member of the faculty:

> At the University of Chile they had much more interest in the national economy. At the Catholic University economics has always been concerned with scientific advances. We did not touch upon politics. Here professors did not belong to political parties. At the University of Chile, students came out more mature, better prepared for political life. We recognized we had to relate our courses to the national reality but we did not feel very guilty because we were teaching them very good techniques. (interview by the author, Montecinos 1988)

Despite disclaimers like the one just quoted, the Chile project paid attention to policy matters (human capital, inflation) from the start. Chicago Professor Simon Rottenberg, designated in 1956 as responsible for the project in Santiago, conducted research on the social security system, planting the seeds of what decades later would be one of Chile's key privatizing reforms (Valdés 1989, pp. 207–10).

The project was unmistakably political, although the Chicago economists polished their image of technical independence by insisting that the practice of economics should be free of favoritism and partisan biases. Statism was branded unnecessary and destabilizing (Kast 1984) but when the Chicago group took control of the state, they centralized decisions as never before. In the name of fiscal sanity and efficiency, unpopular measures were enforced with revolutionary vehemence. They argued that past policies had led to inefficiencies and false expectations. Redistributive measures had favored well-organized pressure groups, they said, leaving the poor untouched. In 1975, for example, Finance Minister Jorge Cauas, a former economics professor, Central Bank official and World Bank expert, introduced a new economic strategy with an aggressive anti-inflationary plan as its centerpiece. That early use of 'shock therapy' was duly recognized as a historic turning point. Many wondered whether under democratic conditions such a socially regressive policy would have been at all possible. Even part of the entrepreneurial elite suffered the consequences of rigid economic prescriptions. Others saw these policies as the successful beginning of the triumph of market orthodoxy: inflation declined from an annual rate of 600 percent in 1973 to less than 100 percent in 1977. The restructuring program worsened income distribution, defenders argued, but in the long run it improved the country's economic outlook.

With Pinochet the economists' methods and language became institutionalized conventions at the core of the regime's political discourse. The Chicago Boys even persuaded unlikely allies like Jaime Guzmán and his followers, a group of conservative lawyers whose vision for Chile's future followed Franco-style corporatism rather than US-based economic theories.[16] The ideas of Hayek and Michael Novak, the American conservative Catholic philosopher, were embraced by these lawyers as part of their anti-statist platform.

Over time, a growing pool of economists trained in the free-market catechism was deployed to all corners of the administration, including regional and local governments. Contrary to their own precepts, Pinochet's economists followed clientelistic social policies at the municipal level. This strategy enlarged the regime's power base among the poor (Huneeus 2000, p. 373).

The influence exerted by the Chicago group waned with the crisis of the early 1980s.[17] Serious policy errors were made partly because rapid liberalization proceeded without effective supervision and partly because criticisms were silenced and debates forbidden. In spite of their oscillating power, these economists remained central to the regime's identity and legacy. Speaking of Chile's Chicago Boys, University of Chicago Professor and Nobel laureate Gary Becker (1997) said:

> In retrospect, their willingness to work for a cruel dictator and start a different economic approach was one of the best things that happened to Chile. . . . Chile went from a pariah nation controlled by a dictator to an economic role model for the whole undeveloped world. Chile's performance became still more impressive when the government was transformed into a democracy. . . . Their teachers are proud of their richly deserved glory.

Many stars of the profession took the side of the Chilean revolution as a transformative watershed that would for ever disempower their rivals in the discipline as well as charlatans of various types. Milton Friedman's endorsement was unequivocal: 'I do not consider it as evil for an economist to render technical economic advice to the Chilean Government, any more than I would regard it as evil for a physician to give technical medical advice to the Chilean Government to help end a medical plague' (cited in Letelier 1976).[18] Sanctified in the name of science, the combination of free market and political repression sacrificed social justice but many were enthralled by the prospect of defeating collectivistic ideologies.[19] The rapid rise of consumer capitalism (from high-end goods for the rich to imported used garments for the poor) gave tangible signs that the glaring promises of national development would indeed be realized.

Money Doctors

Chilean economists moved from their latecomer status at mid-century to that of heralds of the profession's wisdom in the neoliberal era in part thanks to the mythology surrounding money doctors, archetypes of the cross-national diffusion of economic dicta. Money doctors, operating at the intersection of politics and economics, are more than a simple remedy for a lack of local expertise. They spread ideas, mobilize alliances and peddle investments and loans – along with threats for non-compliance. As Drake (1994) has argued, money doctors act, above all, as connecting mechanisms in the international economic system. Their outsider status is seen as a guarantee of independence when domestic politics enter a stalemate and creditors demand policy uniformity and guarantees of good debtor behavior.

The shadow of Chile's first money doctor, Jean-Gustave Courcelle-Seneuil (1813–92), hovered over policy debates long after he left Chile in 1863. This French free-market doctrinaire and finance specialist, recognized as the father of generations of orthodox economists,[20] was hired by the government in 1855. His international reputation stemmed from his translation of John Stuart Mill's *Principles of Political Economy* and his work at the French Finance ministry. At the University of Chile, Courcelle-Seneuil exerted great influence as a professor of political economy and as an adviser on fiscal policy, banking legislation and foreign credit negotiations.[21]

Over the years Chile made other calls to foreign financial experts. Ambivalence toward these economic wizards, however, was pervasive. As policy brokers, they often served as scapegoats for failures. They were also targets of resentment over hierarchies of power and professional prestige. 'Poor Courcelle-Seneuil!' commiserated Albert Hirschman, for 'virtually every serious ill subsequently experienced by the Chilean economy, from inflation to monoexportation, has been traced to him' (Hirschman 1963, p. 166).

In the interventionist climate of the 1960s, not even the perspicacious Hirschman could have foreseen that by century's end, intrepid descendants of Courcelle-Seneuil would find themselves not the targets of nationalists' wrath, but the carriers of globalism, acting in the money doctor role, responding to the calls made by, or in the name of other ailing nations.

The phenomenon of 'Chile-mania' (Krugman 2005) caught steam when the World Bank, the International Monetary Fund and other arbiters of 'good economics' bestowed more praise than opprobrium on Chilean crusaders of economic liberalism. They had not just reshaped their nation's consciousness and institutions according to the principles of methodological individualism, but from the heart of the developing world the Chilean marketeers appeared to remake economics' modern orthodoxy into a more palatable international canon.

Despite the persistently insidious representation of poor countries as unable to devise technically informed policies,[22] there are early twentieth-century antecedents of Chile's recent well-connected economic experts. As Kenneth P. Jameson (2005) has shown, Latin American economists at that time, although not formally schooled in the discipline and overlooked by historians, made significant contributions by participating in international conferences (that is, the Pan American Congresses, the League of Nations) and producing capable analyses that sometimes contradicted those of their foreign counterparts. The Chilean Guillermo Subercaseaux was one such contributor. As a delegate to the Second Pan American Scientific Congress of 1915–16, Subercaseaux opposed Princeton Professor Edwin Kemmerer's proposal for a Latin Union monetary unit based on the US gold dollar (Jameson 2005). He authored several economic treatises (his 1912 *El Papel Moneda* was published in Paris) and his international connections were extensive, having joined economics associations in the US, Belgium, France and Germany. At the Universidad de Chile, he was an enthusiastic promoter of economics teaching (his 1916 *Manual de Economía Política* had several editions) and as Finance Minister, Subercaseaux championed protectionist policies, attacking Courcelle-Seneuil and his Chilean disciples for the loss of mining resources at the hands of foreign capitalists (Glaser 2003, p. 168, Herrera 1946).

Behind the wave of modernizing reforms in the 1920s, as Patricio Silva has made clear, there was a team of competent technocrats, mostly engineers led by Pablo Ramírez. A brilliant parliamentarian and later Finance Minister, Ramírez saw the combination of economic mismanagement and growing social unrest as the product of oligarchic governance and imperialist domination. Ramírez's recipe for Chile's troubled economy included the creation of a more professionalized public bureaucracy, progressive social legislation of the kind being adopted in Europe, the creation of national industries and the protection of Chile's interests in the foreign-controlled mining sector (Silva 1998). His nationalism recognized, however, the benefits of foreign financing and international alliances. He met with President Herbert C. Hoover, himself a mining engineer and internationally-minded technocratic modernizer who was made an honorary member of the Instituto de Ingenieros de Chile when he visited Chile as president-elect in 1928.

Frequently, the foreign money doctors' proposals resemble ideas previously advanced by the country's own specialists. For example, the creation of the Chilean Central Bank has been credited to the famous Edwin W. Kemmerer, an advocate of the gold standard and balanced budgets with vast international experience and who was supported by foreign investors (Eichengreen 1994). Yet a similar measure had been sponsored by Guillermo Subercaseaux before Kemmerer's mission had even landed in Chile (Glaser 2003, p. 170). Interestingly, Ramírez later justified his own initiatives as being in line with Kemmerer's ideas.

The Klein Saks mission to Chile in the mid-1950s was again prompted not so much by the lack of local expertise as by the need to satisfy foreign creditors and internal political realities (Ffrench-Davis 1973, pp. 25–6; Sierra 1969, p. 54). The country was then facing an inflationary crisis aggravated by declining export earnings and investments and labor mobilizations against an unpopular government. Klein-Saks, a private financial firm with experience in Latin America, proposed measures previously offered by Central Bank officials. The Chilean political right, weary of the ideological leanings of Chile's own economic experts, welcomed the orthodox credentials of the Klein-Saks firm and its connections with the US government and the International Monetary Fund, master of external conditionality.

In these cases, foreign advisers were not so much a substitute for local expertise as a multifaceted political device.[23] Chile's dependence on external counsel declined with the proliferation of local specialists endorsed by an increasingly internationalized economics profession and no longer relegated to the receiving end of transnational economic advice.

Bureaucratic Power

Economics turned into a desirable, well-remunerated profession even before it was formally recognized as an autonomous discipline. Although in the 1940s the School of Law at the *Universidad de Chile* was still a powerhouse in the teaching of political economy and economic policy courses

(Luis Enrique Marshall and Daniel Martner, authors of two influential economics textbooks in 1936 and 1941 respectively, were among the most respected and influential scholars), the bureaucratic reach of professional economists was fast surpassing that of lawyers, engineers and other competing professionals. By the end of that decade, the separation of law and economics was clearly established and economists were successfully colonizing the academy, politics and the state (Muñoz 1993).

The economists' skills and vision were embraced within the public bureaucracy early, especially in agencies with a strong tradition of meritocratic recruitment. Several of the first economics graduates were considered for cabinet-level appointments in the 1950s although not until 1961 was a formally-trained economist sworn in as minister. In the 1950s and 1960s the influence of economists was still moderate and the support from politicians was often ambivalent and contested, but by the 1970s it was a well-established trend to have economists at the top of the economic bureaucracy.

Since then, economists with graduate degrees in foreign universities have constituted a large and influential 'critical mass' and cabinet-level appointments favor them even in areas like labor, health and education or in purely political posts. Less internationally-connected individuals, who never worked abroad, did not study or teach in foreign universities and who cannot converse comfortably about technical matters with foreign and domestic interlocutors, have practically vanished from the shortlist of candidates for Finance and Economy Ministers.

Several of the first professional economists were hired by the *Corporación de Fomento de la Producción* (CORFO), a powerful agency created under the Popular Front government in 1939 to advance industrialization through the creation of large enterprises (electricity, steel, oil) and through investments in manufacturing, mining, agriculture and other sectors. CORFO pioneered economic research, national accounting and development planning (Montecinos 1988).

At the Central Bank, economists forged the earliest and most extensive web of transnational connections. Interactions with multilateral institutions, external investors and creditors and other central bankers afforded these economists privileged access to sources of professional prestige.[24] During the Bank's early decades, a German economist, Herman Max, was enlisted to head the Research Division. He greatly contributed to the development of academic research, mentoring many young economists and transforming the Bank's library into one of Chile's best in economics.[25] Upon his retirement in 1959, Max was replaced by Jorge Marshall, the first Chilean with an economics doctorate (Harvard, 1957). Marshall, who had served previously on the staff of the International Monetary

Fund in Washington, remained at the Central Bank until the 1970s and later was a professor at the Universidad de Chile where he enjoyed a sizeable reputation.

Other stars of the profession benefited from the standing and privileges accorded to Bank economists. Consider, from a very long list of possible examples, the case of Felipe Herrera, who in 1946 had been awarded the Claudio Planet Lavín prize for the best thesis in economic science at the School of Law (Tomassini 1997, p. 76).[26] Upon graduation, Herrera was offered a teaching position in economic policy and hired by the Central Bank. He studied at the London School of Economics with a scholarship from the British Council between 1950 and 1951 and was appointed Finance Minister in 1953. An early disseminator of Keynesian ideas and an enthusiastic supporter of Latin American economic integration, Herrera authored many books and held prominent international posts. He became the first president of the Inter-American Development Bank in 1960, where he stayed until 1971 overseeing an institution that aspired to be an alternative to the Washington-controlled IMF and World Bank.

The international connections and prestige of the Central Bank were enhanced by the Bank's own scholarship program, which allowed many of its economists to study abroad. In recent years the Central Bank is said to resemble a prestigious academic department, with over 25 holders of economics doctorates doing high-caliber research, a well-regarded economics journal among other in-house publications, and a series of professional conferences that attract international experts and academics.[27]

In 1989, a few days before the presidential election that ended the military period, a law changed the bank's statute, severing its ties to the Finance Ministry. It has been argued that the bank's autonomy strengthened the technical nature of appointments. According to the new rules, board members could not be removed for ten years. All 13 individuals appointed to the board since 1990 have been economists; of them four have PhDs, four are doctoral candidates and four hold MAs or equivalent degrees (Céspedes and Valdés 2006).

The number of economists at the core of the economic bureaucracy rose markedly in the 1960s. The Budget Bureau, for example, had been created in 1927 but was first headed by an economist in 1954. Sergio Molina held the post until he became Finance Minister a decade later. After its reorganization in 1960, this agency acquired ample powers and enlarged its pool of budgetary analysts. The new staff pressed the adoption of internationally-accepted budgetary techniques, although not always successfully, as in the case of a bill sent to Congress in 1969 to introduce a new budgeting system based on PPBS. The proposal was opposed by political and entrepreneurial interests and defeated. Government agencies with expansionary agendas challenged the new, tighter budgetary rules by hiring their own experts in an effort to regain budgetary autonomy and bypass the Budget Bureau.[28] Another strategy was to negotiate foreign loans directly, a task facilitated by well-placed Chilean economists in Washington, Felipe Herrera among them.

The next major change in budgetary rules came in 1975 (*Ley Orgánica de la Administración Financiera del Estado*, D.L. 1263), when Congress was closed, the press was under government control and the anti-statist Chicago Boys occupied key positions in the bureaucracy. A series of fiscal reforms, including a regressive new tax system and drastic budget cuts were introduced without opposition (95 000 public employees were dismissed during Pinochet's first four years). During this period, however, the Budget Bureau was among the agencies that lost some of their traditional authority to ODEPLAN, an increasingly influential policy center. At the heart of the Chicago Boys network, ODEPLAN promoted and monitored cost–benefit analysis and project evaluation as a methodology to rationalize public spending and played a major role in the restructuring of the public sector.

In the mid-1960s, the creation of ODEPLAN, the *Oficina de Planificación Nacional*, had enormously increased the demand for economists. A group of US-trained economists set up to develop state-of-the-art modeling for which ODEPLAN signed a collaborative agreement with the Center for International Studies at MIT. Eduardo García d'Acuña, one of ODEPLAN's high-ranking economists (PhD from MIT), worked in that project. Rosenstein-Rodan, Carlos Díaz Alejandro, Edmar Bacha and Lance Taylor were among the MIT representatives. Not even the Finance Ministry had a comparable technical staff.

Those lofty endorsements notwithstanding, ODEPLAN's political and financial resources remained modest during its first decade.[29] President Frei supported planning but he was above all a fiscal conservative and kept ODEPLAN as a supra-ministerial agency in the office of the presidency. Facing a split between moderate and radical reformist factions in the administration, Frei was reluctant to share his authority with a powerful planning ministry. As other ministries created their own planning divisions and regional governments established theirs as well, the demand for economists kept growing.

President Allende elevated ODEPLAN to the status of autonomous ministry but it was the planning-averse Chicago Boys under Pinochet who gave ODEPLAN greatest power. ODEPLAN also became the preeminent recruitment tool for young economists, sending scores of them to train at the University of Chicago. ODEPLAN imposed strict prescriptions in all policy areas arguing that the scientific method should

Table 4.1 Ministers of Finance and Economy, 1990–2006

Ministers of Finance	Ministers of Economy
Foxley (PhD Wisconsin)	Ominami (PhD U. Paris)
Aninat (PhD Harvard)	Marshall (PhD Harvard)
Marfán (PhD Yale)	García (PhD Berkeley)
Eyzaguirre (PhDc Harvard)*	Leiva (PhDc Berkeley)*
Velasco (PhD Columbia)	de Gregorio (PhD MIT)
	Rodríguez (PhD Boston)

Note: *PhD candidate.

replace the previous irrational and obsolete models of decision-making. Even the regime's generals found it difficult to transgress these new rules (Montecinos 1988).

After the economic crisis of the early 1980s the government acknowledged serious policy errors and a pragmatic accommodation with interest groups led to policy adjustments (Silva 1996). Although the Chicago Boys lost some of their enormous sway, the power of economists in Chile's bureaucracy was not diminished. Since 1990 the Ministries of Finance and Economy continued to employ many economists with doctoral credentials from prestigious universities. All subsequent Finance Ministers and all but three Economy Ministers have been alumni of doctoral programs in economics, as shown in Table 4.1.[30]

These ministers' terms in office were often bracketed by academic appointments in Chile and abroad. The distinction between academic and non-academic economists in Chile is closer to the European than to the US model (see Frey and Eichenberg 1993). At times, the government has drained economics departments of most of their faculty, as happened in 1964 when President Eduardo Frei took office, again in the 1970s when the Chicago Boys moved from the Catholic University to the state apparatus, and yet again in the 1990s when those opposed to Pinochet left opposition research centers to fill government jobs. Table 4.2 lists Ministers of Finance and Economy with active academic careers.[31]

Economists and Political Democratization

Much controversy has been prompted by the marriage of democracy and market economics under the auspices of a center-left technocracy (Puryear 1994; Silva 1991). The technocratic phenomenon in Chile, however, contrary to common manifestations, is not confined to the bureaucracy. Indeed, one of its distinctive features is that it permeates the entire

Table 4.2 Ministers of Finance and Economy, who were also economics professors, 1961–2006

Ministers of Finance	Tenure	Ministers of Economy	Tenure
Molina	1964–68	Escobar	1961–63
Cauas	1974–76	Vuksovic	1970–72
de Castro	1976–82	Matus	1972–72
de la Cuadra	1982–82	Cademártori	1973–73
Lüders	1982–83	de Castro	1975–76
Escobar	1984–85	Baraona	1976–78
Foxley	1990–94	Federici	1979–80
Eyzaguirre	2000–06	Lüders	1982–83
Velasco	2006–	Passicot	1983–84
		Marshall	1992–93
		Leiva	1998–2000
		de Gregorio	2000–01
		Rodríguez	2001–06

administration as well as the legislature, political parties, and even social movements (Montecinos 1998a, 2003).

While Congress was closed, outlawed political parties looked for new principles of legitimation to challenge the alleged irresponsibility and ineptitude of politicians and reconstitute a viable party system. Dialog among economists facilitated interparty negotiations by enhancing an image of pragmatism and credibility as part of a campaign to modernize party structures and leadership (Boeninger 1997, p. 369). Opposition economists had impressive credentials and contacts with foreign foundations; their research centers helped voice criticisms against government policies (Puryear 1994). The political right also had economists who favored compromise and a more 'rational' approach to politics. Symbolically, the technification of political leadership reduced anxiety over the risks of an unpredictable democratization (Montecinos 1998b).

After 1990, the preservation of Chile's lofty place in international rankings of economic performance came to be regarded as integral to political realignments among long-proscribed parties. Pinochet's economists became active members of right-wing political parties and dispersed to recently-created private universities and conservative think tanks. On the center-left, political parties continued their display of economists to signal compliance with the new rituals of free-market governance and their commitment to what has been called the 'post-revolutionary left' (Roberts 1998, p. 188).

From pensions to unions to schools and neighborhoods, institutions had already been deeply changed by market reforms for which Chileans paid a heavy price. The reforms would not be rolled back (Foxley 1987). The crux of the policies adopted by Pinochet's successors rested on balancing social spending and macroeconomic stability. The pre-coup adversarial political culture was transformed. Moderation and compromise bridged the previously gaping ideological divide that for decades pitted market advocates against state partisans. The economists' role in this change contributed to their own political rise.

A strong indication of this rise is their growing presence in electoral politics. While economists formally appeared as advisers to presidential candidates as far back as 1958 (drafting the economic platforms of Frei and Allende), today the number of economists at the top of Chile's political roster is among the highest anywhere. They are newspaper columnists and party propagandists. Economists are also running as party candidates and they are holders of high office. President Ricardo Lagos (1999–2006), a socialist, had an economics doctorate from Duke.[32] In 1999, the third election since the transition to civilian rule, Lagos and his main rival, the conservative economist Joaquín Lavín (MA from the University of Chicago), evenly divided the electorate. Lagos prevailed with 51.3 percent of the vote in the second round.[33] Michelle Bachelet, the winner of the 2006 presidential campaign and a medical doctor, is the only major presidential candidate in recent years without formal training in economics, but she, like all the other frontrunners, counted on the advice of teams of economists with PhDs.

In striking contrast with the heavy reliance on political parties in the pre-coup period, the personalization of political campaigns and the enormous weight of public opinion polls since the transition to democracy have made it easier for economist-politicians to gain electoral competitiveness. Candidates now emphasize their own credentials and image, avoiding explicit references to party affiliation.

The economists' jurisdiction also extended rapidly into the legislative branch after 1990. The ascending pace was much faster than in the executive, where economists conquered new positions gradually over a period of several decades. This 'technocratic spillover' into the legislature is particularly clear in the composition of the Finance committees, the most powerful in both the Senate and the Chamber of Deputies (Montecinos 2003).

Historically the Chilean Congress has been characterized as an unusually professionalized and technically competent legislature, but in the pre-1973 Congress there was only one economist, Deputy José Cademártori of the Communist Party. By contrast, in 2000 most members of the Finance Committees of the Senate (5 members) and the Chamber of Deputies (13 members) were economists, as seen in Table 4.3.

Table 4.3 Congressional finance committees, 2000

Senate 5 members	%	Chamber of Deputies 13 members	%
Economists	80	Economists	54
Lawyers	20	Lawyers	23
Others	0	Others	23
Total	100	Total	100

Source: Montecinos (2003).

One could expect that eventually economists will also influence the judiciary. Indeed, legal education in Chile has already introduced economics training,[34] and calls have begun to increase the economic literacy of judges trained under the supposedly anti-market bias of Continental legal traditions (Saavedra and Soto 2006, pp. 59–63). The largest and more internationalized private law firms have started to incorporate economists in their staff (interview material). Dezalay and Garth (2002, p. 40) trace the trend among Latin American lawyers to invest in economic expertise to the debt crisis of the 1980s.

The Business of Economics

Traditionally, Chilean economists were more attracted to policy-making than to the private sector, with the exception of the Chicago Boys who as early as the 1960s were working for business conglomerates and creating private consulting firms. CESEC was one that achieved some prominence advising Jorge Alessandri, the conservative candidate in the 1970 presidential campaign (Fontaine Aldunate 1988, p. 32). Yet it was during the Pinochet period that the boundaries between various segments of the economists' professional labor market grew more porous.

The alliance of technocratic, military and business elites that internationalized the economy in the 1970s and 1980s used the suspension of democratic practices to their own benefit in audacious ways. While economists advertised their policy-making style as economic rationalization to eliminate past abuses of incompetent, self-interested bureaucrats and politicians, opaque practices were used to privatize state industries, pension funds and financial services. Without public debate and congressional oversight, Pinochet's marketeers came to 'privatize themselves' (Mönckeberg 2001). Often, the transfer of public patrimony ended up in the hands of a few well-placed officials and their associates who joined the ranks of foreign conglomerates. While a new, more transnational local business class was formed, charges of preferential treatment were furiously contested: 'If people are earning money, it is because they are productive and efficient', said Alvaro Bardón, a top government economist (Constable and Valenzuela 1991, p. 192). The distinction between technocrats and capitalists faded (Silva 1996, p. 141).

Business opportunities were sometimes linked to the commercialization of expertise as consulting firms began to employ prominent economists. For example, Professor Harberger was hired in 1981 by Rolf Lüders, one of his former students, business executive and future Finance Minister, to study the real estate market (Fontaine Aldunate 1988, p. 167). Harberger and another disciple, Ernesto Fontaine, an economics professor at the Catholic University, formed Harberger Limitada in1987 (Délano and Traslaviña 1989, p. 15). Currently, the participation of prominent economists in business ventures is quite common. Moneymaking activities have turned many academic and government economists from mere professionals into prosperous entrepreneurs, wealthy financiers and corporate executives.

The emergence of business economists has coincided with a growing specter of fraud and dishonesty involving policy-makers. As in other countries in the region (Conaghan 2005), marketization and corruption have advanced hand-in-hand.[35] The probity record that made generations of Chileans so proud is being questioned as never before (OECD 2007). Several corruption scandals involving high-ranking officials under and after Pinochet have been aired in the press and the courts in recent years. New anti-corruption legislation and administrative measures have been introduced, however, and Chile retains its high-ranking position in international comparisons. The Transparency International index places Chile 22nd in the world in 2007, ahead of all other Latin American countries (Transparency International 2007).

ECONOMICS EDUCATION

The extraordinary ascent of economists in Chile could not have been possible without substantial support for economics education. The state played a major role but so did the vast web of international contacts that Chilean economists forged over time. Many Chileans obtained financial aid from the universities they attended, since economics departments abroad largely depend on the recruitment of international students. Over half of graduate students in economics in the US are foreigners; a very large percentage of them receive funds working as teaching or research assistants, especially after they reach the dissertation stage (Aslanbeigui and Montecinos, 1998).

The School of Commerce and Economics at the University of Chile was founded in 1935 by Pedro Aguirre Cerda. In a preview of present-day merging of economic expertise and presidential politics, the election of 1938 elevated Aguirre Cerda to the presidency as the Popular Front candidate. He prevailed in a tight contest against the conservative Gustavo Ross who competed with a successful record as Finance Minister.[36]

Soon after the school's creation, in 1942, a commission report on economics teaching recommended the inclusion of courses in statistics and econometrics. Substantial curricular changes were made to strengthen economic theory partly at the urging of Flavián Levine, who had registered the year the school opened and became an indefatigable reformer and Keynes's admirer. Keynesianism was further strengthened with Felipe Herrera's *Fundamentos de la Política Fiscal* (1951), published after his return from the London School of Economics.

Despite the lack of library and other resources (Levine ordered his own library collection from London which he paid for with money from a lottery prize; see Muñoz 1993, p. 17) gradually, larger and more capable cohorts of economics students enrolled. Law students were being encouraged to study economics to raise the level of economic expertise in the legal profession and soften the competition from the newly minted 'commercial engineers'.[37] The promising Ricardo Lagos, for example, got his law degree with an influential and fiercely debated thesis, the first systematic analysis of the concentration of economic power in Chile.[38] In the fluid professional landscape of the period, engineers resisted the label 'commercial engineering' which they regarded as an unacceptable usurpation of their credentials, but to no avail. To this day, the title is awarded to economics and business administration graduates.

A measure of internationalization was achieved early with the arrival of Ernest Wagemann, a Chilean-born economist who had achieved professional success in Germany. He returned in 1949 to direct the Instituto de Economía at the University of Chile. Another influential figure in the internationalization of the profession was Joseph Grunwald, an economics professor at Columbia University who joined the faculty at the University of Chile in 1954 and stayed for seven years (Valdés 1989, p. 156). As director of the Instituto de Economía, he gave new impetus to economic research and strengthened ties with universities in the US. The Chileans Aníbal Pinto and Osvaldo Sunkel, who studied at LSE in the late 1940s became prominent exponents of the CEPAL school, also infused economics education with up-to-date disciplinary trends.

Although economics education gained in stature in the 1940s, it was not until 1951 that a commercial engineer directed the school of economics, replacing lawyers and engineers. And it was only in 1955 that an economist, Luis Escobar Cerda, was named dean of the Facultad de Ciencias Económicas. By this time, more full-time professors had been hired and economics as a field of specialization had been separated from the more practical area of business administration, a change Escobar instituted after his stay at Harvard in the mid-1950s (Escobar 1991, pp. 27–32). This enhanced the intellectual prestige of the former, but did little to benefit the latter, which did not engage in research and had limited success recruiting future businessmen; on-the-job training in family-owned firms was then preferred to formal academic training.

The *Facultad de Comercio y Ciencias Económicas* at the Catholic University was less prestigious, although it was older (founded in 1924). For the first two decades most courses focused on commerce and accounting, despite a series of curricular changes in 1928, 1931 and 1942. All twenty members of its faculty were part-time, mostly lawyers and civil servants self-taught in those subjects (Escobar 1991, p. 15; Vial 1999, pp. 12, 19). Graduates at the Catholic University began to be awarded the title of 'commercial engineers' in 1942 in response to students' perceived disadvantages when compared to their counterparts at the University of Chile (Vial 1999, p. 13). Although dominated by Chicago graduates since the early 1960s, there was a short-lived period of doctrinal pluralism that, according to Vial (1999, p. 217), was prompted by the Ford foundation. In 1971 funding for the graduate program was conditioned on the hiring of Osvaldo Sunkel and Sergio Molina, former Finance Minister under Frei (both joined the faculty). At the time, the left-leaning Eduardo García, previously employed by ODEPLAN, was the interim chair of economics. About one-third of the department faculty had resigned or left the country in response to the university reforms of 1968 and the election of a socialist president two years later (Vial 1999, p. 218). The Chicago-trained professors saw Chile moving in a dangerous direction. In addition to ideological reasons, new opportunities emerged in the private sector as impatient entrepreneurs sought professional advice to defend themselves against the rising tide of reformism.

Although only two universities trained professionals in the discipline, the number of commercial engineering graduates grew steadily, from less than 100 in 1960 to 286 in 1980 (Montecinos 1988, p. 410). According to one estimate, the number of economists in Chile rose from 121 in the early 1960s to 727 in 1970 (Valdés 1989, p. 269). By the early 1980s, the field's popularity was at a new peak with enrollment reaching 6000 students (Sanfuentes 1981). As the education reform of 1980 opened the way to private universities, the total number of institutions of higher education went from eight in 1980 to 64 in 2004, with 11 universities offering economics as a field of specialization within commercial engineering. As many as 24 000 students were enrolled in commercial engineering that year. About 300 students were specializing in economics and the rest in business administration (Larroulet and Domper 2006).

The overall increase in the number of students reflects in part a rise in the number of foreign economics students. The first significant expansion of international students occurred after the University of Chile created a graduate-level economics program, ESCOLATINA (*Escuela de Estudios Económicos Latinoamericanos*), in 1957. By then, economics teaching in Chile was considered the best in the region. (Buenos Aires had been regarded as the best in the first decades of the 20th century (Love 1996, p. 122). Already in 1953, in the context of a conference of Latin American schools of economics held in Santiago, Raúl Prebisch, the head of CEPAL, proposed the creation of a 'pilot school of economics' for the training of Latin American economists in Santiago, a task to which CEPAL was committed (Valdés 1989, p. 164).

The number of foreign professors rose as well after ESCOLATINA was created, and so did the level of foreign funding. In 1965, for example, the Ford Foundation sponsored a comprehensive exchange agreement between the University of Chile and the University of California (Chile–California program) to improve training and research in agricultural economics.

ESCOLATINA is said to have lived its golden years in the late 1960s. In 1967/68, Edgardo Boeninger, the head of the Facultad de Economía, oversaw an important curricular reform that made ESCOLATINA more attractive as an alternative to graduate studies in the US. Students were chosen among capable applicants through a carefully managed selection process. Professors traveled to various countries in the region to test and interview prospective students. ESCOLATINA teaching corps included several foreign professors. In 1968, foreign faculty members included: Henri Bruton, Carlos Díaz-Alejandro, B. Henrick, A. Martin, G. Beijaut, Ann Zammit, M. Schubick, John Strassma, Solon Barraclough, Marcos Mamalakis and Keith Griffin.[39] In addition, several of the new Chilean PhDs joined the faculty: Carlos Massad, Carlos Hurtado, Oscar Muñoz and Ricardo Lagos among others.[40]

The Catholic University, too, was improving the quality of economics training thanks to the exchange agreement with the University of Chicago. That agreement required that all students enrolled in Chicago. Initially, the offer of an exchange with Chicago was made by an official of the US Embassy in Santiago to the University of Chile, but it was rejected out of concerns regarding academic pluralism. The decision was correct, according to Luis Escobar Cerda, then the head of the economics department, and also unavoidable: 'It would have been like sending all the students to the University Patrice Lumumba in the Soviet Union. What could have happened in Chile after 20 years?' (Escobar Cerda 1991, p. 34).

The 1960s was a period of heated curricular debates. Gaping cleavages within the profession mirrored and reinforced broader ideological battles and the growing polarization of party politics. As the Chicago school became established, on the left, students and professors demanded more radical approaches to the study of economic development. Those recently returned from graduate schools in the US argued that the judicious use of neoclassical ideas and sophisticated technical instruments should complement CEPAL-style structuralism, then the dominant theoretical view. Following student mobilizations and class boycotts, the *Facultad de Economía* at the University of Chile eventually split in 1971; two schools emerged with different curricula and separate campuses. The left controlled the Northern Campus (*Sede Norte*), which focused on Marxist political economy. The Christian Democrats dominated the Western Campus (*Sede Occidente*). Even the library was divided without much of a quarrel. A professor I interviewed explained that 'most people were just not interested in what was been taught at the other campus' (Montecinos 1988).

An account of the international connections of economics in Chile must also consider the active role played by European universities and other institutions, which sustained resistance to Amcricanization, at least temporarily. Deep ties to Continental Europe relied partly on connections between the Chilean class-based multi-party system and several counterparts in Europe. The Christian Democrats, for example, developed various forms of collaboration with the German, Belgian and Italian Christian Democratic parties. The church's influence over education and economic doctrines was also important,[41] as were its ties to political parties, labor movements and the press. At DESAL (Center for Latin American Economic and Social Development), for example, the Belgian Jesuit Roger Vekemans exerted enormous influence over the funding and orientation of education abroad, and so did the Centro Bellarmino.

In sum, transnational ties with the US and Europe informed tensions among Marxist, social democratic and conservative visions of economics and development, pitting critics and defenders of capitalism against one another. These ties also often placed Chile at the core of international actions in Latin America.

Economics Students Abroad

Chileans began to enroll in graduate economics programs abroad in the 1940s. The trend accelerated in the 1960s remained focused on the United States and England, although Spain also attracted students beginning in

Table 4.4 MIDEPLAN scholarships for economists, 1981–2006

US		UK		Spain		Others	
No.	Institution	No.	Institution	No.	Institution	No.	Country
19	Chicago	8	LSE	3	Complutense	2	Germany
17	UCLA	7	Cambridge	3	Polit. Cataluña	2	Belgium
13	Boston	3	U. London	2	Barcelona	2	France
9	Harvard	3	Warwick	2	Navarra	1	Italy
9	Berkeley	3	U. York	10	Others	1	Australia
9	MIT	12	Others			1	Japan
53	Others						
139	Total	36	Total	20	Total	9	Total

Source: www.MIDEPLAN.cl/admin/docdescargas/centrodoc/becas.

the late 1980s. Government sponsorship complemented external funding primarily through two scholarship programs: one at the Central Bank and the other at MIDEPLAN (the former ODEPLAN). Of the total of 2009 scholarships that MIDEPLAN awarded in the 1981–2006 period, 204 went to economics students. Less than a third of them enrolled in universities outside the US, and within the US the concentration is also striking, as illustrated by the data in Table 4.4.

Economists employed at the Central Bank had access to a separate and highly prestigious scholarship program. Data for the 1977–2001 period show that a total of 39 economists received financial support (usually for three years) to attend the universities shown in Table 4.5.

Several observations can be made regarding the data on scholarships presented below, in addition to the concentration of economics students in US universities. First, no scholarships were given to study economics in Latin America or other less developed regions; Chileans overwhelmingly target world-class institutions. Second, Chicago attracted the largest number of students, as expected. UCLA's second place is explained by the role played by the move there in 1984 of Arnold Harberger, a patron of Chilean economics since the 1950s (Fontaine Aldunate 1988). But other major universities are also represented. Over time, the community of foreign-educated economists has become less uniform than the 'Chicago Boys' label would suggest, but sufficiently homogeneous to facilitate collegiality and a public image of great cohesiveness. Economists in Chile are perceived – and see themselves – as an exclusive and cosmopolitan club, in which membership is reserved for those who have passed the rigorous initiation rituals of the PhD. Third, the sheer number of economists with

Table 4.5 Central Bank scholarships, 1977–2001

Number	University
8	Chicago
7	UCLA
14	Other US Universities*
4	Universities in Spain**
5	Universities in UK***
1	University in Germany
39	Total

Notes:
*NYU (3); MIT (2); Minnesota (2); Harvard (1); Columbia (1); Boston (1); Rochester (1); University of Pennsylvania (1); Georgetown (1)
**Autónoma de Madrid (1); ESADE 2); IESE (1)
*** Cambridge (3); University of London (1); Reading (1)

Source: Central Bank.

doctoral degrees, or who have attended graduate programs without completing the PhD is so high that their impact can hardly be underestimated. There is no official estimate but economics doctorates are very numerous, considering the country's population.[42] Anecdotal evidence indicates that it is common among economists to encourage their children to enroll in economics programs abroad, much as military officers, lawyers or physicians have traditionally motivated theirs to join their professions. As mentioned earlier, the possession of a PhD in economics is a winning ticket to enter the country's political elite and international policy and financial circles.

Historically, most foreign-trained economists have returned to Chile. Unlike other Latin American economists whose countries offered less attractive professional opportunities, jobs in Chile abounded and salaries were competitive for those working as government advisers, university professors or international civil servants. Economists' expertise was valued and rewarded with competitive salaries. Several multilateral agencies with offices in Chile not only offered prized working conditions but also the prestige of semi-diplomatic status. Aside from a dynamic job market, the professional milieu in Chile was intellectually and politically exciting.

Economics graduates have returned to Chile also because scholarships provided by government and academic institutions require recipients do so for a specified length of time (typically doubling the number of years they spend abroad). In fact, during the 1970s and 1980s when the Chicago Boys had full control of the policy apparatus and most Chileans went to the University of Chicago (only four students went to Chicago between 1990 and 2006 with MIDEPLAN scholarships), students were often urged to enter government service before they had completed their doctoral degrees.[43] By the 1990s pressures for premature return had declined considerably. Students are currently compelled to complete their programs. The most desirable positions in academic and government institutions are out of reach without a PhD in hand, and without a doctoral degree even the chances of political success are limited.

A sign of the value now accorded to the doctoral degree is the adoption of more stringent recruitment and evaluation standards for academic economists. Their profile indicates that in recent years they are much more likely to have completed their doctorates; they have more opportunities to teach graduate level courses; they face a more competitive labor market; they are expected to be active in research, participating in international conferences and publishing regularly in leading professional journals. Economics departments have been experimenting with various incentive systems to promote among their faculty a commitment to applied but technically sophisticated research, as well as high standards of excellence in teaching.

A 1971 report on the impact of the Ford Foundation on the development of economics in Chile (cited in Valdés 1989, p. 270) states that the number of economics professors had gone from 32 to 79 between 1960 and 1971, with a significant increase in the percentage of full-time faculty as well as in the number of PhDs (16), MAs (16) and ABDs (14). Thirty years later, the faculty at the country's main economics programs looks much changed, although the evolution has been far from linear.

When the Department of Economics at the University of Chile was in the hands of the Chicago Boys, scarce mention was made of alternative viewpoints, 'except in caricatured and distorted versions . . . taken out of context' (Sunkel 1993, p. 3). The enforcement of intellectual conformity led to resignations and politically-motivated dismissals. 'What is the academic logic behind the fact that those with only a Master's degree exclude from the university others who have a PhD?', protested Patricio Meller, who had joined CIEPLAN (Meller 1987). CIEPLAN belonged to a network of independent research centers, a kind of parallel academic system that kept economic researchers in good international standing and preserved a measure of academic pluralism alive during the years of authoritarian rule.[44] The international prestige of Chilean universities languished for several years under the control of government-appointed authorities, some of them active-duty generals and admirals. Economics, however, rose in popularity among students seeking promising careers in government and businesses. ESCOLATINA was replaced in the 1980s by a less advanced program.

Table 4.6 Faculty credentials, Department of Economics, University of Chile

University	Profesores investigadores
UCLA	4 PhD
Maryland	3 PhD
Columbia	2 PhD
Duke	1 PhD
U. Pennsylvania	1 PhD
U. California	1 PhD
Minnesota	1 PhD
Oxford	1 PhD
U. College, London	1 PhD

Source: *Memoria 1998–99*, Departamento de Economía, Universidad de Chile.

Table 4.7 Faculty credentials, Centro de Economía Aplicada (CEA), University of Chile

University	Profesores investigadores
Berkeley	4 PhD
MIT	3 PhD
Cambridge	1 PhD
U. Pennsylvania	1 PhD
Minnesota	1 PhD
Boston	1 PhD
Cornell	1 PhD

Source: CEA: *Activity Report 2005–2006,* Facultad de Ciencias Físicas y Matemáticas, U. de Chile.

In 1992, only two professors in the economics department at the University of Chile had completed their doctoral degree. But less than a decade later, of the 20 profesores investigadores, 15 had PhDs in economics, one was a doctoral candidate, and one had a PhD in mathematical modeling. Only one member of the faculty had stopped with a Master's degree (Minnesota).[45] The diversity of degrees had increased as well; there were graduates from as many as seven US universities, and two held degrees from universities in the UK (Table 4.6).

At the *Centro de Economía Aplicada* (CEA) of the University of Chile, generally recognized as the most rigorous economics center in the country, all *profesores investigadores* have a PhD in economics (Table 4.7). CEA is housed within the Department of Industrial Engineering: half of its 12 professors have undergraduate degrees in engineering, and most of its students come from the School of Engineering. Their graduates are regularly admitted to top foreign universities and find employment at national and international organizations. CEA is primarily a graduate-level program. Its curriculum and research agenda have a strong mathematical emphasis, but technical sophistication is combined with an explicit commitment to apply economic theory to development issues as well as to participate and influence public policy debates. Opinion articles by CEA staff appear regularly in the press. One of the most widely read is the column by Eduardo Engel, who remains affiliated to CEA as a research associate although a few years ago was offered a professorship at Yale, where he is currently a member of the famous Cowles Foundation (previously Cowles Commission). The publication record of CEA faculty in national and international journals is enviable. Several members of the faculty were associated with CIEPLAN, the prestigious opposition think tank that played a major role challenging economic policies in the 1970s and 1980s.

Two other graduate-level programs are offered jointly by the Universidad Alberto Hurtado and Georgetown University, both Jesuit institutions. One of these programs, the Master of Applied Economics, is aimed at professionals in the social sciences, law and engineering and has lower mathematical requirements. Their Master of Arts in Economics, which began in 1987, is unique in that its students simultaneously obtain an academic degree in a US university. Georgetown counts as approved the first year of studies in Santiago for those who choose to register in the doctoral program in Washington. All nine faculty members hold doctoral degrees from almost as many foreign universities (Table 4.8).

Four decades after it became the cradle of the Chicago School in Latin America, economics at the Catholic University remained heavily dominated by the Chicago Boys. In 2000, ten of its faculty members were Chicago graduates. No other economics program at the time had so many professors trained in the same university. More tellingly, no one with an economics degree from Chicago was then teaching at the other three institutions. In 2000, of a total of 21 professors, only 12 had PhDs.[46] Six years later, however, the faculty profile at the Catholic University had changed significantly. New hires were required to have completed their doctorates and the range of universities represented in the list of faculty credentials was broader, as shown in Table 4.9. The Chicago group is also dominant in many of the private universities that emerged in the 1980s (that is, Universidad del Desarrollo, Universidad de los Andes, Universidad Finis Terrae and Universidad Andrés Bello, among others).

Table 4.8 Faculty credentials, Master of Arts in Economics, ILADES/ Georgetown, Universidad Alberto Hurtado

University	Full-time Professors
Cambridge	1 PhD
Minnesota	1 PhD
Michigan	1 PhD
Cornell	1 PhD
Georgetown	1 PhD
Texas A&M	2 PhD
U. of London	1 PhD
U. Pennsylvania	1 PhD

Source: Prospectus, Master of Arts in Economics, Departamento de Economía y Administración, Universidad Alberto Hurtado.

Table 4.9 Faculty credentials, Departament of Economics, Catholic University

University	Full-time Professors
Chicago	1 PhD
MIT	1 PhD
Harvard	1 PhD
Georgetown	1 PhD
UCLA	1 PhD
Maryland	1 PhD
Cornell	1 PhD
Oxford	1 PhD
Berkeley	1 PhD
Minnesota	1 PhD

Source: Webpage Departamento de Economía, Universidad Católica de Chile.

The data show that in the absence of a single system for academic ranking, each program uses its own titles, academic hierarchy and promotion scale. Traditionally, it was uncommon for professors to move from one program to another and the two main universities had a strong tendency to hire their own alumni, as illustrated in Table 4.10, but this pattern is becoming more flexible as faculty recruitment comes to rely primarily on the candidates' foreign credentials.

The economics programs reviewed above share important similarities in terms of faculty profile. Only six of the professors listed had completed

Table 4.10 Economics professors with undergraduate degrees from the same university, 2000

University of Chile	Catholic University
73% are U. Ch. alumni	71% are U.C. alumni

their graduate studies in Europe, all in the UK. Until very recently, women were, by and large, absent from these institutions, in part because few studied abroad. Female professors are concentrated at CEA: Alejandra Mizala (PhD Berkeley), Pilar Romaguera (PhD Boston), Andrea Repetto (PhD MIT), Viviana Fernández (PhD Berkeley), and María Soledad Arellano (PhD MIT). ILADES/Georgetown employs only Marcela Perticara (PhD Texas A&M), and at the Catholic University there is also one woman among the full-time faculty, Bernardita Vial, an alumna of its own MA program.

There is growing pressure to increase the publication record of economics faculties. Until recently, it was common for academic economists to publish in the journals sponsored by their own departments. Salaries are currently linked to the number and type of publications (US standards are used) to reward publishable research and discourage lucrative external consultancy not acceptable in academic journals (interview material). The process has proven highly complex due to conflicting demands made on the faculty. On the one hand, they must publish, although teaching requirements are typically three courses per year. On the other, their research must generate income to help finance the department, a problem that dates back to the education reform of the early 1980s, when public funding for primary-level education was increased at the expense of universities. But not all economics departments face the same level of financial pressure: at the Catholic University, faculty salaries are comparatively high because of generous private contributions to the *Facultad de Economía y Administración* and because the business school subsidizes the economics department.

Economics departments engage in a variety of consultancy projects for international organizations, private and public clients.[47] 'It is not a bad system', argued an economics professor I interviewed, 'it obliges universities to work on issues that are relevant to the country'. In this view, financial pressures generate a desirable combination of applied research and technical rigor, avoiding the much criticized tendency toward esoteric and abstruse research. Others were less confident regarding the benefits of this arrangement, and thought instead that the system leads to perverse effects. For example:

- universities are doing much of the research that state institutions need but are not prepared to conduct themselves;
- the state is indirectly financing academic research but it imposes its own priorities;
- professors, especially at the junior level, must reconcile these conflicting demands, often at the expense of their teaching, their area of specialization, or/and their personal lives;
- professors are enticed to take consultancy activities that are academically irrelevant but highly remunerative. External contracts sometimes pay several times their university salaries;
- professors are expected to complete a certain number of projects every year even though articles submitted to prestigious journals may take years to appear, either because of higher rejection rates or long waiting lists for accepted articles;
- serious conflicts of interest may arise between the results of academic research and the clients' expectations which may prevent the publication of research results.

Graduate Economics Programs in Chile

Chile has several Master's programs in economics and two doctoral programs. The idea of creating a doctoral program at the University of Chile was first discussed at the American Economic Association meeting in New Orleans in 1997, where economists from of ITAM (Mexico) and Di Tella (Argentina) approached Eduardo Engel of CEA. Engel was initially concerned about the ability of a regional program to compete with doctoral programs in the US but the proposal was approved and funding secured. Two students (from Ecuador) were admitted in September 2000, and I was told that the program would be considered a success if at least six students were admitted every year. This doctoral program, which has agreements with ITAM and the Universidad Di Tella, seeks to 'strengthen the economics discipline in the region, educating economists with a solid foundation in economic theory and a deep knowledge of Latin American economies'. The original idea was that students would attend courses in each academic center during three four-month periods. After completing their courses, students would work on their dissertations under the guidance of a professor chosen from any of the three academic centers. This was an expensive design. Transportation costs, especially, would have been high. Many seemed to doubt its long-term financial viability and the continuous institutional support required from all the universities involved. The complexity of academic politics was an important factor as well: rivalries between the two MA programs at the University of Chile had to be addressed to generate a new scheme of cooperation between them. The collaboration among institutions in the three countries continues, although it has been implemented in a more flexible framework.

To avoid being left out, and under strong pressure from the university authorities, the Department of Economics at the Catholic University promptly initiated efforts to create its own doctoral program. Currently, both universities compete for government funds from MECESUP (*Fondo Competitivo para el Mejoramiento de la Calidad y el Desempeño de la Educación Superior*) to finance their respective doctorates.

Chile's best students will continue to apply to universities outside the region. Those who are less likely to enroll in doctorates abroad (including women with family responsibilities and faculty members from provincial universities) will find local training attractive. Chile's doctoral programs offer valuable research opportunities for academic economists (who would be more motivated to keep up with the latest developments in the field) and the possibility of conducting applied research that is relevant to the region.

Although Chile's MA programs offer a similar curriculum, their areas of specialization vary. The University of Chile, as mentioned before, offers two Master's programs in economics. One is the Magister en Economía (*Facultad de Economía y Administración*), with approximately 20 students admitted annually, that offers specialization in international economics, regulatory economics, industrial organization, labor economics, the economics of social policy, and natural resources. The second program is the Magister en Economía Aplicada at CEA (*Departamento de Ingeniería Industrial, Facultad de Ciencias Físicas y Matemáticas*), which enrolls about ten students per year.[48] For its part, the Catholic University offers a *Magister en Economía* with four areas of specialization: financial economics, applied macroeconomics, public policy, and economic theory. In addition, the Master of Arts in Economics, offered jointly by ILADES/Georgetown, admits around 15 students of a total of about 70 applicants.[49]

In their contents and requirements, these MA programs are considered the equivalent of the first year in a doctoral economics program in the US. Typically, the first year includes two courses in macroeconomics, two in microeconomics, and econometrics courses. 'We are mainstream', said a professor interviewed for this study. 'We teach the same things that are taught at Chicago', explained another, 'although our foreign students sometimes expect that in Chile they will study economics for the poor'.

Despite similarities in terms of theoretical orientation and technical rigor, there is, however, an important difference between graduate level economics education in Chile and in the US. The Chilean programs advertise themselves as giving particular emphasis to applied research, with a focus on issues that are specific to Latin America. During the second year, in which students take elective courses and prepare their theses, they are exposed to such topics as public finances, electric regulation, and labor economics, from a 'Latin perspective', in the words of an interviewee.

Is there enough demand to justify all these graduate programs in a country the size of Chile? MA programs that are linked to undergraduate economics programs can rely on a regular flow of students (such is the case of the Department of Economics at the University of Chile and its counterpart at the Catholic University). Undergraduate economics students are able to obtain a graduate degree with very little additional time and tuition expenses. The MA prepares them well to continue on to doctoral programs abroad. CEA is considering the creation of an undergraduate program, but the idea is controversial, since the University of Chile already has an undergraduate economics program. Foreign students are a crucial source for recruitment, just as they are in the US (Aslanbeigui and Montecinos 1998).

Foreign Economics Students in Chile

To a degree, the ample opportunities Chileans have had to study economics in foreign countries have been matched by the opportunities foreign students have had to study economics in Chile. Chile's international prestige in economics education brought hundreds of Latin Americans there to attend graduate programs, starting with ESCOLATINA. With the creation of the *Magister en Ciencias Económicas*, the first of its kind in the country, not only foreign but also Chilean students began to enroll in larger numbers.

At the Catholic University the flow of foreign economics students began with the creation of PREL (*Programa en Economía para Estudiantes Latinoamericanos*) in 1965. A two-year undergraduate economics program for Latin American students, PREL was funded by the Ford and Rockefeller foundations and with scholarships provided by USAID. It was expected that PREL students would receive a better education than was available in other Latin American countries and they would then enroll in graduate studies in the US at a lower cost than if students applied directly to universities in the US. By 1970, 60 students from ten Latin American countries had attended PREL (Valdés 1989, pp. 270, 275).

Two other programs at the Catholic University attracted large numbers of foreign students. PIMA (*Programa Interamericano de Macroeconomía Aplicada*) had over 200 students between 1990 and 1997 with funding from the Inter-American Development Bank and various Central Banks and Finance ministries in the region. CIAPEP (*Curso Interamericano en Preparación y Evaluación de Proyectos*), created in 1976 in an agreement between the Catholic University and ODEPLAN, offered 11-month courses, which 800 Chileans and 100 foreign students had attended until 1997. Also 2800 students had registered in one-month courses between 1979 and 1997 (Vial 1999, p. 276).

At the University of Chile, the *Magister en Economía* enrolled 36 foreign students, or 27 percent of the total of 133 students between 1990 and 2001. They came from Ecuador (10), Peru (9), Central America (6), Bolivia (6), Colombia (2), Argentina (1), and from other countries (3). CEA, in addition to the Master's in Applied Economics, offers a Master's in Management and Public Policy, which recruited 144 foreign students, or 73 percent of total admissions between 1995 and 2001, from as many as 21 Latin American and Caribbean countries. In 2005, however, the proportion of foreign students represented only about 40 percent of the total.

Foreign students also represent a significant number (61 percent in 1987–2005) of the students at the Master of Arts in Economics at ILADES/Georgetown. Peru, Bolivia and Argentina sent the largest numbers (18, 12 and 9 percent, respectively), although students also came from other countries in the region. External funding was crucial: the Konrad Adenauer Foundation provided US$400 000 for the first two years of this program. The Inter-American Development Bank financed ten scholarships per year (until 1998); also the Ford Foundation, USAID, the Organization of American States, and the Chilean government provided scholarships.

In sum, Chile is not only a country with many foreign-educated economists but also a destination for international students. These two trends constitute a virtuous circle for the growth and prestige of the profession and explain the transnational character of the academic and applied professional markets of Chilean economics. The attractive conditions for scholarly and applied professional practice gather in prestigious members of the discipline and maintain a steady flow of new capable entrants, setting this site apart from competitors in other Latin American countries. At its own scale, Chile seems to replicate within the region some of the conditions that have made American economics the world center of the profession.

Economics Journals

Considering the country's size, the number of economics journals published in Santiago is surprising. One of the first specialized journals was *Panorama Económico*; created by Aníbal Pinto in 1947, it became a major

Table 4.11 *Economics journals in Chile in the 1990s*

Journal	Initiated	Institution
Cuadernos de Economía	1963	Catholic University
Estudios de Economía	1973	University of Chile
Colección Estudios	1979	CIEPLAN
Análisis Económico	1986	ILADES
Economía Chilena	1997	Banco Central

Source: Meller and Bravo (2000).

Table 4.12 *Articles published in top 50 economics journals, 1996–2000*

Institution	No. of articles	%
CEA	13.8	46.1
Economics, Catholic U.	3.8	12.8
Central Bank	4.5	15.0
Economics, U. of Chile	1.3	4.4
Other	4.0	13.3
Total	30.0	100.0

Source: CEA, Departamento de Ingeniería Industrial, Facultad de Ciencias Físicas y Matemáticas, Universidad de Chile, Informe de Actividades, 1999–2000.

outlet for economic debates in the coming decades. By the 1990s, five specialized journals were published (Table 4.11),[50] not counting the CEPAL journal, or the numerous Working Papers series dealing with economic issues.

As the peer review process acquires greater significance, editorial board members, reviewers and contributors became more diverse and more international. In 1999, for example, *Cuadernos de Economía* was given a new name: *Cuadernos de Economía: Latin American Journal of Economics*. Some of these journals, particularly those affiliated with universities, are publishing articles by authors from other countries. Economics professors are no longer submitting most of their work to in-house journals (Interview material). CEA is ranked the highest, in terms of the number of articles published in the top 50 economics journals (based on the Social Science Citation Index) (Table 4.12). An analysis of a total of 1280 economics articles published in Chilean journals between 1963 and 1996 (Meller and Bravo, 2000) indicates a notable increase in the number of articles, especially in the 1990s (Table 4.13). Over time, the topics addressed also changed. In the 1990s, compared with the 1960s, there were

Table 4.13 Articles in economics journals in Chile

	No. articles/year	No. published journals
1960s	12	1
1970s	25	2
1980s	50	4
1990s	70	4

Source: Meller and Bravo (2000).

fewer articles on economic development. The number of microeconomics articles increased, and articles on macroeconomics are less frequent than in the 1980s. This has been explained as the result of Chile's success in inflation control and the general consensus on measures to maintain macroeconomic balance (interview material) but it also reflects general trends in the profession beyond Chile. Articles on environmental issues, as expected, are more numerous in recent years, but the neglect of economic history shows no improvement. Articles reflect shifting priorities and current debates, but there is also a certain level of institutional specialization; for example, CIEPLAN had a distinctive emphasis on income distribution and institutional issues.

CONCLUSION

The fervor that economic ideas induce in Chile's political discourse seems as fit for anthropological analysis as it is fit for studies of political economy; no narrative of Chilean economics can omit that kinship, and any profile of the country's history would be weakened without references to the evolution of economics.

The prospects of reviving the traditions that for most of the past 100 years sought to challenge the legacy of nineteenth-century French pro-market money doctor Courcelle-Seneuil have dimmed. The past and the present of Chilean political identities have grown farther apart, as if separated by the fall of lava or the gaping crack of a quake. Chile is no longer the country that for decades pained commentators with its runaway inflation and slow growth rates. Its economists boast about new trade agreements with dozens of countries in all continents, years of budget surpluses, the technical refinement of economic legislation and innovative monetary policies. The specter of a democracy beholden to bickering factions of experts and competing economic ideologues seems to have been left behind. Chile's triumphant appearance in press headlines and international rankings of economic performance makes it less able to retrace the steps of its former self, when it was driven not by the advocacy of market competition but by the championing of planning; when it was known by its anti-capitalist reforms and mass mobilizations rather than by its export potential or its display of modern highways, malls, and top tourist destinations.

Compliance with conventional standards of the economics profession is advertised for professional and political reasons: economists can improve their occupational prospects and their access to professional networks only if they hold the 'right' professional degrees and only if they are fluent in the formal, abstract language of their most prestigious peers in the field. More than most, Chileans seem convinced that governments risk financial disaster if they appoint economic teams without the appropriate credentials (Markoff and Montecinos 1993).

Chilean economists have been particularly receptive to homogenizing currents in economics. Few economists in Chile are willing to defend, much less revive, the legacy of economic heterodoxy that gave fame and power to their predecessors just a few decades ago. They seem certain that on the road to development and prosperity there are no paths leading back to the statist past, no detours to economic nationalism and no shortcuts to economic populism.

A detailed reading of recent developments in Chilean economics, however, illustrates the emergence of unexpected trends. Even when the rituals, assumptions and rhetoric of the academic mainstream are wholeheartedly adopted, the emulation process seems filled with creative surprises, unanticipated adaptations and therefore hopeful possibilities for the rise of a 'new economics'.

Rescuing the center–periphery metaphor of yesteryear, it is perhaps not too audacious to suggest that, as happened in the last century, innovations in economic theory are likely to occur as a result of pragmatic accommodations and policy innovations in the periphery (Love 1996; Montecinos and Markoff 2001). While academic institutions in the center remain rigidly constrained by their promotion systems and not prone to examine the perversity of their incentive structure, that task seems to be left to outside critics or disgruntled colleagues. Could Chile again play a major role in nurturing debates about the mission, paradigms and methods of economics, as it did half a century ago? Given the continuous leading status of Chilean economics in the region – measured in terms of the professional credentials of policy elites, the number of foreign students enrolled in economics programs, or the influence of Chilean economists in international policy and financial circles – novel ideas and practices could have repercussions in the rest of the region.

First, consider the eclectic approach to economics education being adopted by all graduate programs in Chile. Without explicitly renouncing economic orthodoxy, these programs define their mission as a distinctive attempt to incorporate 'applied economics' in the curriculum. There is no document discussing the need for curricular reforms, and questions about the existence of informal debates regarding curricular contents were systematically dismissed by economists I interviewed: 'Those who are exploring other ideas do not have a synthesis that could influence the curriculum', I was told. Whatever discussions exist refer only to the length of the program (possibly reducing the undergraduate program to four years), or the need to emphasize work-related skills (that is, English proficiency). Yet, it is clear that economics programs in Chile are at least in part designed as an alternative to the type of training offered in universities in the US, an issue much discussed in the 1950s and 1960s (see Pinto and Sunkel 1966, among others).

Second, the fluid line between academic and government economists suggests not only that applied research with a clear focus on issues relevant to Latin America has regained status but that interdisciplinary work may also be revalued. The data presented above indicates that Chilean economists move back and forth between government and academic centers, and that the research agenda of academic economists is heavily influenced by the needs of the state. Moreover, economists in Chile are now more engaged in microeconomic research and practice. They may have been taught to appreciate precision and the importance of general equilibrium models but they have lived the uncertainties of real politics and the complexities of bureaucratic life. They are ministers, party leaders and Congress members. Economists may have experienced intense quarrels with physicians, teachers and architects as they tried to demonstrate to them how their evaluation systems were defective and their productivity records lacking. Could this mesh of theory and practice within Health, Labor, Education and Housing ministries be brought to the classroom in ways that would be impossible for purely academic economists?

Third, the proliferation of graduate level programs in Chile could be explained as a defensive strategy to employ the growing ranks of well-trained economists returning to an already crowded professional labor market. But this explanation is insufficient if the extent and diversity of foreign funding is considered. As in the past, foreign foundations and international organizations seem willing to disburse substantial funds to sustain and promote economics education in Chile. During the Cold War, Chile became a regional center for the study of economics: the country had an ambitious foreign policy and a highly competitive multiparty politics. Free-market missionaries, apostles of social Catholicism and other third-way reformists were betting that their grants, scholarships and loans would tip the political balance in Chile and serve as a demonstration effect to stop the leftist contagion in Latin America. The reputation of Chilean universities remains relatively high, and the credentials of economics professors have been enhanced in the past decade. If external funding continues to strengthen the export of economics from Chile to other Latin American countries (most foreign students come from neighboring countries but others from Central America and the Caribbean), innovations taking place in Chile eventually may affect the profession elsewhere.

Finally, if predictions about student recruitment in graduate economics programs in Chile are correct, the number of qualified women with postgraduate degrees will continue to rise. In Chile, as elsewhere, there are few women economists, and a woman in a position of professional prestige is a rarity (Albelda 1997; Montecinos 2001). Economists think of humans as self-interested and rational maximizers, involved in exchanges with equally motivated and unconnected actors. Because economic models do not include the impact of cultural values, power and coercion, they do not adequately explain the unequal rewards of men and women, the biased distribution of resources within families, or women's limited ability to participate in markets and respond to price signals. Economists tend to neglect, undercount and undervalue the work women perform in nonmarket contexts, and frequently promote policies that are overtly (even if not deliberately) biased against women's interests. A larger contingent of women economists in academically prestigious and politically powerful positions will not necessarily challenge the theoretical foundation and masculine identity of neoclassical economics, but it could make it easier to think of gender as an important dimension of economic life. This would indeed be a major reform in the world of economists and a blow to neoliberal notions of economics. With the election of Chile's first woman president in 2006, a glimpse of those possibilities appeared. In the private pension system reform, the main social transformation of her presidency – whose fiscal implications are the most significant of the past two decades[51] and which was just recently approved by the Chilean Congress, market rules were kept in place but greater gender equity was achieved, as the President demanded.

Thus Chilean economics continues to trace novel constructs. Unsuspecting observers may attribute this to pure luck, the confabulation of hidden interests or the ambition of individual economists manufacturing their own grandeur. As seen in this chapter, the legacy of half a century of economics in Chile points to a chain of multiple connections, some – but not all – internal to the profession and some – but not all – internal to that country's life.

NOTES

1. I thank John Markoff and Richard Frushell for valuable comments on an earlier version of this chapter.
2. See, among others, Bitar (1986); Bosworth et al. (1994), Castañeda (1992), Collins and Lear (1995), Edwards and Edwards (1987), Ffrench-Davis (1999), Foxley (1983), Griffith-Jones (1981), Harberger (1997), Hojman (1993), Larraín and Meller (1991), Mamalakis (1976), Meller (2000), Mesa-Lago (2000), Molina (1970), OECD (2003), Ramos (1986), Stallings (1978), Zammit (1973).
3. Marshall, Martner, Piñera, Escobar, Tokman and Landerretche are just a few names that exemplify these meritocratic dynasties.
4. Literature on economists during the military government include Constable and Valenzuela (1991), Fontaine (1988), Huneeus (2000), E. Silva (1996), P. Silva (1991).
5. Under President Eduardo Frei, Chile became the 'darling of US policy makers' receiving nearly US$2 million from the CIA in covert projects to infiltrate student and labor groups, influence political campaigns and destabilize radical reformism (Sigmund 1993, p. 35).
6. Economist W.W. Rostow, sometimes known as the 'high priest of counterinsurgency' (Lodewijks 1991, p. 296), worked for the State Department and later served as national security adviser to President Lyndon Johnson. He was the author of the influential linear stages theory of development.
7. Consider, for example, that the region's most renowned economist, Raúl Prebisch, CEPAL's first Secretary General, was forced by exile to rebuild his professional legacy in Chile instead of in his native Argentina. In Mexico, economics education at UNAM, the largest program, was assailed for its deficiencies even 'at its height of technicality in the 1950s and 60s' (Babb 2001, p. 91). As late as 1968, no Brazilians had obtained a doctoral degree in economics (Dezalay and Garth 2002, p. 99). See also Biglaiser (2002, p. 275) for data on US AID's generous funding to Chile, compared with Argentina and Uruguay between 1961 and 1970.
8. In addition, the Organization of American States in 1962 sponsored the creation in Santiago of the Inter-American Center for Statistical Training (CIENES). Its international prestige attracted students and government officials from around the region. Between 1966 and 1985, CIENES Master's program in mathematical statistics had 394 graduates, only 43 percent of whom were Chileans (del Pino 2006).
9. Prebisch, who died in Chile in 1986, was honorary member of the School of Economics at the University of Chile and was named Doctor *Honoris Causa* by the Catholic University of Chile.
10. One of the top graduates of CEPAL's first course (1952–53), the Chilean Osvaldo Sunkel was then sent to study at the London School of Economics. Traveling in Europe he met Gunnar Myrdal, Jan Tinbergen, Hans Singer and Nicholas Kaldor (Burger 1998, p. 93).
11. A Chilean, Luis Alamos, was among the handful of Latin American representatives to the preliminary meetings in Atlantic City before the Bretton Woods conference of 1944.
12. The Chilean Raúl Sáez coordinated the Committee of Nine, a group of experts at the Inter-American Committee for the Alliance for Progress. W.W. Rostow, Celso Furtado and Roberto Campos were also members.
13. While under Allende's predecessor Chile had, on average, US$300 million in private short-term credits, only US$30 million were available by his second year in office (Valenzuela 1978, p. 56).
14. In 1980, as president of the Centro de Estudios Públicos, Jorge Cauas went to Friburg University to invite Hayek to serve as honorary president of this newly created Chilean think tank, a post he held until his death. Hayek went to Chile in 1981 when the Societé (of which he was the founder) had a regional meeting there. A general meeting was organized in Chile again in 2000. The journal *Revista de Estudios Públicos* became a

well-respected conservative outlet which often published the work of famous foreign libertarians and local academics.

15. When Chile broke away from the Andean Pact in 1976, a career diplomat was appalled by the economists' unsophisticated diplomacy. Arguing that the mistaken policies of Chile's partners were at fault, they had basically insisted that Chile had to leave the regional integration scheme because 'they were all idiots!' (interview material, Montecinos 1997b).
16. Guzmán, a charismatic law professor, helped an emerging right-wing movement (Gremialismo) gain many adepts to oppose the 1968 student mobilizations. Economics student leaders of this period who were studying economics (Miguel Kast, Felipe Lamarca, Cristián Larroulet among others) occupied powerful government posts under Pinochet. Kast spearheaded the social security reform upon his return from the University of Chicago in the early 1970s, although José Piñera is generally given the credit (Huneeus 2000, p. 404; Piñera 1991).
17. Many of the Chicago Boys were replaced in 1983 in the midst of the worst economic debacle since the Great Depression. A conservative politician said with relief: 'Finally economics is spoken about in Spanish' (Escobar 1991, p. 128).
18. Friedman's endorsement came at a price, however. Protestors followed him all the way to the ceremony in which he was awarded the Nobel Prize.
19. In private, however, the praise was sometimes more temperate. Consider a 1981 letter from Hayek to Margaret Thatcher in which he refers to Chile as 'an example of economic reform from which we can learn many lessons. However, I am sure you will agree that, in Britain with our democratic institutions and need for a high degree of consent, some of the measures adopted in Chile are quite unacceptable' (quoted in Hoover, 2003, p. 213).
20. An early and influential Chilean disciple was Congressman Zorobabel Rodríguez, a conservative Catholic journalist, author of the 1894 *Tratado de economía política.*
21. It was in Chile that he wrote *Traité théorique et pratique de l'Economie Politique*, two volumes published in Paris in 1858 (Villalobos and Sagredo 1987, pp. 61–2, cited in Vial 1999, p. 21).
22. Consider the anecdote recounted by former President Ricardo Lagos, an economist, about his 1920s predecessor Arturo Alessandri (Massis and Hidalgo 1999, p. 52). The Finance Minister is said to have asked president Alessandri if he wanted the report on the state of public finances 'with or without a deficit'.
23. Drake (1994) has helped disaggregate the 'money doctoring' phenomenon. It has been a ploy to circumvent entrenched domestic interests, a signal of creditworthiness to external investors and lenders, an alternative to homegrown advice, a convenient scapegoat for the authorities' unfulfilled promises and a conditionality mechanism for capital-starved countries.
24. Two example of Chile's active participation in those networks: in 1946 Chile became the first customer of the World Bank by applying for a US$40 million loan to finance a variety of government projects (Kraske 1996, p. 30) and Chile hosted the Second Meeting of Central Bank Experts of the American Continent held in 1949.
25. Dr Max participated in the creation of the *Instituto de Economía* at the University of Chile, in 1943, an initiative shared with Flavián Levine and Enrique Marshall.
26. In 1945, as president of the student association at the University of Chile (FECH), Felipe Herrera attended a World Youth Congress in London and traveled with a Chilean delegation to the United States and various countries in Europe and Latin America establishing important contacts for his future career as an economist.
27. See, for example, the book series on 'Central Banking, Analysis, and Economic Policies' of the Central Bank of Chile.
28. In his analysis of decision-making during the Frei administration, Peter Cleaves (1974, pp. 89–99) grouped economic agencies into two major coalitions: a 'restrictive' coalition focused on inflation control, which consistently enjoyed the president's support and a 'developmentalist' coalition dealing with agrarian reform and other medium-term plans.

29. ODEPLAN's promising origins faltered with the unexpected death of economist Jorge Ahumada in 1964. Well respected in international circles and influential in the design of Frei's government program, he was consensus-maker in the Christian Democratic Party even among those who thought him excessively concerned with stabilization. Burger (1998) reviews Ahumada's significant but relatively little known career.
30. The Budget Bureau has been in the hands of foreign-trained economists as well. The Director post has been held by José Pablo Arellano (PhD Harvard), Joaquín Vial (PhD U. of Pennsylvania), Mario Marcel (PhDc Cambridge) and Alberto Arenas (PhD U. of Pittsburgh).
31. A list of other economics professors with ministerial-level positions would include Alberto Baltra, Guillermo del Pedregal, Edgardo Boeninger, Carlos Massad, Eduardo García d'Acuña, Luis Arturo Fuenzalida, Jorge Selume, Alvaro Bardón, among many others.
32. Consider, in addition to Lagos's multidimensional, stellar career (Massis and Hidalgo 1999) the case of Minister Alejandro Foxley, a Christian Democratic 'technopol' with a PhD from Wisconsin (Giraldo 1997), or those of José and Sebastián Piñera, both conservative presidential candidates with economics PhDs from Harvard.
33. Lavín's presidential candidacy had been initially challenged by the economist Sebastián Piñera, who had earlier lost his bid for a Congressional seat to Evelyn Matthei, an economist who at some point was also included among possible presidential candidates (Boylan 1997).
34. For example, in 1993, the University of Chile began offering an economics program for lawyers (Post-título en Economía y Finanzas para Abogados).
35. Various scandals involving high-level economic officials have made headlines throughout the region. General Pinochet's long-protected image of austerity and integrity rapidly dissolved in 2004 when an investigation by the US Congress disclosed the existence of millions of dollars hidden in secret foreign bank accounts (US Senate Report 2005).
36. Aguirre Cerda served as the first dean of the Escuela de Economía y Comercio of the University of Chile between 1935 and 1939.
37. Influential lawyer-economists were Professors Luis Enrique Marshall (author of *La Ciencia de la Economía*), Daniel Martner (who studied in Bonn, taught public finances and served as Finance Minister in the 1920s) and Alberto Baltra, one of the founders of the School of Economics (later its Director, a Senator, Economy Minister and consultant for the United Nations).
38. This information was kindly provided by Oscar Muñoz, academic director of ESCOLATINA between 1965 and 1969.
39. Foreign students and professors were also important at the Center for Socio-economic Studies (CESO), an interdisciplinary institute with a Marxist leaning, connected to the School of Economics at the University of Chile.
40. Generations of Catholic politicians and social thinkers referred to the 1891 and 1931 papal encyclicals *Rerum Novarum* and *Quadragesimo Anno*.
41. Of the total of 1402 scholarships that ODEPLAN/MIDEPLAN granted between 1981 and 2001, the areas of economics and administration combined received the highest percentage (296 scholarships), exceeding the number of scholarships to students in the social sciences and law (250), natural sciences (216), and engineering (143).
42. Many prominent Chicago Boys who came back with a Master's degree or without completing the dissertation occupied influential posts. Lists of government and academic economists still include the title 'PhDc', or ABD.
43. It is estimated that on average about US$1 million a year in foreign funds went to think tanks in Chile between 1975 and 1980 and about US$3 million annually between 1980 and 1988 (Puryear 1994, p. 52).
44. In addition, this program employed eight instructors with an MA in economics: seven of them graduated from the Magister en Economía at the University of Chile and one from the Magister ILADES/Georgetown.

45. Several members of the first generation of Chicago Boys have already passed the university retirement age, but their contracts have been extended. They enhance the prestige of the program, and the university is loath to facilitate their transfer to the recently created private universities (interview material).
46. In 1998–99 the Economics Department at the University of Chile conducted a total of 65 research projects; 65 percent of them were commissioned by ministries and other government agencies. In addition, the Unidad de Encuestas of that Department of Economics conducted a total of 23 surveys, 43 percent of which were contracted by government agencies.
47. The Departamento de Ingeniería Industrial also has the Magister en Gestión y Políticas Públicas. The Facultad de Economía y Administración, at the University of Chile has three other graduate level programs: the Magister en Administración, the Magister en Finanzas and the MBA for the Americas (the latter is part of an agreement between the University of Chile and Tulane University).
48. The Universidad de Concepción offers two MA programs, one in Applied Economics and one in Environmental Economics.
49. *Colección Estudios CIEPLAN* was temporarily discontinued in the late 1990s. *Economía Chilena* was founded in 1997.
50. See Arenas de Mesa et al. (2008).

REFERENCES

Albelda, Randy (1997), *Economics and Feminism: Disturbances in the Field*, New York: Twayne Publishers.

Alvarez-Rivadulla, María José, John Markoff and Verónica Montecinos (forthcoming), 'The Trans-American Market Advocacy Think Tank Movement', in Adolfo Garcé and Gerardo Uña (eds.), *Think Tanks and Public Policies in Latin America*, Ottawa: International Development Research Center (IDRC).

Arenas de Mesa, Alberto, Paula Benavides, Leonardo González and José L. Castillo (2008), 'La reforma previsional chilena: Proyecciones fiscales 2009–2025', Santiago: Ministerio de Hacienda, Dirección de Presupuestos, Estudios de Finanzas Públicas.

Aslanbeigui, Nahid and Verónica Montecinos (1998), 'Foreign Students in US Doctoral Programs', *Journal of Economic Perspectives*, **12** (3), 171–82.

Babb, Sarah (2001), *Managing Mexico. Economists from Nationalism to Neoliberalism*, Princeton: Princeton University Press.

Barber, William J. (1997), 'Postwar Changes in American Graduate Education in Economics', in A.W. Coats (ed.), *The Post-1945 Internationalization of Economics*, Annual Supplement to Vol. 28 *History of Political Economy*, Durham and London: Duke University Press, pp. 12–30.

Becker, Gary (1997), 'What Latin America Owes to the "Chicago Boys"', *Hoover Digest*, 4, reprinted from *Business Week*, June 9, 1997, p. 22.

Biglaiser, Glen (2002), 'The Internationalization of Chicago's Economics in Latin America', *Economic Development and Cultural Change*, **50** (2), 269–86.

Bitar, Sergio (1986), *Chile. Experiment in Democracy*, Philadelphia: Institute for the Study of Human Issues.

Boeninger, Edgardo (1997), *Democracia en Chile. Lecciones para la gobernabilidad*, Santiago: Editorial Andrés Bello.

Bosworth, Barry P., Rudiger Dornbusch and Raúl Labán (eds) (1994), *The Chilean*

Economy. Policy Lessons and Challenges, Washington, DC: The Brookings Institution.
Boylan, Delia M. (1997), 'The Rise and Fall (and Rise?) of a Technopol. The Evelyn Matthey Story', in Jorge I. Domínguez (ed.), *Technopols: Freeing Politics and Markets in Latin America in the 1990s*, University Park PA: The Pennsylvania State University Press, pp. 195–227.
Burger, Hilary (1998), 'An Intellectual History of the ECLA Culture, 1948 to 1964', PhD dissertation, Department of History, Harvard University.
Castañeda, Tarsicio (1992) *Combating Poverty: Innovative Social Reforms in Chile during the 1980s*, Oakland, CA: ICS Press.
Céspedes, Luis Felipe and Rodrigo Valdés (2006), 'Central Bank Authonomy: The Chilean Experience', *Journal Economía Chilena*, **9** (1), 25–47.
Cleaves, Peter (1974), *Bureaucratic Politics and Administration in Chile*, Berkeley, CA: University of California Press.
Collins, Joseph and John Lear (1995), *Chile's Free-Market Miracle. A Second Look*, Oakland, CA: The Institute for Food and Development Policy.
Conaghan, Catherine M. (2005), 'El ascenso y la caída de los neoliberales en los países de los Andes centrales', in Jairo Estrada Alvarez (ed.), *Intelectuales, tecnócratas y reformas neoliberales en América Latina*, Bogotá: Universidad Nacional de Colombia, Convenio Andrés Bello – Colciencias.
Constable, Pamela and Arturo Valenzuela (1991), *A Nation of Enemies. Chile under Pinochet*, New York: W.W. Norton.
Contreras Claudia, Gonzalo Edwards and Alejandra Mizala (2006), 'La productividad científica de economía y administración en Chile. Un análisis comparativo', *Cuadernos de Economía*, **43** (128), 331–54.
Délano, Manuel and Hugo Traslaviña (1989), *La herencia de los Chicago Boys*, Santiago: Ediciones del Ornitorrinco.
del Pino, Guido (2006), 'International Cooperation in Statistics Education in Latin America: The Chilean Experience', http://www.stat.auckland.ac.nz/~iase/publications/17/1E2.
Dezalay, Yves and Bryant G. Garth (2002), *The Internationalization of Palace Wars. Lawyers, Economists and the Contest to Transform Latin American States*, Chicago: The University of Chicago Press.
Dornbusch, Rudiger and Sebastian Edwards (1994), 'Exchange Rate Policy and Trade Strategy', in Barry P. Bosworth, Rudiger Dornbusch and Raúl Labán (eds), The Chilean Economy. Policy Lessons and Challenges, Washington, DC: The Brookings Institution, pp. 81–115.
Drake, Paul (1994), 'Introduction. The Political Economy of Foreign Advisers and Lenders in Latin America', in Paul W. Drake (ed.), *Money Doctors, Foreign Debts, and Economic Reforms in Latin America from the 1890s to the Present*, Wilmington, DE: A Scholarly Resources Inc., pp. xi–xxxiii.
Eckaus, Richard and Paul Rosenstein-Rodan (eds) (1973), *Analysis of Development Problems. Studies of the Chilean Economy*, Amsterdam: North-Holland Publishing Co.
Edwards, Sebastián (2003), 'Latin American and US Universities: A Forty Years Analysis', *Cuadernos de Economía*, **40** (121), 399–412.
Edwards, Sebastián and Alejandra Cox Edwards (1987), *Monetarism and Liberalization: The Chilean Experiment*, Cambridge, MA: Ballinger.
Eichengreen (1994), 'House Calls of the Money Doctor: The Kemmerer Missions in Latin America, 1917–1931', in Paul W. Drake (ed.), *Money Doctors, Foreign*

Debts, and Economic Reforms in Latin America from the 1890s to the Present, Wilmington, DE: A Scholarly Resources Inc., pp. 110–32.
Escobar Cerda, Luis (1991), *Mi testimonio*, Santiago: Editorial Ver.
Ffrench-Davis, Ricardo (1973), *Políticas económicas en Chile: 1952–1970*, Santiago: Ediciones Nueva Universidad, Universidad Católica de Chile.
Ffrench-Davis, Ricardo (1999), *Entre el neoliberalismo y el crecimiento con equidad. Tres décadas de política económica en Chile*, Santiago: DOLMEN Ediciones.
Fontaine Aldunate, Arturo (1988), *La historia no contada de los economistas y el Presidente Pinochet*, Santiago: Zig-Zag.
Fourcade-Gourinchas, Marion and Sarah Babb (2002), 'The Rebirth of the Liberal Creed: Paths to Neoliberalism in Four Countries', *American Journal of Sociology*, **108** (3), 533–79.
Foxley, Alejandro (1983), *Latin American Experiments in Neo-Conservative Economics*, Berkeley: University of California Press.
Foxley, Alejandro (1987), *Chile y su futuro, Un país posible*, Santiago: CIEPLAN.
Frey, Bruno and Reiner Eichenberger (1993), 'American and European Economics and Economists', *Journal of Economic Perspectives*, **7** (4), 185–93.
Gallego, Francisco and Norman Loayza (2002), 'The Golden Period for Growth in Chile: Explanations and Forecasts', Santiago: Banco Central de Chile, Documento de Trabajo N. 146.
Giraldo, Jeanne K. (1997), 'Development and Democracy in Chile: Finance Minister Alejandro Foxley and the Concertación's Project for the 90s', in Jorge I. Domínguez (ed.), *Technopols: Freeing Politics and Markets in Latin America in the 1990s*, University Park, PA: The Pennsylvania State University Press, pp. 230–75.
Glaser, Elizabeth (2003), 'Chile's Monetarist Money Doctors, 1850–1988', in Marc Flandreau (ed.), *Money Doctors: The Experience of International Financial Advising, 1850–2000*, London and New York: Routledge, pp. 166–89.
Griffith-Jones, Stephanie (1981), *The Role of Finance in the Transition to Socialism*, London: Frances Pinter.
Harberger, Arnold (1997), 'Good Economics Comes to Latin America, 1955–95', in A.W. Coats (ed.), *The Post-1945 Internationalization of Economics*, Annual Supplement to Vol. 28, *History of Political Economy*, Durham and London: Duke University Press, pp. 301–11.
Harvey, David (2005), *A Brief History of Neoliberalism*, Oxford: Oxford University Press.
Herrera, Felipe (1946), 'Esquema de las tendencias de política económica en Chile', *Anales de la Facultad de Derecho*, **XII** (44–51), http://www.analesderecho.uchile.cl/CDA/an_der_articulo/0,1361,SCID%253D2101%2526ISID%253D186,00.html.
Herrera, Felipe (1951), *Fundamentos de la Política Fiscal*, Santiago: Editorial Jurídica de Chile.
Hira, Anil (1999), *Ideas and Economic Policy in Latin America. Regional, National and Organizational Case Studies*, Westport and London: Praeger.
Hirschman, Albert O. (1963), 'Inflation in Chile', in Albert O. Hirschman, *Journeys toward Progress: Studies of Economic Policy-Making in Latin America*, Westport, CT: Greenwood Publishing Group, pp. 159–223.
Hojman, David (1993), *Chile. The Political Economy of Development and Democracy in the 1990s*, London: Macmillan.

Hoover, Kenneth R. (2003), *Economics as Ideology: Keynes, Laski, Hayek and the Creation of Contemporary Politics*, Oxford: Rowman and Littlefield Publishers Inc.
Huneeus, Carlos (2000), *El régimen de Pinochet*, Santiago: Editorial Sudamericana.
Jameson, Kenneth P. (2005), 'Exchange Rate Regimes: Latin American Economic Analysis before the Depression', Department of Economics, University of Utah, www.econ.utah.edu/activities/papers/2005_2006.pdf.
Johnson, Harry (1977), 'Economics and the Radical Change: The Hard Social Science and the Soft Social Reality', in Joseph Ben-David and Terry Nichols Clark (eds), *Culture and Its Creators*, Chicago: University of Chicago Press, pp. 97–118.
Kast, Miguel (1984), 'Relaciones del la política económica de la administración del Estado de Chile: el Estado empresario y el principio de subsidiariedad', *Estudios Públicos*, **13**, 211–28.
Koljatic, Mladen and Mónica Silva (2001), 'The International Publication Productivity of Latin American Countries in the Economics and Business Administration Fields', *Scientometrics*, **51** (2), 381–94.
Kraske, John (1996), *Bankers with a Mission. The Presidents of the World Bank, 1946-1951*, Washington, DC: The World Bank.
Krugman, Paul (2005), 'Pride, Prejudice, Insurance', *The New York Times*, November 7, 2005.
Larraín Felipe and Patricio Meller (1991), 'The Socialist-Populist Chilean Experience: 1970–1973', in Rudiger Dornbusch and Sebastián Edwards (eds), *The Macroeconomics of Populism in Latin America*, Chicago: The University of Chicago Press, pp. 175-214.
Larroulet, Cristián and María de la Luz Domper (2006), 'La enseñanza de la economía y la administración en las instituciones de educación superior', Santiago: Libertad y Desarrollo, Serie Informe Económico 169.
Leonard, Robert J. (1991), 'War as a "Simple Economic Problem": The Rise of an Economics of Defense', in Craufurd D. Goodwin (ed.), *Economics and National Security: A History of Their Interaction*, Annual Supplement to Volume 23, *History of Political Economy*, Durham: Duke University Press, pp. 261–83.
Letelier, Orlando (1976), 'The Chicago Boys in Chile: Economic Freedom's Awful Toll', *The Nation*, 28, August.
Lodewijks, J. (1991), 'Rostow, Development Economics and National Security Policy', in Craufurd D. Goodwin (ed.), *Economics and National Security: A History of Their Interaction*, Annual Supplement to vol. 23, *History of Political Economy*, Durham, NC: Duke University Press, pp. 285–310.
Lodewijks, J. (2001), 'Roy Weintraub's Contribution to the History of Economics', in Seteven G. Medema and Warren Samuels (eds), *Historians of Economics and Economic Thought. The Construction of Disciplinary Memory*, London and New York: Routledge, pp. 320–35.
Love, Joseph (1996), *Crafting the Third World: Theorizing Underdevelopment in Rumania and Brazil*, Stanford: Stanford University Press.
Mamalakis, Marcos (1976), *The Growth and Structure of the Chilean Economy: From Independence to Allende*, New Haven and London: Yale University Press.
Markoff, John and Verónica Montecinos (1993), 'The Ubiquitous Rise of Economists', *Journal of Public Policy*, **13** (1), 25–53.

Marshall, Luis Enrique (1936), 'La Ciencia de la Economía', *Anales de la Facultad de Derecho*, **II** (8).
Martner, Daniel (1941), *Tratado de Hacienda Publica: Curso de Ciencias Económicas*, Santiago: Ediciones Universidad de Chile.
Massis, Diana and Giullermo Hidalgo (1999), *Lagos. El Hombre – El Político*, Santiago: Editorial Planeta.
Meller, Patricio (1987), 'Una revisión de la crisis de la ciencia económica', Santiago: CIEPLAN.
Meller, Patricio (1990), 'Revisión del proceso de ajuste chileno de la década del 80', Santiago: CIEPLAN *Colección Estudios*, **30**, 5–54.
Meller, Patricio (2005), *La Paradoja Aparente: Equidad y eficiencia. Resolviendo el Dilema*, Santiago: Aguilar Chilena de Ediciones SA.
Meller, Patricio (2000), *The Unidad Popular and the Pinochet Dicatatorship. A Political Economy Analysis*, New York: St. Martin's Press.
Meller, Patricio and Claudio Bravo (2000), 'Análisis historiográfico de la literatura económica chilena', Santiago: CIEPLAN, *Serie Estudios Socio/Económicos*, 4.
Mesa-Lago, Carmelo (2000), *Market, Socialist, and Mixed Economies. Comparative Policy and Performance. Chile, Cuba, and Costa Rica*, Baltimore and London: The Johns Hopkins University Press.
Molina, Sergio (1970), *El proceso de cambio en Chile. La experiencia 1965–1970*, Santiago: Editorial Universitaria.
Mönckeberg, María Olinia (2001), *El saqueo de los grupos economicos al Estado Chileno*, Santiago: Ediciones B
Montecinos, Verónica (1988), 'Economics and Power. Chilean Economists in Government: 1958–1985', PhD dissertation, University of Pittsburgh.
Montecinos, Verónica (1997a), 'Economists in Political and Policy Elites in Latin America', in A.W. Coats (ed.), *The Post-1945 Internationalization of Economics*, Durham: Duke University Press, pp. 279–300.
Montecinos, Verónica (1997b), 'The New Chilean Economic Diplomacy and the Chile–Pacific Relationship', paper presented at the XX International Congress of the Latin American Studies Association, Guadalajara, Mexico.
Montecinos, Verónica (1998a), 'Economists in Party Politics. Chilean Democracy in the Era of Markets', in Miguel A. Centeno and Patricio Silva (eds), *The Politics of Expertise in Latin America*, London: Macmillan, pp. 126–41.
Montecinos, Verónica (1998b), 'The Symbolic Value of Economists in the Democratization of Chilean Politics', in Kurt von Mettenheim and James Malloy (eds), *Deepening Democracy in Latin America*, Pittsburgh: University of Pittsburgh Press, pp. 108–22.
Montecinos, Verónica (2001) 'Feminists and Technocrats in the Democratization of Latin America: A Prolegomenon', *International Journal of Politics, Culture and Society*, **15** (1), 175–99.
Montecinos, Verónica (2003), 'Economic Policy-Making and Parliamentary Accountability in Chile', Geneva: UNRISD, Democracy, Governance and Human Rights, Programme Paper 11.
Montecinos, Verónica and John Markoff (2001), 'From the Power of Economics Ideas to the Power of Economists', in Miguel Angel Centeno and Fernando López-Alves (eds), *The Other Mirror. Grand Theory through the Lens of Latin America*, Princeton: Princeton University Press.
Morandé, Felipe (1986), 'Consensos y disensos entre economistas', Santiago: Universidad de Santiago, Departamento de Economía, Documento de Trabajo 15.

Muñoz Gomá, Oscar (ed.) (1993), *Historias personales, políticas públicas*, Santiago: Editorial Los Andes and CIEPLAN.
OECD (2003), *Economic Surveys: Chile*, Paris: Organisation for Economic Co-operation and Development.
OECD (2007), 'Chili – Phase 2: Rapport sur la mise en oeuvre de la Convention de l'OCDE sur la lutte contre la corruption', http://www.oecd.org/LongAbstract/0,3425,fr_33873108_39418658_39550491_1_1_1_37447,00.html.
Palacios, Jorge (1979), *Chile: An Attempt at Historic Compromise*, Chicago: Banner Press.
Pinto, Aníbal and Osvaldo Sunkel (1966), 'Latin American Economists in the United States', *Economic Development and Cultural Change*, **15** (1), 79–86.
Piñera, José (1991), *El cascabel al gato. La batalla por la reforma previsional*, Santiago: Empresa Editora Zig-Zag.
Porzecanski, Roberto (2005), 'Alliance for Progress or Alianza para el Progreso? A Reassessment of the Latin American Contribution to the Alliance for Progress', MA thesis on Law and Diplomacy, http://fletcher.tufts.edu.
Puryear, Jeffrey M. (1994), *Thinking Politics. Intellectuals and Democracy in Chile, 1973–1988*, Baltimore: The Johns Hopkins University Press.
Ramos, Joseph (1986), *Neoconservative Economics in the Southern Cone of Latin America, 1973–1983*, Baltimore: The Johns Hopkins University Press.
Roberts, Kenneth M. (1998), *Deepening Democracy? The Modern Left and Social Movements in Chile and Peru*, Stanford: Stanford University Press.
Rosenthal, Gert (2004), 'ECLAC: A Commitment to a Latin American Way toward Development', in Yves Berthelot (ed.), *Unity and Diversity in Development Ideas. Perspectives from the UN Regional Commissions*, Bloomington, IN: Indiana University Press, pp. 168–232.
Saavedra Eduardo and Raimundo Soto (2006), 'Toward a Modern State in Chile: Institutions, Governance, and Market Regulation', in Patricio A. Aroca and Geoffrey J.D. Hewings (eds), *Structure and Structural Change in the Chilean Economy*, New York: Palgrave Macmillan, pp. 35–67.
Sanfuentes, Andrés (1981), 'La investigación económica actual en Chile', Santiago: Corporación Universitaria.
Sierra, Enrique (1969), *Tres ensayos de estabilización en Chile*, Santiago: Editorial Universitaria.
Sigmund, Paul E. (1993), *The United States and Democracy in Chile*, Baltimore: The Johns Hopkins University Press.
Silva, Eduardo (1996), *The State and Capital in Chile. Business Elites, Technocrats and Market Economics*, Boulder, CO: Westview Press.
Silva, Patricio (1991), 'Technocrats and Politics in Chile: From the Chicago Boys to the CIEPLAN Monks', *Journal of Latin American Studies*, **23** (2), 385–410.
Silva, Patricio (1998), 'Pablo Ramírez: A Political Technocrat Avant-la-Lettre', in Miguel A. Centeno and Patricio Silva (eds), *The Politics of Expertise in Latin America*, London: Macmillan, pp. 52–76.
Stallings, Barbara (1978), *Class Conflict and Economic Development in Chile, 1958–1973*, Stanford: Stanford University Press.
Sunkel, Osvaldo (1993), *Development from Within. Toward a Neostructuralist Approach for Latin America*, Boulder, CO: Lynne Rienner Publishers.
Tomassini, Luciano (1997), *Felipe Herrera. Idealista y realizador*, Santiago: Banco Interamericano de Desarrollo y Fondo de Cultura Económica.

Transparency International (2007), http://www.transparency.org/policy_research/surveys_indices/cpi/2007.
US Senate Permanent Subcommittee on Investigations (2005), 'Money Laundering and Foreign Corruption: Enforcement and Effectiveness of the Patriot Act. Supplemental Staff Report on US Accounts Used by Augusto Pinochet'.
Valdés, Juan Gabriel (1989), *La Escuela de Chicago: Operación Chile*, Buenos Aires: Grupo Editorial Zeta S.A. [1995, *Pinochet's Economists. The Chicago School in Chile*, Cambridge: Cambridge University Press].
Valenzuela, Arturo (1978), *The Breakdown of Democratic Regimes. Chile*, Baltimore: The Johns Hopkins University Press.
Vial Correa, Gonzalo (1999), *Una Trascendental Experiencia Académica. Una Historia de la Facultad de Ciencias Económicas y Administrativas de la Pontificia Universidad Católica de Chile y la Nueva Visión Económica*, Santiago: Fundación Facultad de Ciencias Económicas y Administrativas, Pontificia Universidad Católica de Chile.
Villalobos, Sergio and Rafael Sagredo (1987), *El proteccionismo económico en Chile*, Santiago: Siglo XXI.
Williamson, John (1994), 'In Search of a Manual for Technopols', in John Williamson (ed.), *The Political Economy of Policy Reform*, Washington, DC: Institute for International Economics, pp. 3–28.
Zammit, J. Ann (ed.) (1973), *The Chilean Road to Socialism*, Sussex: Institute of Development Studies, University of Sussex.

5. Colombia: economics, economic policy and economists

Luis Bernardo Flórez Enciso[1]

This chapter deals with the evolution of economic theories and policies in Colombia in the past half a century, assessing some of the key problems and solutions devised by Colombian economists during this period. I examine the priorities given to various issues as well as the context in which debates and economic policy-making took place.

Economic debates in Colombia followed, albeit with less intensity, debates in the rest of Latin America. Until the late 1970s, those debates centered on development models and strategies; since then, the focus has been on short-term adjustment programs, and reforms aimed at opening the economy, financial and trade liberalization, and privatization.

In the 1990s, however, measures taken to open the economy and reduce government intervention and regulation led to more intense, polarized controversies between neoliberal currents, adept to the recommendations of the Washington Consensus, and social-democratic currents, based on neo-structuralist approaches.

Unlike the rest of the region, Colombia did not experience episodes of hyperinflation nor did it have typically populist periods. Instead, an implicit social pact between government, entrepreneurs and workers managed to avoid price increases above the 30 percent mark. This was the result of an institutionalized economic policy system characterized by gradualism and pragmatism that aimed at preserving basic balance among basic macroeconomic variables. In political terms, there was an agreement between the two main political parties – liberal and conservative – known as the 'National Front', that provided ample space for an independent technocracy in charge of macroeconomic policy. This arrangement remained in place even after the National Front came to an end.

COLOMBIA IN THE LONG TERM

In the course of the twentieth century, Colombia registered profound economic changes. Between 1925 and 1945, real GDP doubled and between 1945 and 1995 it increased tenfold. Today, the Colombian economy is ten times larger than 50 years ago in terms of its capacity to produce goods and services. The size of the economy grew at a steady pace (the average growth rate in the past 75 years stayed at around 4.5 percent annually) starting with a small base and very low income levels. The 'golden period' of economic growth took place in the first half of the 1920s and in the postwar decade. There was another period of dynamic growth from the early 1960s until the late 1970s. Since 1980, however, economic growth has declined when compared with previous periods.

Per capita income grew almost continuously, except during the crisis of the late 1990s. Yet, in the long run, per capita increase in GDP has been slightly lower than 2 percent per year. This means that part of the effort to grow and expand productive capacity has gone to generate income for a population that has been increasing at around 2.5 percent per year – although the rate of population growth has declined due to demographic transition and corresponding changes in social patterns, especially in the second half of the past century.

The processes of economic growth and urbanization led to deep changes in the structure of production, but these transformations weakened towards the end of the 1970s.[2] In 1925, agriculture represented 60 percent of total GDP; the share of agriculture fell sharply in the next thirty years. While in 1965, agriculture was 25 percent of total production, currently it is only around 15 percent. The manufacturing sector, in turn, more than doubled its share of GNP between 1925 and 1975 due to the industrialization process, particularly since 1945. Yet, after 1975, its participation stalled at around 20 percent of GDP, an indication of limited diversification, slow incorporation of new productive activities and long-term innovativeness. For its part, the government sector remained at about 5 percent of GDP until the 1950s. After that, it began to grow faster than the economy as a whole, so that by 1995 it represented 10 percent of GDP. Finally, the large service sector (modern and traditional) increased its share of GDP from 8 percent in 1975 to 30 percent today. In other words, the restructuring of the national economy has led to an important decline of agriculture in favor of a greater 'tertiarization' with a weak industrialization and less vibrant structural changes in production patterns.

In terms of exports, during the first half of the twentieth century, Colombia was a rather open economy (measured as the relationship between exports and GDP). Between the 1950s and the early 1980s, the export ratio fell drastically, reaching less than 15 percent of GDP, a sign of low dynamism and the dominance of 'inward-looking' development. Of course, short periods of coffee exports booms had a positive effect on growth and savings. But since the mid 1980s, the export rate practically doubled, becoming the leading factor in economic growth. This became associated with a more diversified export structure, although still heavily dependent on primary products, agricultural and mining.

Regarding inflation, for three decades, until 1950, annual average rates were below 6 percent; there was a private central bank that followed, during part of this period, the gold standard. Since then and until 1963, the objective of monetary policy was to promote economic development. Average inflation rates almost doubled. Between 1963 and 1971, when monetary policy was in the hands of the government-controlled Monetary Board, multiple quotas were created to favor the private sector. Starting in 1972, annual average inflation rates were about 22 percent, due to indexations, accumulated price inertia and monetary increases. After 1991, with a more autonomous central bank, inflation rates fell to one digit. Inflation has been especially low since the late 1990s. The current annual rate is less than 6 percent.

The historical evolution in economic and social matters has interacted with notable cultural changes brought about by huge technological advances and the powerful forces of globalization. Also, drug trafficking has had devastating economic, political and social effects. According to Steiner (1997), net income associated with narcotics exports was highest in the first half of the 1980s, representing about 7 percent of GDP and 70 percent of total exports (according to estimates, not the official balance of payments figures). In the 1990s it declined to about 3 percent of GDP and 25 percent of total exports.

THE POLITICAL AND ECONOMIC CONTEXT

During the second half of the twentieth century, the Colombian institutional and regulatory system was based on a mixed economy oriented towards growth and stability. Although each administration produced its own development plans, policy decisions were focused on short-term circumstances and macroeconomic policies. In the words of Miguel Urrutia, one of the most prominent policymakers in Colombia, who served as head of the National Planning Agency, Minister of Mining and Energy and head of the Banco de la República (the Central Bank), 'both political parties support a mixed economy, but have been reluctant to establish state enterprises outside of public utilities and natural resource exploitation' (Urrutia 1988, p. 156). The 1990s, however, marked a swift conceptual change toward reducing state interventionism, even in those sectors.

Two different phases can be identified in terms of the role of the state in national development, the role of economic institutions and the extent of state regulations. The first phase, between the 1950s and the 1970s, which we could call more *Cepalino* (after CEPAL, the Spanish acronym for the UN Economic Commission for Latin America), gave higher priority to import substitution policies, complemented by an early support to export diversification. The regulatory framework included a variety of controls, subsidies, targeted credits and protectionist tariff regimes. Planning agencies elaborated plans to help guide that strategy, and a growing number of public agencies were created to implement policies and regulations. Monetary agencies combined the goals of price stability and productive development through the creation of production quotas, selective borrowing and inflationary subsidies for the public and private sectors. As in other countries, foreign exchange restrictions and the need for external financing imposed limitations on economic policy decisions and increased the leverage of multilateral institutions on internal economic processes.

The second phase, starting in the 1970s, brought criticisms to the previous policy framework, advancing a neoliberal view of development, with fewer state regulations, controls, subsidies and protectionist tariffs. Short-term planning, with an emphasis on project evaluation and macroeconomic adjustment programs, became more prominent. Monetary authorities gave priority to the control of inflation. The gradual dismantling of the institutions and regulations of the previous period was clearly accentuated in the course of the 1990s.

In both periods, short-term crises and booms led to stabilization policies whose instruments were not necessarily consistent with the then predominant theories and visions of development. Paradoxically, this has been at the roots of policy continuity and pragmatism as well as the remarkable stability of the economy's main variables. Two factors were crucial: the exchange regime adopted in 1967 after several years of internal economic turmoil and institutions in the coffee sector.

Indeed, the broad consensus around the exchange regime, which lasted from 1967 to 1991, was an essential source of the stability that set Colombia apart from other Latin American countries. There may have been differences in emphasis, but the flexibility to manage scarcity and abundance of foreign exchange was widely valued. The system was so flexible that in periods of currency appreciation or excessive devaluations, it was possible to use a variety of policy instruments to make necessary corrections, introduce compensatory measures for affected sectors and resume a path of stability in real exchange rates (Jaramillo et al. 1999).

Given the political, social and economic influence of coffee, this sector's regulations and institutions had a major impact on macroeconomic management and economic stability. Through the National Federation of Coffee Growers (*Federación Nacional de Cafeteros*), this sector's leaders played a major role in policy negotiations. After all, as late as the 1980s, coffee represented half of Colombian exports.

At the risk of offering a somewhat simplified picture of the diverse and complex political and institutional context in which the Colombian economy has developed, and of the economists' role in that process, I will distinguish two main periods: the National Front (1958–74) and the 1990s, in which structural reforms were implemented.

NATIONAL FRONT, TECHNOCRACY AND POLICY-MAKING

The National Front was an agreement between the two main political parties to alternate in power while excluding other political forces. In an effort to put an end to a long period of violent confrontations, the National Front turned to less ideological party stands, and instituted parity in the bureaucracy and in elective offices. 1974 marked the formal conclusion of the pact, but the losing party retained representation in top government posts until the 1980s.

Because the National Front was more a mechanism to consolidate the power of economic elites than a formula for economic and social development, major reforms were not to be expected: no property or income redistribution took place and there was no reconfiguration of the economic functions of the state. The priorities were, instead, to increase economic growth with social policies and state services for the poorest groups; political agreements on regional budgetary allocations were used as 'palliative steps to calm and control the lower income groups' (Berry 1980, p. 292; Leal 1984).

Thus, in its political dimension, the system emphasized clientelistic relations. Political leaders, especially at the regional level, built political and electoral machines based on the distribution of budgetary resources. In its economic dimension, this arrangement favored a highly autonomous technocracy in charge of macroeconomic policies that was largely insulated from political pressures, technically qualified, imbued of a 'rationalizing' mission, and quite free from party commitments and radical ideological postures. This technocratic consensus was reinforced by the lack of a clear ideological differentiation between the main political parties, especially in their economic programs.

In their relationship with entrepreneurial groups, economic policy agencies operated through a complex set of subsidies, specific credit and budgetary programs, with shifting sectoral priorities but in a context of relative macroeconomic stability (Urrutia 1991). These interrelations, in turn, were nurtured and strengthened by the fluid movement of top-level technocrats between the public and private spheres.

The National Front contributed to 'depoliticize the government structure [and] advance political modernization in the form of a more technocratic state' (Cepeda and Mitchell 1980, p. 237). It should be noted, however, that this was a selective rather than a generalized phenomenon; various public agencies, either because of their functions or for their direct involvement with regions, are operated through clientelistic networks, with the consequent loss of policy coordination and coherence.

It is in this political context that the 'technocratic elite', or the economic team, as it was later known, established relationships with international multilateral agencies. These agencies influenced the decision-making process for the following four reasons, according to Cepeda and Mitchell (1980): first, the presence of a large number of national experts (especially economists and engineers) who alternated between posts in Colombia and in international agencies; second, through consultative groups and technical missions, agreements were reached regarding the design of economic policies and their external funding; third, multilateral entities played an active role in the creation of more technical, autonomous public institutions (74 of them were established between 1954 and 1974), which received preferential loans and technical assistance; fourth, these agencies contributed to formulate priorities for external borrowing and public investment, strengthening domestic technical capacity and the potential to evaluate foreign loans.

Initially, the design and organization of government economic agencies was made with the contribution of foreign technical missions and foreign experts, especially in the areas of planning, programming, taxation, monetary and exchange regulations. These missions constituted the preferred instrument for the diagnosis and formulation of vast economic reforms. It was only later that Colombian experts began to assume a dominant role.[3]

Since the 1960s, economists' involvement in decision-making took place in a pragmatic and non-ideological context. Party membership did not influence the basic course of economic policies, although it led to different emphases and different combination of policy instruments. The National Front 'removed many basic issues in development policy from direct exposure to political debate, . . . increasing the probability that aspects of economic strategy could be defined and addressed as technical in nature . . . technical qualifications became the main prerequisite for individuals to have access to policy design' (Cepeda and Mitchell 1980, p. 245). Top-level technocrats strengthened their autonomy and their public role was not conditioned on party affiliation and not subject to detailed congressional scrutiny. The Congress was more interested in the regional distribution of budgetary resources than in the overall analysis of economic policies. These conditions were maintained after the National Front ended.

What are the factors behind this technocratic consensus? In addition to the bureaucratic and political coalitions emerging from the National Front pact and the complex, exclusionary political and institutional system it generated, some authors have highlighted other reasons: first, the characteristics of the technocrats' academic training, mostly based on the neoclassical economic tradition (especially at the Universidad de los Andes); second, the role of FEDESARROLLO, founded in 1970 as an independent private economic research center and actively involved in policy design and in the training of researchers and national leaders (Meisel 1996).

FEDESARROLLO was spearheaded by Rodrigo Botero (former Economy Minister under President Lleras Restrepo and the first Finance Minister under President López Michelsen in 1974) and Manuel Carvajal, a prominent entrepreneur. FEDESARROLLO's main mission has been to analyze and debate economic policy, for which it organizes periodical seminars and events. It publishes *Coyuntura Económica*, a journal of ample circulation.[4]

FEDESAROLLO was initially funded by the Ford Foundation and Colombian entrepreneurial groups. Later, funding came from income from contracts with public and private entities to conduct research and consulting. FEDESARROLLO is quite possibly the country's most influential economic research center, having more international exchanges with foreign think tanks than any other. It should be noted that, since the 1970s, government economic teams have been led by former FEDESARROLLO directors and researchers, many of whom have also been leaders of interest group associations. Top Colombian economists have had high levels of mobility, serving as Finance ministers, members of the Board of the Central Bank, FEDESARROLLO researchers and international officials. In fact, for the past two decades, of a total of eleven Finance ministers, six have occupied positions in international organizations. There are strong connections between undergraduate economics degrees obtained at the Universidad de los Andes and graduate studies in the United States. Seven of the last eleven Finance ministers studied first at the Universidad de los Andes and later enrolled in economics graduate programs in the United States. As indicated in Table 5.1, six members of the Board of the

*Table 5.1 Economists and economic policy, 1980–2004**

Name of official	Undergr.	Graduate		Finance Ministers	Board of Central Bank	Other public posts	Fed[b]	International				Dean/ Professor Andes
	Andes[a]	US	Europe					IMF	WB	IDB	E[c]	
Eduardo Wiesner	X	X		1980–82		X		X	X	X		X
Roberto Junguito	X	X		1983–84; 2002	X	X	X	X				X
César Gaviria	X			1987–88		X						
Luis F. Alarcón	X	X		1989–90						X		X
Rudolph Hommes	X	X		1990–94		X		X	X			X
Guillermo Perry	X	X		1994–96		X	X		X			
José A. Ocampo		X		1996–97		X	X				X	X
Antonio Urdinola	X	X	X	1997–98		X	X					
Juan C. Restrepo			X	1998–2000		X						
Juan M. Santos			X	2001–02							X	
Alberto Carrasquilla	X	X		2003–04	X	X	X					X
Sergio Clavijo	X	X			X	X		X				X
Carlos C. Argáez	X	X			X		X					
Fernando Tenjo	X		X		X	X				X		X
Juan J. Echavarría	X	X	X		X	X						

Leonardo Villar	X	X	X	X	X	X			X
Miguel Urrutia		X		X	X	X			
Antonio Hernández[d]		X		X		X			
Luis B. Flórez[d]			X	X	X				
Salomón Kalmanovitz		X		X					
Eduardo Sarmiento	X	X			X	X		X	X
Eduardo Lora			X			X	X		

Notes:

* The table is in no way exhaustive, but intended as illustration only. Thus, for instance, it does not include information about other members of the economic team, in particular, those who during this period served as directors of the National Planning Department.

[a] Universidad de los Andes.

[b] FEDESARROLLO.

[c] ECLA.

[d] Undergraduate studies at the Universidad Nacional.

Source: Elaborated from respective CVs.

Central Bank had teaching positions or were Deans of Economics at the Universidad de los Andes.

In Colombia, debates on economic issues were less fierce than in the rest of Latin America, although they generally followed similar lines. In the 1950s, economic policy was guided by recommendations made by a technical mission sponsored by the World Bank, 'Bases for a Development Program in Colombia' (Currie 1951). This, a pioneer mission in developing countries, prepared a comprehensive program for economic and social development with the participation of sectoral experts from the World Bank, the International Monetary Fund (IMF), and specialists in taxation and budgetary matters (Richard Musgrove, among others). The mission was led by Professor Lauchlin Currie, a distinguished Canadian economist who had worked as an economic adviser in the Roosevelt administration and later persecuted in the United States during the McCarthy era. Currie had designed during the New Deal years a reactivation strategy which was based on the concept of net public spending.

Currie wrote the World Bank's mission final report which contained an exhaustive diagnosis of the country's economy showing that its main problems were the underutilization and inefficient use of land and agricultural labor and the lack of integration of the national market. To address the first issue, various tax schemes were proposed – and promptly rejected.[5] An infrastructural program was partially financed by the World Bank. As a result of the Mission's proposal, a National Planning Council was set up, a predecessor of the National Planning Department (DNP), which led to the adoption of important changes in exchange policies.[6] The Currie report, according to Urrutia, one of the staunchest critics of Currie's thesis, 'showed the first generation of Colombian economists how it was possible to apply economic theory to the specific problems of their country' (Urrutia 1988, p. 165).

The role played by Lauchlin Currie in Colombian economics deserves a more detailed discussion. Although CEPAL's ideas and prescriptions had many followers, no one exerted greater influence over this country's economic policy than Currie. Indeed, his theses represented a break with other schools of economic thought (Flórez 2002). On the basis of his theoretical insights and policy experience, Currie designed a development strategy for Colombia that could be generalized to other countries. After the World Bank mission was over,[7] he carried out other studies of Colombia's regions without the sponsorship of a multilateral organization. Currie promoted economic research at the Universidad Nacional; from the *Centro de Investigaciones para el Desarrollo* (CID), he advanced the concept of cities within cities as a method of urban planning, according to which production centers and urban services would be located close to employment sites. (The urban development plans of Bogotá and Manizales derived from this approach.) Currie's work at the University inspired a group of economists who later created FINES, a research institution for the debate of national issues.

For the following 30 years, Currie continued to work on the elaboration of economic concepts and diagnoses eventually presenting a complete, coherent theory of growth (Sandilands 1990). Unfortunately, Currie's contributions have not been fully understood by his critics. His theoretical explanation centered on the effects of market size and growth rate (real demand in Say's terms) on the generation and full exploitation of internal and external economies of scale, the adoption of more productive and profitable technologies, specialization and changes in proportional use of factors. All these elements, taken together, would generate new increases in real demand, in a dynamic and cumulative trend. From this perspective, Currie criticized traditional neoclassical growth models (according to which production functions had constant returns to scale and technical progress was exogenous) as well as later theories of endogenous growth (in which growth is the result of investments in physical and human capital leading to externalities and economies of scale). Currie argued that although endogenous theories were superior because they specified the components of the production function, they remained tied to old conceptions in which growth depended on previous increases in those components. On the contrary, he said, external economies and economies of scale, the degree of specialization, technological change and the relative remuneration of productive factors depended upon the market's size and growth rate. A remarkable implication of this contribution was Currie's formulation of an alternative theory of income distribution that pointed to the irrelevance and lack of realism of neoclassical theory based on the marginal productivity of factors.

Currie's many ideas have been neglected by mainstream economics. Krugman (1994) has highlighted two reasons why dominant schools of economic thought ignored theses like Currie's, Hirschman's and those of other development theorists. First, they were not expressed with technical rigor, as understood by mainstream economists, that is in the language of formal, mathematical models, 'that were increasingly becoming the unique language of discourse of economic analysis' from the 1970s on. Secondly, only when such concepts as external economies and increasing returns to scale could be modeled did their general theoretical relevance and practical importance begin to be recognized, as demonstrated by the theories of endogenous growth. Krugman's question regarding the benefits that could have been obtained but for these two methodological obstacles, remains unanswered.

Despite the relative lack of acrimonious disputes among economists in Colombia in the 1960s and early 1970s, there were contrasting views on development. In the 1960s, development strategies were based on the tenets of CEPAL, which highlighted two principal obstacles to economic growth: capital and foreign currency shortages and the low productivity of the agricultural sector due to land tenure patterns. CEPAL recommended a policy of imports substitution, new export incentives, greater external financing and agrarian reform policies. This diagnosis served as the basis for the Ten Year Development Plan, formulated in Colombia at the beginning of the 1960s (*Departamento Administrativo de Planeación*, 1960). As mentioned earlier, specific projects, especially in infrastructure, received significant external funding through the Alliance for Progress.

The main critic of this plan was Currie, who thought the plan lacked a rigorous analysis and did not adequately justify the assumption that savings and foreign currency scarcity were key restrictions. He also complained about the diagnosis of agricultural problems and the absence of specific policy proposals. In 1963, Currie presented an alternative program – known as Operación Colombia – which recommended the massive creation of jobs in urban areas through housing construction, public services and a long-term financing system to guarantee the real value of loans and interests (Currie 1968). The government did not accept Currie's proposal, but the CEPAL-inspired plan did not fare much better. In spite of the availability of foreign loans and technical assistance, a deep economic and inflationary crisis in the early sixties conspired against the implementation of the plan. Currie viewed the Plan CEPAL as a stillborn effort that contributed to the discrediting of global planning. Ironically, Currie's criticisms later targeted the Planning Department itself: 'nobody knew for sure what it did, yet the idea spread that a theoretically competent group was dealing with important issues' (Currie 1984, p. 123). This posture probably explains the intense criticism and rejection that Currie suffered in the coming decade.

Many economists of various ideological persuasions participated in this debate, which in its most fundamental aspects dealt with opposing views on the agrarian problem and its solutions (Arrubla 1976). For CEPAL's adherents, the issue amounted to agrarian reform and incentives for small farmers to increase agricultural productivity and food supply. For Currie, on the contrary, the problem was the excessive competition between commercial and traditional agriculture and the limited mobility of rural labor, which obstructed capitalist development in the countryside, keeping most producers impoverished. Under these circumstances, increasing agricultural productivity and the amount of cultivated land would lead to more poverty among the rural population, given the low elasticity of demand for agricultural products. The solution to the agrarian problem, in Currie's opinion, rested on the creation of urban jobs.[8]

Another controversial issue, before the 1967 adoption of a flexible approach to currency management, had to do with the accumulated deterioration in the exchange rate. Abrupt devaluations were often accompanied by complementary trade liberalization or import controls, as recommended by the IMF. Probably, the most telling controversy in this respect was generated by the 1962 devaluation, which was introduced to cope with serious external and fiscal imbalances, declining economic growth and rising inflation. In November of 1962, after lengthy discussions, the exchange rate was adjusted. The main pressure groups, however, had anticipated the benefits of this measure or had protected themselves against its costs, including wage, price and tariff increases. The debate, which involved congressional and party leaders, was essentially a political one. Economists' voices were marginal, since the profession had still limited influence. As one of the protagonists of this debate later said, the management of the crisis was so deplorable that for many years the term 'devaluation' came to be considered offensive and barred from the economic policy lexicon (Vélez et al. 1962).

During the first half of the 1970s, the development model was based on the ideas and proposals that Currie had been reiterating. They were adopted in the Development Plan '*Las Cuatro Estrategias*' during the administration of President Pastrana Borrero (1970–74) of the National Front (Departamento Nacional de Planeación 1972).[9] According to this diagnosis, labor demand had to increase in sectors with high growth potential, such as construction and exports. Policy efforts should center on reorienting savings toward construction, a sector with multiplying effects on job creation and economic growth. A system for savings and housing was devised, based on an inflation-protecting mechanism known as Constant Purchasing Power Unit or UPAC (*Unidad de Poder Adquisitivo Constante*), in which savings and loans were adjusted according to variations in the price index.

Arguments against Currie's leading sectors strategy and UPAC's inflationary effects were voiced by FEDESARROLLO and others. Professor Gustav Ranis, one of the theorists of dualism, was invited to give further credence to the critics' position during a seminar organized to debate these issues (CORP 1972).[10] In theoretical terms, Currie's diagnosis based on the concept of insufficient real demand was seen as flawed. It was contended that in order to absorb excess agricultural labor it was necessary to increase agricultural productivity and generate a surplus that could then be invested in the industrial sector. Furthermore, construction, a 'consumer' good and not a productive investment would have weak effects on growth and it would encourage more rural–urban migration, thus worsening unemployment in cities.

Currie's answer and that of the Plan's supporters showed that basic concepts had been misunderstood. In particular, the difference between excess monetary demand, with its inflationary effects, and insufficient real demand, in a context of low productivity and low mobility of the agricultural labor force, had not been adequately interpreted. During the following years, as prices soared, the supposed inflationary bias of UPAC seemed to be confirmed. Amid the controversy, Francisco Ortega, a notable monetarist and later a Central Bank manager, stated that the validity of monetarist theories could be questioned in view of Colombia's inflationary experience; he argued that the impact of climate and other factors should be further explored (Ortega 1974). Currie's camp dismissed UPAC's role in price increases, counter-arguing that expansionary monetary and fiscal policies were the real factors behind inflationary trends (Hernández 1974).

Under President López Michelsen (1974–78), the economic debate focused on trade initiatives and financial liberalization (based on McKinnon's thesis of 1974) as well as higher interest rates to promote capital accumulation.[11] Criticisms came, primarily, from economists with a Keynesian or CEPAL-like orientation. Since then, economic debates have centered – sometimes exclusively – on macroeconomic adjustment, especially after the international crisis of the early 1980s and after Colombia's adoption, in 1984, of fiscal and exchange measures designed to face the dramatic worsening of all economic indicators.

One of the main figures in these debates was José Antonio Ocampo, Colombia's most distinguished economist who also enjoys the highest level of international prestige.[12] From the Center for Economic Research at the Universidad de los Andes (CEDE), Ocampo organized a symposium critical of orthodox adjustment. In his view, the severe crisis of the 1980s revealed the enormous weaknesses of the neoliberal policies implemented in Latin America: 'If in the seventies we witnessed the decline of neo-Keynesianism and the traditional CEPAL approach, in the last few years we have seen the crumbling of neoliberal economic models, which to various degrees in different countries have been replacing those schools of thought' (Ocampo 1984). At the 1984 symposium there was clear opposition to financial laissez-faire, to the inflationary and recessive consequences of devaluation and to monetary policies in a context of regulated prices.[13]

The excessive focus on short-term issues was also objected because it resulted in price stability without economic growth. President Barco (1986–90), a liberal leader of strong social convictions, acknowledged the need for economic stability, but questioned the short-term bias of the existing policies and their negative impact on production and employment. Barco's economic team, formed by socialdemocratic economists (some had stayed from the previous administration), was charged with consolidating economic stability while simultaneously boosting the anti-poverty programs announced during the presidential campaign. Among other members of this team were César Gaviria, María Mercedes Cuellar, Luis Fernando Alarcón, Antonio Hernández and Luis Bernardo Flórez. Barco's strategy was based on the concept of the 'social economy': incentives to private investments would lead to higher, sustainable rates of economic growth, public investment would be reoriented, and social programs to fight absolute poverty would receive high priority (Departamento Nacional de Planeación 1987).

At this time, Colombia still had a mixed economy system with high levels of state intervention and regulation. Privatization and radical economic liberalization were not yet part of the policy agenda; no one was advocating those measures. It is telling that, in 1987, another major debate was organized by Ocampo (of FEDESARROLLO) and Eduardo Sarmiento (of Universidad de los Andes, who had worked with Currie and also at the National Planning Department and FEDESARROLLO) to challenge the thesis of Balassa and other authors who had served as inspiration for the Washington Consensus (Balassa et al. 1986). Participants in this seminar insisted on the importance of continuing the import substitution strategy, pointing to the dangers of an indiscriminate opening of the economy and the costs of financial liberalization. Mention was made of the important role of the state in society and strategies were proposed, among other things, to complement export promotion and the development of internal markets, the gradual and selective elimination of controls, the use of compulsory mechanisms to increase internal savings, the continuation of existing policies to face foreign debts while resisting the liberalizing policies advocated by the World Bank, and increases in public investment with high social return, even if it meant higher taxes (Ocampo and Sarmiento 1987).[14] It must be noted that, in the 1990s, FEDESARROLLO radically shifted its stance and came to defend the very ideas that had been condemned at the 1984 gathering.

In early 1990, the government of President Barco initiated a series of changes in the development model to increase competitiveness, strengthen the export sector and stimulate productive restructuring. This program gave exports the leading role in economic growth with a gradual policy of economic opening and competitive exchange rates (CONPES 1990).

Between 1990 and 1994, under President Gaviria, an economist and politician with vast experience as Barco's Finance Minister and Government

Minister (and later Secretary General of the Organization of American States), the opening of the economy became the axis of the new development model. Its implementation was accelerated, together with wide-ranging reforms aimed at market deregulation and liberalization. The idea that excessive state interventionism had led to inefficient economic performance justified changes in the financial, labor and exchange markets. New regimes were introduced in the areas of taxation, foreign investment, trade, debt, and eventually social security. New laws led to the replacement of traditional interventionist tools. The privatization of state firms, concessions to the private sector and direct subsidies to demand phased out the managerial functions of the state. A new ideological profile emerged instead of Colombia's historic preference for pragmatic and gradual economic adjustments. Apart from confrontations dealing with the fast pace of liberalization and deregulation, another major debate occurred in the second half of the 1990s regarding macroeconomic imbalances. The exchange rate system adopted by the Central Bank and the 1998 rise in interest rates, critics charged, had caused the deep economic crisis at the century's end.

THE POLITICAL AND ECONOMIC REFORMS OF THE 1990s

At the beginning of the 1990s, Colombia, far from experiencing an economic crisis, had consolidated its macroeconomic stability with higher levels of economic growth and persistent reductions in the unemployment and poverty rates. The only worrying factor was the acceleration of inflation above what was then considered acceptable levels (annual rates of 26–28 percent). That was the price the Barco administration paid for adopting a policy of active devaluation aimed at sustaining a gradual opening of the economy. Unlike other Latin American countries, the urgency to introduce market reforms did not stem from the need to adopt major stabilization and adjustment programs. From a long-term perspective, however, it was necessary to face the weakening of the economy and adapt to the new global environment. The urgency was coming from a crisis of governance, the lack of legitimacy of representative institutions unable to secure law and order and guarantee citizens' rights. The influence of drug trafficking on institutional performance and on the structure of income and spending was significant.

In 1991, vast political reforms were formalized in a new constitution, which on the basis of a broad social and political consensus established new citizens' rights, new avenues for their participation and new institutions. The 1991 constitution may be viewed as a system with four pivotal components, which were not necessarily consistent: more market-based economic growth; more participatory democracy, solidarity and governability; rule of law as a prerequisite for equality and social justice, and inflation control as a condition for economic stability (Flórez 2001b). Thus, at the beginning of the nineties, Colombia had two significant structural reforms: an economic reform, conceptually akin to the Washington consensus, and the other, a major political and institutional reform.

It must be noted that, although the political reform reflected a broad consensus among traditional political forces and new social movements – including demobilized guerilla movements which participated in the constitutional assembly – the content and orientation of the economic reforms did not rely on those political agreements. The agreements behind the new political model had no equivalent in the area of economic reforms. On the contrary, the latter were adopted without much public debate, while society was focused on the implementation of political changes. Gradually, two positions became more clearly delineated, which in their most pure versions we could call a social-democratic camp – defending the precepts of the political and institutional reforms, and the neoliberal camp – supporting economic liberalism.

This new confrontation had no precedent in the traditional political divisions between liberals and conservatives. As an illustration, consider that President Samper (1994–98) and his predecessor Gaviria, both members of the Liberal party, pursued different policy strategies. President Samper, deviating from the neoliberal approach followed under Gaviria, implemented development policies with an emphasis on social equality.[15] He negotiated with representatives of economic and social interests to sign a pact on prices, wages and productivity that would complement macroeconomic policies. Thus, lower rates of inflation would be achieved without big sacrifices in employment and production. The support for technological development, human capital formation and productive modernization would make the economy more competitive and economic openness more sustainable. The modernization of infrastructure and communication received greater impulse to strengthen exports and domestic production. Various social investment programs were introduced to link economic growth with more equitable social development. The seriousness of the crisis and the depth of political polarization that accompanied the Samper government, however, tarnished the great achievements of this period.

Since then, debates have stressed the differences between the contents and objectives of the 'economic model' under way and the corresponding 'constitutional model'.[16] The new economic model was intended to open up space for market mechanisms and private initiatives in areas previously reserved to the state, which would then play a more limited and subordinate role. The constitutional model included guidelines for state intervention leading to greater equity, guaranteeing access to basic goods and services, especially among lower income groups. Thus, while the constitutional model tended to strengthen the state, the neoliberal economic model weakened it. While the first model demanded more public spending, the second reduced it. The first recognized new social rights, the second limited them. The first tried to combine efficiency with equity, the second sought to subordinate equity to efficiency. This lack of coherence caused enormous tensions and acute fiscal and exchange imbalances that compromised the political legitimacy of the constitutional model as well as the consistency and credibility of the economic model. The redistribution of power and resources mandated by the new constitution was compounded by globalization's encroachments on national policy autonomy to further debilitate Colombia's governance (Misas 2002).

In Colombia as well as in Latin America as a whole, the twentieth century concluded with the type of disputes that had informed economic thought for much of it: protectionism vs free trade; shock vs gradualism; selectivity vs universality; decentralization vs centralism; and interventionism vs deregulation. But new topics also emerged in the context of reforms; among others, the independence of the Central Bank.

The Debate on Central Bank Independence

The 1991 constitution considered autonomy and independence for the Central Bank (*Banco de la República*). For some, this represented the triumph of monetarism. The view that no long-term trade-off could exist between inflation and growth had gained acceptance in an international theoretical and ideological environment that assumed a significant correlation between low inflation and greater Central Bank independence, and between lower inflation and greater economic growth. The Central Bank's role in preserving the value of the currency could not be jeopardized by attempts to coordinate monetary with overall economic policy (Misas 2002). For others, dissatisfaction with the results of past monetary and credit policies was paramount: inflation had been persistent, if moderate, monetary policy had been used to finance fiscal deficits; the monetary authority had used discretionary, arbitrary decisions to impose inflationary taxes. They also argued that the Central Bank had become an institution that issued loans at subsidized rates, instead of being a monetary authority. From this perspective, the most positive and substantial change introduced by the 1991 constitution was to prohibit the Central Bank from lending to the private sector (Hernández 2001). Critics faulted the new

Central Bank regime for favoring the control of inflation at the expense of other economic policy objectives, such as reacting with more flexibility to new economic crises (Cuevas and Pérez 2001).

This controversy led new proposals for constitutional reform. One proposed restoring the Central Bank to its previous role as a development bank: instead of limiting monetary policy to inflation control, the Bank would issue loans to priority sectors at subsidized rates. This would imply, in turn, reinstating the integrity of macroeconomic management, with the Finance Minister as the principal policy actor (Agudelo 2001). An alternative proposal recommended an increase in the Bank's autonomy, awarding high priority to the control of inflation, even excluding the Finance Minister from membership on the Bank's Board of Directors (Alesina et al. 2000).

Other Debates in the 1990s

Despite the huge concentration of land in the hands of paramilitary groups and drug traffickers, agrarian reform or plans for structural changes in this sector were not part of the political and economic agenda of the 1990s. Instead, the agenda was dominated by other issues: the technological transformation of some sectors, export diversification, trade expansion, foreign investments, and deepening trade and financial liberalization.

The deep recession of the late 1990s was unusually harsh for Colombian standards. This led many economists to reconsider their positions as they discussed the causes and symptoms of the recession, the vulnerability of Colombia's economy in a more open economic environment and the transmission mechanisms of external crises. Dissension has been strong in terms of the selectivity and the pace of economic reforms, the role of the state, and the relationship between liberalization, growth and equity, despite a relative consensus regarding the need to open up the economy. Some authors claimed that a new social and economic order was urgently needed because economic globalization had exacerbated social exclusion and the concentration of wealth (Restrepo Botero 2003).[17] The effects of the liberalization of capital flows also generated questions about the new economic model, especially after the Asian crisis of the late 1990s. Critics of neoliberalism argued that the model resulted in unstable economic growth and employment, making compensatory measures necessary to limit the spread and impact of external shocks. Furthermore, trade or capital barriers would be advisable policy measures, contrary to what Washington Consensus precepts indicate and what globalization enthusiasts say.

Yet those adhering to neoclassical economics seem to regard those ideas as absolute true. A Finance Minister expressed his views in Darwinian evolutionary terms: 'all of the world's wealth is being created as . . . a result of competition' (Carrasquilla 1999a). In this perspective, the market is seen as the only true model; state intervention in production, investment or the financing of social spending is perceived as dysfunctional.

Ex-post assessments of the market model were especially contentious in the late 1990s, when economic and social indicators were negative despite a drop to one-digit inflation rates. Economic debates, although technical on the surface, were primarily ideological and political in nature. As Ocampo has said:

> Controversies on the Colombian economy in the nineties have not been separate from the country's general process of polarization. Opinions on economic liberalization go from those who believe that it represents the start of the disaster to those who think it was not radical enough. Worse yet, manichaeism has penetrated deeply in these debates. Economic trends in the nineties, more than in any previous stage in our economic history, have been analyzed in terms of heroes and villains. (Ocampo 2001, p. 11)

THE ROLE AND EDUCATION OF ECONOMISTS

Parallel to changes in economic policies and theories there has been a gradual transformation in the education of Colombian economists and in their role in society. The teaching of economics partly emerged as an attempt to correct excessive empiricism in economic analysis. The professionalization of economics coincided with the expansion of Colombia's economic base, which required the managing of complex phenomena. Simple empiricism was not enough (Universidad Nacional 1968). The Institute for Economic Science was created in 1945. Its founder was Professor Antonio García, a notable Colombian thinker who made important contributions to the theoretical and historical analysis of Latin American economies. From a perspective that anticipated the latinamerican dependency school, Professor García's rich conceptual framework and detailed knowledge of Latin America explained how international structures of domination and dependence caused structural underdevelopment (García 1972).

In the 1960s, the restructuring of economics education in the country's main universities was gradually placed in the hands of economists trained abroad, primarily in the United States. Specific agreements and economists associated with outside missions also brought foreign professors to Colombian universities.[18]

Since the 1970s, public agencies (such as the National Planning Department, the National Statistics Department, DANE, and decentralized ministries and institutes) as well as private entities (large firms and interest associations) demanded more specific skills for economists. Simultaneously, Currie's proposals on the education of economists were made public. He called for a new academic system in which the first years would be devoted to general education and basic concepts. Greater specialization and in-depth study of authors would come later, when students would be spending less time attending lectures and more on developing their own research skills (Currie 1965). These recommendations were taken into account at the Universidad de los Andes and at the Universidad Nacional, although not without debates and political confrontations. Professor Currie complained about the hostility, at best indifference, toward scientific processes in less developed countries:

> One of the results of being an underdeveloped country is the disadvantaged conditions under which scientists work: they are not given the place they deserve and are not listened to. Sometimes I wonder what would have been the fate of the 'General Theory of Employment' if Keynes had been a Latin American and had written in Spanish. . . . Perhaps if I had published the basic theory of Operación Colombia as a professor in Harvard or Cambridge, under the arid title 'Accelerated Development Through Induced Structural Changes' I would have received a more respectful acceptance in Colombia. (Currie 1963, p. 1)

Between 1970 and 1980, the teaching and professionalization of economic science were progressively institutionalized. The university acquired an important role in the analysis of the country's economic problems. As one of the most lucid, sharp and polemic economists of the 1980s and 1990s said, research coming from universities centered on economic development and its determinants (among others, the theories of dependency and imperialism), industrialization and its connected problems, the agrarian question, as well as economic history and economic policy, which was also studied at FEDESARROLLO, the National Planning Department and the Central Bank (Bejarano 1997).

In the early 1980s, theoretical specialization and analytical formalism were more stressed, particularly by neo-Keynesian groups at the Universidad de los Andes and by neo-Marxists and neo-Ricardians at public universities, especially at the Universidad Nacional, the Universidad de Antioquia and the Universidad del Valle. Since the mid-1980s, due to curricular changes and the greater influence of foreign-trained economists, neoclassical theory gained ground, at the expense of Keynesian, neo-Keynesian and Marxist orientations (González 1999). This shift led to new priorities in research and economics education. We must note that since 1983–84, the Colombian economy went through successive adjustments that weakened the import substitution model, stimulating interest

Table 5.2 Policy-makers in macroeconomic area, 1958–2000

Categories	1958–1982	1982–2000	1958–2000
Policy-makers[a]	30	32	62
Policy positions[b]	34	38	72
Policy-makers with economics Ph.D.	3	9	12
Finance Ministers	16	11	27
DNP Directors	13	12	25
Central Bank managers	5	3	8
Central Bank Board members	0	12	12
More than one post	4	6	10

Notes:

[a] Policy-makers include: Finance Ministers, National Planning Department (DNP) Directors and Central Bank managers and members of the Board.

[b] The number of posts is greater than the number of policy-makers because some individuals have occupied more than one position.

Source: Palacios (2001).

in new research areas, accelerating the decline of theories that had guided debates in the 1960s. At the same time, the importance of economists in decision-making was increasingly evident. Economists' advanced training was seen as the basis for their leading role in economic policy (see Table 5.2). A similar trend can be observed at the *Centro de Investigaciones para el Desarrollo* of the Universidad de los Andes and at FEDESARROLLO.

Economics Education

Initially, economics education in Colombia was limited to specialization programs offered by public institutions that trained professionals in law and commerce at the Universidad Nacional and the Universidad de Antioquia. The economics program at the Universidad de los Andes, which was founded in 1948, started offering industrial economics, a combination of industrial engineering and business administration. In the 1960s, professionalization increased and economics acquired a more distinctive profile; differentiation from law and other academic careers was consolidated, the training of economists became more specialized and greater emphasis was given to economic theories and policies. Universities stressed different schools of economic thought, but the quality of economics education still varied markedly, although less so at the seven main universities. The curricular reform of the 1970s, promoted by Lauchlin

Currie at the Universidad Nacional, reduced the number of courses and increased attention to research.[19] A rigid structure gave way to a flexible, liberal system in which debate and reasoned discussions were the norm. The new program not only included courses in the social sciences and the humanities but also economic theory in its three basic paradigms: classical, neoclassical and Keynesian.

By the 1980s, the economics curriculum had clearly achieved a separate identity. Currently, there are 98 economics programs in the country. All the main economics programs offer similar course contents, albeit with differences in the level of depth assigned to the various topics. The curriculum is typically centered upon principles of economics, microeconomics, macroeconomics and introduction to the Colombian economy, in addition to quantitative courses. Also included are courses in applied economics, economic policy, fiscal and monetary theory and policy, international trade and international economics. History lost importance in economics education, as neoclassical economics favoring mathematical formalism became dominant (González 1999). Faculty appointments vary: the main economics programs tend to employ full-time professors-researchers, whereas part-time professors are common in the other schools. This results in unequal levels of training for the new generation, despite similarities in curricular content and structure.

The number of economics students has increased significantly. In 1985, there were 3000 first-year students; by the mid-1990s, the number had risen to 5100. In 2002, higher education enrollment was down and the preference for studying economics also declined. The Universidad Nacional and Universidad de los Andes, however, increased their enrollment (Table 5.3).

Evolution of Economics Education

At the master's level, economics education has flourished. The number of graduates went from 31 to 138 between 1990 and 2002 (Table 5.4). In 1996, the Universidad Nacional initiated a doctoral program in economics following a system similar to European doctorates, with a significant research component. This program requires at least one semester of research in a foreign university; currently, agreements have been signed with the Universidad de Salamanca and Alcalá de Henares. Four students have graduated and there are 24 students registered, the majority of whom are professors in public universities. No foreign students have enrolled until now.

The Central Bank has been a major source of funding to study economics abroad: 122 scholarships between 1982 and 2004 (45 for Bank's officials

Table 5.3 Evolution of economics education in Colombia

University	Enrollment					
	Year	Max.	Applic.	1st yr.	Last yr.	Grads.
Total	1985	4966	4818	3026	2031	1886
	1990	5122	6422	3856	1453	1836
	1995	7093	11132	5160	2228	1641
	2000	6764	9168	3306	1989	2080
	2002	8151	8625	3359	1836	2147
Andes	1985	100	120	47	24	24
	1990	110	199	83	37	37
	1995	110	344	104	85	85
	2000	249	291	139	83	83
	2002	152	321	152	106	106
Nacional*	1985	160	284	175	90	63
	1990	143	287	113	80	73
	1995	256	1608	247	45	51
	2000	323	1829	298	97	97
	2002	330	1747	263	90	90

Note: * Until 1990, data refers to economics students at the Bogotá Campus and agricultural economics students at the Medellín Campus. Since 1995, both locations have had an economics program.

Source: Elaborated from data provided to the author by the Ministry of Education.

and 77 for people employed by other public entities). Currently, there are 35 individuals enrolled in foreign economics programs. The Central Bank's policy is to allow prospective students to choose the program they plan to attend. About two-thirds of those who have received Bank's scholarships to pursue a PhD abroad went to universities in the US.

Economic Research and Publications

Research projects on Colombia's economy, society and economic history have multiplied since the 1970s. Some, especially at FEDESARROLLO, relied on economic orthodoxy; others followed Keynesianism, Marxism, CEPAL and dependency approaches. In academic circles, intense political and ideological struggles stimulated economic debates (Kalmanovitz 1986).

The FEDESARROLLO group published a book in 1971, *Lectures on Colombian Economic Development*, with original studies on income distribution, economic growth, employment, monetary and fiscal policy,

Table 5.4 Economics students and programs: Colombia, 1960–2002

	1960–75	1980	1990	2000	2002
All Economics Programs (N)	16	32	58	96	98
Economics Students (N)	N.A.	N.A.	11649	15384	13643
Last-year Econ. Students	6358	1644	1453	1989	2080
Last-year High Ed. Stud.	N.A.	N.A.	43274	80939	75085
Economics graduates					
Universidad Nacional	708	18	39	51	97
Universidad de los Andes	240	31	37	83	106
MA Econ. Programs (N)	N.A.	5	8	11	13
All MA Econ. Graduates	N.A.	N.A.	31	105	138
MA Econ. Graduates Universidad Nacional	N.A.	0	3	18	24
MA Econ. Graduates Universidad de los Andes	N.A.	0	21	10	24
Total MA Graduates	N.A.	N.A.	791	1319	1741

Note: N.A.: Not available.

Source: Data provided to the author by the Ministry of Education.

planning, and the external and agrarian sectors, which quickly became a widely used text. The authors included both foreign academics with vast experience on Colombia (such as Albert Berry) and Colombian economists who would later occupy influential policy positions: Miguel Urrutia, Eduardo Wiesner, Francisco Ortega, Roberto Junguito, Guillermo Perry, Antonio Urdinola and Eduardo Sarmiento. Since then, many research projects have been completed on various aspects of Colombian reality: economic history (José Antonio Ocampo) agriculture (Roberto Junguito) and macroeconomics (Ocampo, Eduardo Lora and others).

In the 1970s, the National Statistics Department – DANE – conducted studies on industrial concentration in Colombia (Gabriel Misas, Alberto Corchuelo), agrarian development, criticisms to dependency theory, and economic history (Salomón Kalmanovitz). The Research Center of the Universidad de Antioquia produced works on unemployment, industry and economic cycles (Juan Felipe Gaviria, Santiago Peláez, Hugo López).

And independent journals such as *Cuadernos Colombianos* published essays on history, economic development and economic policy (Jesús Antonio Bejarano, Alvaro Tirado, Germán Colmenares, Carlos Esteban Posada and Luis Bernardo Flórez).

Over time, economic research and publications became more concentrated in the following institutions: FEDESARROLLO, Universidad de los Andes, the *Asociación Bancaria de Colombia*, journals of the Universidad Nacional and Universidad de Antioquia, and the journals of the *Contraloría General*, DNP and *Banco de la República*. Although the emphases varied, the main research topics were macroeconomic policy, the sectoral and regional aspects of Colombia's economic structure, as well as economic theories. Among the main economics journals, all with very limited circulation, are: *Desarrollo y Sociedad*, published by the Universidad de los Andes (founded in 1979, has 52 issues); *Ensayos de Política Económica*, published by the Central Bank (since 1982, 44 issues); *Cuadernos de Economía*, published by the Universidad Nacional (39 issues since 1979); and *Lecturas de Economía*, published by the Universidad de Antioquia (59 issues since 1980). The first two journals have been characterized, especially in the 1990s, for spreading the neoclassical paradigm. The last two journals, with a heterodox profile, are open to different schools of thought while openly challenging neoclassical theory.

FEDESARROLLO publishes the journal *Coyuntura Económica* (33 volumes) and *Coyuntura Social* (29 issues); in addition, it conducts surveys of entrepreneurs and of the national economy. For its part, the *Contraloría General de la República* publishes the bi-monthly *Economía Colombiana*, which recently celebrated its fiftieth anniversary; this journal focuses on macroeconomic topics, sectoral policy and public administration and has a wide circulation among academic circles and in public institutions.

The authors of a recent essay on the trajectory and current state of economic research show that from the theoretical and political debates of the 1960s and 1970s – about the development of capitalism in Colombia – the attention shifted in the 1980s to short-term issues and, in more recent years, to technical formalism, the use of increasingly sophisticated modeling techniques that try to come up with the best econometric and statistical results, without addressing the relevance of theoretical precepts (Jalil and Salazar 1999).

Two of the most prominent authors of the first period were Mario Arrubla – a perceptive analyst identified with dependency theory whose 1963 book was widely debated – and Lauchlin Currie. Among the most notable authors in the second period is José Antonio Ocampo, whose contributions to economic policy debates and his heterodox ideas have been amply recognized.

Finally, the era of technical formalism includes works on general equilibrium models, theories of endogenous growth and rational expectations. Prominent analysts include former minister Juan Luis Londoño and the current Finance Minister, Alberto Carrasquilla, as well as economists at the DNP and at the Central Bank. The Bank's journal *Ensayos de Política Económica* is illustrative of this period, with its 'tradition of technical virtuosity and independence regarding the government economic policy, which over time has intensified, constituting a small discursive community, built around econometric expertise and the determination to derive policy recommendations from ever more refined econometric tests' (Jalil and Salazar 1999, p. 169).

The consolidation of academic and scientific communities has been slow. Academic debates have been limited, both within and between universities. Colombian economists remain primarily oriented toward public policy topics, working mostly for government agencies or consulting firms. After studying these issues, Jesús Antonio Bejarano made the following observations, valid until now:

> There seems to be a number of researchers, grouped in a few centers, which do not communicate, do not debate, and do not exchange the results of their work, except through publications. They do not contrast their results, do not criticize each other; in other words, these groups operate in virtual isolation. Thus, their scientific production does not have the cumulative character that is typical of scientific progress. Perhaps an explanation for the lack of community must start by acknowledging that in Colombia true academic careers do not exist. Instead, what exist are life cycles of academics who for various reasons do not persist in their research programs. Moreover, there are no incentives for competitiveness among academics, nor is there a culture of debate that could be stimulated by users of research results (for example, around the counterpoint between different schools of thought), as it indeed happened until the mid-1980s. (Bejarano 1999 pp. 190–91)

CONCLUDING REMARKS

By the middle of the twentieth century, economic debates and policy decisions in Colombia followed closely those observed in other Latin American countries. Yet the intensity of debates was lower due to the country's relative macroeconomic and price stability and the institutional agreements reached between the liberal and conservative parties, the main political groups. Colombia, at the end of the 1950s and during the 1960s, formulated development plans that, like other countries in the region, followed CEPAL's diagnoses; several of the policy recommendations made by CEPAL were implemented. Alternative strategies proposed by

Lauchlin Currie resulted in a new development stage during part of the 1970s. In the 1980s, Colombia joined international currents towards trade liberalization. In the 1990s, globalization led to the dominance of free market models, although with specific political and economic features.

Unlike the rest of Latin America, Colombia did not experience an economic crisis in the early 1990s. On the contrary, by the late 1980s it had consolidated its macroeconomic stability in the context of higher economic growth with reductions in unemployment and poverty rates. The urgency of reforms in Colombia did not originate in the need to adopt adjustment programs recommended by the International Monetary Fund. What prompted a process of reforms was the urgency of solving a governance crisis and the lack of representativeness of institutions. The 1991 constitution included profound political reforms, establishing new rights, new institutions and new forms of citizen participation.

These changes were accompanied by the not always positive influence of economists. Particularly influential has been a group of economists – mostly graduates of the Universidad de los Andes, with graduate studies in North American universities, several of them linked to FEDESARROLLO – who have constituted a technocratic group in top economic policy positions. Parallel to the transition from development debates to macroeconomic stabilization there have been changes in the education and role of economists. Since the 1980s, for example, the main universities have emphasized theoretical specialization and analytic formalism, strengthening neoclassical theory at the expense of Keynesian and Marxist orientations.

At the risk of oversimplification, it seems that a synthesis of current debates leads one to see a repetition of the controversies that took place in the past century: How much protectionism? How much free trade? What level and scope should state intervention and regulation have? How gradual or immediate should the opening toward international markets be? (This is an important issue as Colombia begins to negotiate a free trade agreement with the United States.) How much public spending should go to the armed forces and how much to social investment? All these debates continue to be imbued in deep, unresolved conflicts involving drug trafficking, paramilitary and guerrilla groups.

NOTES

1. I thank the able collaboration of Mauricio Castillo Benítez in the preparation of this chapter.
2. According to Ocampo (1992), although the accumulation of factors (labor and capital) as well as productivity 'explain' quantitative increases in economic growth, the country's various phases in economic growth have been determined by the interrelationship

between foreign currency availability and structural changes in the structure of production. Thus, periods of currency scarcity and loss in the dynamism of structural change weaken the pace of growth and productivity increases. Whereas the former was an important factor between 1950 and 1970, since then, the latter has become the main restriction.

3. For an evaluation of the approaches and results of the main foreign missions, see Currie (1984).
4. FEDESAROLLO's initial technical team was partly formed by former members of the National Planning Department (among them, Roberto Junguito and Guillermo Perry, who later served as Finance ministers) who had resigned at the beginning of the Pastrana administration due to disagreements over the orientation of economic and planning policies (Gómez Buendía, 1995).
5. At the time, Colombian policies relied heavily on CEPAL's ideas. Support from the Alliance for Progress and political circumstances gave preference to a type of agricultural development based on small-sized land units.
6. The Council was formed by three Colombians close to President Roberto Urdaneta Arbeláez. It also included Albert Hirschman, hired by the World Bank as an adviser and later Currie, who joined the Council after finishing a study of Colombian regions. Disagreements and confrontations between Currie and Hirschman were intense, especially in the areas of monetary policy, industrial protectionism and agrarian reform (Sandilands 1990). It must be remembered that Hirschman's studies of the Colombian case and this experience in particular influenced his thinking on development theories and policies.
7. Currie became a Colombian citizen and lived most of the rest of his life in Colombia.
8. At the time, Currie's position was interpreted by CEPAL's followers and leftist economists as a defense of landowners' interests. Yet Currie also received support from leaders of the liberal left, such as Alfonso López, Colombia's president from 1974 to 1978.
9. Although Currie and Pastrana knew each other from the 1960s, the '*Cuatro Estrategias*' plan was partly possible thanks to the intervention of Roberto Arenas Bonilla, a leader of the liberal party and one of Currie's admirers. President Pastrana had initially followed the recommendations of the International Labor Organization mission led by the economist Dudley Seers, which had been working under President Lleras Restrepo (1966–70). Arenas Bonilla became Director of the National Planning Department and cabinet member in the Pastrana administration.
10. In addition to Ranis, other critics included policy-makers Miguel Urrutia and Guillermo Perry and the academics Guillermo Calvo and Jorge García.
11. President López's first economic team included Rodrigo Botero as Finance Minister and Miguel Urrutia as Director of the National Planning Department. Since then, debates began to more explicitly pit supporters against opponents of 'neoliberal development models' (De La Torre 1982).
12. Ocampo has been Director of FEDESARROLLO, professor and researcher at Yale and Oxford universities, Minister of Agriculture, Director of the National Planning Department and Finance Minister. Between 1998 and 2003 he served as Executive Secretary of CEPAL and is currently UN Deputy Secretary General for Economic and Social Affairs.
13. Foreign participants included distinguished economists: Carlos Díaz-Alejandro, Lance Taylor and Edmar Bacha, whose attendance was possible thanks to Ocampo's own academic connections.
14. Economists contributing to the published collection of seminar papers included, in addition to the editors: Javier Fernández, Antonio Urdinola, Jorge Méndez, Carlos Caballero, Manuel Ramírez, Roberto Junguito and Eduardo Lora, all among the country's most prominent economists, several of whom were also leaders of interest associations, directors of FEDESARROLLO, international officials and government policy-makers. I am not suggesting that all these economists felt equally identified with

the set of the above mentioned policy proposals. Each addressed specific topics, but they all shared a critical view of Balassa's thesis.

15. Samper served as Development Minister under President Gaviria until discrepancies with the government economic team on the pace of economic opening led to his resignation. A group of his economic advisers (Ocampo, Perry, Cecilia López, Gamarra and Flórez) and other social-democratic economists then elaborated a government program for his presidential bid.
16. Paradoxically, several of the economists who collaborated with President Gaviria in the 1991 political reforms later became severe critics of its results, especially the decisions adopted by the Constitutional Court to justify and implement those reforms.
17. Participants in these debates also included members of Congress, interest groups and former public officials. The latter denounced in harsh terms the economic policy decisions made during these years (Misas 2002; Restrepo Botero 2003).
18. These connections, however, cannot be compared to those existing in Chile or Mexico, because there was no major interest in financing groups of students to study at Chicago or other American Universities. There was no particular ideological bias attached to the academic training of the sort that made the 'Chicago boys' style notorious in other countries.
19. Thanks to the contacts of Professor Currie, the Universidad Nacional brought foreign economics professors to give lectures and helped some students to start graduate programs in the United States and Europe.

REFERENCES

Agudelo Villa, Hernando (2001), 'Recesión y autonomía del Banco de la República', Bogotá: SEAP.

Alesina, Alberto et al. (2000), 'The Central Bank in Colombia', Bogotá: Fedesarrollo.

Arrubla, Mario (ed.) (1976), *La agricultura colombiana en el siglo XX*, Bogotá: Colcultura.

Balassa, Bela et al. (1986), *Hacia una renovación del crecimiento económico en América Latina*, México: El Colegio de México.

Bejarano, Jesús Antonio (1997), 'La investigación económica en Colombia', *Cuadernos de Economía*, 27, Bogotá: Universidad Nacional de Colombia.

Bejarano, Jesús Antonio (ed.) (1999), *Hacia dónde va la ciencia económica en Colombia*, Bogotá: Tercer Mundo Editores.

Berry, R. Albert (1980), 'The National Front and Colombia's Economic Development', in R. Albert Berry et al., *Politics of Compromise: Coalition Government in Colombia*, New Brunswick: Transaction Books.

Carrasquilla, Alberto (1999a), 'Toro de lidia y modelo económico', *Economía Colombiana y Coyuntura Política*, 275, Bogotá: Contraloría General de la República.

Carrasquilla, Alberto (1999b), *Estabilidad y gradualismo: Ensayos sobre la economía colombiana*, Bogotá: Tercer Mundo Editores.

Cepeda Ulloa, Fernando and Christopher Mitchell (1980), 'The Trend towards Technocracy: The World Bank and the International Labor Organization in Colombian Politics', in R. Albert Berry et al., *Politics of Compromise: Coalition Government in Colombia*, New Brunswick: Transaction Books.

CONPES (1990), 'Programa de modernización de la economía colombiana', Bogotá: Departamento Nacional de Planeación, Documento DNP-2465-J.

CORP (1972), *Controversia sobre el Plan de Desarrollo*, Bogotá: Editorial La Oveja Negra.

Cuevas, Homero and Mauricio Pérez Salazar (2001), 'La economía política de la Constitución de 1991', Bogotá: Universidad Externado de Colombia.

Currie, Lauchlin (Director) (1951), *Bases de un programa de fomento para Colombia*, Mission sponsored by the World Bank, Bogotá: World Bank.

Currie, Lauchlin (1963), *La responsabilidad de los economistas en la programación nacional,* Bogotá: Fundación para el Progreso de Colombia.

Currie, Lauchlin (1965), *La enseñanza de la economía en Colombia*, Bogotá: Ediciones Tercer Mundo.

Currie, Lauchlin (1968), *Desarrollo económico acelerado*, México: Fondo de Cultura Económica.

Currie, Lauchlin (1984), *Evaluación de la asesoría económica a los países en desarrollo: El caso colombiano*, Bogotá: CEREC.

De La Torre, Cristina (ed.) (1982), *Modelos de desarrollo económico: Colombia 1960–82*, Bogotá, Editorial La Oveja Negra.

Departamento Administrativo de Planeación (1960), *Colombia: Plan general de desarrollo económico y social*, Bogotá.

Departamento Nacional de Planeación (1972), *Las cuatro estrategias*, Bogotá.

Departamento Nacional de Planeación (1987), *Plan de economía social 1987–1990*, Bogotá.

Departamento Nacional de Planeación (1991), *La revolución pacífica: Modernización y apertura de la economía*, Volume I, Bogotá.

FEDESARROLLO (1971), *Lecturas sobre desarrollo económico Colombiano*, Bogotá.

Flórez E., Luis Bernardo (2001a), 'Economía y estado social de derecho', Bogotá: ASOCAJAS.

Flórez E., Luis Bernardo (2001b), 'Colombia tras diez años de reformas políticas y económicas', *Cuadernos de Economía*, 34, Bogotá: Universidad Nacional de Colombia.

Flórez E., Luis Bernardo (2002), *El legado de Currie,* Bogotá: Universidad de los Andes.

García, N. Antonio (1972), *Atraso y dependencia en América Latina: Hacia una teoría latinoamericana del desarrollo*, Buenos Aires: Librería El Ateneo.

Gómez Buendía, Hernando (ed.) (1995), *Economía y opinión: 25 años de Fedesarrollo*, Bogotá: TM Editores.

González, Jorge Iván (1999), 'La fetichización del currículo y la absolutización del libro de texto', in Jesús Antonio Bejarano (ed.), *Hacia dónde va la ciencia económica en Colombia*, Bogotá: Tercer Mundo Editores.

Hernández G., Antonio (1974), 'El Plan y la inflación', *El Plan de Desarrollo Colombiano en Marcha*, Seminar of the Sociedad Colombiana de Economistas, directed by Lauchlin Currie, Bogotá: Departamento Nacional de Planeación.

Hernández G., Antonio (2001), 'La Banca Central en la Constitución de 1991', Bogotá: Academia Colombiana de Ciencias Económicas.

Jalil, Munir and Boris Salazar (1999), 'El estado de la investigación académica: Del vacío a la comunidad virtual', in Jesús Antonio Bejarano, (ed.), *Hacia dónde va la ciencia económica en Colombia*, Bogotá: Tercer Mundo Editores.

Jaramillo, Juan Carlos, Roberto Steiner and Natalia Salazar (1999), 'The Political Economy of Exchange Rate Policy in Colombia', Bogotá: Fedesarrollo.

Kalmanovitz, Salomón (1986), 'Notas para una historia de las teorías económicas en Colombia', *Ciencia, Tecnología y Desarrollo*, 3–4, Bogotá.

Krugman, Paul (1994), 'The Fall and Rise of Development Economics', in Lloyd Rodwin and Donald A. Schon (eds), *Rethinking the Development Experience*, Washington, DC: Brookings Institution.

Leal Buitrago, Francisco (1984), *Estado y política en Colombia*, Bogotá: Siglo XXI Editores.

McKinnon, Ronald (1974), *Dinero y capital en el desarrollo económico*, México: CEMLA.

Meisel, Adolfo R. (1996), 'Why no Hyperinflation in Colombia?: On the Determinants of Stable Economic Policies', *Borradores Semanales de Economía*, 54, Bogotá: Banco de la República.

Misas Arango, Gabriel (2002), *La ruptura de los 90: Del gradualismo al colapso*, Bogotá: Universidad Nacional de Colombia.

Ocampo, José Antonio (ed.) (1984), *La política económica en la encrucijada*, Bogotá: Editorial Presencia.

Ocampo, José Antonio (1992), 'Reforma del Estado y desarrollo económico y social en Colombia', *Análisis Político*, 17, Bogotá.

Ocampo, José Antonio (2001), *Un futuro económico para Colombia*, Bogotá: Alfaomega.

Ocampo, José Antonio and Eduardo Sarmiento (eds) (1987), *¿Hacia un nuevo modelo de desarrollo?: Un debate*, Bogotá: Tercer Mundo Editores.

Ortega, Francisco J. (1974), 'Política monetaria y precios', *El mercado de capitales en Colombia 1974*, Bogotá: Asociación Bancaria–Banco de la República.

Palacios, Marco (2001), *De populistas, mandarines y violencias: luchas por el poder*, Bogotá: Colección Grandes Temas, Editorial Planeta.

Restrepo Botero, Darío I. (ed.) (2003), *La falacia neoliberal: Crítica y alternativas*, Bogotá: Universidad Nacional de Colombia.

Sandilands, Roger (1990), *Vida y política económica de Lauchlin Currie*, Bogotá: Legis Editores.

Steiner, Roberto (1997), 'Los dólares del narcotráfico', *Serie Cuadernos de Fedesarrollo*, 2, Bogotá.

Universidad Nacional de Colombia (1968), 'El economista ante el desarrollo nacional', Congress of Economists, Bogotá.

Urrutia, Miguel (1991), 'On the Absence of Economic Populism in Colombia', in Rudiger Dornbush and S. Edwards (eds), *The Macroeconomics of Populism in Latin America*, Chicago: The University of Chicago Press.

Urrutia, Miguel (1988), 'The Changing Nature of Economic Planning in Colombia', in Miguel Urrutia and Setsuko Yukawa (eds), *Development Planning in Mixed Economies*, The United Nations University.

Vélez García, Jorge et al. (1963), *Devaluación 1962: Historia documental de un proceso*, Bogotá: Ediciones Tercer Mundo.

6. From nationalism to neoliberalism: conflict and consensus in the history of Mexican economics

Sarah Babb

> Theories created in the great centers of capitalism should not be submissively applied [to less developed countries]. . . . Each theoretical adaptation should be made after careful analysis, with our feet planted on our own soil and with a clear vision of the primary needs and the legitimate aspirations of the people. (Jesús Silva Herzog, co-founder of the UNAM School of Economics, in *A un joven economista mexicano*, 1967)

> A demand curve is the same here, in China, in the United States, in Russia and wherever. And where prices are higher, the producers will produce a higher quantity, it doesn't matter where. (ITAM economist, 1997)

Once upon a time, economists in Mexico were notorious for their populist rhetoric and socialist proclivities. Mexico's first economics program at the National University was run by self-taught economists dedicated to the ideals of the Mexican revolution, and deeply suspicious of the purported benefits of untrammeled markets. Today, in contrast, Mexican economics has become a profession that would be unrecognizable to its original founders. Professors at Mexico's leading economics programs have PhDs from highly-ranked universities in the United States and England; they publish in international journals and attend conferences overseas. The economics programs in which they teach are famous for producing the high-level public officials who promoted the free-market reforms popularly known as 'neoliberalism'. In this respect, Mexico strongly resembles other countries in Latin America and elsewhere in the developing world, where economic reforms, technocratic governments and Americanized economics professions have been observed as parallel trends (Coats 1996).

For a number of compelling reasons, Mexico is often viewed as a case apart from other Latin American cases. Its unique history of stable single-party authoritarianism, its long border with the United States and its revolutionary past are some of the most salient factors that make Mexico an exceptional case. The history of Mexican economics told in this chapter, however, reflects fundamental similarities with the rest of Latin America – similarities that have increased rather than decreased over time. This chapter is based on a larger project on the history of Mexican economics (see Babb 2001) and draws an eclectic array of sources of information, including interviews, news media and archival material. At the center of the project are 287 undergraduate theses from the two most historically important Mexican economics programs: the public National University (UNAM) and the private Autonomous Technological Institute of Mexico (ITAM). Whereas the UNAM was home to Mexico's first and historically most influential economics program, the ITAM program has more recently become the most important source for government technocrats involved in liberalizing reforms.

The journey of Mexican economics from nationalism to neoliberalism did not follow a steady trajectory; rather, it was punctuated by episodes of conflict and consensus, reflecting changes in the social, political and economic context. Two social-structural factors, in particular, will be considered in this chapter. The first is the dominant role of the state in the profession's formation and ongoing evolution. In contrast to the economics in the United States, which has historically found institutional support within a decentralized national network of private and state-funded colleges and universities, Mexican economics was always a 'statist' profession, depending on the government for most of the resources that sustained it, including funding for university programs, jobs for graduates and scholarships. For this reason, the historically changing agenda of the Mexican state was a key factor influencing how the profession evolved. The second structural factor is the relationship between the state and different social groups. In particular, when levels of conflict between the state and the Mexican private sector were high, the economics profession became more fragmented and polarized. In contrast, when there was relative consensus between the state and the most conservative segment of big business, Mexican economics converged to a more unified position.

THE MEXICAN CONTEXT

Until recently, Mexico was an anomaly in Latin America – a country in which the same political party, the Institutional Revolutionary Party (PRI), had ruled for more than half a century. The origins of the PRI dated back to the first decades of the Mexican revolution, when a series of military leaders struggled to unify the country fragmented by rival military powers and disparate social groups. The solution that was forged in the 1920s and consolidated in the 1930s was a party that officially incorporated labor, peasant and 'popular' sectors. In name, the system was democratic; in practice, however, Mexican corporatism was used to buy off potentially dissenting leaders, to repress opposition and to engineer electoral victories (cf. Hansen 1971).

The ideology of the ruling party was difficult to characterize. The party itself was always an umbrella for a variety of different interests and tendencies. In rhetoric, at least, political leaders paid lip-service to the egalitarian ideals of the Mexican revolution. In practice, the closest the party came to realizing this rhetoric was under the administration of Lázaro Cárdenas, who promoted nationalizations, land redistributions and other populist measures during the Depression. By the 1950s, the rhetoric remained, but the policies were much more pragmatic, focusing on fostering foreign direct investment, industrialization and the modernization of agriculture.

Its political uniqueness notwithstanding, in the realm of economic policy, Mexico mostly followed the historical trends of other Latin American nations. Beginning in the 1930s, the government began to endorse state-led development policies, including the protection of domestic industries from foreign competition, the channeling of selective credit to private projects through a state development bank and public ownership of petroleum and other industries. Starting in the 1950s, these statist policies were accompanied by a strong government commitment to sound (some would say orthodox) macroeconomic policies, with the result that Mexico had impressively low levels of inflation from 1954 through 1970. This period, known as 'stabilizing development', was characterized by strong economic growth (over 6 per cent) and rising inequalities, as some social groups prospered more than others (Hansen 1971).

The economic policies of the 1970s represented both a continuation of and a break with these postwar policy trends. On the one hand, state involvement in Mexican economy and society increased, with major investments in social programs and education and later major increases in the budget of state-owned industries, particularly the lucrative petroleum company. Economic growth during the 1971–81 period averaged over 7 percent; inflation, which fluctuated between 20 and 40 percent between 1973 and 1981, was higher as well (Gil Díaz 1984). On the other hand, these policies were partly made possible by the unprecedented availability of low-interest loans from international banks (Gil Díaz 1984; Frieden 1991). As elsewhere in Latin America, by the beginning of the 1980s, Mexico was plagued by an enormous external debt, the consequences of which are still being felt today.

The 1970s also marked the breakdown of the consensus that had been built between the state and private sector during the postwar decades.

Particularly during the presidency of Luis Echeverría (1970–76), Mexican business organizations were increasingly antagonized by populist rhetoric and policies (Bazdresch and Levy 1991). Although the presidency of José López Portillo (1976–82) was initially seen as more friendly to business interests, private sector leaders became increasingly frustrated with high inflation and macroeconomic instability. The death-blow to state–business relations was dealt in 1982, when in response to escalating crisis, the López Portillo administration imposed currency controls and nationalized the private banking sector.

The outbreak of the debt crisis at the beginning of the 1980s established the conditions for an unprecedented turnaround in economic policy. A decline in international petroleum prices and a sharp rise in global interest rates made it impossible for the Mexican government to continue to service its debts. Consequently, there was a long series of painful negotiations between the Mexican government and its private creditors, the United States Treasury and the International Monetary Fund. Deflationary fiscal and monetary policies implemented to re-establish balance with the international economy contributed to a sharp economic downturn. Soon thereafter, Mexico embarked on a nearly complete reversal of its previous commitment to state-led development. Public enterprises were privatized, trade barriers were lifted and subsidies and price controls removed. A free trade agreement with the United States and Canada was signed and legislative and constitutional changes were implemented to make Mexico more attractive to foreign investment.

In Mexico, as elsewhere in Latin America, the 1980s were a 'lost decade' of stagnant and even negative growth. However, despite numerous predictions to the contrary, the Mexican economy since then has shown little signs of improvement. A modest pickup in economic activity in the early 1990s was interrupted by the peso crisis in 1994–95, which was followed by a 6 percent contraction of the economy. Growth picked up for several years thereafter, but was close to zero in 2001 and 2002 (INEGI 2004). The recent Carnegie report on the Mexico's experience under NAFTA indicates that there has been a net loss of employment and decline in wages since the beginning of the 1990s (Audley et al. 2003). Like a number of Latin American nations, Mexico has recently consolidated a transition to full electoral democracy: the victory of Vicente Fox in 2000 signified the final crumbling of Mexico's single-party system. But throughout Latin America, this opening to democratic politics seems to have been accompanied by a narrowing of possible economic policies (cf. Kurtz 2004; Weyland 2004). None of Mexico's three major political parties – including the left-of-center PRD – have proposed a coherent alternative to the 'neoliberal' policies currently in effect.

THE FOUNDING OF TWO PROGRAMS

Mexican economics was a child of the state that was consolidated in the wake of the revolution of 1910–17. The founders of the economics program at the National University (UNAM) in 1929 were government officials and other individuals who had played an important role in the construction of post-revolutionary institutions. The program, which was expanded to become a full-fledged economics department in 1934, was explicitly aimed at training aspiring state functionaries and was advertised as such: an announcement for the new program explained that 'Economics graduates can occupy the most important administrative posts in the Federal and local government because their knowledge is especially oriented toward this end' (*El Economista* 1929, p. 6). The majority of the first professors at the School of Economics were full-time employees of the public sector: salaries were simply too low at the UNAM to live on and full-time professors in economics were nonexistent. These so-called 'taxi' professors were famous for identifying promising students and offering them jobs in public administration (Camp 1980). By 1939, there were already 271 economics students at the UNAM, many of whom worked in government jobs while simultaneously taking classes (UNAM 1981, p. 255). The recently-established Fondo de Cultura Económica (Foundation for Economic Culture) gave Mexican students access to economic literature from around the world through publishing translations of foreign books, as well as articles translated for the journal *Trimestre Económico*. The *Trimestre* soon also became an important forum for publishing original works by Mexican and Latin American authors (Loyo 1988).

While the Mexican state was taking a more active role in promoting economic growth and development in the 1930s, it was simultaneously solidifying its mass base under the populist presidency of Lázaro Cárdenas. Many of the founders and first professors of the National School of Economics were supporters of Cárdenas and influenced by Marxist and other socialist ideas. A few of the state-builders involved in the foundation of UNAM economics (most notably Miguel Palacios Macedo and Manuel Gómez Morín) were more conservative in their views. The evidence suggests that these individuals soon came to feel outnumbered and uncomfortable at the fledgling program and subsequently ceased to participate; there is no evidence of the participation of these individuals in UNAM activities after the early 1930s.

Thus, from the very beginning, the UNAM economics department became a magnet for left-leaning taxi professors. In a study of the graduates of the UNAM School of Economics through 1961, Camp (1975) finds that of the 15 most notable professors selected by interviews and published

Table 6.1 Most-cited authors, UNAM, 1934–45

Name	N	%
Karl Marx	10	13.3
Adam Smith	8	10.6
Gustavo Cassel	4	5.3
David Ricardo	4	5.3
John Strachey	4	5.3
Ernst Wagemann	4	5.3

Note: Total N=75 (theses with theoretical cites = 44%).

materials, 11 were leftists of some stripe; nine of these 11 'leftist' professors reached middle- to high-level government posts during their careers (Camp 1975, pp. 140–41). These tendencies seem to have been reproduced among the students: the most cited author among the undergraduate theses of 1934–45 was Karl Marx (see Table 6.1). However, it should also be noted that Marx was in company with a number of less revolutionary classical authors, including Adam Smith and David Ricardo. The rhetoric of the theses, too, revealed somewhat more pragmatic tendencies: only three of the 75 theses from this period mentioned socialism approvingly, with two disapproving and a resounding 70 not mentioning the issue at all.

The theses suggest that although the UNAM economics program had a leftist slant, it could hardly be characterized as communist or even socialist. Nevertheless, the Mexican business elite wanted to have nothing to do with it. Not only did the 'social economics' taught at the UNAM have anti-capitalist undertones, but it provided little training in the skills that businesses might find practical, such as management and accounting. As a result, UNAM economics graduates found jobs in government, not in the private sector.

A private sector group known as the Mexican Cultural Association formed to propose the founding of a new school of economics untainted by the leftist ideology of the UNAM program. Members of the Association included the Mexican Central Bank, seven large private banks and several large companies from the Northern industrial city of Monterrey, including the Monterrey Iron and Steel Smelting Company and the Moctezuma beer company. The 1930s had been a period of growing conflict between the state and groups within the private sector who felt threatened by the government's populist rhetoric and policies. Decades later, a prominent member of the Association's Board of Directors in the 1940s, Aníbal Iturbide, recalled that

> The ideas of the government of General Cárdenas . . . had an important influence in the ideological development of Mexican life and politics, which to us seemed most unfortunate for the search for a balanced development of the country . . . we thought that to encourage the industrial development of Mexico we had to try to change people's mentality, because it was predominantly a socialist, leftist mentality, which is what predominated in the political sphere. . . . This was essentially the reason that impelled us to create the Technological Institute of Mexico, having as its goal the creation of a School of Economics from which would graduate the men who would in the future manage both the private and public economies of Mexico. (Negrete 1988, p. 9)

To this end, in 1946, Mexico's first private economics program was founded at the Technological Institute of Mexico (ITM, which would become the officially autonomous ITAM after 1962). Now Mexico had two economics programs, apparently at opposite ideological poles.

THE MIRACLE AND THE CONVERGENCE OF MEXICAN ECONOMICS

Unlike the turbulent decades after the Revolution, the postwar period in Mexico was characterized by relative social peace as well as the impressive economic growth popularly known as the 'Mexican Miracle'. After the great social upheavals of the Cárdenas administration, the focus of Mexican government policy turned from social issues and redistributive politics to the task of promoting economic development. The United Nations Economic Commission for Latin America (ECLA) never became as important in determining economic policies in Mexico as it did in other Latin American countries. Although ECLA luminary Raúl Prebisch served on the board of the *Trimestre Económico* for many years, advice from the ECLA was not always welcomed or heeded by the Mexican government (Babb 2001, pp. 76–7). Nevertheless, the economic policies of postwar Mexico – particularly its commitment to import-substituting industrialization – bore a general family resemblance to ECLA prescriptions. The policy framework responsible for the 'Miracle' was generally characterized by a commitment to industrial protection, a high level of direct state involvement in many areas of the economy (notably in the petroleum industry and electric power) and the promotion of industry through the industrial Development Bank. No longer were Mexican presidents supporting workers in their strikes against employers and making threats about expropriation. On the contrary, postwar Mexican government policy was good for business: it kept taxes and wages low, expanded infrastructure and protected domestic industries from foreign competition.

These policies were implemented and managed by a growing developmentalist bureaucracy, in which the services of economists became increasingly important (Pallares 1952). Economists were rarely in top government positions, which were still monopolized by lawyers and other amateur economic policymakers, but their voices became increasingly important (Vernon 1963). Meanwhile, economics programs in private schools flourished as businessmen became more educated about the role and functions of economists in the private firm. Unlike the ITM, however, other private economics programs (such as that of the Monterrey Technological Institute) were founded with much less ideological agendas, focusing on practical business economists. For example, the Monterrey Tech's original economics curriculum (established in 1954) required over 15 percent of total class hours in accounting, more than 21 percent in law and over 16 percent in administration: in addition to their special skills as economists, 'Tech' graduates were supposed to serve as versatile 'jacks of all trades' within the private sector. Meanwhile, during the relatively placid political era of the Mexican Miracle, the initially polarized UNAM and ITAM economics programs converged toward a common vision.

The UNAM

In keeping with the spirit of the times, after 1940 the UNAM School of Economics became more careerist and less contentiously leftist. In 1941 the program revised its curriculum in order to 'suppress all those aspects of exaggerated radicalism that it contained, in order to achieve a more technical and complete teaching of economics' (words of UNAM Rector De la Cueva cited in Pallares 1952, p. 103), beginning a trend toward 'technification' that would continue for the next two decades.

The outstanding rhetorical themes of UNAM economics theses from 1958 reflected the postwar Keynesian/developmentalist consensus. Although Keynes was the most cited author among the UNAM theses of 1958, these citations co-existed with a widespread belief that underdeveloped countries like Mexico needed a different set of policy prescriptions. As one author asserted, 'The economic structure of [developing] countries is quite different from that of developed ones, if one considers that they are characterized by an economy based fundamentally on primary activities and with an incipient level of industrialization' (Hernández 1958, p. 12). This idea that there were fundamental differences between developed and developing countries appeared in a striking half of the 1958 theses.

As a result of these fundamental differences, a new role for government was required. In the words of one UNAM thesis author, 'The abstentionist role that was traditionally demanded of the state has ceased to be valid. The supervision of the capitalist system depends in large measure upon state intervention in economic life, since government action tends to cover the system's deficiencies by maintaining the economy at adequate levels' (Cervantes 1958, p. 102). As a result of this new focus on the role of the government in the economy, there were no 1958 theses that failed to mention state intervention either in theory or in practice, with more than half expressing strong support for such intervention. In contrast to the theses of the earlier period, none of the 1958 theses mentioned socialism, either approvingly or disapprovingly. The issue of capitalism versus socialism, it seems, was dead: the question of the hour was how best to foster *capitalist* development in Mexico, an idea very much in keeping with the developmentalist philosophy being promoted at the ECLA at the time. Although none of the 1958 theses cited Raúl Prebisch, 18 percent cited Juan Noyola, an ECLA economist who taught for a number of years in the UNAM economics program.

The ITM

Whereas the UNAM School of Economics was founded as a program with socialist overtones, the ITM had been established as a bastion of pro-business conservatism. However, a comparison between the 1958 UNAM theses and theses written by ITM economics students from 1956 to 1960 reveal that the similarities between the two programs apparently outweighed the differences. For one thing they cited the same authors: just as at the UNAM, the most-cited theoretical author at the ITM was Keynes – with the second-most cited author being Ragnar Nurkse, a Swedish development economist whose analyses were similar to those of the ECLA structuralists.

Finally, Table 6.2 shows that ITM theses took positions on state interventionism that were nearly identical to those taken in UNAM theses, with 50 per cent strongly interventionist and 37.5 per cent moderately interventionist (see Appendix for explanation of how position on state intervention was measured). As one author explained:

> I do not in any way uphold the traditional doctrine of *laissez faire–laissez passer* in its purest form, since although social and economic liberty should exist, one cannot deny the function of the state as a regulator and promoter of development. [I therefore] recognize certain social and economic intervention as necessary. (García 1959, p. 47)

Thus, by the late 1950s there appears to have been a single Keynesian or developmentalist 'policy paradigm' in Mexico, which was simultaneously upheld at the UNAM and the ITM. This common view of the role of the

Table 6.2 Positions on state intervention, UNAM 1958 vs ITAM 1956–60, theses

	UNAM 1958 N(%)	ITAM 1956–60 N(%)
Less Intervention Advocated	0	0
	(0)	(0)
Existing Interventions	6	6
	(37.5)	(37.5)
More Intervention Advocated	10	8
	(62.5)	(50)
No Position on Intervention	0	2
	(0)	(12.5)
Total	16	16

Note: χ^2=2.22, $\alpha > 0.05$.

government in the economy was made possible by consensus between the state and the private sector, founded in the pronounced evolution of the postwar Mexican state away from its revolutionary origins.

This postwar consensus goes a long way toward explaining why the Chilean and Mexican economics professions of the late 1950s looked so different. Postwar Chile was a multi-party democracy and lacked an authoritarian corporatist state to stamp out social conflict, foster economic growth and guarantee macroeconomic stability. In contrast to Mexico, postwar developmentalism in Chile produced relatively low levels of economic growth and high levels of strikes and other social conflict. Inflation was a perennial plague generated by unresolved distributional issues, a substitute for civil war. As early as the late 1950s, many Chilean economic elites were fed up with state-led development, exasperated by inflation and ripe for a new theoretical paradigm – a paradigm that came to them through an exchange program between the private Catholic University and the University of Chicago (Montecinos 1988; Valdés 1995). As a result, Chilean economics began to split at a time when Mexican economics had reached an unprecedented level of convergence.

THE BREAKDOWN OF DEVELOPMENTALISM AND THE SPLITTING OF MEXICAN ECONOMICS

When the postwar consensus began to break down, the unity of Mexican economics broke down along with it. By the early 1970s, most economists and public officials agreed that the old development strategy was no longer working and that import substituting industrialization had created serious, long-standing imbalances in the Mexican economy. Meanwhile, an ideologically diverse student movement arose to oppose social injustice and political repression in Mexico. In 1968, the brutal massacre of a student movement gathering at Tlatelolco plaza served to further radicalize the movement.

The populist policies of Presidents Echeverría (1970–76) and López Portillo (1976–82) responded to both domestic political concerns and new developments within the international economy. Both presidencies were known for increased government intervention and spending, made possible by unprecedented access to international financing. The growing integration of international financial markets facilitated financing through loans from First World banks (and later, portfolio investors) (Frieden 1991). By 1982, the external debt stood at over 36 percent of Mexico's Gross Domestic Product or 92.4 billion US dollars (Gil Díaz 1984; Bazdresch and Levy 1991, pp. 246–9).

Fueled by foreign financing and the boom in petroleum revenues, increased government spending in the 1970s increased public sector employment opportunities for economists (Lozano Hernández 1988). At the same time it was increasingly a particular *kind* of economist that was most favored: namely, those trained at private or elite public institutions (such as the ITAM or Colegio de México) and/or with postgraduate degrees from foreign universities. This was partly for technical reasons – particularly the growing complications of administering international debt (Centeno 1994, p. 93). However, the fact that economists were increasingly at the *top* of economic ministries – rather than serving as assistants to ministers – indicates that there was also an important symbolic dimension to the rise of foreign-trained economists in Mexican public administration (Markoff and Montecinos 1993). These young technocrats were fluent in English and had important old-school ties with foreign banks and multilateral institutions – in short, they had what it took to ensure that the money kept on coming. By 1980, the heads of the Ministry of Finance, the Ministry of National Patrimony, the development bank and Central Bank were all foreign-trained economists.

These highly visible trends in the profile of government policymakers were accompanied by a less visible trend that would have greater significance over the long term: an enormous increase in government scholarships to study abroad. One aspect of Echeverría's expansive higher education policy was the foundation of the National Council for Science and Technology (CONACYT) in 1970 for the purpose of funding training and research in the service of economic development. The Council was

Table 6.3 Theoretical citations, UNAM 1976 vs ITAM, 1974–79

UNAM 1976, n = 50 (Theses with theoretical cites = 76%)		ITAM 1974–79, n = 43 (Theses with theoretical cites = 86.05%)	
Name	N	Name	N
Karl Marx	5	Gary Becker	8
Paul Baran	4	Milton Friedman	7
Raymond Barre	4	Harry Johnson	7
Frederich Engels	3	John M. Keynes	5
Celso Furtado	3	Paul Cagan	4
Osvaldo Sunkel	3	Heinz Robert Heller	4
		Robert Musgrave	4
		Paul Samuelson	4

able to fund graduate economics study abroad on a scale that dwarfed previous programs. For example, in 1973 alone there were 48 Mexicans studying economics abroad with Science and Technology grants (CONACYT 1973, p. 86).

Table 6.3, which depicts the most-cited authors at the UNAM and ITAM in the late 1970s, shows that the 'breakdown' of Mexican developmentalism was reflected in a polarization of economics programs. While the UNAM became a bastion of Marxism and dependency theory, the ITAM evolved into a US-style economics program, with a particular affinity toward the University of Chicago.

The UNAM

Under the Echeverría administration in the early 1970s, leftist activism within the university was tolerated, public education budgets skyrocketed and public university admissions exploded. The student movement took advantage of this atmosphere of greater tolerance to demand radical changes in the curricula of different departments of the UNAM and greatly increased participation of students and professors in academic policy. A set of curriculum changes implemented within UNAM economics in 1975 were designed to satisfy movement demands and remade the School's program into an essentially Marxist one. Among numerous other changes, the new program required students to take *seven* semesters of 'political economy', or Marxist economics.

In this way, the student movement transformed the UNAM economics program into a very different institution than it had been in the 1950s. For the radicalized students of this era, to work for the government was to work for the enemy. As a result, the new study program deliberately de-emphasized practical training for aspiring state functionaries – previously the program's reason for existence. The delinking of public university curricula from government employment was noted with concern by members of the National College of Economists, the official professional organization of Mexican economists and formal bridge between the economics profession and the Mexican government. In 1978, the organization held a meeting to discuss the shortcomings of the curricula at the UNAM and other public economics programs. Some participants complained of the dogmatism of programs which excluded mainstream theoretical tendencies and even modern Marxist authors (Ramírez 1978, p. 12). Others complained that UNAM graduates had deficient preparation in economic theory, mathematics and research skills and lacked foreign language proficiency, 'an indispensable instrument for the study of current works and of great use in professional life' (Fernández 1978, pp. 24–5).

One of the biggest problems, however, was the sheer size of the UNAM economics program, which by the mid-1970s had more than 4000 students, in contrast to fewer than 1000 in 1958 (UNAM 1981). The size of the program both devalued UNAM economics degrees and decreased the efficacy of existing mechanisms of selection. The program had never had particularly strong formal selection mechanisms or standards; rather, its prior success had relied on the informal mechanisms of personal relationships developed between 'taxi professors' and their students. But the 'massification' of the UNAM made such relationships more difficult to establish; moreover, the extreme politicization brought on by the students alienated taxi professors, who became increasingly annoyed by constant protests and accusations that they were servants of imperialism; many deserted the UNAM and a number of them began to offer classes in more congenial environments, such as that of the ITAM. Branded (not always fairly) as Marxist malcontents, with devalued degrees and lacking the political connections they had previously enjoyed, UNAM economics graduates began to face a marked disadvantage on the job market. They had never been very successful at getting jobs within the private sector; now, however, even the Mexican government was cautious about hiring them (see Consultores 1993).

The ITAM

While UNAM graduates had historically gone into public sector careers, graduates of the ITAM (renamed after being made autonomous in 1962) tended to go to the private sector. However, it was a group of ITAM students who went into government jobs that were ultimately to have the greatest impact on the program's future trajectory. Where government employment was concerned, a particularly important employer of ITAM economics graduates was the Central Bank.

The employment of early ITAM economics graduates by the central bank was logical given their mutual disaffinity for leftist ideology, as well as the Banco's role in the school's foundation. ITAM graduates from this period rose to high positions within the Central Bank and subsequently taught classes that provided more ITM graduates with the possibility of Central Bank employment. The Central Bank was an organization within the Mexican government with a particular interest in cultivating economic talent and in incorporating international standards of economic expertise. As part of its commitment to international standards, the Banco de México had a scholarship program for sending its personnel to study abroad in economics and other fields. This is the first large-scale Mexican government scholarship program sponsoring foreign training in economics. The Banco de México was also a key organizational sponsor for the foundation of the economics graduate program at the Colegio de México in the 1960s (Babb 2001, p. 92).

The Americanization of the ITAM can ultimately be attributed to the efforts of two ITAM graduates who subsequently became Central Bank officials and studied abroad with Central Bank scholarships. During the 1960s and 1970s, under the directorship of Gustavo Petricioli (who had studied at Harvard) and Francisco Gil Díaz (who had studied at Chicago), the ITAM program became much more mathematical and rigorous and the faculty came to include more Central Bank officials and economists who had studied abroad. These professors, including Directors Petricioli and Gil, helped their students obtain positions at the Central Bank and admission to foreign economics programs, where they were financed both through the Central Bank scholarship program and through other programs (Interview Petricioli 2/3/97).

By 1976, the University of Chicago was the single most important destination for ITAM graduates pursuing postgraduate study abroad and the two most-cited theoretical authors of 1976 theses were Gary Becker and Milton Friedman. In contrast to its famous counterpart, the Catholic University in Chile, however, the Chicago influence at the ITAM did not result from a formal exchange program between the two universities. Rather, it was an artifact of Francisco Gil Díaz's directorship of the Economics Department during the 1970s, which naturally encouraged many students to apply to Chicago and encouraged Chicago to admit Mexican students recommended by Dr Gil Díaz. By the 1990s, the ITAM had lost its Chicago-school focus and undergraduate theses were simply citing American authors from a variety of institutional sources.

Table 6.4 ITM/ITAM theses' use of mathematical modeling, 1956–60, 1974–78 and 1994

	ITM 1956–60 N (%)	ITAM 1974–78 N (%)	ITAM 1994 N (%)
Formal Mathematical Models Used	1 (6.25)	32 (74.42)	35 (94.59
Formal Mathematical Models Not Used	15 (93.75)	11 (25.58)	2 (5.41)
Total	16 (100)	43 (100)	37 (100)

Note: $\chi^2 = 42.68$, $\alpha < 0.005$.

Looking retrospectively upon the history of the ITM/ITAM economics program, the most striking change over time was the dramatic increase in level of methodological sophistication between the late 1950s and 1994. Table 6.4 shows that whereas in 1956–60, only a single thesis utilized mathematical models to express economic concepts, between 1974 and 1978, nearly three-quarters utilized formal mathematical models; by 1994, these numbers had increased even further. The use of econometric analysis of data also increased dramatically during this period.

Thus, the ITAM economics program faithfully represented the shifts in international professional standards toward a more quantitative and theoretical approach. Consequently, since the 1970s the ITAM has been on the 'cutting edge' of economics as it is being practiced in the United States. Today, the ITAM economics faculty is renowned for its prestigious foreign credentials. Particularly within the ITAM's Center for Economic Research (CIE in Spanish), faculty publish in top international journals, including the *American Economic Review*, the *Journal of Economic Perspectives* and the *Journal of Economic Theory*.

NEOLIBERAL TRANSITION AND THE VICTORY OF AMERICANIZED ECONOMICS

Whereas escalating domestic conflict was at the root of the splitting of Mexican economics into opposing camps in the 1970s, it was primarily the international environment that contributed to the triumph of Americanized economics over the two decades that followed. As a number of scholars have observed, the outbreak of the debt crisis in 1982 marked a turning-point for economic policy in Latin America. On the one hand, multilateral organizations began a new era of 'policy-based lending', in which financial support was offered in return for commitment to government downsizing and conservative monetary policy; on the other hand, the increased need to foster foreign investor confidence provided indirect incentives for governments to pursue liberalizing reforms (Frieden 1991; Kahler 1992; Stallings 1992; Maxfield 1997). At the same time, the debt crisis had an impact on the profile of economic policymakers in Latin America. To negotiate with the US Treasury and the IMF and inspire the confidence of foreign investors, it made tremendous sense to staff the top levels of government with English-fluent economists trained at American universities, in a show of 'ceremonial conformity' to international standards (Markoff and Montecinos 1993; Schneider 1998).

The definitive rise of US-trained economists to the heights of government power occurred during the presidential administration of Miguel De la Madrid (1982–88). In 1981, rising international interest rates and falling international petroleum prices were leading to speculation about the impending devaluation of the peso and widespread capital flight. Different factions of foreign-trained economists within the Mexican policy bureaucracy favored distinct approaches to Mexico's blossoming debt crisis: a group of 'radical developmentalists' associated with the López Portillo government and an opposing group of fiscal and monetary conservatives. This latter group was mostly comprised of individuals with long careers within the financial-sector bureaucracy – particularly the Central Bank – and who had received graduate training in economics in the United States. The radicals, in contrast, had worked in the Ministry of National Resources (which was in charge of the rapidly-expanding parastate industries) and other areas of the Mexican government and often had studied economics at Cambridge University in England – a hotbed of Keynesian and 'post-Keynesian' thinking.

A crucial event in determining which group of technocrats prevailed was President López Portillo's selection of Miguel De la Madrid as the ruling party's official candidate for the presidency, which essentially anointed him to be Mexico's future president.[1] Whereas during the 1970s, the ruling party had supported candidates who promised to restore its domestic legitimacy, its most pressing problems after 1981 were international, rather than domestic. It was no longer peasants, workers and radicalized students that the party needed to impress, but multilateral agencies, foreign lenders and government officials – all of whom needed to be mobilized to help bail Mexico out. De la Madrid was ideal: he had a Master's degree in Public Administration from Harvard and was described in the foreign business press as 'a friend of bankers and businessmen' ('The New Hero' 1981, p. 68).

Even before assuming the presidency in November 1982, De la Madrid was allowed to appoint two Yale-trained economists to head the Finance Ministry and Central Bank. The newly-appointed Finance Minister, Jesús Silva Herzog, immediately began to steer the Mexican government toward a negotiated settlement with the IMF, the United States Treasury and the banks. This course was vehemently opposed by the 'radical' British-trained economists, who favored imposing capital controls and were even rumored to be discussing forming a debtor nations' cartel and defaulting. However, with the IMF and US Treasury on their side, the Yale-trained fiscal conservatives prevailed. In return for the financial support of these external organizations, Mexico pledged to implement a package of harsh IMF structural adjustment measures.

Toward the middle of the 1980s, international circumstances once again favored the policy program of those favoring a more market-oriented course. On the issue of free trade, there were particularly deep disagreements within the government – with the fiscally conservative developmentalists within the Ministry of Commerce on one side and the 'free traders' in the Mexican Central Bank on the other. The Commerce Ministry was headed by an economist who had studied at the University of Melbourne in Australia rather than in the United States, who advocated only gradual and selective opening to international free trade and was generally in favor of an active state in a mixed economy (Kraft 1984; Heredia 1996).

In contrast, a younger generation of foreign-trained officials at the Central Bank was made up of more fervent believers in market forces. The most important of these was a University of Chicago graduate Francisco Gil Díaz – one of the key figures in the Americanization of the ITAM in the 1970s. Gil Díaz had numerous allies within the administration, including Pedro Aspe, an MIT-trained economist at the Ministry of Budget and Planning and Chicago-trained Herminio Blanco in the President's Office of Economic Advisors. In 1984, the Central Bank began to disseminate policy proposals in favor of accelerated trade opening. Later that year, following close collaboration with officials in the Central Bank and Finance Ministry, the World Bank granted Mexico the first 'Trade Policy Loan' in the Bank's history, which provided Mexico with a series of loans in return for comprehensive trade liberalization (Heredia 1996). In 1986, the Reagan administration further strengthened the hand of international financial institutions and free traders within the Mexican government by announcing that it would not negotiate on Mexico's behalf with international banks unless Mexico 'implemented substantive structural reforms', and arrived at a new agreement with the IMF ('Silva Lining' 1986). With such powerful international allies to help them argue their case, the free trade technocrats within the Mexican government won. In 1987 the

Mexican government implemented a program of trade liberalization that went far beyond GATT requirements in both degree and type of opening. This agreement was essentially a prelude to the North American Free Trade Agreement, which was implemented in 1994.

The US-trained economists whose views emerged during the De la Madrid administration were promoted to top policy positions during the subsequent administrations of Carlos Salinas (1988–94) and Ernesto Zedillo (1994–2000), where they continued the neoliberal revolution begun in the early 1980s (see Table 6.5). Although not an 'economist' in the purest sense (his Harvard degree was in political economy and government), Salinas was well-versed in US-style neoclassical economics from his years at Harvard and had strong alliances with US-trained economists in public administration. Zedillo, on the other hand, received a PhD in economics from Yale and since ending his term as president has become director of the Center for the Study of Globalization at his alma mater; he was and remains an 'economists' economist'. Such internal distinctions not withstanding, it is clear that the debt crisis and its aftermath empowered economic experts of a particular sort – those who had studied in the United States and whose views were most likely to coincide with those of the international organizations with which the Mexican government was negotiating. Economic policymakers who did not fit this profile found themselves marginalized, while those who did remained as political players.

During this period, the ITAM, which specialized in sending students to study economics in the United States, became disproportionately successful at placing its graduates in powerful government positions (see Table 6.5). In the three administrations spanning 1982–99, ITAM economics graduates in top positions included two Finance Ministers (Gustavo Petricioli and Pedro Aspe) and a Central Bank Director (Miguel Mancera). These individuals represented the tip of the iceberg: each top post occupied by an ITAM graduate provided multiple opportunities for other US-trained ITAM graduates at lower levels. Moreover, by the 1990s, the liberalization of the Mexican financial sector was creating jobs for ITAM graduates within banks, brokerage houses and consulting firms, where the ability to 'translate' the Mexican context for foreign investors was similarly rewarded (Babb 2001 p. 164).

Since at least the 1980s, it has been necessary to have a graduate degree – preferably from the United States or England – to be considered 'an economist' in Mexico. Because the ITAM had become so successful sending its graduates to study abroad, it was only natural for this once-marginal school to acquire tremendous prestige disproportionate to its small size. The ITAM's prestige, combined with the proliferation of jobs

Table 6.5 *Characteristics of top economic policymaking slots[a] by presidential administration*

Presidency (term)	Top econ. policy slots	Undergrad. econ. degree	Undergrad. at private Mexican school	Foreign graduate training	Foreign graduate training econ.
	N	N	N	N	N
Avila Camacho (1940–46)	5	0	1	0	0
Aleman (1946–52)	5	0	0	0	0
Ruíz Cortínez (1952–58)	4	1	0	0	0
López Mateos (1958–64)	5	1	1	1	1
Díaz Ordaz (1964–70)	5	1	0	1	1
Echeverría (1970–76)	9	2	0	4	2
López Portillo (1976–82)	12	4	0	7	4
De la Madrid (1982–88)	7	6	2	7	5
Salinas (1988–94)	5	4	2	5	4
Zedillo (1994–2000)	8	7	2	8	7

Note: [a] Total number of slots for each presidential administration equal the number of top policy positions, multiplied by the number of individuals who occupy those positions during a given administration. Thus, the data for an individual who occupies two positions at different times during the same administration, are counted twice. Top policy positions are defined as the President of the Republic, Minister of Finance, Minister of Commerce and Central Bank Director (throughout the entire period) and Minister of the Presidency (1958–76) and Minister of Budget and Planning (1976–92).

Source: Assorted news media for more recent information.

for US-trained economists in the Mexican government, led many economics programs in Mexico to emulate the ITAM's recipe for success; today, young would-be technocrats have a variety of highly-Americanized economics programs from which to choose, including the Monterrey Tech, the Ibero-American University, the Autonomous University of Nuevo León and the Center for Economic Teaching and Research (CIDE). Many of these programs are, like the ITAM, privately funded. A solid preparation in US-style economics and English, along with letters of recommendation from professors with American PhDs, help graduates of these programs secure admission to foreign graduate programs, financed by scholarships from the Mexican government and other sources. However, the ITAM seems to be maintaining its reputational 'edge' over these other programs; a recent survey administered by the newspaper *Reforma* found that the ITAM economics program was still considered to be the best in the country (Tomasini 2004).

CONCLUSION

In December 2000, Vicente Fox, of the right-wing National Action Party (PAN) was sworn in to the Mexican presidency. This definitively ended more than half a century of single-party rule and marked a fundamental change in the Mexican political system. However, as far as the economics profession is concerned, the Fox presidency also represented some important continuities. Economists trained in the United States were, once again, in charge of economic policy. The source of the degrees was slightly different: in contrast to the Ivy League purity of the PRI administrations, two of Fox's top technocrats had had degrees from the University of Oregon and the University of Pennsylvania. Still, the ITAM continued to be extremely influential: the Minister of Finance under the Fox Administration was Francisco Gil Díaz, famous for his promotion of US-style economics within the ITAM and his promotion of free trade in the government during the mid-1980s.

Thus, there is little reason to believe that Mexico's democratic transition is bringing fundamental changes in the profiles of economic policymakers. This may seem surprising, given economics' historic association with the Institutional Revolutionary Party (PRI). It should be remembered, however, that recent generations of technocrats were never known for their partisan commitments (cf. Centeno 1994 p. 125). Even more importantly, as long as the state remains committed to creating confidence within the international financial community and pursuing market-friendly policies, foreign-trained economists are likely to remain at the helm of economic policy. Even a government led by the center-left PRD would be unlikely to change this state of affairs: as one ITAM economist asked rhetorically, 'Who are going to be their interlocutors? When they have to deal with the IMF, the IMF is going to say, 'send me someone I can talk to' (Interview Bassols 1/19/99). In other words, US-trained economists are likely to continue to be at the highest level of economic policy, irrespective of the party in power.

Having economists in top policy positions, in turn, guarantees the future of the profession as a whole, because it is the state (and not the private sector) that remains the single most important constituency for the Mexican economics profession. Powerful government positions give US-trained economists influence over the deployment of government resources that subsidize and contribute to the ongoing Americanization of the profession. Many of these resources are channeled through the National Council for Science and Technology (CONACYT), Mexico's analogue to the National Science Foundation in the United States. For example, the Council finances the National System of Researchers (SNI), which subsidizes the salaries of Mexican academics in different fields based on their research and publications. In a nation where most universities pay low salaries that force academics to seek secondary employment, the SNI creates a space and incentive for academic research. The Council also administers subsidized professorships (*cátedras*) for outstanding teachers and 'repatriation' scholarships to bring Mexicans studying abroad back to Mexico. Such programs enable the Mexican government to encourage the development and ongoing dominance of the most internationalized version of Mexican economics.

The Council is the cornerstone of an edifice of government-sponsored support for higher education that has enabled social sciences to flourish in Mexico perhaps more than in any other Latin American country. In part because of this generosity, Mexico seems not to have suffered from the same degree of 'brain drain' as other Latin American countries; indeed, academics have come to live and work in Mexico from around the world (including the United States and Europe) because of the agreeable working conditions. In addition to jobs within the government and academia, over the past two decades, a number of US-trained economists have found employment in the private financial sector and consulting firms, where fluency in English and international training are at a premium; there, they may continue in their roles as diplomats to the international financial community. For example, after serving out his term as Finance Minister under the Salinas Administration, Pedro Aspe co-founded a Mexican financial services firm specializing in attracting foreign investors to Mexican companies (Interview Sales 8/2/99).

However, the boom years for economists in Mexico may be drawing to a close, and there are signs that we may soon see more Mexican economists seeking employment abroad. First, subsidies to social science through the National Council ultimately depend on governments' willingness to spend scarce fiscal resources on scholarship. This willingness should not be taken for granted. The PAN, for example, has been somewhat less committed to supporting abstruse academic pursuits than the more highly-technocratic PRI and the National Council on Science and Technology recently announced a significant cutback in fellowships to study abroad. Second, the Mexican economy has not been performing particularly well, which is almost certainly limiting the growth of new job opportunities for economists in the private sector and academia. Finally, after decades of generous government support for scholarships abroad, it seems likely that there is an oversupply of foreign-trained economists in Mexico. It would be ironic to see neoclassical Mexican economists exiled from their native country by the impersonal forces of supply and demand.

Whether or not there is an exodus of Mexican economists to American and British universities, a major change in the general contours of the profession is unlikely. Once torn apart by social conflict, economics in Mexico seems to have converged, just as it did in the 1950s, upon a relatively unified core, with agreed-upon standards of evaluation and methods. But in contrast to the 1950s, the source of this convergence is external rather than internal; it is based primarily on the power of international forces rather than the influence of domestic social groups. Only a change in the international environment – or a resurgence in the power of domestic relative to international forces – could bring about a major change in the profession's orientation.

APPENDIX: STUDY OF UNAM AND ITM/ITAM THESES

A central source of information for this research project was a selection of 287 undergraduate theses from the public Autonomous National University of Mexico (UNAM) and the Autonomous Technological Institute of Mexico (ITAM, but called the ITM before being made officially autonomous in 1962). Whereas I was unable to find historical collections of syllabi, the undergraduate theses of Mexican economics programs are available to the public in university libraries. Rather than describing course content, the theses are exercises in applied theory and method and indicate the general approach to economic problems that students learned during their five years of undergraduate education – and generally what skills they would bring to the job market.

In Mexico (and throughout Latin America), an undergraduate degree in economics is much more specialized than the liberal arts 'major' of American universities; to receive a full licentiate degree (*licenciatura*), students must typically complete a thesis to demonstrate their mastery of the discipline. Thus, the theses represent a historical record of what students were expected by their thesis advisors to have learned and thought. By analyzing the rhetorical content, methods and citation patterns of these theses from these two key programs – and by placing them in their historical context – I sought to understand how and why Mexican economics changed over time.

My method was to thoroughly read the introduction and conclusion of each thesis, where main theoretical points and citations were made and skim the middle for methodological approaches. I coded each thesis for theoretical citations, methodology and various rhetorical features (most importantly, position on government intervention in the economy). I did not code theoretical citations for whether authors were cited in a positive or negative light. Thus, the citation data do not necessarily indicate whether students who cited them agreed or disagreed, since they may have been cited negatively. Rather, these citation patterns indicate which authors the students thought were important to cite because of their scholarly contributions and thus tell us about the students' intellectual frame of reference. For example, Marx was traditionally seen as important at the UNAM, but was only rarely cited at the ITAM. The opinions of students concerning the *content* of economic theories were measured through analyzing the students' rhetoric concerning certain key issues, rather than through theoretical citation patterns.

I selected theses from four key periods in the history of Mexican economics for consideration in my study, to show the evolution of the economics programs over time: (1) The first years of the UNAM program (or rather, the years when the first UNAM economics theses were submitted), from 1934 to 1945; (2) The stabilizing development period of the postwar years; (3) The era of populism and social conflict of the late 1970s; and (4) The neoliberal period which began approximately in the mid-1980s and continues until the present. The total number of theses analyzed was 287 (191 from the UNAM and 96 from the ITM/ITAM).

For the first decade of the UNAM program (1934–45) and 1958, I reviewed all available theses. However, after 1970 the UNAM economics program became prohibitively large; therefore, for the years 1976 and 1994, I chose a random sample of 50 theses. Due to the very small size of the ITM/ITAM during its first decades, I chose to review theses from a range of years for comparison to the UNAM in the late 1950s and 1970s. Thus, UNAM theses from the year 1958 are compared to ITM theses from the years 1956–60 and UNAM theses from the year 1976 are compared to ITAM theses from the years 1974–78. By 1994, the ITAM program was producing graduates in sufficient quantities that I opted to investigate theses from a single year rather than a range of years.

NOTE

1. Until very recently, the official party candidate was selected by the outgoing President through a process shrouded in mystery known as the *destape* (or 'unveiling'). It is therefore impossible to know for certain why any PRI Presidential candidate is selected – including De la Madrid. Given the dire situation of Mexico's finances by the end of 1981, however, it seems reasonable to assume that López Portillo selected De la Madrid as the candidate best-suited to deal with international financiers. It was certainly not because of his political popularity, since De la Madrid – like Salinas and Zedillo after him – had never held public office.

REFERENCES

Audley, John J., Demetrios G. Papadmetriou, Sandra Polaski and Scott Vaughan (2003), *NAFTA's Promise and Reality: Lessons from Mexico for the Hemisphere*, Report of the Carnegie Endowment for International Peace.

Babb, Sarah (2001), *Managing Mexico: Economists from Nationalism to Neoliberalism*, Princeton, NJ: Princeton University Press.

Bazdresch, Carlos and Santiago Levy (1991), 'Populism and Economic Policy in Mexico, 1970–1982', in Rudiger Dornbusch and Sebastián Edwards (eds), *The Macroeconomics of Populism in Latin America*, Chicago: University of Chicago Press, pp. 223–62.

Camp, Roderic A. (1975), 'The National School of Economics and Public Life in Mexico', *Latin American Research Review*, **10** (3), 137–51.

Camp, Roderic A. (1980), *Mexico's Leaders: Their Education and Recruitment*, Tucson: The University of Arizona Press.

Centeno, Miguel Angel (1994), *Democracy within Reason: Technocratic Revolution in Mexico* (1st Edition), University Park: Pennsylvania State University Press.

Cervantes Delgado, Alejandro (1958), 'Aspectos del gasto público y de la tributación en México', UNAM economics thesis.

Coats, A.W. (ed.) (1996), *The Post-1945 Internationalization of Economics*, Durham, NC: Duke University Press.

Consejo Nacional de Ciencia y Tecnología (CONACYT) (1973), Informe de labores, México: CONACYT.

Consultores de Estudios y Proyectos, S.C. (1993), *Perfil del economista demandado en el mercado de trabajo*, Mexico: Consultores de Estudios y Proyectos.

El Economista (1929), February 16, p. 6.

Fernández Lozano, Ma. Teresa (1978), 'La formación del economista en México', *El Economista Mexicano*, **12** (3), 21–6.

Frieden, Jeffrey A. (1991), *Debt, Development and Democracy: Modern Political Economy in Latin America, 1965–1985*, Princeton: Princeton University Press.

García Duarte, Alberto (1959), 'El desarrollo económico de los países subdesarrollados', ITM economics thesis.

Gil Díaz, Francisco (1984), 'Mexico's Path from Stability to Inflation', in Arnold C. Harberger (ed.), *World Economic Growth*, San Francisco: Institute for Contemporary Studies, pp. 333–76.

Hansen, Roger D. (1971), *The Politics of Mexican Development*, Baltimore: The Johns Hopkins Press.

Heredia, Blanca (1996), 'Contested State: The Politics of Trade Liberalization in Mexico', Doctoral Dissertation in Political Science from Columbia University.

Hernández de la Mora, Jenaro (1958), 'Los gastos corrientes del gobierno Federal', UNAM economics thesis.

Instituto Nacional de Estadística Geográfica e Informática (INEGI) (2004), Statistical information on http://ww.inegi.gob.mx.

Interview, Antonio Bassols 1999, January 19.

Interview, Gustavo Petricioli 1997, February 3.

Interview, Carlos Sales 1999, August 2.

Kahler, Miles (1992), 'External Influence, Conditionality and the Politics of Adjustment', in Stephan Haggard and Robert R. Kaufman (eds), *The Politics of Economic Adjustment: International Constraints, Distributive Conflicts, and the State*, Princeton, NJ: Princeton University Press, pp. 89–138.

Kraft, Joseph (1984), *The Mexican Rescue*, New York: Group of Thirty.

Kurtz, Marcus (2004), 'The Dilemmas of Democracy in the Open Economy: Lessons from Latin America', *World Politics*, **56** (2), 262–302.

Loyo, Engracia (1988), 'La lectura en México, 1920–1940', in Josefina Zoraida Vazquez y Vera (ed.), *Historia de la lectura mexicana*, México: El Colegio de México, pp. 243–94.

Lozano Hernández, Wilfrido (1988), *30 años de la vida profesional: generación 1953–1957*, México: UNAM.

Markoff, John and Verónica Montecinos (1993), 'The Ubiquitous Rise of Economists', *Journal of Public Policy*, **13** (1), 37–8.

Maxfield, Sylvia (1997), *Gatekeepers of Growth: The International Political Economy of Central Banking in Developing Countries*, Princeton, NJ: Princeton University Press.

Montecinos, Verónica (1988), 'Economics and Power: Chilean Economists in Government, 1958–1985', PhD dissertation, Department of Sociology, University of Pittsburgh.

Montecinos, Verónica and John Markoff (2001), 'From the Power of Economic Ideas to the Power of Economists', in Miguel Angel Centeno and Fernando López Alves (eds), *The Other Mirror: Grand Theory through the Lens of Latin America*, Princeton, NJ: Princeton University Press, pp. 105–50.

Negrete, Sergio (1988), 'Entrevista a Aníbal de Iturbide, fundador de la Asociación Mexicana de Cultura', *Opción*, **8** (40), 9–11.

Pallares Ramírez, Manuel (1952), *La Escuela Nacional de Economía: Esbozo histórico 1929–52*, México: UNAM.

Ramírez Hernández, Guillermo (1978), 'Problemática de la enseñanza y la investigación económica en México', *El Economista Mexicano*, **12** (3), 9–17.

Schneider, Benjamin (1998), 'The Material Basis of Technocracy: Investor Confidence and Neoliberalism in Latin America', in Miguel Angel Centeno and Patricio Silva (eds), *The Politics of Expertise in Latin America*, New York: Macmillan Press, pp. 77–95.

Silva Herzog, Jesús (1967), *A un joven economista mexicano*, Mexico: Empresas Editoriales.

'Silva Lining' (1986), *The Economist*, March 22, pp. 80–81.

Stallings, Barbara (1992), 'International Influence on Economic Policy: Debt, Stabilization and Structural Reform', in Stephan Haggard and Robert R. Kaufman (eds), *The Politics of Economic Adjustment: International Constraints, Distributive Conflicts, and the State*, Princeton, NJ: Princeton University Press, pp. 41–88.

'The New Hero' (1981), *The Economist*, October 3, pp. 68–9.

Tomasini, Carlos (2004), 'ITAM: Ofrecen experiencia y personal reconocido', *Reforma*, August 18, p. 14a.

UNAM, Secretaría General de Administración, Dirección General de Servicios Auxiliares, Departamento de Estadística (1981), Cuadros estadísticos 1929–1979, México: UNAM.

Valdés, Juan Gabriel (1995), *Pinochet's Economists: The Chicago School in Chile*, Cambridge, UK: Cambridge University Press.

Vernon, Raymond (1963), *The Dilemma of Mexico's Development: The Roles of the Private and Public Sectors*, Cambridge, MA: Harvard University Press.

Weyland, Kurt (2004), 'Neoliberalism and Democracy in Latin America: A Mixed Record', *Latin American Politics and Society*, **46** (1), 135–58.

7. The United States: an economist's economy

Marion Fourcade[1]

Nowhere, perhaps, is the world of economic knowledge production as large and diverse as it is in the United States. More than any other nation, the United States is an economist's economy. This may sound surprising given that economists in this country rarely hold political positions. Larry Summers' tenure as Treasury Secretary (1999–2001) was, after all, more the exception than the rule. For all its prestige, the political influence of the Council of Economic Advisers remains limited (Bernstein 2001), and rarely translates into any form of long-lasting individual influence, due to the very short-term nature of appointments. Compare this to the extraordinary inroads made by economists in Latin American political systems, described in this volume, or even to the relatively common involvement of economics professors in national politics all over continental Europe (Frey and Eichenberger 1993).

But if economists do not rule America, economics does – to a quite significant extent. It rules in policy, where microeconomic criteria of efficiency often serve as a standard for evaluating the legitimacy of all sorts of programs and regulations when other criteria have been pushed aside; it rules in the courts, where economic expertise has become closely enmeshed with a wide range of legal questions, from racial discrimination to antitrust law; it rules in business, where economic and financial tools often guide firm governance and reform (Baumol and Faulhaber 1988). Finally, economists enjoy a prominent place in the media, too, as the inevitable source of commentaries on the latest statistics and policy decisions to the assertion of authority on any topic of public interest – be it medical decisions, environmental choices, or the behavior of criminals. How can we explain this paradox of economics' deep penetration of American society and economy without a capture of its dominant institutions?

DISCIPLINARY STRENGTH: ACADEMIC ECONOMICS

To answer this question, we must consider the distinctive historical path by which economic knowledge came to establish its presence in academic, policy and business institutions in the United States. Economics constitutes today one of the strongest pillars of higher learning in American universities, with a well established scientific style and a secure academic niche that extends well outside of economics departments into almost all professional schools. Paradoxically, such a situation would have seemed less than certain in the middle of the nineteenth century. Compared with the intense intellectual activity then going on in Europe, and the ambitious claims economic writers there made on matters of public interest, the United States looked rather like a backwater (Barber 1993).

Disciplinary economics in America started quite late, but change happened fast. Until the 1880s, discourse on economic issues remained dominated by traditional elites – lawyers, doctors, educators, and businessmen. The absence of serious advanced training in the subject[2] led many young Americans to get doctoral degrees in Germany, where the historicist school was dominant. Upon their return from Europe, these graduates filled up the positions that were opening in a higher education sector in rapid expansion. With the university revolution gaining steam at the end of the nineteenth century, the number of specialized teaching posts in political economy grew rapidly, from three chairs in 1880 to 51 in 1900 (Coats 1985, p. 1700). The creation of the American Economic Association in 1885 (which broke away from the American Historical Association) consolidated the ascent of academic economists, and further established their role at the vanguard of the transformation of American higher education.[3] Professional publications, often linked to particular universities, followed these developments. The *Quarterly Journal of Economics* was launched at Harvard in 1886; in 1892 the *Journal of Political Economy* was founded at Chicago, and in 1911 the American Economic Association started an in-house journal, the *American Economic Review*.

The expansion of the university system became the driving force in the rapid institutionalization of economics and other social sciences, supported as the beacons of secular moral progress in American society. Indeed the first generation of what we may call 'professional economists' sought explicitly to use their newly found social position in order to mobilize support for social and economic reform. As Mary Furner's (1975) classic work has shown, however, the most radical among them often found their aspirations seriously thwarted by university trustees and administrators, many of them members of the economic elite, who wanted to draw a line between political activism and scholarly behavior. Hence American economics bifurcated early on into two main roads, both of which stemmed in part from scholars' efforts to shelter their work against political attacks, and in part from societal demands. On the one hand, the emerging field evolved toward a model of 'ivory tower' scholarship, focused on high scientific claims and the assertion of disciplinary sovereignty (the success of marginalism in the early part of the twentieth century may be an example, and the vogue of Walrasian economics, particularly among left-wing scholars, after World War II may be another). On the other hand, economists turned toward providing expertise of an increasingly applied sort to businesses and public agencies. Hence the reform activism of the first generation of American economists, for all the difficulties it encountered, nonetheless helped establish the legitimacy of technical, expert discourse *vis-à-vis* audiences in policy and business – in other words it shaped the particular nature of American academic professionalism.

Since the nineteenth century university revolution, economics has occupied a particularly prominent place at America's most prestigious institutions of higher education. In 1926, economics represented the largest group of majors at Stanford, the second largest at Harvard and the third largest at Yale (Reuben 1996, p. 209). At the turn of the twenty-first century, over 11 percent of undergraduate degrees awarded by Harvard went to economics majors (source: Harvard University Registrar's Office). In addition, economics diffused to other academic units, such as business schools, later law schools and public policy schools. The intimate association between economics and the business curriculum is perhaps most striking. Today, for instance, there are almost as many economics PhDs teaching in the top 20 business schools as there are teaching in the top 20 economics departments (Committee on the Status of Women in the Economics Profession 2004).

Many authors since Tocqueville (2000 [1835/1840]; for example Hofstadter 1963) have noted that egalitarianism in American political culture makes intellectual privilege suspect, so that intellectual institutions have had to establish their claims to legitimacy through formal criteria: American academia is more tightly professionalized along disciplinary lines than other systems of higher education (Abbott 2001). Like other social scientists, American economists came to rely on the doctorate as a marker of professional identity early on, as a way to carefully craft their jurisdiction against the intrusion of lay people and non-experts in a country with a weak administrative tradition (Fourcade 2009). Even today, economics departments award a larger proportion of PhDs (as a proportion of higher degrees awarded) than any other social science. One consequence of this 'culture of professionalism' (Bledstein 1976) was the centralization of disciplinary control in those universities, which train the largest number of graduate students. The top 20 universities award half of the doctorates in the field, out of 120 PhD-granting institutions (Gumport 1993, p. 273). They are thus in a strong position to exert significant influence over the methods and problems deemed appropriate, as well as the relative value of professional credentials. To a large extent, these definitions and hierarchies (also reproduced at the international level) determine access to journals,[4] employment prospects and other rewards. Network analyses of different disciplines have indeed shown that, somewhat ironically for a discipline focused on competition, the economics labor market is rooted in a clear hierarchy and tight solidarity among leading institutions, to a much greater extent than other disciplines except, perhaps, philosophy (Han 2003; Healy 2006; Lamont 2009).

Besides the rigid organization of the 'buying' and 'selling' of new PhDs, other mechanisms that contribute to tight disciplinary control include the existence of highly coveted prizes, such as the 'Nobel' prize or the Clark medal (which rewards outstanding research accomplishments by a US-based economist under the age of 40), the frequently non-blind review process (Baron and Hannan 1994),[5] the 'oligarchic' or top-down governance of the American Economic Association (which contrasts markedly with the more democratic and decentralized governance of the American Sociological Association)[6] or elitist gate-keeping in access to research funds. Intellectually, the highest rewards go – by and large – to virtuosity in model building or statistically clever empirical work.

The Improbable Intellectual Trajectory of American Economics

On its face, this path would have been hard to predict at the turn of the twentieth century, and even well into the interwar period. American economics was more eclectic then. Institutionalism was fighting with neoclassical economics for the 'soul' of the discipline (Yonay 1998). The University of Wisconsin, with its tradition of reformist involvement, was an intellectual powerhouse on a par with its rivals in Cambridge, MA and Chicago. Institutionalist economists occupied prominent positions in the profession, sometimes at the helm of its most important institutions – the National Bureau of Economic Research (NBER), the American Economic Association, and scholarly journals.

The boundaries between institutionalism and neoclassical economics were never too clear either. During the 1920s and 1930s for instance, it was not uncommon among self-identified institutionalists to rely on the scientific rhetoric of marginalism to avoid controversies with university administrators and funding agencies (Ross 1991; Biddle 1998). Even later, some important postwar personalities arguably continued to bridge the two categories in their own work: perhaps most interesting, given the topic of this book, is the case of Milton Friedman, who counted prominent institutionalists (Arthur R. Burns, Wesley Clair Mitchell, John Maurice Clark and Simon Kuznets) among his mentors (along with his Chicago teachers and classmates), and who would end up writing (with Anna Schwartz), a *Monetary History of the United States* (1963) in a classic institutionalist vein.

In any case, by the 1940s the differences between these practices of economics were somewhat obsolete, as both parties confronted the mathematical and econometric revolutions, largely imported from Europe and mostly attributable to the work of a (then) small and still fairly marginal institution, the Cowles Commission for Economic Research.[7] The greatest impetus for the diffusion and legitimation of more formal approaches also came from the growing incorporation of economists (some of them still based at Cowles and other similar institutions) into the machine of government. Input–output analysis, national accounting and linear programming techniques were thus all largely developed in the context of contractual or in-house work for government agencies. So was game theory. As Mirowski (2002a) has brilliantly shown, the latter field expanded dramatically as a result of lavish Defense Department funding – during World War II, and continuing after the outbreak of the Cold War (also see Bernstein 2001).

Scholars have pointed out that political factors were also important to understand the post-war mathematization of American economics: repeating the pattern first enacted at the turn of the century, economists suspect of Marxist or left-wing Keynesian leanings found themselves harassed, prosecuted and dismissed as their political views came under suspicion during the McCarthy era (Morgan and Rutherford 1998).[8] Mathematics did not always offer protection against such mistrust: indeed the ill-treatment extended to mathematical scholars with socialist sympathies, such as future 'Nobel' prize winner Lawrence Klein. Still, the whole institutional apparatus that supported economic research – including, quite prominently, the National Science Foundation – clearly found in the emulation of the rhetoric and methods of the natural sciences a valuable way to persuade funders and defend economics against the attacks of lay people and politicians (see McCloskey 1985; Gieryn 1999; Mirowski 2002b).

Thus a highly abstract and formalized theoretical core gained increasing standing over empirical applications during the post-war period (Leontief 1982; Whitley 1984). By the late 1980s, American graduate students in economics had come to perceive analytical ability to be more important than knowledge of the economy for professional advancement (Klamer and Colander 1990). Formalism and abstraction also enabled modern economics to evolve into a truly 'universal' science. The language of mathematics and, above all, the increasingly tight assumptions about rationality facilitated the imperialistic diffusion of modern economics to other countries (Markoff and Montecinos 1993; Fourcade 2006) and disciplinary domains, including sociology, history, political sciences and most remarkably, perhaps, the law – a process especially pronounced in the United States. Characteristically, non-orthodox economists in this country (for instance Marxist economists) are just as likely to use mathematics as their neoclassical peers.

By the 1990s, however, the nearly exclusive *theoretical* emphasis, which had risen to prominence in the 1960s–1970s (to the point where it attracted strong criticisms both from within and from without the discipline),[9] started to weaken significantly. Several convergent trends explain this shift: the growing availability of large-scale data, the revolution in computing power, the generalization of econometric training, and – intellectually – the triumph of Chicago price theory. The percentage of empirical papers in the top three American journals (*American Economic Review*, *Quarterly Journal of Economics* and *Journal of Political Economy*), which had stayed constant at around 30 percent from 1960 until 1975, started rising in the 1980s (to about 40 percent in 1990) and jumped to 57 percent in 1992 (Figlio 1994). The representation of American economics as a theoretical, high status core surrounded by a low-status, empirical periphery is thus largely outdated. Modern American economics has reconnected with the original empiricist orientation of its institutionalist founders, although the empiricist projects are now carried out from within a much more homogeneous analytical paradigm and with the assistance of considerably more sophisticated technical tools.[10] And this, to a large extent, explains the discipline's extraordinary power in shaping today's policy debates, and in providing expertise to corporations, courts, and governments at all levels. In a very different way, the recent success of 'Freakonomics' (Levitt and Dubner 2006), which consists in taking trivial empirical problems and addressing them in a 'clever' (if irrelevant) manner, with minimal theoretical intervention, is perhaps also exemplary of this new trend.

AMERICAN ECONOMISTS AND AMERICAN GOVERNMENT

As pointed out earlier, American economists rarely cast their discourse in an explicitly political frame and usually refrain from holding political office. In the United States, unlike Europe or Latin America where political careers are not uncommon, political involvement is often presented as incompatible with standards of professionalism (Frey and Eichenberger 1993). The institutional pressures to keep science and politics separate are such that political appointments, while clearly sought after – the state remains, here as elsewhere, an essential source of 'symbolic capital' (Bourdieu 1998) – are at the same time represented by purists (particularly those coming out of the University of Chicago) as dangerous threats to scientific reputations.[11] Hence the ritualistic emphasis on the separation between academic work and partisanship (the theme of the ivory tower) and the strict rules governing ties between academics and politics: (academics' involvement in government is usually limited to rotations of a few years.) To a certain extent, however, these defensive practices mask the reality of a deep involvement of economists in American public policy.

Although the Progressive Era and the experience of World War I had legitimated greater government economic activism and improvements in economic and statistical information (Nelson 1987), before the New Deal, only a few government agencies employed a permanent staff of economic experts. The 1920s had also witnessed important technocratic experiments, which helped cement a particular organizational nexus of relationships involving government agencies, philanthropic foundations and research institutes (Barber 1985).

It is with Franklin D. Roosevelt, however, that the reliance on social-scientific professionals became far more extensive. With the academic labor market devastated by the Great Depression, many young graduates turned to employment opportunities in government. Institutionalist economists had a particularly noticeable (though often short-lived) influence on early New Deal measures on planning, labor and agricultural organization, and social security (Stryker 1989; Dobbin 1993; Biddle 1998). After 1937, a group of American Keynesians at Harvard and Tufts University helped articulate a rationale for using the budget to stimulate economic activity (Stein 1996; Weir and Skocpol 1985). With the advent of World War II, the contribution of economists to government planning, rationalization and military strategy expanded further. As an indication of the profound change underway, the proportion of authors of economic articles in the main academic journals who held government appointments jumped from 2.7 percent in 1932–33 to 16.8 percent in 1942–43 (Stigler 1965, p. 45).[12] A young Milton Friedman worked in the Treasury Department. John Kenneth Galbraith headed the Office of Price Administration, which supervised the rationing of production and price controls. Simon Kuznets and Robert Nathan prepared projections for military production for the War Production Board. At the Office of Strategic Services, Edward Mason 'assembled a stunning array of some of the nation's leading economic authorities' and future stars of the profession. (Bernstein 2001, pp. 79–80)

As Mirowski (2002a) has shown, military operations, goals and financing remained central to the connections between economists and government throughout the Cold War, with powerful intellectual consequences (also see Porter 1995; Bernstein 2001).

The (greatly disputed, to be sure) creation, in 1946, of the Council of Economic Advisers (in the White House) and the Joint Economic Committee (in Congress), signaled the institutionalization of the contribution of economic knowledge to the formulation of economic policy.[13] The CEA has come to play an important role in policy debates, although its actual influence has been highly variable, depending mainly on the President's willingness to take its recommendations seriously (Tobin and Weidenbaum 1988, p. ix)[14] as well as on the competition of groups of economic experts in other government agencies (the Treasury, the Federal Reserve and the more recently established National Economic Council).

The fact is that, with formal institutions in place, interactions between academics and government are much more common in the United States than the 'Ivory Tower' metaphor suggests. Universities encourage the public visibility of their members. And the fragmented and non-specialized structure of the US government allows it to easily incorporate outsiders into public service (Weir and Skocpol 1985). Still, the nature of the involvement of economists in US government remains quite noticeably distinctive in comparative perspective. Many other Northern countries have no similar practices or have institutionalized them only very partially and recently. In France, policy design has been traditionally the prerogative of a special class of state administrators. In England, administrative training has a much less formal character, and is rooted primarily in elite socialization and long tenures on-the-job. The United States, by contrast, exemplifies a political culture that refuses to single out the state as the ultimate locus of political sovereignty by separating 'state knowledge' from other forms of knowledge, and relies on externally validated outsiders (that is, primarily, the professions) to legitimize government action (Fourcade 2009).

The 1960s and 1970s are often regarded as the Golden Age of economists in US policymaking (Bernstein 2001), both in terms of the profession's ambition ('we believed we could change the world', one interviewee from the Brookings Institution told me) and in terms of its actual visibility. The use of macroeconomic models and the institutionalization of cost–benefit analysis drove much of the demand for economists at all levels of government, whose rise Figure 7.1 documents. The success of the 1964 ('Keynesian') tax cuts vindicated Keynesian macroeconomics, and seemed to demonstrate the effectiveness of economic expertise. The enthusiasm, however, was short-lived. The economy started to slow down in the late

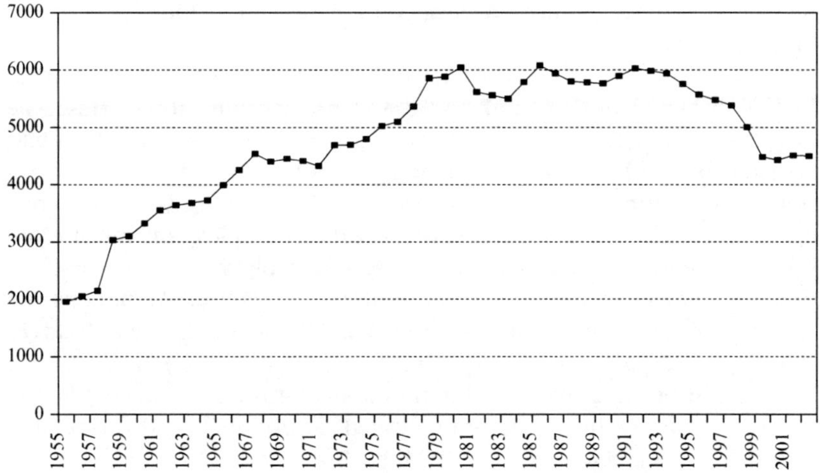

Source: United States Office of Personnel Management, (1967–1999).

Figure 7.1 Number of economists in US government, 1955–2002

1960s. Sluggish growth, if not recession, became the norm. Combined with the post-Civil Rights cultural backlash, the critique of government action gained momentum. By 1980, the ideas of Milton Friedman had found a highly public platform in a PBS television series, *Free to Choose*, which opened with the chapter 'the power of the market', complete with a reference to the mythical image of America as the land of opportunity.[15] All the while, critics from within the discipline were getting louder and more numerous, de-legitimizing some of the best established policy tools (monetary policy, fiscal policy, econometric forecasts). From a focus on the macroeconomy and growth, economics became increasingly concerned with microeconomic efficiency – applied to industrial regulation, social policies, and the provision of public goods – and, (signaling the imminent triumph of the Chicago approach to the economy) increasingly enamored with a more effective utilization of the price system (Sunstein 2002).

The shift in the nature and orientation of economic expertise also had profound institutional roots in the growing complexity of the field of economic knowledge in the United States. In this country, institutionalized political rules tend to favor the decentralized and competitive organization of policy expertise and research. The fragmentation of the government machine, with numerous jurisdictional overlaps, and the practice of congressional hearings, tends to create a competitive situation within the realm of expertise. In fact, inconsistencies and contradictions are not uncommon across executive agencies, and between the different branches of government.[16]

From the 1970s on, policy-relevant economic research was increasingly contracted out to think tanks and private consulting firms. The movement had begun in the 1960s, with the War on Poverty, which had seen the birth of a number of important non-governmental organizations (for example, the Urban Institute in 1968) alongside new public agencies. By the late 1970s, these organizations had become much more numerous and the field had changed considerably with the diversification of financial support. Corporations also increasingly understood the importance of financing business-friendly social science research. If technical expertise is a central part of policy discourses in modern societies, 'it becomes more and more important for elites to control the process through which data are collected, interpreted, and formulated into policy arguments' (Fisher 1993, p. 36). Corporate activism in the 1970s not only improved the think tanks' financial base, but further legitimized and expanded their policy role (Vogel 1978, 1983, 1989). Indeed, many research institutes emerged (for example, the Heritage Foundation, the Cato Institute) or were strengthened (for example, the Hoover Institution, the American Enterprise Institute) as a result of this new understanding of influence.[17]

It is perhaps not surprising, then, that the vast majority of those think tanks that dealt primarily with economic matters proclaimed their commitment to the promotion of free-market ideas loud and clear (Day 1993). Some of these organizations saw their fortunes grow as the movement to reform government as we knew it gained steam. When Ronald Reagan took office, for instance, as many as twenty research fellows from the conservative American Enterprise Institute joined his administration in high positions. This was somewhat unusual, and indicative both of the growing ideological polarization in American government and of the transformation in the supply of expertise in all domains that accompanied it. The rising mistrust of government action that was the core discourse of the conservative revolution meant that government-based economic information and advice were losing critical support and legitimacy. Government research was now seen as just another form of partisan research that needed to be counterbalanced, either by appealing to organizations that represented different interests, or by relying on outside professionals viewed as 'neutral', such as academics. It is in this context that think tank economists came to assume a prominent social role as experts routinely called upon by government and the media. As Figure 7.2 suggests, however, their social trajectory into this role was different from that of their main competitors in the field of policy knowledge: people working in the non-profit and private

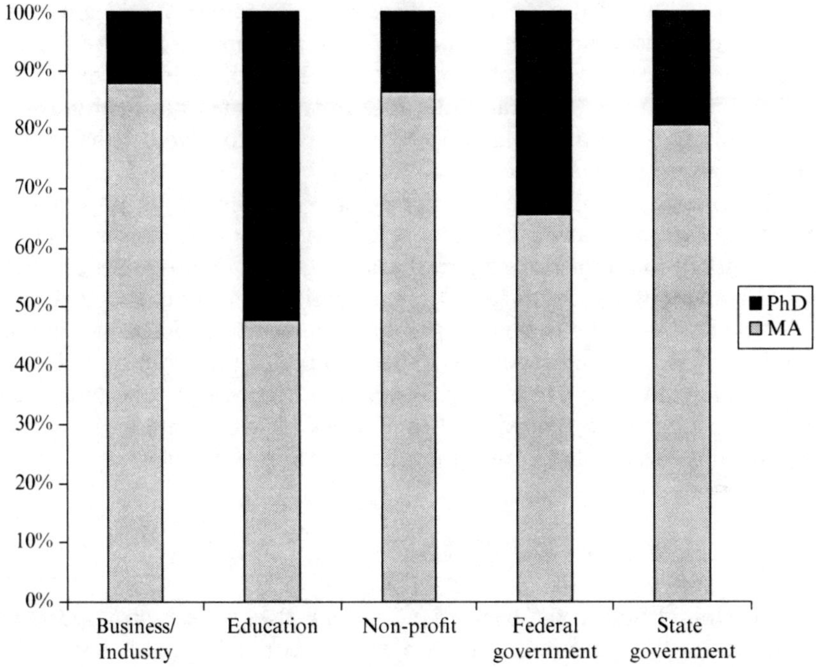

Source: National Science Foundation (2003).

Figure 7.2 Relative proportions of holders of MA vs PhD economics degrees in different employment sectors (as a proportion of all graduate economics degree holders)

sectors, in particular, are much less likely to hold an economics PhD than those located in academia and the federal government.

The enormous growth of policy research organizations, both non-profit and private, has been especially marked in the United States, where it was brought about by the expanding demands for economic policy expertise, the permeability of state structures and the pervasive mistrust of government. Although such organizations also exist in other countries, the visibility and influence they have in the United States is unparalleled.[18] Smith (1991) identified over 1000 think tanks in the United States, with a little more than 100 in Washington alone.

Quasi-academic think tanks like NBER or Brookings participate in academic debates via scholarly publications and conferences, and may have a leading role in diffusing recent scientific developments to broader audiences, acting as bridges between the academic and political worlds.

The more political think tanks walk a much finer line. The legitimacy of their expertise can be much more precarious. Some provide refuge to people who are relatively marginal to the academic world (for example, supply-siders at the American Enterprise Institute, the Cato Institute and the Manhattan Institute), but nonetheless prepared to advocate their positions by all possible means.

The emergence of advocacy think tanks in the 1970s profoundly reshaped the policy analysis field (as older organizations, like Brookings, were pushed to adopt more aggressive strategies to retain influence), but it also had an impact on the overall organization of economic knowledge. Think tanks have challenged the place and authority of academics in the public sphere, pushing experts to either embrace a more openly political stance or, conversely, to engage furiously in boundary work (see Paul Krugman's critiques against the supply-siders, the pop internationalists, and the industrial policy wonks for instance) (Fourcade 2004).

ECONOMICS AS BUSINESS

In the United States, the business world has always been an important employer of trained economists; conversely, economic experts have successfully turned their knowledge into a marketable asset. The profession of 'business economist' was already well institutionalized by the middle of the century, with a robust economic consulting market addressing a variety of topics, from pollution to antitrust to crime control. The liberalization of economic policy (in the area of industrial regulation for instance) has, to some extent, deepened this trend by shifting the burden of oversight from government agencies to private sector consultants and law firms, all of which have increased markedly their employment of economists. Finally, with the financialization of the economy (Krippner 2006), economic expertise has also become much more firmly entrenched in the banking and financial sectors.

In 1985, jobs in business represented a little over 50 percent of the self-identified 'economist' positions in the United States (National Science Foundation 1985). Although the business sector employs a smaller percentage of the highly trained economists than academic institutions, business employment of doctoral economists since 1970 has grown at a much faster pace than any other type of employment – from about 10 percent of all economics PhDs in 1970 to over 25 percent in 2001 (Figure 7.3). This suggests that the educational qualifications of people occupying 'economist' positions in business have risen sharply over the period, at least at the top end, and that the PhD has become an essential professional marker in this

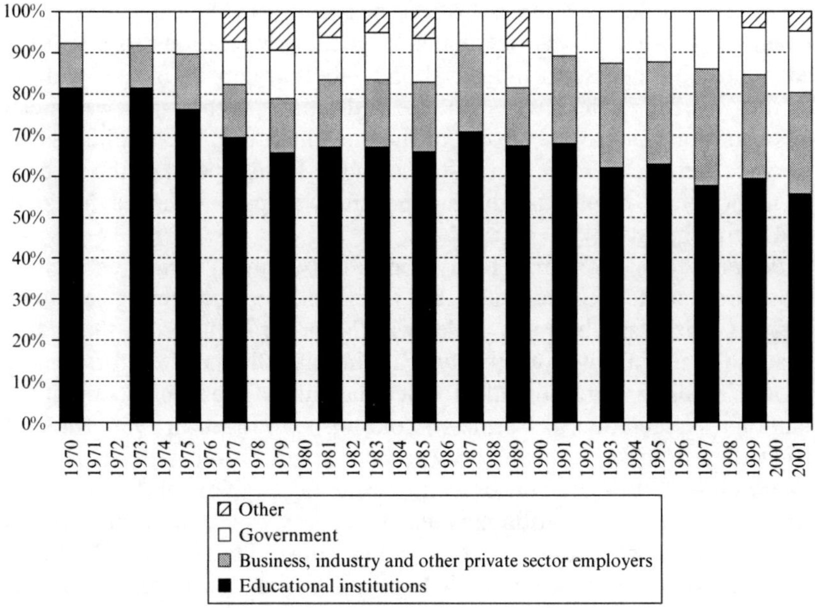

Sources: National Science Foundation, *Characteristics of Doctoral Scientists and Engineers*, 1975, 1987, 1991, 1993, 1995, 1997, 1999 and 2001.

Figure 7.3 Employment sector of US doctoral economists, 1970–2001

sector. Similar trends are evident in other countries, a combination of the persistent rise of credentialization and specialization in modern societies and of the growing demands for economic knowledge coming from the business sector, itself connected to the changing make-up of the economy.

There are two main ways in which the connection between economists and business is relevant here. First is the growing incorporation of academic economics into the business curriculum, which is particularly significant given the latter's exponential growth throughout the twentieth century (as a subject of undergraduate and graduate education, business grew at a much faster pace than higher education in general, including economics). For better or for worse, economic science (and especially financial economics) has become a central component of the education of businessmen, financiers and managers at all levels (Khurana 2007). Second is the emergence of a distinctive niche for professional economics in the business sector. None of these phenomena were entirely new. The creation of the first business schools often involved economics professors. The membership of the earlier political economy clubs and associations clearly shows the keen interest of business elites. In the early part of the twentieth century it was not uncommon for corporations to call upon economists' expertise in industrial and labor organization (particularly as they related to the law) or finance and money (although it was much less common than today). Some of the most high-profile consultants and advisers were academics. For instance Irving Fisher, perhaps the preeminent monetary economist during the interwar period, had a lucrative consulting business.[19]

Private sector economics today comes in two main forms: on the one hand are 'business economists', that is, individuals performing economic services (forecasts, business cycle) within corporations from the industrial, commercial, and, especially, banking and financial sectors. These professionals have traditionally formed the bulk of the membership of the National Association of Business Economists, founded in 1959. Most of what they produce is directed toward the organization itself, its routine functioning and the pursuit of its interests (although in some cases privileged economic information may also be conceived as part of the normal services that corporations reserve to their most elite clients). Chief economic advisers often bring in a network of formal and informal connections with academic or government circles and are a key component of the 'public face' of the corporation, performing important symbolic functions and writing and being reported on frequently in the media (this is particularly true of those economists who operate in the financial world, such as Stephen Roach at Morgan Stanley).

On the other hand are economic consultancy and economic research organizations with various specializations (legal, forecasting, market design) and client bases (governments, courts, corporations). With the rise of statistical and later econometric methods, economists developed a much more sophisticated arsenal of saleable services, databases and tools, all of which came to serve as a basis for the creation of specialized for-profit organizations. For instance, econometric forecasting, which was initially started by academics and federal government agencies under the mantel of Keynesian macroeconomics, was an almost entirely private enterprise by the 1980s. Finance theory produced in business schools during the 1970s was taken up by traders and completely transformed the way the financial markets functioned, getting many scholars heavily involved as investors and consultants in the process, with considerable material benefits for them and, perhaps, considerable negative consequences for the rest of us (MacKenzie 2006).

Most remarkable, perhaps, is the massive expansion of economics in the legal sector (Mercuro and Medema 2006). Because of the character of the legal system in the United States, where administrative and legal rules are constantly subject to challenge and negotiation, corporations face an evolving and ambiguous regulatory environment. Not surprisingly, firms, courts and government offices have all resorted to economists to provide quantifiable standards of decision making. In the last decades of the twentieth century, however, the neo-liberalization of the economy and, in particular, the weakening of the regulatory environment (partly under the influence of the 'law and economics' movement within academia), as well as the reliance on increasingly complex techniques to assess the legal or illegal character of economic actions, have tremendously benefited economists. The *Wall Street Journal* recently summed up the evolution of antitrust the following way:

> Traditionally, trust-busters focused on blatantly illegal behavior, such as price-fixing, leaving little leeway for an economist's interpretation once the facts were established, observes Howard University law professor Andrew Gavil. More recent cases, such as the one against Microsoft Corp. in the late 1990s, have involved tricky calculations of how much consumers might be damaged by a company's market domination. (Anders 2007, p. A1)

CONCLUSION

Elsewhere (Fourcade 2009) I describe the production of economic knowledge in the United States as a case of 'scientific and merchant professionalism'. This formula is meant to depict the two main elements I have discussed in this chapter. On the one hand, the relative institutional isolation of universities, their vulnerability to political criticism, particularly in the 1900s and 1950s, have helped cement the scientific evolution of American economics toward mathematical and statistical technique, and marginalize more descriptive and literary forms of intellectual work. On the other hand, the American government's reluctance to internalize the production of policy-relevant research and the decentralized and competitive character of political and administrative decision-making in this country have provided ample room for economists to exercise their skills in the public domain under the mantel of applied expertise. Coupled with the primacy of extra-administrative (mainly legal) mechanisms in the governance of the US economy, these factors have also ensured the far-ranging commercialization of the skills and ideas of economists, toward both government (at all levels) and private corporations. This does not mean that the designs of economists always win in the American economy – they do not. Policy, after all, remains an eminently political process. But the techniques and approaches of economists have become part and parcel of the competition over this process in a manner that, perhaps, has no parallel elsewhere.

NOTES

1. My deepest thanks to Verónica Montecinos and John Markoff for very constructive comments, and to María José Álvarez for her able research assistance.
2. Teaching in political economy, introduced in 1817, was originally controlled by clergymen until almost the end of the nineteenth century (O'Connor 1944, p. 106; Barber 1993; Coats 1993, p. 349).
3. Economists, for instance, were also at the forefront of efforts to establish the American Association of University Professors early in the twentieth century (Coats 1985).
4. Journal articles constitute the standard form of scholarly output. Dissertations consist generally of three articles, not necessarily related to one another.
5. In the non-blind system, reviewers know the identity of the authors of the reviewed paper. Examples of non-blind journals in economics include some of the top journals, such as *American Economic Review, Journal of Political Economy, Review of Economic Studies.*
6. A key difference between the two associations is the role of the nominating committee – appointed by the association's president in the American Economic Association and voted on by the membership at large in the American Sociological Association.
7. See Mirowski (2002a). The Cowles Commission had been established in the 1930s to support the newly founded Econometric Society, an association of mathematicians, statisticians and mathematical economists that became the main center for the development of large-scale macroeconometric models and a crucial influence in shaping American economics in the post-war period. First housed at the University of Chicago (1939–55) and then at Yale (1955–82), the commission helped incorporate a large group of mathematically-inclined refugee scholars from Continental Europe. One-third of the recipients of the Nobel Prize in economics between 1969 and 1990 had been formally associated with the organization.
8. Paul Baran at Stanford, Paul M. Sweezy at the University of New Hampshire, Howard Bowen at the University of Illinois, among others.
9. The rise of mathematical economics attracted severe critiques both from within and from outside the discipline (Leontief 1971, 1982; Bell 1981; Colander and Brenner 1992; Aslanbeigui and Montecinos 1998) that argued that much of academic economics had become useless and irrelevant. The profession reacted to these complaints with the creation of the *Journal of Economic Perspectives*, and in 1988 the president of the American Economic Association appointed a Commission on Graduate Education in Economics (COGEE report, Krueger 1991; Hansen 1991).
10. In the words of a labor economist: 'I think the field is about as healthy as it has ever been. It may be too empirical. . . . But for economics that's incredibly positive because it just stops in the track the baloney of people who have theories and theories' (Professor, Ivy League University. Interviewed by author on May 17, 1999).
11. The heavily ideological 'supply-siders', a group of maverick economists involved with the Reagan revolution, came, with a few exceptions, from the fringes of the profession: journalism, consulting firms and conservative think tanks (Campbell 1998).
12. The journals of Stigler's study were: *Quarterly Journal of Economics*, the *American Economic Review*, the *Review of Economics and Statistics* and *Econometrica.*
13. The CEA consists of three principal members with a staff of 12 to 20 professional economists, all of them generally drawn from academia. Because the CEA is a purely advisory body, it represents no major challenge to the more powerful economic agencies, such as the Treasury and the Bureau of the Budget (Weir 1989).
14. Harvard professor Martin Feldstein, Council chairman under President Reagan, was dismissed after public disagreements over budget deficits. At the time, the White House considered abolishing the institution altogether.
15. The series served as a basis for a bestseller book, published with Rose Friedman (1990 [1980]).
16. Stuart Eizenstat (Executive Director of the White House Domestic Policy Staff from

1977 to 1981) recalls: 'When we had to decide on the Administration's position on the advisability of raising the minimum wage in 1977 we could expect widely differing economic estimates from the Departments of Labor and Commerce on the impact of a rise in the minimum wage, because each saw the world differently, and their economic assumptions reflect those differences' (1992, p. 66). Also see Allen (1977, p. 86) on the lower status and prestige of government economists.

17. Hence Vogel (1989, p. 226) states that by the early 1980s 'the hostility of business to government was articulated differently; instead of rhetorical denunciations of big government, it now was expressed in terms of relatively sophisticated and well-documented analyses of the economic effects of specific government policies on business and of criticisms of the scientific basis of health and safety regulations'.
18. *The Economist* (1989) summarizes well this discrepancy: 'In Washington, think tanks have large, grand offices. In London they are strictly hole-in-the-wall jobs, occupying a few town houses in Westminster'.
19. Fisher's reputation, however, was tarnished by his optimistic predictions on the eve of the Great Depression.

REFERENCES

Abbott, Andrew (2001), *Chaos of Disciplines*, Chicago, Ill.: University of Chicago Press.

Allen, William R. (1977), 'Economics, Economists and Economic Policy: Modern American Experiences', *History of Political Economy*, **9** (1), 48–88.

Anders, George (2007), 'An Economist's Courtroom Bonanza', *Wall Street Journal*, March 19, p. A1.

Aslanbeigui, Nahid and Verónica Montecinos (1998), 'Foreign Students in US Doctoral Programs', *Journal of Economic Perspectives*, **12** (3), 171–82.

Barber, William J. (1985), *From New Era to New Deal: Herbert Hoover, the Economists, and American Economic Policy, 1921–1933*, Cambridge: Cambridge University Press.

Barber, William J. (1993), 'Political Economy and the Academic Setting before 1900: An Introduction', in William J. Barber (ed.), *Breaking the Academic Mold: Economists and American Higher Learning in the Nineteenth Century*, New York: Transaction Publishers, pp. 3–14.

Baron, James N. and Michael T. Hannan (1994), 'The Impact of Economics on Contemporary Sociology', *Journal of Economic Literature*, **32** (3), 1111–46.

Baumol, William J. and Gerald R. Faulhaber (1988), 'Economists as Innovators: Practical Products of Theoretical Research', *Journal of Economic Literature*, **26** (2), 577–600.

Bell, Daniel (1981), 'Models and Reality in Economic Discourse', in Daniel Bell and Irving Kristol (eds), *The Crisis in Economic Theory*, New York, NY: Basic Books.

Bernstein, Michael A. (2001), *A Perilous Progress: Economists and the Public Purpose in America*, Princeton, NJ: Princeton University Press.

Biddle, Jeffrey (1998), 'Institutional Economics: A Case of Reproductive Failure?', in Mary S. Morgan and Malcolm Rutherford (eds), *From Interwar Pluralism to Postwar Neoclassicism*, Durham, NC: Duke University Press, pp. 108–33.

Bledstein, Burton (1976), *The Culture of Professionalism: The Middle Class and the Development of Higher Education in America*, New York: W.W. Norton and Company.

Bourdieu, Pierre (1998), 'Rethinking the State: Genesis and Structure of the Bureaucratic Field', in *Practical Reason*, Stanford, CA: Stanford University Press, pp. 35–74.

Campbell, John L. (1998), 'Institutional analysis and the role of ideas in political economy', *Theory and Society*, **27**, 377–409.

Coats, A.W. Bob (1985), 'The American Economic Association and the Economics Profession', *Journal of Economic Literature*, **23** (4), 1697–1727.

Coats, A.W. Bob (1993), *British and American Economic Essays. Vol. II: The Sociology and Professionalization of Economics*, London and New York: Routledge.

Colander, David and Reuven Brenner (1992), *Educating Economists*, Ann Arbor: University of Michigan Press.

Committee on the Status of Women in the Economics Profession (American Economic Association) (2004), 'Report of the Committee on the Status of Women in the Economics Profession'. Available at http://www.cswep.org/annual_reports/2004_CSWEP_Annual_Report.pdf (last accessed: June 19, 2007)

Day, Alan J. (1993), *Think Tanks: An International Directory*, London, UK: Longman Group.

Dobbin, Frank (1993), 'The Social Construction of the Great Depression: Industrial Policy during the 1930s in the United States, France and Britain', *Theory and Society*, **22**, 1–56.

Eizenstat, Stuart E. (1992), 'Economists and White House Decisions', *Journal of Economic Perspectives*, **6** (3), 65–71.

Figlio, David (1994), 'Trends in the Publication of Empirical Economics', *The Journal of Economic Perspectives*, **8** (3), 179–87.

Fisher, Donald (1993), *Fundamental Development of the Social Sciences: Rockefeller Philanthropy and the United States Social Science Research Council*, Ann Arbor: The University of Michigan Press.

Fourcade, Marion (2004), 'Paul Krugman: The Wicked Economist?', *Footnotes. Newsletter of the American Sociological Association*, May.

Fourcade, Marion (2006), 'The Construction of a Global Profession: The Transnationalization of Economics', *American Journal of Sociology*, **112** (1), 145–94.

Fourcade, Marion (2009), *Economists and Societies. Discipline and Profession in the United States, Great Britain and France*, Princeton, NJ: Princeton University Press.

Frey, Bruno S. and Reiner Eichenberger (1993), 'American and European Economics and Economists', *Journal of Economic Perspectives*, **7** (4), 185–93.

Friedman, Milton and Rose Friedman (1990 [1980]), *Free to Choose: A Personal Statement*, New York: Harcourt Brace.

Friedman, Milton and Anna Schwartz (1963), *A Monetary History of the United States 1867–1960*, Princeton, NJ: Princeton University Press.

Furner, Mary (1975), *Advocacy and Objectivity. A Crisis in the Professionalization of American Social Science, 1865–1905*, Lexington, KY: The University Press of Kentucky.

Gieryn, Thomas F. (1999), 'The US Congress Demarcates Natural Science and Social Science (Twice)', in *Cultural Boundaries of Sciences: Credibility on the Line*, Chicago: University of Chicago Press, pp. 65–114.

Gumport, Patricia J. (1993), 'Graduate Education and Organized Research in the

United States', in Burton R. Clark (ed.), *The Research Foundations of Graduate Education: Germany, Britain, France, the United States, Japan*, Berkeley: The University of California Press, pp. 225–60.

Han, Shin-Kap (2003), 'Tribal Regimes in Academia: A Comparative Analysis of Market Structure across Disciplines', *Social Networks*, **25** (3), 251–80.

Hansen, W. Lee (1991), 'The Education and Training of Economics Doctorates: Major Findings of the Executive Secretary of the American Economic Association's Commission on Graduate Education in Economics', *Journal of Economic Literature*, **29** (3), 1054–87.

Healy, Kieran (2006), 'Specialization and Status in Philosophy', Unpublished Manuscript. Department of Sociology, University of Arizona.

Hofstadter, Richard (1963), *Anti-Intellectualism in American Life*, New York: Alfred A. Knopf.

Khurana, Rakesh (2007), *From Higher Aims to Hired Hands: The Social Transformation of American Business Schools and the Unfulfilled Promise of Management as a Profession*, Princeton, NJ: Princeton University Press.

Klamer, Arjo and David Colander (1990), *The Making of An Economist*, Boulder, CO: Westview Press.

Krippner, Greta (2006), 'The Financialization of the American Economy', *Socio-Economic Review*, **3** (2), 173–208.

Krueger, Anne O. (1991), 'Report of the Commission on Graduate Education in Economics', *Journal of Economic Literature*, **29** (3), 1035–53.

Lamont, Michèle (2009), *How Professors Think: Inside the Curious World of Academic Judgment*, Cambridge, MA: Harvard University Press.

Leontief, Wassily (1971), 'Theoretical Assumptions and Unobserved Facts', *American Economic Review*, **61** (1), 1–7.

Leontief, Wassily (1982), 'Academic Economics. Letter to the editor of *Science*', *Science*, **217**, July 9.

Levitt, Steven and Stephen J. Dubner (2006), *Freakonomics: A Rogue Economist Explores the Hidden Side of Everything* (revised and expanded), New York: William Morrow/Harper Collins.

MacKenzie, Donald A. (2006), *An Engine, Not a Camera*, Princeton, NJ: Princeton University Press.

Markoff, John and Verónica Montecinos (1993), 'The Ubiquitous Rise of Economists', *Journal of Public Policy*, **13** (1), 37–68.

McCloskey, Donald N. (1985) *The Rhetoric of Economics*, Madison, WI: University of Wisconsin Press.

Mercuro, Nicholas and Stephen Medema (2006), *Economics and the Law: From Posner to Postmodernism and Beyond*, Princeton, NJ: Princeton University Press (Second Edition).

Mirowski, Philip (2002a), *Machine Dreams: Economics Becomes a Cyborg Science*, Cambridge: Cambridge University Press.

Mirowski, Philip (2002b), 'Cowles Changes Allegiance: From Econometric Empiricism to Cognition as Intuitive Statistics', *Journal of the History of Economic Thought*, **24**, 165–94.

Morgan, Mary S. and Malcolm Rutherford (1998), 'American Economics: The Character of the Transformation', in Mary S. Morgan and Malcolm Rutherford (eds), *From Interwar Pluralism to Postwar Neoclassicism*, Durham, NC: Duke University Press, pp. 1–26.

National Science Foundation *Characteristics of Doctoral Scientists and Engineers*, 1975, 1987, 1991, 1993, 1995, 1997, 1999 and 2001.

National Science Foundation (1985), *Science and Engineering Personnel: A National Overview*, Surveys of Science Resource Series, NSF #85-302.

National Science Foundation (2003), Division of Science Resources Statistics, Scientists and Engineers Statistical Data System (SESTAT), preliminary estimates, http://sestat.nsf.gov.

Nelson, Robert H. (1987), 'The Economics Profession and the Making of Public Policy', *Journal of Economic Literature*, **27**, 49–91.

O'Connor, Michael J.L. (1944), *Origins of Academic Economics in the United States*, New York: Columbia University Press.

Porter, Theodore (1995), *Trust in Numbers: The Pursuit of Objectivity in Science and Public Life*, Princeton, NJ: Princeton University Press.

Reuben, Julie A. (1996), *The Making of the Modern University*, Chicago: University of Chicago Press.

Ross, Dorothy (1991), *The Origins of American Social Science. Ideas in Context*, Cambridge: Cambridge University Press.

Smith, James Allen (1991), *The Idea Brokers. Think Tanks and the Rise of the New Policy Elite*, New York: The Free Press.

Stein, Herbert (1996), *The Fiscal Revolution in America: Policy in Pursuit of Reality*, 2nd edn, Washington, DC: American Enterprise Institute.

Stigler, George J. (1965), 'Statistical Studies in the History of Economic Thought', in *Essays in the History of Economics*, Chicago: University of Chicago Press, pp. 31–50.

Stryker, Robin (1989), 'Limits on Technocratization of the Law: The Elimination of the National Labor Relations Board's Division of Economic Research', *American Sociological Review*, **54** (3), 341–58.

Sunstein, Cass (2002), *The Cost–Benefit State. The Future of Regulatory Protection*, Chicago: American Bar Association.

The Economist (1989), 'President Arafat goes to Paris', November 25, p. 37.

Tobin, James and Murray Weidenbaum (eds) (1988), *Two Revolutions in Economic Policy: The First Economic Reports of Presidents Kennedy and Reagan*, Cambridge, MA: The MIT Press.

Tocqueville, Alexis De (2000 [1835/1840]), Democracy in America, Chicago, IL: University of Chicago Press.

US Office of Personnel Management (1967–1999), *Characteristics of Federal White-Collar Workers*.

Vogel, David (1978), 'Why American Businessmen Distrust Their State?', *British Journal of Political Science*, **8**, 45–78.

Vogel, David (1983), 'The Power of Business in America: A Re-Appraisal', *British Journal of Political Science*, **13** (1), 19–43.

Vogel, David (1989), *Fluctuating Fortunes. The Political Power of Business in America*, New York: Basic Books.

Weir, Margaret (1989), 'Ideas and Politics: The Acceptance of Keynesianism in Britain and the United States', in Peter A. Hall (ed.), *The Political Power of Economic Ideas: Keynesianism across Nations*, Cambridge: Harvard University Press, pp. 53–86.

Weir, Margaret, and Skocpol, Theda (1985), 'State Structures and the Possibilities for Keynesian Responses to the Great Depression in Sweden, Britain, and the United States', in Peter Evans, Dietrich Rueschemeyer and Theda Skocpol (eds), *Bringing the State Back in*, Cambridge: Cambridge University Press, pp. 107–63.

Whitley, Richard (1984), *The Intellectual and Social Organization of the Sciences*, Oxford: Clarendon Press, pp. 53–86.

Yonay, Yuval P. (1998), 'The Struggle over the Soul of Economics: Institutionalist and Neoclassical Economists', in *America Between the Wars*, Princeton, NJ: Princeton University Press.

8. Economics, economists and politics in Uruguay

Adolfo Garcé[1]

INTRODUCTION

In this chapter I will show that the 'ubiquitous rise of economists' to high posts in government noted by Markoff and Montecinos (1994) took place in Uruguay as well, but was comparatively limited and delayed.

During the second half of the twentieth century in Uruguay, economic growth slowed down, income distribution worsened and the political system went through very important changes. According to Sebastián Torres (2003), between 1946 and 1996 among Latin American countries 'Uruguay's 1.7 percent GDP growth rate was the lowest' (see Table 8.1). This slow growth has led to a relative impoverishment. According to Gabriel Oddone (2005) 'towards the middle of the 1950s Uruguay's gross national product per capita was similar to that of Belgium and Denmark; in 2001 it was only about one third as large'.

Two other features have characterized the economic evolution of Uruguay since the 1950s. First, Uruguay started to abandon the import-substitution industrialization (ISI) model, and opened and deregulated its economy. Second, from the beginning of the 1960s, its relation with international financial institutions like the IMF, the IDB and the World Bank became very important due to the size of the external debt. For example, following the severe financial crisis that took place during 2002, the country had an external debt equivalent to 90 percent of its GDP.

At the social level, inequalities grew during the same period. According to Luis Bértola (2005), a long period of improvement in income distribution in Uruguay (1910–60) was followed by increasing inequality. This tendency was especially marked during the authoritarian regime (1973–84). But Uruguay is still the most egalitarian country in Latin America as measured by the Gini coefficient. According to the criteria used in the United Nations Reports on Human Development Uruguay is among the countries with high human development.

At the political level, since the 1950s Uruguay has gone through

Table 8.1 GDP growth rates in Latin American countries, 1945–1996

Country	Rate (%)
Argentina	3.0
Bolivia	2.9
Brazil	6.1
Chile	3.6
Colombia	4.9
Costa Rica	5.4
Dominican Republic	5.2
Ecuador	5.1
El Salvador	3.6
Guatemala	4.3
Mexico	5.2
Nicaragua	3.0
Panama	3.0
Paraguay	4.7
Peru	3.7
Uruguay	1.7
Venezuela	4.2

Source: Torres (2003).

three main phases. From the mid-1950s until 1973, the political parties weakened – as did democracy. The political dynamic became highly polarized and an unexpectedly strong guerrilla movement (MLN-Tupamaros) was launched. This phase finished with the breakup of democracy in June 1973. From that point until the end of 1984 the country was governed by the military. During this second period leftist parties, labor unions and student organizations were strongly repressed. The third phase started in 1985 with the reestablishment of democracy. During the following 20 years, the Colorado Party and the National Party alternated in power. But in the national elections of October 2004, for the first time in Uruguay's history, the left achieved power.[2]

Historians such as Juan Pivel Devoto realized that a key nineteenth-century issue was the stormy relationship between 'caudillos', whose leadership dates to the struggle for national independence, and 'doctors', that is, the university-trained elite of lawyers reluctant to be subordinated to them. Other scholars (José Pedro Barrán, Benjamín Nahum, Ulises Graceras, and Alción Cheroni, among others), analyzing the years when the modern Uruguayan state was built, showed the central role of engineers during the first two decades of the twentieth century. Aldo Solari, Carlos Real de Azúa, Ángel Rama, and others studied the role of educated professionals in the following period. More recently, some researchers have studied the relationship between experts and politics in the reform of social policies during the authoritarian regime (Papadópulos 2001; Castiglioni 2005) or during the 1990s (De Armas 2002).

The major conclusion from this literature is that conflict between experts and politicians has been more common than cooperation in Uruguay. Conflicts were especially difficult during the nineteenth century. During that century's last three decades, many factors, among them the rise of positivism (in its Spencerian version), encouraged a degree of reconciliation between intellectuals and politicians. But the ending of the legal order by the coup of 1933 was the starting point of a new cycle of estrangement between intellectuals and politicians. Little by little, intellectuals abandoned their sympathy for the traditional parties, and tended to shelter in universities and to cultivate their vocation for public affairs in journals and essays. This tendency to estrangement became significantly worse during the 1960s when intellectuals, very influenced by the Cuban, decisively shifted to the left. Since the end of the authoritarian regime in 1984 intellectuals have tried to cooperate with the government. However, political and ideological differences and the deep wounds left by the 1960s and 1970s have been obstacles not easily removable (Garcé 2000).

A major work on the history of Uruguayan economics is Celia Barbato's (1986) pioneering treatment of the discipline until the mid-1980s. One of Barbato's most important conclusions is that the development of economics in Uruguay was comparatively late. Another valuable work is the volume put out at the 70th anniversary of the Faculty of Economics and Administration (FCEA) that contains new information on the discipline's evolution (FCEA 2002). Lara Robledo (2002) studies the dynamics of cooperation and conflict between economists and the military during the authoritarian period (1973–84) from a political scientist's standpoint. The most extensive contribution to these topics is Glen Biglaiser (2002a, 2002b). In an earlier publication (Garcé 2003) I presented a general view of the access of economists to the most important economic posts in government, and explained this process in terms of changes in the supply of and demand for economists within the political system.

In this study I draw on previous work and expand on how and why the supply of experts in economics grew and on the dynamics of demand for economists from the political system. I will show that the relatively modest character of the rise of economists in Uruguay has occurred because both supply and demand have been less strong than in other countries. But this analysis must be complemented by an understanding of the development of economics in Uruguay, taking into account the debates among different economic traditions and their impact on party doctrines.

I distinguish three phases. The first ran from 1932, when the Faculty of Economics and Administration (FCEA[3]) was created, up until 1954. During this period the institutional bases for an economics profession in Uruguay were established. At first there was simply a lack of economists. The FCEA was largely training accountants and not economists. But some state agencies and the Ministry of Economy needed economists.

The second stage began in 1954 and lasted until 1973. Against a background of stagnation and inflation Uruguayan economics was consolidated, both in research and teaching. Economists and accountants were clearly differentiated. Both the supply of and demand for economists grew, as well as the interactions between economists and politicians, under the prevalence of the CEPAL structuralist paradigm. The political parties were highly influenced by the growing profession.

During a third period beginning in the early 1970s economics experienced significant transformations. The quality of the education of economists improved (especially through postgraduate courses abroad), research centers multiplied, and so did theoretical pluralism. Many economists became involved in politics and gained access to high executive or legislative posts. Nonetheless, the process was less notable than in other countries.

THE FORGING OF ECONOMICS

The Creation of FCEA

Until the 1930s the teaching of economics had taken place in the Faculty of Law. Research was largely an individual matter without institutional support. The chair in Political Economy of the Faculty of Law was the main vehicle for the diffusion of economic ideas. Between its creation in 1861 until 1932, this chair was occupied by Carlos de Castro, Pedro Bustamante, Carlos Labandeira, Martín Aguirre, Carlos María de Pena and Eduardo Acevedo (FCEA 2002, p. 14). There was also a School of Commerce, founded in 1903, but it was oriented to training accountants. Meanwhile, research in economics was advanced by the valuable but isolated efforts of such intellectuals as José Pedro Varela, Angel Floro Costa, Adolfo Vaillant and Julio Martínez Lamas.

In the mid-1920s a public debate began in connection with the need to improve scientific understanding of national economic problems. The most important promoter of the creation of a Faculty of Economics was the accountant Mariano García Selgas, a congressional representative from the National Party. According to the bill (1924) that was to set up the FCEA: 'It is time for our country to have a teaching institution fully capable of training professionals, just like other countries in the forefront of civilization. There is an urgent need for the scientific study of economics and finance as well as administrative, commercial and industrial management'. This legislation was passed by the Chamber of Deputies in 1927, but it was not until July 13, 1932 that legislative enactment was complete.

It is remarkable that the plan to create the FCEA did not originate in a context of crisis. On the contrary, the 1920s was a time of good feeling, with a euphoric climate that reached its peak during the 1925 centenary of national independence. But the crisis of 1929 did play a role in the law's final approval. The violent fall in GDP caused by the weakening of external demand for Uruguayan exports and the abrupt rise of unemployment generated a strong demand for diagnoses and solutions grounded in technical knowledge.

Paradoxically, in its first decade, the FCEA did not train experts in economics, but accountants. To carry out institutional change within the context of the strong budgetary restrictions of the early 1930s, the old School of Commerce was reconstituted as a Faculty of Economics. What this meant in practice was that whoever wanted to study economics had to first obtain a degree in accounting and then go on to complete two one-year Research Seminars. As a capstone, it was necessary to present a 'thesis on a juridical, financial, economic or administrative' subject. Those graded 'very good' or better would be given the degree of 'Doctor in Economic Sciences and Administration'. The curricular reform in 1944 did not make deep changes to this scheme. In fact, almost all graduates of the FCEA during that first phase graduated as accountants (*contadores*). Only five students actually earned this Doctorate (Barbato 1986, p. 130).

Classes began in 1935 and the first graduates got their diplomas in the late 1930s. Among them were Juan Eduardo Azzini, Nilo Berchesi and Luis Faroppa. During the following two decades they played a decisive part in the institutionalization of the discipline, the introduction of new theoretical perspectives and the promotion of research. In 1944, at the request of Dean Luis Mattiauda, the curriculum was reformulated. One of the main reforms was the creation of institutes for economic research. Around 1950 the following institutes were functioning: the Institute of Finance, directed by Azzini; the Institute of Banking and Monetary Economics, directed by Faroppa; the National Income Institute, directed by Carlos Quijano, and the Statistics Institute directed by Alfredo Fernández (FCEA 2002, pp. 86–7). The most dynamic and influential of them all would be the Institute of Banking and Monetary Economics. Its name was changed in 1953 to the Institute of Economic Theory and Policy and in 1963 it fused with the

National Income Institute to become the Institute of Economics (FCEA 2002, p. 87).

Quijano's role was very influential in the consolidation of economics in Uruguay during this period. He had a calling for politics and worked as a lawyer and journalist. A strong admirer and heir of José Enrique Rodó (author of the influential Latinamericanist essay *Ariel*), leader of a small socialist and democratic faction of the National Party, Quijano contributed in many ways to the slow but persistent legitimation of economics in Uruguay. However, his training in economics was incomplete. After graduating as a lawyer in Montevideo, he studied economics at the Sorbonne (1924–26) but he did not finish his studies. He took the chair of Political Economy at the Faculty of Law in 1936 and directed the Research Seminar for doctoral candidates. He promoted the first systematic program of research on national income. He was important in diffusing economic ideas through two publications that he edited. In 1939 he created the journal *Marcha* (1939–74) that had a very deep influence among university students, intellectuals and politicians. From 1947 until 1958 he also edited the *Revista de Economía* (1947–58), with a more restricted circulation. This journal published texts from the theoretical debates of that era (Barbato 1986, pp. 128–9).

From 1947, when he assumed the second chair in Economics, until the government took control of the University, Faroppa was the key figure in the teaching of economics at FCEA as well as in promoting research. His influence was especially decisive during the 1950s because he was the central figure in spreading ideas associated with CEPAL in Uruguay. In addition, as the director of various institutes for research in economics, he created the first working teams and stimulated the first specialized publications on such issues as inflation, industrialization, exchange regimes and economic policy.[4]

One of the most outstanding characteristics of that epoch was that graduates from the FCEA did not attempt to take postgraduate courses abroad. Neither Azzini nor Faroppa (among the graduates from the first economics curriculum, known as Plan 32, after the year 1932) nor Enrique Iglesias (who studied after the curricular reform of 1944, or Plan 44) sought to continue their training despite having had brilliant grades in their university studies. An important exception was Israel Wonsewer (graduated from Plan 44) who took a postgraduate course at the London School of Economics in 1949 (FCEA 2002, p. 114). Even so, according to Azzini, the directors of the Faculty's various institutes tried to send graduates to work as assistants in research centers in Italy, Belgium, France and Germany (FCEA 2002 p. 143).

Two factors explain this low tendency to pursue postgraduate studies abroad. First, it is important to bear in mind that during the 1930s and 1940s, Europe continued to be the main reference point for Uruguayan culture. During this period, the USA and its university system were not very attractive to Uruguayan intellectuals. But Europe was going through a deep crisis (fascism, Nazism, Spanish Civil War, etc.). Second, the Faculty's expansion allowed the best students guaranteed access to research centers and professorships connected to the FCEA itself. They did not need to make the extra effort to be better trained. In addition, they were frequently recruited by their teachers to work at some of the technical agencies of the public sector.

Demand for Government Economists

The FCEA was not the only possible source of jobs for the graduates. Beginning in the 1930s, the state increased its regulation of economic activity and its provision of social services. State structures, therefore, needed people trained in management and economics. Successive presidents frequently appointed people to executive posts who were considered to be economic experts. Among these appointees were José Serrato,[5] Ricardo Cosio, César Charlone and Eduardo Acevedo Álvarez. Luis Mattiauda, founding Dean of the FCEA, held the post of Health Minister between 1943 and 1945, when President Amézaga was in office.

The Colorado governments of that era soon tried to get party sympathizers Faroppa and Berchesi into their administration. As soon as he had his accounting degree, Faroppa was appointed Adviser to the Finance Minister (1940–45). After that, he was the manager of the most important tax collection agency, the Office of High Profit Tax Collection (1945–50). In 1949 and 1950 he was Technical Consultant for the Comptroller of Imports and Exports. Something similar happened to Berchesi. He was appointed Finance Minister by president Luis Batlle Berres when he turned 30, the constitutionally required minimum age for holding the post. Berchesi was Minister for two years (1949–51), after which he refused any other government responsibility.

A preference for people with a technical profile was clearer in the Finance Ministry (see Table 8.2) than in the *Banco de la República* (BROU). BROU was the other institution with a fundamental role in economic management due to its importance in regulating money and credit. A review of the names of the successive presidents of the Bank shows that the appointment of highly talented professional politicians was the general rule during the whole period (see Table 8.3).

In addition, the Colorado elite began to be replaced in the 1940s. Engineers and experts in public finances had to make way for a new

Table 8.2 Ministers of Finance, 1943–1970, and Economy, 1970–2000

Minister	Profession	Period
Ricardo Cosio	Politician and lawyer	1943–45
Hector Alvarez Cina	Politician and lawyer	1945–46
Ledo Arroyo Torres	Politician and notary	1947–48
Nilo R. Berchesi	Economist	1949–50
Hector Álvarez Cina	Politician and lawyer	1951–52
Eduardo Acevedo Álvarez	Politician and lawyer	1952–54
Armando Malet	Politician and lawyer	1955–56
Amílcar Vasconcellos	Politician and lawyer	1957–58
Juan Eduardo Azzini	Accountant	1959–62
Salvador Ferrer Serra	Politician and lawyer	1963
Raul Ybarra San Martín	Accountant	1964
Daniel H. Martins	Politician and lawyer	1965
Dardo Ortiz	Politician and notary	1966
Carlos Végh Garzón	Engineer and entrepreneur	1967
César Charlone	Politician and lawyer	1968–69
Armando Malet	Politician and lawyer	1970
Carlos M. Fleitas	Politician	1971
Francisco Forteza	Politician	1972
Moisés Cohen Berro	Accountant	1972
Manuel Pazos	Accountant	1973
Carlos Bello	Politician	1973–74
Alejandro Végh Villegas	Engineer and economist	1974–76
Valentín Arismendi	Accountant	1976–82
Walter Lusiardo Aznárez	Accountant	1982–83
Alejandro Végh Villegas	Engineer and economist	1983–84
Ricardo Zerbino	Accountant-economist	1985–89
Enrique Braga	Accountant	1990–92
Ignacio de Posadas	Politician and lawyer	1992–94
Luis Mosca	Politician and economist	1995–99
Alberto Bensión	Accountant-economist	2000

Source: Database of the *Instituto de Ciencia Política*, FCE, UDELAR.

political elite who were focused on electoral competition and the distribution of goods to particular constituencies, rather than on managing state affairs from a technical perspective. Technical logic was ceding ground to political competition. By the end of this first phase, the advance of this particularistic policy-making style left little space for 'scientific' government (Filgueira et al. 2003, pp. 186–8). This style of policy-making continued to prevail into the 1960s, despite increasing claims to the contrary, as discussed in more detail below.

Table 8.3 Presidents of the Banco de la República Oriental del Uruguay, 1943–2000

Name	Profession	Period
Alfredo Baldomir	Military-architect-politician	1943–46
Andrés Martínez Trueba	Politician	1948–50
Alberto Zubiría	Politician and lawyer	1952–54
Francisco Forteza	Politician	1955–58
Solano Amilibia	Politician and notary	1959–63
Francisco Podestá Milans	Politician	1963–64
Julio Solsona Flores	Politician	1965–67
Santiago de Brum	Politician and lawyer	1967–68
Carlos Végh Garzón	Engineer and entrepreneur	1968–69
Armando Malet	Politician and lawyer	1969–70
José Pena	Politician and lawyer	1970–72
Jorge Seré del Campo	Agricultural engineer	1972–76
Abdón Raimúndez	Military	1976–78
Moisés Cohen Berro	Accountant	1978–80
José María Siqueira	Military	1980–82
José Cardozo	Military	1982–83
Emilio Berriel	Accountant	1983–84
Federico Slinger	Accountant	1985–89
Emilio Berriel	Accountant	1990–94
César Rodríguez Batlle	Accountant	1995–99
Juan Ignacio García Peluffo	Economist	2000

Source: BROU Library.

Change of Climate: From Liberalism to Keynesianism

From the point of view of prevailing doctrines, the phase we are analyzing coincides with a developing shift from the liberalism that prevailed up to the beginning of the 1930s to perspectives closer to Keynesianism. The questioning of liberal orthodoxy was imposed by circumstances, as elsewhere. Explaining the overturning of laissez-faire in Uruguay and the rise of interventionism, Faroppa said:

> At the outbreak of the [1929] crisis, liberal economic ideas prevailed among the main political leaders and national advisors. External circumstances progressively required interventionism. Leaders and advisors . . . responded to the circumstances and participated in the creation of institutions like the Import and Export Comptroller, the Autonomous Fund for Amortization, as well as assigning an interventionist role to the Banco de la República, which during

> that period functioned as a central bank and as a commercial bank. This . . . led to an increased demand for experts in management, economics and accounting. This demand was extended and deepened as the end of the decade approached and the Second World War began. (FCEA 2002, pp. 127–8)

The Colorado Party extended interventionism during its period in office while the National Party was still defending economic liberalism. Curiously, the preference of the colorados for state interventionism did not lead to the five-year plans that were very common at the time. In many western countries there had been a debate on planning during the 1930s and 1940s, but not in Uruguay. This is surprising because one of the characteristics of the Colorado Party since José Batlle y Ordóñez's presidencies (1903–06 and 1911–15) was a strong faith in experts, especially engineers.[6] At least in principle, the strong rationalism of the batllista tradition offered a good institutional home to the logic of planning that during the Marshall Plan era quickly spread in Europe and in numerous Latin American countries, from Chile and Colombia to Argentina and Brazil (Garcé 2002). To the colorados, 'planning' carried strong negative connotations, for they associated it with the authoritarian systems of the region (like peronism and varguism) and of the world (like fascism or communism).

The blancos, as supporters of the National Party are known, also rejected planning but for other reasons. In the view of the major faction inside the party (known as herrerismo), government should not be based on theories or doctrines but sensitivity and pragmatism. The blancos were in this the opposite of the colorados. They felt close to peronism but not to 'scientific government'. The following passage allows us to understand the extent to which Luis Alberto de Herrera – the most important party leader of this period – did not trust theories and specialists. In a memorable parliamentary debate, he said: 'Solving these matters through doctrine and with books – you can always find a book to prove that it's now night time – seems to me beside the point. I am a man who believes in facts. Each day I am, happily, less an academic and do not allow myself to be seduced by abstract observations or pure doctrine, however simple and dazzling, because they do not resolve concrete issues' (Garcé 2002, p. 33).

Of course, for both parties, accepting planning had a high political cost. Blancos as well as colorados built and reproduced their political loyalties fundamentally through particularistic mechanisms. The parties of that era dedicated most of their political energy to negotiating with the state in order to satisfy the demands of groups of voters. Planning was in opposition to this style of politics.

Summary

Despite the creation of the FCEA, the number of economists did not significantly increase in this first period. In fact, the new faculty graduated accountants almost exclusively. But the creation of the FCEA (1932) and the formation of the first research teams (between 1944 and 1950) established the institutional basis for the takeoff of economics in later years. The political system demanded experts in economics to manage some ministries and technical agencies. Nonetheless, a particularistic approach to distributing goods and benefits prevailed over technical criteria in public policies.

THE LEGITIMATION OF ECONOMICS, 1954–73

The second phase started in 1954 with the second reform in the economics curriculum. That was the point at which the development model that had been followed since the 1930s seemed exhausted. When presenting the new curriculum, Dean José Domínguez Noceto explained the need for change: ‘It has been rightly said that the institutional bases of all of social life are being shaken. Even though these issues cannot be dealt with exclusively from an economic perspective, economic theory and policy – the specific area of our research – are central to the posing of this problem’ (FCEA 2002, p. 56).

During the two decades that followed the 1954 reform, economics was consolidated as an autonomous discipline. Economic research carried out in that period had a strong impact on the political debates of the 1960s. The sense of a country in crisis generated a rising demand for diagnoses and alternatives and economics had a central position in these discussions. This phase ended in 1973 with the breakdown of democracy.

The Differentiation of Economists and Accountants

The curricular reform of 1954, promoted by Dean José Domínguez Noceto, constituted a turning point in Uruguayan economics. This reform was a first step in separating the training of economists and accountants. According to the new curriculum, accountants and economists would take 26 courses in common. After that, those who chose to be economists were to take four additional courses. This would be followed by a monograph, the final step towards a degree as ‘Accountant-Economist’. Another option led to certification as ‘Accountant-Public Finance Specialist’ (FCEA 2002, p. 57).

Between 1959 and 1969 the FCEA had 285 graduates, 240 with degrees as 'Accountant-Public Finance Specialist' and 45 as 'Accountant-Economist' (Barbato 1986, p. 155). Both tracks involved training in economics, and the training was more advanced than it was for the cohorts that graduated under Plans 32 and 44. The level of training was raised in mathematics and statistics, and the teaching of sociology and the history of economic thought were introduced (Barbato 1986, p. 131).

The decisive moment in the separation of economists' and accountants' training was the reform of 1966, carried out at the request of Dean Wonsewer. The new curriculum established a shared basic program of only two years duration, after which differentiated courses would be introduced. The difference in training was also symbolically reflected in the degrees obtained: Public Accountant and Economist. Although there was an increase in the demand for economists, the curriculum established that economists could also graduate as Public Accountants if they passed four additional subjects (FCEA 2002, pp. 64–5).

Throughout this period more research was carried out. The Institute of Economic Policy and Theory played a central role in fostering research in the 1950s. Under the direction of Faroppa, the small research team composed of Iglesias, Wonsewer and Alberto Tisnés gained much prestige and became a reference point for politicians. For that reason, the relationship between economists and policy-makers was extremely close. For example, in 1956, the Institute of Economic Theory and Policy of FCEA actively participated in the preparation of the August 3 decree simplifying the exchange regime. In the same year, the government offered Faroppa the Finance Ministry. His response shows the deep mistrust toward government of the Uruguayan intellectuals of the day. Faroppa made his taking the position contingent on a long series of conditions. Two of them, highly contentious for the colorados, were never accepted: the creation of a central bank and the development of an income tax (Garcé 2002, p. 31). After negotiations with this economist failed, the government instead looked for a politician.

The Impact of the Alliance for Progress

During the first phase (1932–54) the progress of economics was not strongly affected by external developments. The clearest indicator of this is that in Uruguay foreign 'money doctors' played no significant role in the 1930s, unlike other countries. But at the beginning of the 1960s, economic research in Uruguay did experience strong foreign influence. In August 1961, the Carta de Punta del Este was signed and the Alliance for Progress was launched. To access US funds through this program, a Latin

American government had to present a 'comprehensive and well-conceived national program for the development of its own country' (Levinson and de Onís 1970, p. 351). The Uruguayan government took advantage of this extraordinary opportunity and supported the creation of the Commission of Investment and Economic Development (CIDE), a think tank that was to formulate the needed plans. Finance Minister Azzini appointed Enrique Iglesias as Technical Secretary of the Commission. CEPAL, OAS and IDB offered technical support. To formulate 'scientific' plans, it was essential to gather basic information. A census was carried out and for the first time national income and expenditure accounts were calculated. On the basis of these studies the first global diagnosis of the Uruguayan economy was written in 1963. In 1964 and 1965, sectoral plans were prepared.

The experience of planning stimulated a true leap forward in Uruguayan economics with regard to the availability of information and the required human resources. To prepare the plans, it was necessary to generate a great deal of information that had not previously existed. Between 1961 and 1963 a trustworthy historical series of GDP and national accounts were elaborated for the first time. Apart from collecting a great quantity of information, the experience of planning encouraged the training of many qualified people. This last point needs to be highlighted. Dozens of *técnicos* were trained, many of whom went on to have important responsibilities (Garcé 2002). Participants in this experience included Ricardo Zerbino, Alberto Bensión, José Gil Díaz, Alberto Couriel and Danilo Astori, who were to have a very significant role in political life and in government during the following decades.

The experience of the CIDE also facilitated the creation of stronger links among the growing community of Uruguayan economists and those from abroad. As in the previous period, graduates from the FCEA did not pursue doctorates. However, contacts with academic centers and planning agencies from other countries took place regularly. In July 1958, an official delegation from the FCEA took part in the Conference on Economic Development in Santiago de Chile. At the beginning of the 1960s, Iglesias and Bucheli, for instance, visited France for a closer perspective on the French planning system, contacting François Perroux.[7] Other economists, younger than Bucheli and Iglesias, like Couriel, Samuel Lichtensztejn, Zerbino and Astori, chose to improve their knowledge of planning techniques at CEPAL's ILPES in Chile. Around 1969, 16 out of the 34 who graduated from the plan 1954 had taken further courses abroad, mainly at ILPES in Chile and in France (Barbato 1986).

Unlike the cases of Chile or Argentina, there was no systematic plan to train neoliberal economists. In Uruguay, at least during those years, no initiative similar to 'Project Chile' was implemented (Biglaiser 2002a).

Project Chile was an agreement among the Catholic University, the US government and the University Chicago to train liberal economists in order to counter the strong development of the CEPAL school. An agreement with Chicago had been rejected by the University of Chile for ideological and political reasons before it was accepted by the Catholic University.[8] It is very likely that, a project of this type would have been firmly rejected at FCEA because faculty and students harbored deep anti-imperialist sentiments. Alejandro Végh Villegas, who earned a PhD in Political Economy at Harvard in 1958, was the only Uruguayan at the time who studied economics in the US.

Economists, Government and Institutional Reform

In this period there was a curious paradox. Economics was developing strongly as a field. Nevertheless, there was no increase in the participation of economists in the cabinets or even in the post of Finance Minister. Even so, institutional changes made in the context of the Constitutional Reform in 1966 generated a very important opportunity for economists to influence policy-making, especially in the economic area.

During these years, the prestige of economics grew considerably. Many people were eagerly following CIDE's progress in developing a plan, from the educated public to the more modern politicians, as well as the more far-sighted businessmen. This latter group was keen on leaving behind the particularistic and short term policymaking that had been characteristic of Uruguayan public policies from the mid-1940s onwards.

Despite growing social support for an increasing rationalization of policymaking, including support for a greater public role of economists, there was no actual increase in the number of economists in government posts. Consider the participation of economists in the ministries. Unlike the 1930s and 1940s, governments did not turn to economic experts. The only ministry in which expert economic advice was sought was Finance. In 1958, after 93 years, the National Party was able to regain control of government. Surprisingly, the new government appointed accountant Azzini as Finance Minister.[9] The most noteworthy thing about this episode is that Azzini's appointment occurred because he was an expert. Although Azzini was not active in the party, the National Party needed to entrust the Finance Ministry to somebody technically qualified to manage a complicated financial and economic situation. During 1957 and 1958, Azzini and his team of assistants in the Institute of Finance of the FCEA had prepared a document ('For the New Government') that contained a set of reasonable and technically-based recommendations (Azzini 1983, p. 95).

One of those recommendations was the liberalization of exchange policy. After his first year in government, Azzini got the Law of Monetary and Exchange Reform passed (December 1959), which began a long cycle of liberal reforms in Uruguay (Filgueira et al. 2003). As previously mentioned Azzini was one of the creators of the CIDE and galvanized Uruguay's experiment in economic planning. Though strongly challenged because he signed Uruguay's first Letter of Intent with the IMF, Azzini managed to stay in office during the government's four-year term.

After Azzini, appointing economists as Finance Ministers was less frequent and less contentious. The second presidency with a National Party majority (1963–66) sometimes sought politicians, other times entrepreneurs, and less often economists – and when they tried to appoint economists had little success. President Gestido (1967) also hoped to appoint Iglesias Minister of Finance, but when Iglesias refused, he appointed Carlos Végh Garzón, an engineer and business leader who supported limited economic planning. After Gestido died, President Jorge Pacheco (1968–71) sought politicians (like Armando Malet), entrepreneurs (like Végh Garzón) and experts in economic management (like César Charlone).

Throughout this second phase both blancos and colorados tried on many occasions to appoint economists as ministers but, except for Azzini, were not successful. Faroppa (in 1956) and Iglesias (in 1964 and 1967) refused such posts. To explain this it is necessary to recall again the tradition of mutual animosity between intellectuals and politicians. During the 1950s and 1960s, this opposition was especially difficult. Being part of government implied jeopardizing academic prestige in the eyes of colleagues. Party politics was seen as a basically corrupt activity, oriented to selfish interests. Azzini's example is revealing. After being minister and member of the board of directors of BROU, he was expelled from the FCEA and accused of corruption.

There was no increase of economists in already existing positions. The most important development was the creation of two new institutions that served as a platform for the advance of economists during the following period. On May 1, 1967 a new constitution came into force. This document brought about major institutional changes. It reinstated a single-person executive, replacing the nine-member body that had functioned from 1951 to 1966. It increased the number of ministries. And it established two key bodies of great importance for the relationship between economists and politics in Uruguay: the Budget and Planning Agency (OPP[10]) and the *Banco Central* (BCU).

The Budget and Planning Agency is one of the great institutional innovations of the constitutional reform. The first proposals for creating agencies for economic and budgetary planning were presented in the 1940s. Tomás Berreta had strongly argued for planning during the electoral campaign that brought him to the presidency in 1946. When he died after only five months in office, it was Berchesi in the Treasury Ministry (1949–51) who made planning a central issue on the political agenda. Berchesi's attempts failed because the Colorado Party associated planning with authoritarianism. But the question of planning was taken up again by Minister Azzini in the context of the Alliance for Progress.

One of the main legacies of the planning carried out by the CIDE between 1961 and 1965 was to have laid the groundwork for the future institutionalization of planning. The Budget and Planning Agency drew on the CIDE experience. In fact, after the preparation of the major development plans was completed by CIDE in October 1965, *técnicos* who continued to work on smaller projects made up its first staff in 1966. During its first years, OPP even had the same location as CIDE.

In March 1967 President Gestido appointed Faroppa to direct OPP. Here, too, we can recognize the deep conceptual continuity between CIDE and OPP. Although there were important ideological differences between Iglesias and Faroppa, both shared CEPAL's structuralism.[11] In a climate of increasing violence and authoritarianism, Faroppa soon resigned. But, with few exceptions, from that point on the general rule has been that OPP is headed by an economist. From its creation in 1967 until the present this agency has been expanding its role in economic management. It became the most important advisory office within the Presidency as well as a producer of specialized knowledge.[12]

The creation of the *Banco Central* also had many consequences for the careers of economists. Until 1967 the duties later carried out by the *Banco Central* were performed by the *Banco de la República Oriental del Uruguay* (BROU). In 1935, after a very important public debate about the value of creating a central bank, agreement was reached on creating an Emission Department within BROU with the specific task of guiding monetary policy.

The idea of creating a central bank was introduced again into public debate in the 1950s by Benito Nardone, the leader of the Rural Movement.[13] At the beginning of the 1960s, this proposal gained more support when it became part of the package of institutional reforms recommended by CIDE. The final impetus for the *Banco Central* came with the financial crisis of 1965. The Bank was created as part of the 1966 constitutional reform and formally established in early 1967. BROU continued to be a very important institution, particularly because of its considerable involvement in industrial, commercial and farming credit.

The first president of the *Banco Central* was Iglesias. Like Faroppa in the Budget and Planning Agency, and for the same reasons, Iglesias directed the Bank only briefly. He was appointed in May 1967 and resigned in July 1968. After this resignation, the Bank was directed by entrepreneurs or politicians, not by economists, at least during the period we are examining. As we will see later, the Bank was very important in the development of Uruguayan economics. First of all, it allowed monetary policy to be depoliticized and managed by technical criteria. Second, it became a center for specialized knowledge, like OPP. And finally, it had a strong influence in shaping a group of liberal economists who played a central role during the third phase.

The Cycle of Developmentalist Ideas

The 1954–73 period corresponds to the growth, apogee and crisis of developmentalist thought in Uruguay. Since its inception in 1948, CEPAL exerted a strong influence among Uruguayan economists. Its first meeting took place in Montevideo. CEPAL structuralism was the dominant paradigm in economics teaching and its texts were widely used in economics courses, particularly those taught by Faroppa.[14] Between 1960 and 1967, CEPAL and FCEA collaborated on a series of courses on economic development for civil servants and private sector personnel: *Cursos Intensivos de Capacitación en Problemas de Desarrollo Económico* (Barbato 1986).

CEPAL developmentalism remained unchallenged for about a decade. By the mid-1960s, however, many planning specialists believed that CIDE's experience had failed. Political parties were blamed for their unwillingness to support the implementation of development plans. Yet CIDE left an important legacy. It generated a large amount of information on the country's social and economic situation. It initiated an ambitious reform agenda. It facilitated important institutional changes, including the creation of the BCU and the OPP. And it introduced the ideas of CEPAL into the ideology and policy proposals of the most important political parties (Garcé 2002).

When economists became disillusioned with the developmentalist approach, some turned to the left, embracing Marxism and dependency theory, or to the right, toward economic liberalism (Garcé 2002). Some leftist economists distanced themselves from the government and moved to the Economics Institute at FCEA, ending Faroppa's long period of leadership. Figures like Raúl Vigorito, Raúl Trajtenberg, Alberto Couriel, Samuel Lichensztejn, Luis Macadar, Julio Millot, Juan J. Pereira, Nicolás Reig, Octavio Rodríguez and José Santías conducted important research projects, among them, *El proceso económico del Uruguay*, published in July 1969.[15] The studies carried out at the Institute were influential, especially in the formulation of the first program of the Frente Amplio, the left-wing coalition formed in 1971.

Simultaneously, another group of economists trained at CIDE followed the opposite ideological trajectory and espoused free market doctrines. They decided to stay at the Budget and Planning Agency and did not join the University. The most important were Bensión, Zerbino, Juan José Anichini, José Puppo and Gil Díaz. Some of the domestic factors accounting for this group's shift in allegiance were CIDE's unsatisfactory planning experience, the success of the price stabilization program of 1968, the contacts with Alejandro Végh Villegas and Ramón Díaz in the Budget and Planning Agency,[16] and the outstanding political and ideological leadership of Jorge Batlle. Batlle was a key figure when economic liberalism had few partisans in Uruguay's intellectual circles. Those who publicly defended liberalism, such as Azzini, Berchesi or Daniel Rodríguez Larreta, were marginalized in academia. Not even entrepreneurs had a coherent free market discourse, as they were also attracted to the idea of indicative planning (Rivarola 2003).

Those shifting toward economic liberalism were disappointed by the Cuban revolution but impressed by neighboring Brazil's economic stabilization and growth following the military coup of 1964 (Garcé 2002, pp. 132–7). Roberto Campos, President Castelo Branco's Minister of Planning, considered the intellectual father of the 'Brazilian miracle', offered a curious mix of developmentalism and economic orthodoxy. He claimed that the state had a crucial role in development and in promoting national industry but he also argued that inflation should be controlled through strong monetary discipline and insisted on the need to facilitate foreign investment (Bielschowsky 1988; Sola 1998).[17]

In 1972, under the direction of Bensión and Zerbino, the Budget and Planning Agency team elaborated the *National Development Plan 1973–1977*, influential during the authoritarian government. At the time, there was considerable cross fertilization between politicians and economists. Developmentalism had penetrated all political parties and was adapted to the ideological traditions of each. In the Colorado Party 'industrialist developmentalism' had emerged around the leadership of Zelmar Michelini, who received technical and political support from Faroppa. In the National Party, under Wilson Ferreira's leadership, developmentalism emphasized agricultural production and the need for relevant reforms. Developmentalism also can be traced in the 'Programmatic Bases' of the Frente Amplio (1971), a combination of developmentalism, dependencia and Marxist ideas (Garcé and Yaffé 2004a).

Summary

Between the economic crisis of 1954 and the interruption of democracy in 1973, economics expanded and gained legitimacy. The FCEA modified its curriculum in 1954 and 1966, drawing a clearer distinction between economists and accountants. Economic research advanced as planning was backed by the Alliance for Progress (1961–65) and the Institute of Economics at FCEA. These changes stimulated new programs and political agendas in the parties. Uruguayan economics and economists gained prestige. In 1972, for the first time, the accountant-economist Samuel Lichensztejn was appointed Vice-Chancellor of the University. Nevertheless, few economists occupied top government posts.

ECONOMICS' MOST RECENT STAGE (1973–2004)

The third phase began under the authoritarian regime (1973–84) and continues to the time of writing. The number of graduates increased, in absolute and relative terms. Postgraduate studies abroad became more common. The quality of economic research improved.[18] From an institutional perspective, the FCEA is still the leading economics center in Uruguay, but no longer the only one. Developmentalism persists, but alongside a much strengthened economic orthodoxy. The interface between economics and the political system has also changed. During this last period, key posts in public agencies concerned with economic affairs have been occupied by economists. As a rule, however, economists have not created their own bases of political support. Zerbino, Bensión, Ariel Davrieux and Luis Mosca did not follow political careers, although all of them were important figures in economic policymaking. Others, however, became active in party politics. Astori and Couriel, for example, directed the Program Committee of the Frente Amplio, and were later elected to the Senate. Over the past decade, they have been important voices speaking for the Uruguayan left.

Economics Takes Off

Between 1973 and 1984, economics, at least within the FCEA, seems to have moved backward, instead of forward. The curriculum adopted in 1977, as well as the one introduced in 1980, tended to make the training of economists and accountants less distinctive. On the other hand, research activities moved out of the FCEA to private centers. These centers played a central role during the dictatorship, allowing social scientists to continue their work (mainly CINVE, CIEDUR and CLAEH).[19] Economics as practiced before the coup was noted for ideological polarization. The military regime considered the discipline 'subversive to the social order'. When professors were identified as close to the Colorado or National Party they

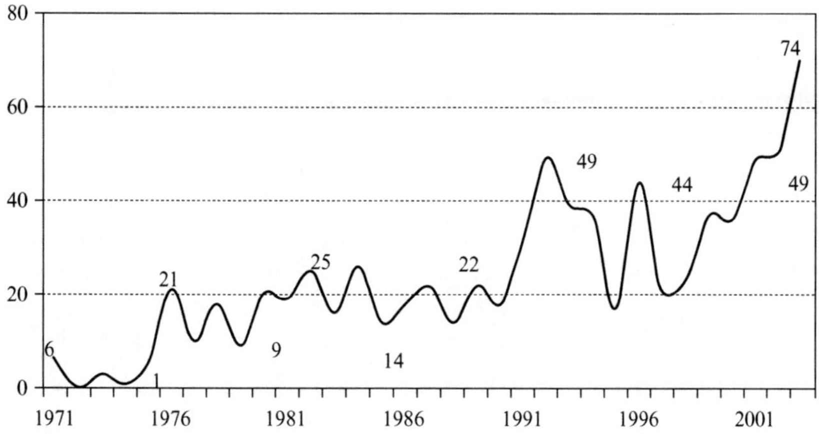

Figure 8.1 Economics graduates from FCEA (annual series), 1971–2003

were expelled. Academics with funding from American foundations such as Ford or Rockefeller were also suspect.

When democracy was reestablished, FCEA Dean Astori initiated yet another curricular reform with three main objectives: first, the restoration of academic pluralism; second, promoting research on Uruguay; and, third, supporting interdisciplinary studies of social problems (FCEA 2002, pp. 76–7).

After two decades of institutional development and greater public legitimacy, economics took off energetically. The number of FCEA graduates grew (Figure 8.1), doubling every ten years (Figure 8.2). These numbers, however, are still relatively low, and the rate of graduation has slowed down since the implementation of Plan 90. It is believed that the requirement of a final monograph (over 200 pages) may explain the limited number of graduates, a topic of debate at FCEA.[20] At the time of writing a new reform of the curriculum is being considered to give the program a more flexible structure. The idea is to introduce a credit system with fewer required courses and more electives to give students greater autonomy.

The 2000 student census shows that the proportion of FCEA students at UDELAR rose to 14 percent (Table 8.4). One of the most revealing indicators of the development of economics is that the proportion of economics graduates doubled between 1971 and 2001.

Since the 1990s newly created private universities have been offering economics degrees, but there have been fewer graduates from these institutions than from the public *Universidad de la República* (Table 8.5). In 2001, 49 economics students graduated from UDELAR (Table 8.6) and

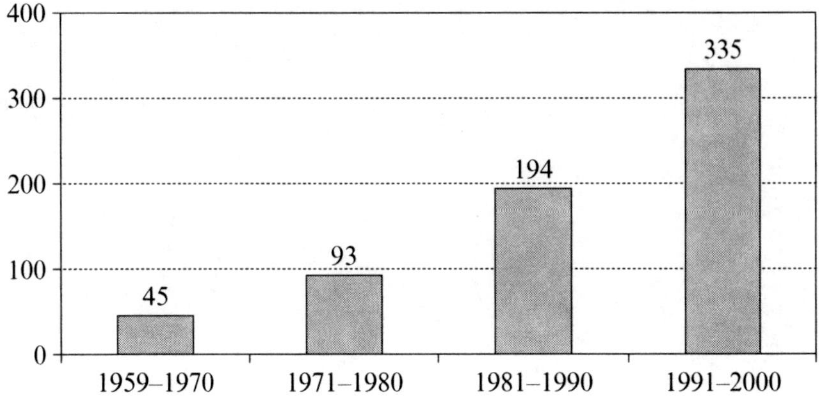

Source: Barbato (1986) and FCEA (2002).

Figure 8.2 Economics graduates from FCEA, 1959–2000 (selected periods)

Table 8.4 Enrollment at FCEA and Universidad de la República (UDELAR)

Year	UDELAR	FCEA	FCEA/UDELAR (%)
1960	15320	1929	13
1968	18610	2161	12
1974	26220	3157	12
1988	61428	7225	12
1999	70156	9997	14

Source: Student Census 2000, UDELAR.

18 from private universities, including 14 from *Universidad de Montevideo*, one from *Universidad Católica* and three from ORT, the country's largest private university (MEC 2003).

From the point of view of the academic curriculum, there are no significant differences between economics graduates from private universities and from FCEA. Both emphasize mathematics, statistics and economic theory. FCEA has nearly 600 professors, but only three of them are full time; 27 percent of FCEA professors have done postgraduate studies and 13 percent hold doctoral degrees.[21] Economics at private universities are more connected to the traditional political parties, the business

Table 8.5 First year students at FCEA and Universidad de la República (UDELAR), 1990–2003

Year	UDELAR	FCEA(*)	FCEA/UDELAR (%)
1990	13975	1340	10
1991	12669	1100	9
1992	12356	1140	9
1993	12145	1195	10
1994	11778	1376	12
1995	13232	1253	9
1996	12617	1224	10
1997	14613	1472	10
1998	14664	1413	10
1999	14257	1430	10
2000	14895	1489	10
2001	15648	1438	9
2002	16400	1468	9
2003	17353	1508	9

Note: (*) FCEA enrollment in economics, accounting and business administration.

Source: Institute of Statistics FCEA (2004).

Table 8.6 Economics graduates compared with UDELAR graduates (selected years)

Selected years	Total graduates (UDELAR)	Economics graduates	Economists/total (%)
1971	1148	6	0.5
1981	2531	19	0.8
1991	4178	32	0.8
2001	4249	49	1.1

Source: Author's computations on the basis of data from FCEA and UDELAR Student Census 2000.

world and US universities than FCEA. Private universities have fewer faculty members but a larger percentage of them have studied abroad. For example, 21 of the 47 instructors in economics and finance at ORT have graduate degrees from foreign universities (five of them have economics PhDs from American universities) (data from web pages and interview material).

Studies at FCEA last five years and at the private schools, four. Private universities are especially concerned about their graduates finding employment because in the last 20 years the demand for economists has not kept up with supply. By contrast, in the pre-authoritarian period the few economics graduates easily obtained good government or university positions. The difficult employment situation has generated strong incentives for junior economists to improve their prospects by obtaining additional professional qualifications. Recently, UDELAR as well as some of the private universities have created Diploma and Master's programs in economics.

Institutional Diversification

The development of economics shows another noticeable feature during this third phase. As already mentioned, professors dismissed by the authoritarian regime who did not leave the country, created several private research centers like CINVE and CIEDUR. These centers have gone through difficult times but are still working.

After the transition to democracy, new public and private institutions emerged devoted to teaching and research in economics. Among them was a new type of private research center exemplified by CERES (Center for the Study of Social and Economic Reality), created in 1995 by Talvi, who that year had obtained a PhD in economics and finance from the University of Chicago.[22] Talvi's idea was to found a think tank able to influence the political agenda and promote free market policies. CERES has achieved a significant public presence, although its permanent research team is small.[23]

At UDELAR, two research poles emerged with different emphases. One of these poles is the old FCEA Institute of Economics, where the heirs of CEPAL structuralism are still dominant. The research topics like economic development, agrarian and labor economics, and economic history. New activities, particularly the influential program on 'Monitoring and Economic Forecasting', headed by Fernando Antía, have helped the Institute regain its dynamism.[24]

The second pole at UDELAR is the Economics Department at the Faculty of Social Sciences (FCS). In 1988, at the request of Vice-Chancellor Lichtensztejn, UDELAR created the Research and Post-graduate Social Science Center (CEIPOS) to promote interaction among social scientists and to support the development of post-graduate programs. In 1991, when the Social Sciences Faculty was created, CEIPOS joined it as its Department of Economics. It aims for high academic standards; nearly 20 of its researchers have obtained doctorates in Europe and the US. This department has always promoted the publication of research in refereed journals, participation in international academic networks, and the pursuit of postgraduate studies abroad through external grants and agreements with foreign universities. Areas of research include international trade, econometrics, labor economics, macroeconomics and finance, industrial organization and topics in microeconomics.

Thus, there is little thematic overlapping between these two units, and until the credit system is introduced, students do not overlap either. Why two entities specialized in economics in the same university? It was a solution to an organizational dilemma. UDELAR created FCS, in August of 1989, to promote research and teaching in the social sciences, including economics. FCEA, however, was experiencing a revival after five decades. The compromise was that FCEA continue with the economics degree and the Economics Institute; FCS, in turn, received CEIPOS, now the Economics Department, and began research in areas that FCEA had no tradition covering.

The Central Bank of Uruguay (BCU) has been important for the development of economics during this third phase. Gil Díaz, the Bank's president between 1974 and 1982, sought to increase contacts between Uruguayan economists and American universities. Between 1976 and 1982, BCU organized postgraduate studies in Montevideo as part of an agreement with Columbia University. The Master's program was directed by Professor Robert Mundell. Professors from Columbia came to Uruguay to teach two or three times a year. Each visit lasted about three weeks (Biglaiser 2002a). In addition, since 1974 the Bank has given financial support to nearly 30 economists to study in foreign universities. BCU's high salaries have been a major help in encouraging their return. Many returnees participate in public policy debates and contribute to the improvement of Uruguayan economics, both in theory and research methods. Thanks to this policy, BCU now has three dozen graduates with advanced academic training. Since 1985, the Bank also has been organizing the Annual Economics Conference, the most important academic event in Uruguayan economics.[25]

As mentioned earlier, in the past 20 years private institutions have begun to offer economics education, after rules regulating private universities were introduced in 1984. The Catholic University was established in 1985. Its Business School offers a degree in economics. The educational supply was expanded further in 1995, when the Universidad de Montevideo and the Universidad de la Empresa were created. ORT-Uruguay is another institution offering economics.

At the time of writing one could say that for the first time Uruguay had numerous institutions offering economics degrees and a variety of public and private research centers. Quasi-monopolistic control by FCEA has been replaced by institutional diversification, but state institutions remain more important than private ones. Despite the efforts of private universities, FCEA is still dominant. In spite of the development of centers like CINVE and CERES, most research is carried out at UDELAR, BCU or the Budget and Planning Agency.

Although private research centers are independent from parties, there is a clear trend toward the emergence of a stronger pro-market group among Uruguay's economists. This is likely to have repercussions in the policy arena, as well as in the linkages between Uruguayan economists and their colleagues in other countries, in and out of Latin America.

Economists in High Political Positions

In Uruguay, the ascent of economists is noticeable but limited. During the third phase, governments have delegated to economists the responsibility for directing key institutions in the economic area, but it has been unusual to appoint economists to non-economic posts, as has happened in some of the cases treated in other chapters. It was only in the two presidencies of Julio M. Sanguinetti that economists got such positions. During his first presidency (1985–89), Sanguinetti appointed Iglesias[26] Minister of Foreign Affairs and Zerbino[27] Economy Minister. During his second presidency (1995–99), Sanguinetti entrusted the Ministry of Economy to economist Luis Mosca and the Ministry of Culture to Lichtensztejn.[28]

By contrast, the military regime (1973–84) and President Jorge Batlle (2000–2004) only named economists as Economy Ministers. Alejandro Végh Villegas was a key figure at both the beginning and the end of the authoritarian regime. When he took office in 1974, Végh began promoting important economic reforms, such as financial liberalization, although he did not introduce major privatizations or deep commercial liberalization (Robledo 2002).[29] Under President Luis A. Lacalle (1990–94) cabinet posts went almost exclusively to politicians. As Economy Ministers he preferred an accountant he trusted, Enrique Braga, and an ideologue of economic liberalism, Ignacio de Posadas. President Jorge Batlle had three Economy ministers: accountant-economist Bensión, economist Isaac Alfie, and during the financial crisis of 2002–03, Alejandro Atchugarray, a prestigious Colorado politician. President Tabaré Vázquez named Danilo Astori as Economy Minister.

During the third phase the Ministry of Economy has always been in the hands of economic experts, except under Lacalle. The *Banco Central* and the Budget and Planning Agency have also been headed by economists (Tables 8.7 and 8.8). Gil Díaz, Juan Carlos Protasi, Ricardo Pascale and

Table 8.7 Presidents of the Uruguayan Central Bank, 1967–2000

Name	Profession	Period
Enrique Iglesias	Accountant	07/1968
Carlos Sanguinetti	Entrepreneur	1969–70
Armando Malet	Politician and lawyer	1970
Nilo Márquez	Accountant	1970–71
Jorge Echevarría	Lawyer	1971–72
Juan Pedro Amestoy	Accountant	1972–73
Carlos Ricci	Accountant	1973–74
José Gil Díaz	Accountant-economist	1974–82
José María Puppo	Accountant-economist	1982–84
Juan Carlos Protasi	Economist	1984–85
Ricardo Pascale	Economist	1985–89
Ramón Díaz	Lawyer	1990–93
Enrique Braga	Accountant	1993–94
Ricardo Pascale	Economist	1995
Humberto Capote	Economist	1996–99
César Rodríguez Batlle	Accountant	2000

Source: Dataset of the *Instituto de Ciencia Política*, FCE, UDELAR.

Humberto Capote played important roles at BCU. Ariel Davrieux was an outstanding figure at the Budget and Planning Agency, where he served under three Colorado presidents – Bordaberry, Sanguinetti and Jorge Batlle.

The presence of economists in posts in charge of economic management is seen by the public as a guarantee of seriousness in the conduct of public finances. A clear demonstration of this is seen in the election campaign in 2004 of the left-wing candidate, Tabaré Vázquez. He announced that his Minister of Economy would be Astori, the former dean of FCEA. Political analysts agreed that this ensured the victory of the Uruguayan left in the first round (Yaffé 2005, pp. 180–81).

In the eyes of politicians and the public, however, economists are not wizards with magic wands. A recent episode illustrates the extent to which the Uruguayan political system can side-step the economists. In the first semester of 2002, a severe financial crisis forced President Batlle to replace economist Bensión as Minister of Economy. Batlle offered the post to Talvi, a Chicago PhD and CERES director, who declined. During the next 24 hours, the media reported that politicians, journalists, political analysts and citizens concerned about the gravity of the crisis preferred a skillful politician over a competent economist. President Batlle finally appointed his main ally in the Senate, Alejandro Atchugarry, a progressive politician

Table 8.8 Budget and Planning Agency Directors, 1967–2000

President of Uruguay	Party in power or regime	Director	Profession	Period
Gestido	Colorado	Faroppa	Accountant	01/03/67–10/10/67
Gestido	Colorado	Luisi (int)	Lawyer	10/10/67–30/10/67
Gestido	Colorado	Manini Ríos	Lawyer	30/10/67–15/02/68
Pacheco	Colorado	Acuña (int)	Accountant	15/02/68–19/03/68
Pacheco	Colorado	Lanza	Lawyer	19/03/68–27/06/68
Pacheco	Colorado	Végh Villegas	Engineer-economist	27/06/68–28/08/68
Pacheco	Colorado	Rodríguez L.	Economist	02/09/68–02/04/70
Pacheco	Colorado	Díaz	Lawyer-economist	02/04/70–26/10/70
Pacheco	Colorado	Lanza	Doctor	09/04/70–26/10/70
Pacheco	Colorado	Servetti	Military	26/10/71–28/02/72
Bordaberry	Colorado	Zerbino	Accountant	01/03/72–13/07/73
Bordaberry	Authoritarian	Cohen Berro	Accountant	13/07/73–12/07/74
Bordaberry	Authoritarian	Anichini	Engineer	12/07/74–21/08/76
Méndez	Authoritarian	Cardozo	Military	01/09/76–04/05/81
Álvarez	Authoritarian	Aranco	Military	14/05/81–02/02/85
Álvarez	Authoritarian	Silveira	–	12/02/85–28/02/85
Sanguinetti	Colorado	Davrieux	Accountant-economist	01/03/85–28/02/90
Lacalle	National	Hughes	Accountant	01/03/90–26/08/91
Lacalle	National	Cat	Engineer	27/08/91–18/10/93
Lacalle	National	De Haedo	Economist	18/10/93–28/02/95
Sanguinetti	Colorado	Davrieux	Accountant-economist	01/03/95–28/02/00
Batlle	Colorado	Davrieux	Accountant-economist	01/03/00–28/02/05

Source: Database of the *Instituto de Ciencia Política*, FCE, UDELAR.

widely respected for his negotiating abilities. When Atchugarry's successful tenure ended, he was frequently mentioned as a probable presidential candidate for the Colorado Party in 2004. (Due to health reasons, he did not accept the nomination.)

Not only has the ascent of Uruguayan economists in government been limited, but relatively few economists have engaged in electoral politics. Apart from Astori and Couriel, who built their political campaigns on prestigious professional and academic careers before joining the Senate in 1989, the other economist in the Senate, elected for the Colorado Party in 2004, is Isaac Alfie, a former Economy minister during Batlle's last two years in office (2003–04.)

Economic Doctrines: Developmentalists and Neoliberals

Economic liberalism is stronger in the third phase, but it is not new. Its revival started at the end of 1960s and by the 1970s had become more widely supported. In the early 1970s, Ramón Díaz and other partisans of economic liberalism reached the conclusion that Uruguay would not adopt market-friendly policies until the citizens demanded them. Their goal was to build that demand by combating interventionism in the realm of public opinion. The journal *Búsqueda*, now the most influential weekly in Uruguay, was a major tool in spreading neoliberal ideas. Its first editorial stated: 'A new socioeconomic doctrine is necessary, with a new idea of the state, and a system of freedom, prosperity and justice; we must start by rejecting the current paternalistic system. This challenge is the reason for our new publication'.[30]

BCU was also a chief contributor to the development of liberal economic thought. As Glen Biglaiser (2002a) has argued, US financial support and graduate academic training were not determinant factors in Uruguay. Domestic actors and processes, rather than US influence or foreign policy, were crucial. The strength of economic liberalism in Uruguay's restored democracy is not explained by the influence of economists, but by that of politicians like Jorge Batlle in the Colorado Party and Lacalle among the blancos.

Although neoliberals have gained influence, developmentalists have continued to be active into the 1990s and beyond. Uruguayan left-wing economists resemble some of their Chilean colleagues, in growing closer to neoliberalism than to developmentalism. Many work as civil servants at the *Banco Central* after studying in graduate programs abroad. But partisans of liberalism have been incorporating perspectives from other traditions, including institutionalism. In sum, there is a process of convergence among groups that had been far apart in the 1960s. Developmentalists take note of monetarist concerns and liberals pay attention to the role of institutions in the operation of markets.

The ideological evolution of the main political parties reveals complex and unstable allegiances to economic doctrines. The Colorado Party has had deep changes since the 1960s, when interventionist ideas prevailed. In the past twenty years, neoliberalism has dominated, and Jorge Batlle is the key figure in this shift. Batlle's radical liberalism must be distinguished from the more moderate and pragmatic ideas of Julio M. Sanguinetti, differences that were reflected in their respective governments (Garcé and Yaffé 2004b, pp. 108–16).

Between 1971 and 1989, the National Party abandoned the economic orthodoxy that had characterized it for decades. This showed the influence of Wilson Ferreira Aldunate, who promoted a developmentalist program. After his death, the liberals, led by Luis Alberto Lacalle (grandson of Luis Alberto de Herrera, the party's principal leader in the twentieth century) recovered control over the party. But again in 2004, the *wilsonistas*, or developmentalists, prevailed over the free-market *herreristas* moving the party toward the center-left.

Economic liberalism has also left its mark on the political left, which in the past 30 years has gone from full acceptance of dependency theory and Marxism to a social-democratic stance. This change, especially evident since 1989, is the result of two factors. First, the collapse of 'real socialism' led to a crisis within the Communist party and to recasting Frente Amplio as a catch-all left party oriented toward winning elections instead of bringing about a socialist and anti-imperialist revolution. Second, the experience of governing Montevideo led the left to abandon ideological rigidity and move towards economic realism. At the end of a long ideological journey, the left developed a program in which elements of the old developmentalism coexist with a commitment to fiscal balance and open trade (http://www.presidencia.gub.uy/; Garcé and Yaffé 2004a).

Summary

During this third phase, more than 800 economists graduated from FCEA (Table 8.9). But the change in Uruguayan economics has been more than quantitative. Post-graduate programs were created and economics education became more diversified as FCEA lost its previous monopoly. Various economic doctrines coexist, although neoliberal ideas gained influence. Economists were given responsibility over key economic agencies, but they have been rarely appointed to head institutions in other policy areas.

CONCLUSIONS

What can the Uruguayan case add to the analysis of the rise of economists in government and politics? It reinforces a simple idea: a large supply of experts and strong demand from the political system are necessary. The supply depends fundamentally on the level of development of economics as a discipline. In Uruguay the number of available economists was very low until the mid-1980s. At that point about 150 economics students had graduated in the country's only economics program.

Institutions and leaders played central roles in making economics

Table 8.9 Economics graduates, FCEA by year and plan, 1971–2003

Year	Plan				Total
	1954	1966	1980	1990	
1971	–	6	–	–	6
1972	–	0	–	–	0
1973	–	3	–	–	3
1974	–	1	–	–	1
1975		5			5
1976	4	17	–	–	21
1977	2	8	–	–	10
1978	3	15	–	–	18
1979	–	9	–	–	9
1980	3	17	–	–	20
1981	1	14	4	–	19
1982	1	11	13	–	25
1983	4	3	9	–	16
1984	3	7	16	–	26
1985	–	5	9	–	14
1986	–	1	17	–	18
1987	–	6	16	–	22
1988	–	3	11	–	14
1989	–	3	19	–	22
1990	–	0	18	–	18
1991	–	3	20	9	32
1992	–	0	31	18	49
1993	–	0	32	7	39
1994	–	1	19	17	37
1995	–	2	12	3	17
1996	–	12	14	18	44
1997	–	–	10	11	21
1998	–	–	2	21	23
1999	–	–	1	36	37
2000	–	–	2	34	36
2001	–	–	1	48	49
2002	–	–	1	50	51
2003	–	–	2	72	74
Total	21	152	279	372	824

Source: *Decanato* (Dean's Office), FCEA (2004).

stronger. It is not possible to understand the Uruguayan case without referring to FCEA, the Institute of Economics, CIDE, the Budget and Planning Agency and BCU, or the impact of journals like *Marcha* and *Búsqueda*. International organizations also played a part, especially

CEPAL in the 1960s. Individuals like García Selgas, Quijano, Wonsewer, Faroppa, Iglesias, Astori, Trajtenberg and Ramón Díaz, among others, were also crucial in raising the stature of economics in Uruguay.

But without significant demand from society and the political system, the public profile of the discipline is unlikely to thrive. The level of demand is affected by three factors. First, in times of economic crisis, the demand for economists tends to rise, although the relationship between severe crises and economists' power is not straightforwardly predictable. The crisis of 1929 prompted the creation of FCEA, whose existence had been proposed at the beginning of the 1920s. Thirty years later, another crisis heightened the visibility of economics, as the authoritarian regime tried to cope with severe trade, financial and fiscal problems in the early 1970s. In the 2002 crisis, however, politicians were named at the top of the economic policy apparatus. Both public opinion and political parties claimed that under the circumstances, political skills were more necessary than economic expertise.

Second, the demand for economists also seems to depend on public attitudes and cultural variables. For decades, Uruguayans held optimistic views of the country's situation, potential and destiny. During the first decades of the twentieth century democratic institutions were consolidated and social development was high. Significant investment in the social sciences did not seem essential (De Sierra 2005). By the mid-1950s, a sense of crisis generated alarm, stimulating the search for new information, diagnoses and specialized knowledge.

Third, the demand for economists in government depends on the ideologies of political parties and presidents. Some are more attentive to the advice of experts. Throughout the twentieth century, the Colorado Party valued rationalism and universalistic theories. At the National Party an attitude of suspicion toward academicism prevailed, a reluctance to accept 'foreign recipes' and a preference for pragmatism and nationalism (De Armas et al. 2003, pp. 88–93). In the early twenty-first century, the left seems closer to the rationalist traditions of the Colorado Party.

The presence of economists in Uruguayan politics and government appeared later, in a more modest measure than in Chile or Argentina. In the Uruguayan political system the interaction between specialized knowledge and public policies is comparatively narrow and unstable (De Armas and Garcé 2000). In the executive branch political considerations tend to prevail over technical criteria. The legislature and the political parties lack technical advisory services. In addition, Uruguay does not have well-established think tanks or schools of government (Bergara et al. 2004).

To sum up, the bridge between knowledge and politics depends on the country's institutional structure, the trajectory of academic disciplines and professions and shifting patterns of prosperity and crisis.[31]

NOTES

1. I would like to thank my colleagues from the Political Science Institute of the Social Sciences Faculty of the *Universidad de la República* (UDELAR) for encouraging me to go deeply into the relationship between experts and politics and for their valuable suggestions. Special thanks for Mariella Torello of the Dean's office in the Faculty of Economics and Administration, who helped me with the data. I thank Jorge Papadópulos for advice about the latest debates on economists and politics. I would also like to thank Verónica Montecinos and John Markoff for their thorough comments on this chapter.
2. In October 2004, Tabaré Vázquez won the Presidential election with 50.4 percent of the votes. Vázquez's political party (*Encuentro Progresista-Frente Amplio*) gained control of the Congress, electing 52 of the 99 deputies and 17 of the 31 senators.
3. *Facultad de Ciencias Económicas y de Administración* (Faculty of Economic and Administrative Sciences).
4. The first publication of the Institute of Banking and Monetary Economics in 1953 was 'Evaluation of prices and inflation growth in Uruguay'. Its authors were Faroppa, Wonsewer and Iglesias.
5. Engineer José Serrato (1868–1960) was a key figure in the first decades of the twentieth century. He was a member of the cabinet during José Batlle y Ordóñez's presidencies, was president of the *Banco de la República* between 1923 and 1927, and a cabinet member during the following two decades.
6. Batlle y Ordóñez was not a positivist, but he did support 'scientific government'. He said at one point: 'if in 1904 I resorted to the army to defend peace, in 1905 I had to resort to the engineers to ensure the progress of the country'. The role of engineers (José Serrato, Víctor Soudriers, Santiago Rivas and Juan Alberto Capurro, among others) in government and in building up the Uruguayan state during the first two decades of the last century has been frequently highlighted by scholars like Barrán, Nahum, Williman, Solari and Rama (Garcé 2002, pp. 27–8).
7. At the request of Iglesias and Wonsewer, the FCEA encouraged the Universidad de la República to give Perroux an honorary doctorate in 1963. Perroux (1903–87) was Professor of Economic Theory in Lyon and Paris and held a professorship at Collège de France between 1955 and 1974. He specialized in the problems of general equilibrium and formulated the theory of 'development poles'. His only Uruguayan connection was through several researchers from the Institute of Economy such as Faroppa and Iglesias.
8. For more, see the chapter on Chile in this volume.
9. The *blancos* had earlier offered that post to Iglesias, but he was barred because he was younger than the constitutionally prescribed minimum of thirty years of age.
10. *Oficina de Planeamiento y Presupuesto* (Office of Planning and Budget).
11. Even at that point, Iglesias was more of an economic orthodox than Faroppa.
12. In fact, OPP and the Presidency share the same building.
13. The Rural Movement dates from the late 1940s. It opposed the ISI model that benefited the urban sector. *Ruralismo* questioned state economic interventionism and called for economic liberalization. In alliance with the *herrerista* faction of the National Party, ruralism was able to win the election of 1958.
14. The powerful influence of CEPAL can be found in CIDE documents and in the works of Faroppa, especially his 1965 book, *El desarrollo económico en el Uruguay*.
15. This work was coordinated by Couriel, Lichtensztejn, Trajtenberg and Raúl Vigorito.
16. Ramón Díaz, a prominent lawyer, was one of the authors of the price stabilization plan implemented under president Pacheco in 1968. In 1970, he served for a short while at BPO. In 1972, Díaz founded *Búsqueda*, currently the most prestigious weekly periodical in the country, which has played a central role in the spread of neoliberal ideas.
17. For more on Campos see the chapter on Brazil in this volume.
18. The FCEA publishes an annual report on the economic situation whose impact is

significant among entrepreneurs and politicians as well as on public opinion more generally.

19. CINVE (Center for Economic Research) began its work in 1974. CIEDUR (Interdisciplinary Center for Development Studies) was created in 1977 by four sociologists. The main difference between them was the degree of specialization in economics. The Latin American Center of Human Economics (CLAEH) dates back to 1957, but during the dictatorship it became more active than earlier.
20. At FCEA there is no entrance exam or tuition. It is financed in part by funds allocated by Congress.
21. The data refers to all FCEA careers, not just economics. I thank FCEA Dean's Office for this information.
22. Talvi has served on the Executive Committee of LACEA, he worked at the Research Division of the Inter-American Development Bank (IDB) in Washington, DC between 1995 and 1997, and was chief economist and Director of the Economic Policy Division of the Uruguayan Central Bank between 1990 and 1995.
23. Of the seven researchers, only one has finished a Master's degree in economics (at the London School of Economics and Political Science).
24. Since 1985, the Institute of Economics has been publishing the *Informe de Coyuntura*, an important reference for entrepreneurs and politicians.
25. For the program of the twentieth Conference, held in 2005, see: http://www.bcu.gub.uy/autoriza/peiees/jor/2005/iees03j30805.htm.
26. Enrique Iglesias was a former Technical Secretary of the CIDE, BCU president in 1967–68, and Secretary General of CEPAL between 1972 and 1984.
27. Zerbino was an accountant-economist with an economic planning diploma from CEPAL-ILPES and Director of the Budget and Planning Agency in 1972.
28. Lichtensztejn was an accountant-economist and former FCEA Dean.
29. At the end of the authoritarian regime, Uruguay was the Latin American country with the second most radical neoliberal reforms (after Chile) according to the IDB's Index of Structural Policies (BID 1997, pp. 103–4).
30. *Búsqueda*, no. 1, April 1972, p. 7 (quoted in Garcé 1997, p. 38).
31. The bibliography on the connections between specialized knowledge and public policies is growing rapidly. A good perspective can be seen in the documents of the 'Bridging Research and Policy' project of the Global Development Network (GDN 2002).

REFERENCES

Azzini, Juan E. (1983), *La historia chica de un ministerio*, Montevideo: Published by the author.

Banco Inter-Americano de Desarrollo (1997), *América Latina tras una década de reformas*, Washington, DC: BID.

Barbato, Celia (1986), 'Economía', in *Ciencia y Tecnología en Uruguay*, Montevideo: Ministerio de Educación y Cultura. Centro de Investigaciones Económicas, pp. 125–61.

Bergara, Mario et al. (2004), 'Political Institutions, Policymaking Processes and Policy Outcomes: The Case of Uruguay', Washington, DC: Red de Centros-BID.

Bértola, Luis (2005), 'A 50 años de la curva de Kuznets: Crecimiento económico y distribución del ingreso en Uruguay y otras economías de nuevo asentamiento desde 1870', Madrid: Universidad Complutense, *Investigaciones de Historia Económica*, **3**, pp. 135–76.

Bielschowsky, Ricardo (1988), *Pensamento econômico brasileiro (1930–1964)*, Río de Janeiro: Contraponto.

Biglaiser, Glen (2002a), 'The Internationalization of Chicago's Economics in Latin America', *Economic Development and Cultural Change*, **50** (2), 269–86.

Biglaiser, Glen (2002b), *Guardians of the Nation? Economists, Generals, and Economic Reform in Latin America*, South Bend, IN: University of Notre Dame Press.

Castiglioni, Rossana (2005), *The Politics of Social Policy Change in Chile and Uruguay. Retrenchment Versus Maintenance (1973–1998)*, New York and London: Routledge.

De Armas, Gustavo (2002), 'Expertos y política en la reforma educativa de Uruguay (1995–1999)', Montevideo, MA Thesis, Instituto de Ciencia Política, Universidad de la República.

De Armas, Gustavo and Adolfo Garcé (eds) (2000), *Técnicos y política*, Montevideo: Trilce.

De Armas, Gustavo, Adolfo Garcé and Jaime Yaffé (2003), 'Introducción al estudio de las tradiciones ideológicas de los partidos uruguayos en el siglo XX', Buenos Aires: *Política y Gestión*, **5**, pp. 77–105.

De Sierra, Gerónimo (2005), 'Social Sciences in Uruguay', *Social Science Information*, London: SAGE Publications, **44** (2 and 3), June/Sept. 2005, pp. 473–520.

Faroppa, Luis A. (1965), *El desarrollo económico del Uruguay. Tentativa de explicación*, Montevideo: CECEA.

FCEA (2002), *La Facultad de Ciencias Económicas y de Administración en los setenta años de su creación legal (1932–2002)*, Montevideo: Banda Oriental.

Filgueira, Fernando, Adolfo Garcé, Conrado Ramos y Jaime Yaffé (2003), 'Los dos ciclos del Estado uruguayo en el siglo XX', in *La política*, Montevideo: Banda Oriental – Instituto de Ciencia Política.

Garcé, Adolfo (1997), 'La conciencia crítica desde Marcha a Búsqueda', in Gustavo De Armas and Adolfo Garcé, *Uruguay y su conciencia crítica*, Montevideo: Trilce.

Garcé, Adolfo (2000), 'Tres fases en la relación entre intelectuales y poder en Uruguay (1930–1989)', in Gustavo De Armas and Adolfo Garcé (eds), *Técnicos y política*, Montevideo: Trilce.

Garcé, Adolfo (2002), *Ideas y competencia política en Uruguay (1960–1973). Revisando el 'fracaso' de la CIDE*, Montevideo: Trilce.

Garcé, Adolfo (2003), 'Economistas y política en Uruguay (1943–2000)', Montevideo: Documento de Trabajo No. 38, ICP-FCS.

Garcé, Adolfo and Jaime Yaffé (2004a), *La era progresista*, Montevideo: Fin de Siglo.

Garcé, Adolfo and Jaime Yaffé (2004b), 'De las ideas a las políticas: programas partidarios, agendas de gobierno y políticas públicas en el Uruguay contemporáneo', *Iberoamericana. Nordic Journal of Latin American and Caribbean Studies*, **34** (1–2), Stockholm: Institute of Latin American Studies, pp. 91–122.

Global Development Network (2002), 'Bridging Research and Policy: Final Project Proposal', GDN, (http://www.gdnet.org/rapnet/).

Instituto de Estadística (2004), 'Análisis de las generaciones Plan 90', Montevideo: FCEA-UDELAR, (http://www.ccee.edu.uy).

Levinson, Jerome and Juan de Onís (1970), *The Alliance that Lost its Way: A Critical Report on the Alliance for Progress*, Chicago: Quadrangle Books.

Markoff, John and Verónica Montecinos (1994), 'El irresistible ascenso de los economistas', *Desarrollo Económico*, **34** (133), 3–29.

MEC (2003), *Anuario Estadístico 2001–2002*, Montevideo: Ministerio de Educación y Cultura.

Oddone, Gabriel (2005), 'El largo declive de Uruguay durante el siglo XX', Doctorate Dissertation, Departamento de Historia e Instituciones Económicas, Universidad de Barcelona.

Papadópulos, Jorge (2001), 'Politics and Ideas in Policymaking: Reforming Pension Systems in Comparative Perspective. The Cases of Uruguay and Chile', Montevideo: paper presented at Jornadas de Economía, Banco Central del Uruguay.

Rivarola, Andrés (2003), *Mirrors of Change: A Study of Industry Associations in Chile and Uruguay*, Stockholm: Stockholm University, Institute of Latin American Studies.

Robledo, Lara (2002), 'Técnicos y militares en Uruguay. Política económica: saber y deber en conflicto', BA Thesis in Political Science, ICP-UDELAR.

Sola, Lourdes (1998), *Idéias econômicas, decisões políticas*, Sao Paulo: Editora Universidade de Sao Paulo.

Torres, Sebastián (2003), 'An Empirical Analysis of Economic Growth for Uruguay and the Latin American Region: 1950–2000', The Hague: Institute of Social Studies, Working Paper Series No. 373.

Yaffé, Jaime (2005), *Al centro y adentro: la renovación de la izquierda y el triunfo del Frente Amplio en el Uruguay*, Montevideo: Linardi y Risso.

9. Epilogue: a glance beyond the neoliberal moment

Verónica Montecinos and John Markoff[1]

FROM ONE MODEL TO ANOTHER

A remarkable thing had happened to Latin American economic ideas and economic policy between the 1970s and the 1990s: the abandonment of what many observers held to be its own distinctive voice. After World War Two, the global climate favored national economic planning by a benign, intelligent and capable state that would correct failures of the market. The visible hands of planners working for national government agencies and international organizations could not only speed the rebuilding of war-ruined Europe but could also build up the economies of countries that had never previously attained Europe's pre-war levels of industrial development, a process in which richer countries would assist those less advanced with a combination of ideas, loans and infrastructural investment. At Bretton Woods in 1944, Keynes himself orchestrated the codification of new global rules in trade and finance and also promoted a system of international cooperation within a fiscally conservative if interventionist framework to be managed by an International Monetary Fund and an International Bank for Reconstruction and Development, soon to be more commonly known as the World Bank. Subsequently, a great deal of faith in planned progress was encapsulated in the design of a series of regional economic commissions connected to the United Nations system.

Among other Latin American economic thinkers, the work of the Economic Commission for Latin America became known far and wide, departing from what A.O. Hirschman called 'monoeconomics' (1981, p. 3) to argue that the economic issues confronting 'peripheral' countries were fundamentally different from those confronting 'core' countries – the major beneficiaries of centuries of global capitalism – at the centers of global wealth and power no matter how much some of those countries may recently have been laid waste by war. Although the World Bank's full name suggested that 'reconstruction' and 'development' could be considered under a common framework, Latin American economists would soon be contending that development needed to be rethought in some very fundamental ways. These economists developed a body of theory tailored to fit their countries' circumstances that supported interventionist development policies. The critique that emerged within CEPAL exerted significant influence, not only beyond Latin America but beyond departments of economics. In the more radical version that came to be associated with the term 'dependency', the creative role of the state in poorer parts of the world was to counter the destructive national consequences of a transnational economic order whose main beneficiaries were in the already wealthy parts of the world. The policy prescriptions emerging from dependency lacked detailed guidance and specificity, although many saw the transition to socialism as the only path to national self-reliance in the capitalist periphery.

Up to the 1970s, thinking about state-guided development seemed to policymakers in many places just common sense. A conservative US president famously announced that all were now Keynesians; in Latin America all seemed developmentalists. If one were to think about what 'Latin American economics' was or ought to be, one would be apt to think about CEPAL and debates within that general framework, despite an increasingly forceful articulation of free-market challenges to that generally accepted wisdom. There had emerged something that seemed a distinctively Latin American perspective on economic issues.

The introduction of Chicago-style economics in the 1950s affected debates over the teaching and practice of economics in several Latin American countries. While mounting resistance to Keynesianism in the US included larger factions within the economics profession, Chicago-style economics was simultaneously affecting debates over the teaching and practice of economics in several Latin American countries. During the 1960s and 1970s, coups in Argentina, Brazil, Chile and Uruguay were widely interpreted as rooted in the incapacity of existing political arrangements to manage the economic challenges posed by what was widely called the 'exhaustion' of prevailing models of development. State-guided development, with its planned projects, industrialization sheltered by tariffs and trade barriers, a growing working class supported by subsidies and price controls, and an awful lot of jobs in government agencies was said to have reached its limits. The democratic politics that permitted, so it was said, vote-hungry political parties to promise so much to so many was redefined as a mix of economically irrational, short-sightedly pandering and dangerously leftist practices, a state of affairs terminated by US-backed militaries.

When the debt crisis shocked Latin American economies in the 1980s, what was left of the doctrinal consensus that sustained pro-industrialization coalitions from Mexico to Argentina was finally blown away. By the 1990s such ideas were no longer dominant, the policies they supported widely abandoned, and the distinctiveness of Latin American economic thought a great deal less obvious – if it could be said to exist at all. Even CEPAL struggled to adapt its thinking to the new circumstances (Rosenthal 2004). Pressed to cut expenditures, attract foreign loans and investments, and find new ways to generate resources to service enormous foreign debts, Latin Americans joined a new consensus that the state was less benign, intelligent and capable of bringing about economic development than recently prevalent views had had it. The advance of the political right to global supremacy seemed unavoidable as did the demobilization of labor and civil society in general. The Hayekian assault on Keynesianism was being presented to the world as the unstoppable cure to the excesses of planning technocracies and collectivist ideologies. 'Less state, more market' could serve as a summary slogan for this change; a slogan that could equally well summarize policy change in the established capitalism of the US, the post-communism of Eastern Europe, the new-style communism of China, and the post-developmentalism of the Third World. The term 'neoliberal' was a catchall expression commonly evoked by critics in talking about such widely dispersed places (Harvey 2005). In all of them, the last quarter of the past century saw well-financed conservative foundations and think tanks advocating libertarian principles and entrepreneurial ideals, pressing for a minimalist state in the media, in the academy and in policy circles, few if any of which embraced the neoliberal label, an identification equally unrecognized among orthodox economists.

One big explanation for these momentous changes could be summed up as 'US hegemony in the post Cold War era'. As Drake (2006) has shown, at the beginning and at the end of the twentieth century, US economic doctrines became more dominant as US dominance rose. The unprecedented and utterly unrivaled military power of the US, its considerable if not quite so overwhelming economic clout, and its continuing image of cultural and sociopolitical success helped spread market economics along with other homogenizing trends. In this thesis a combination of genuine conviction and strong pressures on policymakers in Latin America from Washington, from US-based investors and lenders, and from powerful international institutions themselves to a significant degree agents of US interests has deeply shaped policies. Some followed suit because the ideas seemed to work in the US or elsewhere, some followed suit because there were rewards for doing so, and some followed suit because they were afraid to defy. Some sociologists saw a globalized market-driven standardization reshaping everyday life as the rules of business and work began to regiment entertainment, food, religion, emotions and other realms of everyday life. In this view, common global standards of rationality and for-profit exchanges reached, perhaps irreversibly, a new scale even in areas where tribal rules or family allegiance used to prevail. Calculability, efficiency and predictability became the core principles of human existence. One much-used text spoke of the 'McDonaldization of Society' (Ritzer 2003). Others were less sure this was so new, noting that Marx discerned something of the sort a century and a half earlier. And still others wondered if the claim of global standardization was not much exaggerated, taking note of important local differences in many things, including in the nature of McDonald's itself (Watson 1998).

A second way of describing the whole cluster of changes taking place since the 1970s stresses not US domination over institutions, but the growing role of professional economists in tandem with the domination within the profession of an economics made in the USA. This has been designated 'the Americanization of economics' – indicating that the thinking and methods taught in US courses, the canons enforced in US-based professional journals, the emulation of professional associations and the movement of economists to and from the US have greatly reshaped economics worldwide. And all this has been closely connected to important and congruent policy shifts. As market reforms overshadowed considerations going against individual choice, growth and accumulation, policymaking was depoliticized and references to particular geographies and national traditions vanished. The arenas of competing professions shrank in the face of the economists' imperialistic knowledge claims and their successful conquest of larger intellectual and policy territories. This profoundly shaped the contours of globalization as the current wisdom of the economics profession, elevated as universal truth, is drawn on to explain why things must be the way they are, as in the famous formula 'there is no alternative', commonly attributed to Margaret Thatcher.

Yet another perspective is summarized by labeling the changes as the 'internationalization of economics', recognizing the complex and dynamic relationship between the Americanization of economics and its internationalization (Coats 1997). In some cases the latter amounts to a rejection of Americanization, in others to a partial acceptance of it and yet in others to the adoption of the American model with the addition of distinctive intellectual traditions or a focus on problems that are of particular interest to regions of the world other than the US.

From another angle, the opening of a post-Keynesian era could be interpreted by stressing not so much transformations elsewhere into something like a version of US models but rather a widespread transnational convergence on a common model. Elements of this model include the claim that there is a single economic science valid round the world; that an abstractly conceived *homo economicus* can be understood through that most abstract of theoretical tools, mathematics; that the activities of this universal being leave measurable traces amenable to scrutiny through ever-more refined statistical procedures; and the sorts of academic and professional standards appropriate for training, nurturing and promoting competent economists can follow a transnationally standard pattern. Rather than emphasizing the clout of the US in remaking the discipline beyond its borders, the claim of internationalization suggests a universal science marching forward into truth. If post-World War Two US hegemony was the vehicle propelling economics' Americanization, a major vehicle for internationalization was the tremendous growth in public and private international institutions that brought economists together from many places and focused their attention on many places, helping to diffuse ideas and encouraging policy consensus on transnational issues.

A second mechanism was the relocation of non-US economists to the US, bringing ideas nurtured elsewhere into US discussions. The early stages of the field of development economics, for example, were profoundly shaped by central and east European economists catapulted to the US by Europe's dismal twentieth century. The result of these mid-century migratory trends might be called the Europeanization of US economists in the development and other disciplinary fields. Our chapters have pointed out the very large flows of Latin American graduate students into US economics departments in recent decades. Do we see these students as only taking things back home to the global south or do they also bring something with them northwards?

But transformation of Latin American economics was not just a consequence of the dominant role of the US or of the US economics profession or of an increasingly internationalized economics. The supersession of the ideas and policies of the postwar generation in Latin America was not only made in the USA and in the transnational arena. There were more local roots as well. One must note the powerful significance of evident failure. Despite efforts made to restructure the world economic order, most of the poorer countries found that order hard to change, even at the peak of the bargaining power of some of them during the oil-shock years. Of course, those without oil had limited bargaining power unless they held some commodity equally precious to the rich countries and some collective political capacity to engage in common action. Rather than a period of increased strength, the period that followed the oil price shocks of the 1970s were essentially disastrous for Latin America. There was no transfer of control from rich to poor countries, no increased economic sovereignty for commodity exporting areas.

The policies and practices associated with the theories and

recommendations of CEPAL were supposed to deliver economic growth and greater equality but often delivered neither and nowhere in Latin America actually delivered both. There had been high hopes in many quarters for developmentalist policies, but Latin America was still subject to the enduring problems of underdevelopment, unemployment, inflation, poverty and inequality and the consequent intermittent political turmoil.

As we pointed out at the end of the chapter with which we introduced this volume, Latin America is not the poorest geocultural region on our planet, but it is the one with the greatest inequality. What this means is that a given increment in national income has less payoff in improving citizens' lives than is typical globally, because so much of the benefit goes to so few. (See Hoffman and Centeno 2003 for the data.) No wonder Latin America's intellectuals are often obsessed with a sense of failure, the *fracasomanía* A.O. Hirschman (1975) found so dismaying. Prevalent developmentalist policies largely failed, famously triggering military interventions in Brazil, Argentina, Uruguay and Chile to suppress social unrest, and setting the stage for trying something different. In other countries, horrendous civil wars took their toll, but failed to bring to power revolutionary regimes with their own hopes for development, contributing to the desire to try new directions.

Pulling together the strands of this story: when the debt crisis of the 1980s radically increased the policy leverage of the always very weighty institutions of global finance, those institutions were not only permeated by a very specific set of policy nostrums and were not only endowed with significant enforcement capacities, but Latin American economists and policy-makers, in the rush to follow market signals, all but forgot whatever achievements the import-substitution model of industrialization had brought to the region (Ramos and Sunkel 1993, p. 18). Despite its many flaws, that model had indeed led to a relatively high rate of economic growth, with a regional average above 4.5 percent between 1940 and 1968 (Cardoso and Helwege 1992, p. 98). In the post-war period, larger countries fared better, but by and large, the region's productive capacity improved with agricultural and industrial modernization, and the expansion of social services resulted in higher literacy rates, lower mortality and better access to electricity, housing and water. Yet, as the crisis lingered, policy elites intent on attracting foreign investors and conquering foreign markets came to repudiate earlier rejection of US economics' universalism and helped forge the transnational convergence.

In this book, together with a group of country specialists we carried out a collective study of the economics professions of seven western hemispheric countries: Argentina, Brazil, Chile, Colombia, Mexico, Uruguay and the United States. This has been a comparative enterprise in which we were interested in points of commonality and points of difference in recent trends in professional organization and in the interconnections among professional organization, ideas, and policies. We believe our country chapters have identified many commonalities and many differences. But we have also been engaged in an *anti*-comparative enterprise because we saw these countries not only as seven separate cases but as interconnected. Comparative approaches have typically wondered about social processes robust enough to yield similar effects in disparate settings or about the ways variations in settings lead to varying outcomes. In either version distinct places are taken as separate worlds in which social processes unfold independently of what is happening elsewhere. We might ask, for example, why countries that differed as strikingly in their political histories as Mexico and Argentina or that are as different in the histories of their economics professions as Chile and Columbia all moved, albeit at different times and with varying pace, toward roughly similar changes in professional standards. Or we might ask how the very different employment opportunities for economists in Argentina and Chile lent distinct inflections to those common trends. These are classical sorts of comparative investigation.

But in conceiving this collective work, we also made the bet that in many ways these were not separate cases, that a significant part of what was happening involved social processes that crossed frontiers as professional horizons extended beyond national boundaries. So we looked for ways in which economists and their ideas moved back and forth between the US and various places in Latin America and we also thought about the classroom, the academic journal, the think tank, the scholarly conference, and the international agency as places where economists of different origins encountered each other.

We were therefore interested in many sorts of connections across national frontiers, among them:

- Career paths that include education, academic positions, and posts in international agencies outside one's country of origin.
- The interactions within US institutions of professors and students, both categories that include foreigners in significant numbers.
- The global contexts within which inter-American relations unfold, including economic, ideological, and political situations.
- The growth of international organizations as sites of professional training, economic research and policy-making.
- The growth of transnational think tank networks in which policy-oriented economists connect across national borders.
- US-based efforts by government, foundations, and university departments to reshape Latin American theory and practice.

- Latin American efforts to upgrade their economics professions, partly by conforming to US standards.

But why did we focus on the Americas as opposed to any half dozen individually interesting cases? Because of the distinction of Latin America's economists and their history of innovation in the decades after World War Two; because of the long period in which Latin America has been the recipient (at times the main recipient) of US advice, wanted and otherwise, and even a site of experimentation; because it pioneered the neoliberal turn, which was Chilean before it was Reaganomics. And because early in the twenty-first century the region is pioneering in a rejection of the neoliberal democracy it so recently embraced – in various ways – with as yet unknown consequences. Indeed, some have argued that the apparent revival of social democracy was started by Chile's Concertación coalition (Sandbrook et al. 2007, p. 27).

Our country chapters have examined the neoliberal moment in a half-dozen countries. Our own long introduction has suggested the hemispheric dimensions. We want now and finally to peek ahead, looking beyond the neoliberal moment. Our introduction was lengthy because we had a lot of data, and we presented some of it, on hemispheric connections. This final chapter will be brief because we have no data on the future and because social science speculation on the future is notoriously inaccurate. We are not the first to contend that the early twenty-first century was already the beginning of a post-neoliberal phase, but this contention is itself still a matter of dispute. At least it is obvious that the unanimity with which economists once spoke about market reforms is a lot less conspicuous (Rodrik 2006). While Latin American electorates have with some frequency been voting for parties in opposition to free-market fundamentalism, the new governments are assuming nationally distinct guises. No one, for example, would confuse the policies of Chile's Bachelet with those of Venezuela's Chávez. As of this writing, therefore, it would be foolhardy to speak of post-neoliberal Latin America as headed in a single direction. Nor is it terribly obvious what sorts of policies are ahead as the US attempts to fix its own economy, whose profound troubles came to overtake even the Iraq disaster as the top issue in its 2008 presidential campaign, and even less obvious what sorts of policies it would be promoting on the global stage as it reflects on its recent self-destructive course. And within the economics profession, ongoing debates on how to change graduate education, in Latin America and in the US, also make it foolhardy to predict that future thinking will simply continue past patterns. But once one is convinced that the neoliberal moment is but a moment, it is impossible not to speculate, at least briefly, about what's next.

The trends our chapters documented for one country after another will not simply continue. The conventional wisdom of the neoliberal era looks quite unhinged as more voices are added to the contestations and debates, once the preserve of street activism. The demand for social justice, participation and accountability is no longer regarded as exogenous to the process of economic reforms. In several countries, the public backlash against neoliberalism has brought to power in recent years those who campaigned for a different set of policies. The anti-neoliberal backlash has also penetrated the institutions that converted it into orthodoxy. The unraveling of the Washington Consensus came into public view with the much commented 1999 resignation (some say firing, Benería 2003, p. 8) of Joseph Stiglitz, the World Bank's chief economist. A strong critic of the direction taken by globalization, the 'rebel within', as Stiglitz was known, has scolded the Bank and the IMF for their undemocratic methods and the counterproductive therapies imposed on troubled economies (Chang 2001). The neoliberal recipe was further challenged in 2004, when World Bank president James Wolfensohn (2004) opened a Shanghai conference on 'Scaling Up Poverty Reduction' by stating: 'The Washington Consensus has been dead for years'.

Following economic crises in Asia and Argentina, among other places, the exalted market fundamentalists are reprimanded now as purveyors of bogus science. In Stiglitz's words, 'we should have less confidence in the supposed professional skills of technocrats – or at least less confidence than they have in themselves' (Stiglitz 2003). The discussion has begun to move from a focus on technical solutions of broad applicability and the elimination of distortions in the operation of markets to the understanding of political processes and institutional contexts (Inter-American Development Bank 2006; Bielschowsky 2009). In the present context of 'market reform fatigue', policy activism seems much revived, and even the banned legacies of import-substitution industrialization are being reconsidered (albeit not in its early 'inward-looking' formulation) along with a less ideological and less indiscriminate market liberalization (Ffrench-Davies and Machinea 2007; Rodrik 2007b; Silva 2007).

Although this book has been focused on the recent past we therefore want to conclude by trying to look at the near future, and speculate about the possible emergence of a lot of new thinking in a very short space of time. We stress here three main points: First, there are already in place important critiques of current models of development coming from different quarters. Second, current economic and political trends are likely to strengthen these and other critiques, rather than mitigate them. Third, current trends point to development of the sorts of institutions and networks that might sustain an intellectual shift. We believe there is good reason, in fact, to think that we will see again a 'Latinamericanization' of economics, albeit different from the one that flowered half a century earlier.

CRITIQUE

The critiques are hardly in short supply. There is an environmental critique about the sustainability of current models of development. There is a political-economy critique that argues that current models may produce more wealth, but they also surely produce more poverty on a global scale. There is a social sustainability critique that points to the erosion of social cohesion, including intra- and inter-generational solidarity. There is a democratic critique that argues that the withdrawal of states from economic management shrinks the capacity of citizens to collectively affect the conditions of their lives. There is an efficiency critique to the effect that in certain important arenas, the untrammeled competitive marketplace produces inferior results, as in health care provision. There is a historical critique that reminds us that previous efforts at freeing the market from all restraint in short order generated new market-limiting mechanisms.[2] There is a long-standing sociologists' critique of the unreality of the operations of the abstract Market and State as opposed to the messy interplay of actual markets and actual states. And there is even a growth-oriented critique that argues that inequality itself is an obstacle to economic growth.

Some of these critiques may be on their way to becoming the common sense of the early twenty-first century, others are controversial, and still others fairly esoteric. Some are taken seriously by voters, some by challenging social movements, some by policy wonks, some by governments, and at least one has found a niche in one of the key institutions of neoliberal globalization as World Bank economists fret about whether they had better take inequality seriously if their prescriptions are actually to advance development (World Bank 2005). Consensus on these critiques, and even interest in them, varies. Few could doubt, for example, the environmental critique: current patterns of economic development are clearly unsustainable. But serious scholars divide on whether on a global scale income inequalities have been expanding or contracting since the 1980s as they do on whether the economic inequalities of today came about because some places in getting rich simply left others behind or because what made some rich caused others to become poor. While such critiques engage important issues of policy and tend to be things that political parties and citizens have opinions about, the sociologists' critique of the abstract conceptualization of State and Market is something that few but professors care much about (although some of us are odd enough to care a great deal).

But let us by way of example spend a little time with the feminist critique: Social movements have joined disenchanted scholars in characterizing the current tragedies of environmental depletion, famines, human trafficking, declining life expectancy, and growing gaps in income levels, technological capabilities and quality of life as a pervasive pattern of 'maldevelopment'. Feminist critiques of economics argue that the discipline's narrow focus on competitive markets, its universalistic, individualistic and gender-blind approaches, and its neglect of culture, social norms and power, fail to account for women's distinctive patterns of behavior as consumers and workers, and promote policies that are often stacked against women and other disadvantaged groups (Peterson and Lewis 1999; Benería 2003). The launching of the journal *Feminist Economics* in 1995 was one sign that such critiques would be more than ephemeral.

Women's mobilization and lobbying since the 1970s and feminist complaints of the inadequacies of the economic thinking informing development policies have in fact had some impact. Governments and development agencies now have units that incorporate gender into their planning and monitor compliance in the gathering of disaggregated data and the formulation of programs that target (mainly poor) women as beneficiaries or 'clients'. But it is inadequate to conflate gender inequality with women's lack of productive resources, as if all that disadvantaged women was a lack of human capital and entrepreneurial skills, not limitations on power and autonomy. If the sources of their disadvantages are understood in narrowly-conceived economic terms – as if income gains could erase their subordination within households and communities – we lose sight of the political implications inherent in effective remedy. If, for example, a household is seen as a rational economic actor, one might expect other household members to delight in increasing the access of women to jobs and income as well as access to the education that will help secure superior jobs. The more complex reality, however, is that male partners often resist women's increased autonomy, placing a higher value on mastery than money (Jaquette and Staudt 2006, p. 32). Differently put, the study of gender may perhaps usefully begin with comparing the resources available to women with those available to men, or comparing women's actions and attitudes to men's. But it cannot end with such comparisons because gender is a social relationship, not a separate state. We have to move on to consider the connectedness of the lives of those with more and those with less resources and of those who engage in some activities with those who engage in others. Amartya Sen's concept of 'cooperative conflict' insightfully addresses the complex interaction of resources and power in family arrangements (Sen 1999, pp. 189–203).

Contrary to expectations that macroeconomic reforms, more

decentralized social policies and increased market participation would benefit them, poor women in Latin America, the US, and elsewhere have had to endure a heavier burden. As the privatization of services and the shrinking of safety nets transfer responsibility for people's well-being from the public to the private sphere, women have had to work harder to compensate for falling family income and declining state protection. They have entered paid employment in larger numbers, often migrating when local labor markets cannot accommodate the larger demand for jobs and experiencing wage and promotion discrimination when they do find paid employment. Women also have had to expand their already extensive hours of unpaid labor when health services, elder care and child care are no longer available.

SIGNS OF TROUBLE

These and other critiques might be no more than interesting matter for students of intellectual history to contemplate were it the case that all was well with the world, or at any rate, well enough to sustain the political conditions that in turn sustain neoliberalism. But there is much to suggest that all is not well. Focusing on Latin America, we are very far from the first to point to how widespread are severe economic and political travails. Just to say the names of Colombia, Venezuela, Peru, Ecuador, Bolivia and Argentina is to conjure up images of economic distress along with political and social conflict. Our utter lack of originality here is precisely the point. Very many people, of varying political allegiances, in and out of Latin America, know that something has failed, not the sort of knowledge that engages commitment to the prevailing economic orthodoxy. Even the star case of Chile, which has for some time convinced many in and out of Latin America that neoliberal programs and ideas at least work well somewhere – even that star burns less brightly than before.

Recall that the failure to produce sustained economic growth while reducing income concentration, anywhere in Latin America, was a major catalyst for turning to new ideas in the 1970s and 1980s, which helped give us neoliberalism, the Washington Consensus and Latin American participation in the internationalization of a particular brand of economics. Recall, too, that neoliberalism was Chilean before it was American and that Deng had opened up China to global capital before anyone spoke of Reaganism–Thatcherism, especially notable because changing Chinese practice has been one of the major forces moving the entire world economy since that moment in the late 1970s (Harvey 2005). 'US hegemony' in itself cannot reasonably be called the sole driving force of neoliberalism, unless we conceive it in conjunction with the recessionary circumstances of the 1980s, the hopes for economic recovery of the 1990s, and shifts in dominant interest coalitions in richer and poorer countries (Drake 2006).

But neoliberalism, like developmentalism, failed to produce a satisfactory combination of growth with equity. Although Latin America has spent enormous intellectual and policy energies to remedy inequality, it remains, paradoxically, the world's most unequal region (Hoffman and Centeno 2003; Adelman and Hershberg 2007), a point to which we keep returning. In 2006, 36.5 percent of Latin America's population were poor (195 million people) and 13.4 percent (71 million) were extremely poor by one reasonable set of criteria (ECLAC 2007). Africa is even poorer but it is not so inegalitarian. One very striking set of figures comes from using the UN's Human Development Index as a measure of well-being and then asking how much well-being do countries around the world obtain for a given level of economic development as conventionally measured, say, by Gross Domestic Product per capita. What is striking is that there is less well being in Latin American countries than one would expect on the basis of the world relationship of GDP per capita and the Human Development Index. In other words, as noted earlier, Latin America's truly extraordinary social inequalities mean that development does not very effectively translate into well-being. The same sense of failure that came to haunt Latin American economies and economists a generation ago has returned to haunt them again early in a new century.

As for the US itself, one suspects that the image of that country as the place that got the state/market mix right is looking a bit tarnished in the face of the puncturing of its speculative bubble, the mendacity of its corporate executives and their accountants, the flood of corporate funds financing political campaigns, the enlarging gap of rich and poor, and a swelling public deficit sure to invite the scorn of the global financial institutions trying to convince Third World countries that it is good for them to set their fiscal affairs in order. Not to mention the already well developed reputation for hypocrisy the US has earned in Latin America by advocating a free market for those south of Texas while sheltering US agroproducers with generous subsidies. It is not lost on Latin Americans that US championing of reducing trade barriers, reducing national indebtedness and eliminating favors for domestic producers is far more consistently aimed at them than at itself. Partly because they have been prodded by social movements challenging the consequent impoverishment of rural people, including the new indigenous people's mobilizations in much of the region, Latin American governments have been organizing to try to alter hemispheric trade policies, with their own MERCOSUR rather than the US-favored FTAA (Free Trade Area of the Americas) emerging as one of the world's largest trade blocs.

So there is much reason to believe that students of the region – very much including students *from* the region – will be taking a new look, studying some of the many emerging critiques we have indicated (and developing new ones).

LATINAMERICANIZATION OF LATIN AMERICAN ECONOMICS

But why might new ideas emerge? The worldwide Americanization of economics is undeniable, but local environments continue to affect discursive styles, the institutional organization of professional practices, career patterns and networks, as the previous chapters have amply demonstrated. There remain, however, significant differences in the way economists practice their trade in various national and regional contexts, just as we know that there are significant contrasts between the US and Europe due to differences in market size, university reward systems and definitions of the proper role of economists in public life. The studies in this volume show that Latin American economists have become increasingly similar to their US counterparts, but also that they continue to have a distinctive profile, and one could say much the same of Europe where despite Americanization inroads, recent intra-European economics societies and journals have promoted a trend toward a more homogeneous European economics (Coats 1999, p. 11). That differences diminish does not mean they vanish. The preceding chapters leave one skeptical of assertions that Latin Americans simply replicate what is learned in Ivy League classrooms without adapting to the demands of local constituencies or the specificities of local policy environments.

We have seen that recent changes in Latin American economics have favored the emulation of US mainstream professional norms, but there was a time of great rebelliousness against the professed universal validity of economic theorizing. Heterodox postures led Latin American economists to nurture their own regional professional identities, with their own indigenous interpretations of development, their own training programs and their own justifications for the enhancement of professional competence in policy making.

Such attempts to create a distinctive Latin American economics were displaced with the rise of monetarism and other alternatives to Keynesian ideas. As the push for privatization and deregulation gained momentum, 'old guard' economists were degraded as obsolete, parochial, ideologically biased and technically incompetent. Accused of lack of professionalism, heterodox and radical economists were expelled from university and government positions. These dissenters from the new orthodoxy were not those most likely to be hired in the new private universities, nor to get prominent posts in government. Adopting the standards of 'good economics' was thought to help these countries compete in the global economy, win favor in Washington, and be taken seriously by international organizations, including those dealing with finance and aid. This meant abandoning economic nationalism, 'modernizing' the curriculum and improving the quality of economic research. The academic credentials of economics professors have been upgraded and doctoral degrees from prestigious universities abroad are now the norm in many places. Even government economists are expected to hold graduate titles – and finance ministers are expected to be economists.

The incentive system for academic economists in Latin America has changed: prestige is measured by the number of publications in well-known professional journals and regular attendance at international conferences. Preparing students for entrance to the best graduate schools, primarily in the US, is considered an important mission. Securing the return of foreign-trained economists to teach and practice in their country of origin is also driving reforms in economics education. This means making academic careers in Latin America more attractive, which reinforces efforts to upgrade the quality of university programs. But the growth of high-quality, locally-rooted programs that can offer graduate degrees at home also provides a potential institutional base for once again developing a locally inflected discipline. The prospect of such a scenario is no longer reserved for rebellious minds. In a departure from the recent past, new thinking in the profession is calling for more pragmatism and nuanced contextualization, even among those who maintain allegiance to the neoclassical doctrine (Rodrik 2007b; Galbraith 2008). In fact, some have gone so far as arguing that neoclassical economics might not even dominate the mainstream any longer (Davis 2006).

Latin Americans are struggling to become more competitive in an increasingly internationalized market for economic expertise. The most promising graduates and the most productive faculty members are often lured to well-paid professorships in foreign universities or attracted to employment opportunities in the much expanded private sector, in international banks, multilateral organizations and cosmopolitan think tanks. The expanding think tank network itself is a major support for professional mainstreaming. The most distinguished economics programs in Latin America are enrolling larger numbers of students from neighboring countries, and polishing their marketing strategies by entering exchange agreements with US and European universities. Even economics journals are being refurbished with international editorial boards, new procedures to referee submissions, the elimination of traditional in-house outlets and the publication of more pieces in English.

To say simply that these changes consummate the Americanization of economics in Latin America would be, we think, not quite on target. As in the past, Latin Americans are selectively accommodating and selectively resisting pressures to comply with US-inspired models of economic governance and economic ideas. Already in the 1990s, some saw the 'Washington Consensus' as being challenged by an emerging 'Latin consensus', geared toward improving the distributive effects of market reforms, the creation of more effective regulatory frameworks and the reduction of vulnerability to external shocks. A decade later, the emergence of a post-neoliberal phase predicated on a more pragmatic stance regarding the limits and virtues of both markets and states is much more than mere speculation.

The search for a coherent post-neoliberal paradigm continues with several signs that a revisionist program is not only eroding the most radical versions of economic orthodoxy but that a new regionalization of economics is taking place. The rigidly technocratic, one-size-fits-all policies of the neoliberal interlude are being replaced in response to popular discontent and the resurgence of a politics of contestation across the continent. There is a range of policy approaches that differs on such questions as the extent of privatization, economic nationalism, social spending, trade policy and relations with the US. These differences do not simply distinguish countries where the right has won elections in the early twenty-first century (as in Colombia or Mexico) from those where the left has done so (as in Argentina, Brazil, Chile and Uruguay). There are also considerable differences among the critics of neoliberalism over what should be the next direction, something that shows up in significant differences in policies among countries where those critics have won elections. For those who like pigeonholes, it had become something of a commonplace in the early twenty-first century to distinguish two kinds of left, with Brazil, Chile and Uruguay in one pigeonhole and Mexico, Venezuela, Bolivia and Ecuador in another. At the very least, the confining armor of the neoliberal model has been 'punctured' (Roberts 2007). Some observers discerned an electorally successful New Left that has tried to reduce its dependence from international financial institutions without a radically redistributionist or rampantly populist economic agenda (Moreno-Bri and Paunovic 2006). New forms of regional integration are being pursued but trade liberalization has not been renounced. Although there is more state intervention, fiscal responsibility has not been rebuffed.

The period of disciplinary amnesia that characterized the most radical marketization phases seems to be coming to an end. Pointing to the beginning of a new era, elements from various schools of economic thought are being fused in an effort to avoid the pitfalls of economic autarky, remedy the neglect of politics and history, soften the cost of inequality, and provide states with the resources to govern. CEPAL economists talk about a 'neostructuralism'.[3] They along with other prominent figures from the banned generation have returned to the university and so have leftist intellectuals. Graduate economics programs are combining their externally-validated technical credentials with an applied orientation relevant to regional policy questions and they cooperate across national frontiers. LACEA, a major regional economics association established in 1992, tries to facilitate exchanges among academic economists and policy-makers. In addition to its well-attended annual meetings, LACEA publishes a regional journal focused on high-quality applied research. Its Carlos Díaz Alejandro prize for economics is awarded to research relevant to Latin America. This suggests that what the region's professional elite is trying to accomplish goes beyond pure emulation of US disciplinary norms.

Unlike the 1950s and 1960s, the intent is not to create a 'new economics', different from the economics of the 'North', but to offer a credible and competent complement, even an alternative, to the theory-centered, decontextualized curriculum for which Latin American economists used to fault US graduate programs (Pinto and Sunkel 1966). As it happens, a recent survey of US economics programs suggests that this criticism is significantly less accurate than it would have been in the past since those programs are increasingly stressing empirical research (Colander 2005).[4] That empirical research, moreover, is not just exquisitely refined econometrics but includes laboratory and field experimentation (Kagel and Roth 1995; Harrison and List 2004). Differently put, US economists themselves have been altering their discipline, which probably encourages further critiques. In the past two decades, the very definition of what orthodox economics means has been altered with the growth of new heterodoxies and the revival of old ones (for example, the 20th anniversary of the journal, *Rethinking Marxism. A Journal of Economics, Culture & Society* was celebrated in 2008). Campaigns claiming to shake mainstream economics out of its narrow, self-contained, self-referential framework resulted in the inclusion, it is said, of heterodox economists (Colander et al. 2004, p. vii). And those efforts prompted, among others, the 'post-autistic' movement. Born in 2000 out of a petition by French economics students demanding a more critical, pluralist, reality-based curriculum, this movement has gained significant credibility in segments of the profession and wide international attention. The *Post-Autistic Economics Review* (renamed in 2008 as the *real-world economics review*) already claims almost 10 000 subscribers from over 150 countries. A recent article in this journal affirms the value that the old Latin American school of economic thought might have in the transformation of the discipline (Bianchi 2003). Other international networks are also focusing on the shortcomings of economics education, pressing for greater doctrinal and methodological diversity. Illustrative are ICAPE (International Confederation of Associations for Pluralism in Economics), founded in 1993 and the Association for Evolutionary Economics (AFEE).

Although Latin Americans' presence in international economics circles has expanded greatly beyond the region in recent decades, economists' connections within the region have multiplied as well. Consulting opportunities, academic collaboration and co-authorship with colleagues abroad is common. Research is discussed at various regional conferences and some of these regional gatherings are occasions to nurture linkages with international associations, as in the case of the Latin American Meetings of the Econometric Society. Even those who have been hired in US universities or in the Washingtonian policy establishment try to keep a foot in Latin America. The regionalization of professional labor markets, training programs, journals and associations may not only to some extent shelter networks of economists from US pressures, but also by fostering intellectual interchange among people with diverse national experiences be an important stimulus for creativity. Think tanks proved a major resource undergirding the embrace of neoliberalism, but other think tank networks are supplying resources for a shift in course.

We have seen throughout this book the powerful role a sense of failure has had in reorienting economics. The development of the national professions in Latin America, documented in chapter after chapter, and the growing connections across national borders, also amply documented, now intersect a moment in which many people in many places see multiple, worrisome points of failure. In the early twenty-first century, looking at the global economy, the newspapers were full of fears of near-term food crises in poorer countries, long-term failure to effectively rise to the challenges of global warming, and the frustrating persistence of immiseration despite the benefits to some of globalized trade. Although the US was still often described as 'hegemonic', it could hardly be said to be looking like a model for the rest, not with its speculative bubbles – whose catastrophic risks and eventual crash in 2008 most economists appallingly failed to anticipate and expose – its astronomical debt, its extraordinary trade imbalances and its low rate of saving and investment. And not with its dismal record on what other rich countries took to be basic social services, like health care or education, or even the unglamorous and seriously neglected basic maintenance and repair of roads and bridges. If the US for some had from time to time been seen as a model of freeing individual energies from the dead hand of the stupid, wasteful and corrupt state it was now beginning to look like a place that had gotten a lot of things seriously wrong. It was Europe where redistributive policies were reducing poverty, although issues of immigration and integration were challenging those policies in some places; in the US the most important policy for dealing with the poor was the construction of prisons. So the US model was looking like less of a model altogether in the sense of inspiring would-be developers with an image of how to do it right. Some were wondering if its once-vaunted hegemony amounted to much more than the awesome force at the command of its generals, but even in this arena others were more impressed by the evident brainlessness of its Iraq adventure.

All this suggests a sense of crisis that energizes new ideas, diminishes deference to US prescriptions, and sparks a reconsideration of the role of intelligent regulation, the very thing the US was noted for undoing. There seemed to be few reasons for the US to continue to serve as a model for an enlightened future and no reason for its distinctive social policies to command admiration.

In light of the variety of current critiques one can imagine all sorts of directions in which the renewed attempt to Latinamericanize economics might lead. Intellectual and institutional frameworks might be redrawn to anchor economic ideas and policies in a more ecumenical world order, able to support more democratic and just societies. The extraeconomic dimensions of social life might regain their importance in the reconceptualization of economic expertise, opening spaces for more contextualized, holistic analyses of development. The dominant assumptions in economics, its research methods, rhetorical devices and professional world views might be altered to allow for less technocratic, more humanistic understandings of people's reality. Intra-professional hierarchies that have marginalized those without US economics degrees might be altered, and room made for those who venture into neighboring disciplines with no intention of colonizing them. Above all, a truly Latinamericanized economics, if successful in reclaiming its right to exist, can by itself broaden the scope for innovation and pluralism in the discipline. We hope that it is not just wishful thinking to conclude with the thought that such an outcome would leave us all better off, not just because of greater attention to concrete local needs, and not even just as a model for the 'South' more generally, but for its potential catalytic impact on global thinking about the global social and economic issues ahead.

NOTES

1. An earlier version of this chapter was presented at the annual conference of the Society for the Advancement of Socio-Economics, Aix-en-Provence, June, 2003.
2. Note the surge of interest in Polanyi, whose *Great Transformation* analyzed the abandonment of the utopian project to reorganize society around the self-regulating market in nineteenth century England. The 10th International Karl Polanyi conference was held in Istanbul in 2005. The Karl Polanyi Institute of Political Economy at the Concordia University in Montréal was founded in 1987.
3. Critics contend that contrary to exaggerated claims, the Latin American neostructuralist approach does not amount to a genuine alternative to neoliberalism (Leiva 2008).
4. For example, the John Bates Clark medalist for 2007 (awarded every two years to an influential American economist under the age of 40) was Susan Athey, the first woman to win the prize. Athey, a professor at Harvard, is described in the AEA webpage as 'an applied theorist who has made important contributions to economic theory, empirical economics, and econometrics . . . She has developed tools and techniques that provide the basis for empirical work strongly grounded in sound economic theory.'

REFERENCES

Adelman, Jeremy and Eric Hershberg (2007), 'Desigualdades paradójicas: Ciencias Sociales, sociedad e instituciones en la América Latina', University of Miami, Center for Latin American Studies, Working Paper Series #2.

Benería, Lourdes (2003), *Gender, Development, and Globalization. Economics as if All People Mattered*, New York and London: Routledge.

Bianchi, Ana Maria (2003), 'Concern with Policy Relevance in the Latin American School of Economics', *Post-Autistic Economics Review*, **18**, article 2.

Bielschowsky, Richard (2009), 'Sesenta años de la CEPAL: estructuralismo y neostructuralismo', *Revista de la CEPAL* 97, pp. 173–94.

Cardoso, Eliana and Ann Helwege (1992), *Latin America's Economy: Diversity, Trends, and Conflicts*, Cambridge, MA: The MIT Press.

Chang, Ha-Joon (2001), *The Rebel Within: Joseph Stiglitz and the World Bank*, London: Anthem Press.

Coats, A.W. (1997), 'Introduction', in A.W. Coats (ed.), *The Post-1945 Internationalizing of Economics*, Annual Supplement to Volume 28, *History of Political Economy*, Durham and London: Duke University Press.

Colander, David (2005), 'The Making of an Economist Redux', *Journal of Economic Perspectives*, **19** (1), 175–98.

Colander, David, Richard P. Holt and J. Bakley Rosser Jr. (2004), *The Changing Face of Economics. Conversations with Cutting Edge Economists*, Ann Arbor, MI: University of Michigan Press.

Davis, James B. (2006), 'The Turn in Economics: Neoclassical Dominance to Mainstream Pluralism?', *Journal of Institutional Economics*, **2** (1), 1–20.

Drake, Paul W. (2006), 'The Hegemony of U.S. Economic Doctrines in Latin America', in Eric Hershberg and Fred Rosen (eds), *Latin America after Neoliberalism. Turning the Tide in the 21st Century*?, New York and London: The New Press, pp. 26–48.

ECLAC (2007), *Social Panorama of Latin America*, Santiago: ECLAC.

Ffrench-Davis, Ricardo and José Luis Machinea (eds) (2007), *Economic Growth with Equity. Challenges for Latin America*, Santiago: ECLAC.

Galbraith, James K. (2008), *How Conservatives Abandoned the Free Market and Why Liberals Should Too*, New York: Free Press.

Harrison, Glenn W. and John A. List (2004), 'Field Experiments', *Journal of Economic Literature*, **92** (December), pp. 1009–55.

Harvey, David (2005), *A Brief History of Neoliberalism*, Oxford: Oxford University Press.

Hirschman, A.O. (1975), 'Policymaking and Policy Analysis in Latin America – A Return Journey', *Policy Sciences*, **6**, 385–402.

Hirschman, A.O. (1981), 'The Rise and Decline of Development Thinking', in *Essays in Trespassing: Economics to Politics and Beyond*, Cambridge: Cambridge University Press, pp. 1–24.

Hoffman, Kelly and Miguel Angel Centeno (2003), 'The Lopsided Continent. Inequality in Latin America', *Annual Review of Sociology*, **29**, 363–90.

Inter-American Development Bank (2006), *The Politics of Policies: Economic and Social Progress in Latin America, 2006 Report*, Washington DC: Inter-American Development Bank.

Jaquette, Jane S. and Kathleen Staudt (2006), 'Women, Gender, and Development', in Jane S. Jaquette and Gale Summerfield (eds), *Women and Gender Equity in Development and Practice. Institutions, Resources, and Mobilization*, Durham and London: Duke University Press, pp. 17–52.

Kagel, John and Alvin E. Roth (eds) (1995), *Handbook of Experimental Economics*, Princeton, NJ: Princeton University Press.

Leiva, Fernando Ignacio (2008), *Latin American Neostructuralism. The Contradictions of Post-Neoliberal Development*, Minneapolis: University of Minnesota Press.

Moreno-Bri, Juan Carlos and Igor Paunovic (2006), 'The Future of Economic Policy Making by Left-of-Center Governments in Latin America: Old Wine in New Bottles?', *Post-Autistic Economics Review*, **39** (1), article 1.

Peterson, Janice and Margaret Lewis (1999), *The Elgar Companion to Feminist Economics*, Cheltenham, UK and Northampton, MA, USA: Edward Elgar.

Pinto, Aníbal and Osvaldo Sunkel (1966), 'Latin American Economists in the United States', *Economic Development and Cultural Change*, **15** (1), 79–86.

Ramos, Joseph and Osvaldo Sunkel (1993), 'Toward a Neostructuralist Synthesis', in Osvaldo Sunkel (ed.), *Development from Within. Toward a Neostructuralist Approach for Latin America*, Bouder, CO and London: Lynne Rienner Publishers, pp. 5–19.

Real-World Economics Review (2008), http://www.paecon.net/PAEReview/issue45/whole45.pdf.

Ritzer, George (2003), *The McDonaldization of Society*, Thousand Oaks, CA: Pine Forge Press.

Roberts, Kenneth M. (2007), 'Repoliticizing Latin America. The Revival of Populist and Leftist Alternatives', Washington, DC: Woodrow Wilson Center for Scholars. Update on the Americas, www.wilsoncenter.org/topics/pubs/repoliticizing.roberts.lap.pdf.

Rodrik, Dani (2006), 'Goodbye Washington Consensus, Hello Washington Confusion? A Review of the World Bank's *Economic Growth in the 1990s: Learning from a Decade of Reform*', *Journal of Economic Literature*, **44** (4), 973–87.

Rodrik, Dani (2007a), *One Economics, Many Recipes. Globalization, Institutions, and Economic Growth*, Princeton: Princeton University Press.

Rodrik, Dani (2007b), 'Does Import Substitution Deserve Its Unsavory Reputation?', Dani Rodrik weblog 'Unconventional Thoughts on Economic Development and Globalization', sub.html.

Rosenthal, Gerth (2004), 'ECLAC: A commitment to a Latin American way toward development', in Yves Barthelot (ed.), *Unity and Diversity in Development Ideas. Perspectives from the UN Regional Commissions*, Bloomington, IN: Indiana University Press, pp. 168–232.

Sandbrook, Richard, Marc Edelman, Patrick Heller and Judith Teichman (2007), *Social Democracy in the Global Periphery. Origins, Challenges, Prospects*, Cambridge: Cambridge University Press.

Sen, Amartya (1999), *Development as Freedom*, New York: Random House.

Silva, Eduardo (2007), 'The Import-Substitution Model. Chile in Comparative Perspective', *Latin American Perspectives*, **34** (3), 67–90.

Stiglitz, Joseph (2003), 'Populists are Sometimes Right', in Joseph E. Stiglitz, *I Dissent: Unconventional Economics Wisdom*, Project Syndicate. An Association of Newspapers around the world.

Watson, James L. (1998), *Golden Arches East. McDonald's in East Asia*, Stanford, CA: Stanford University Press.

Wolfensohn, James (2004), 'Washington Consensus Dead', http://www.southcentre.org/info/southbulletin/bulletin80/bulletin80-03.htm#TopOfPage (consulted April 20, 2008).

World Bank (2005), *World Development Report 2006: Equity and Development*, Washington, DC.

Index